The Performance of Human Rights in Morocco

For Roger Allen,
with profound admiration
and as always my
thanks,
Susan Slyomovics

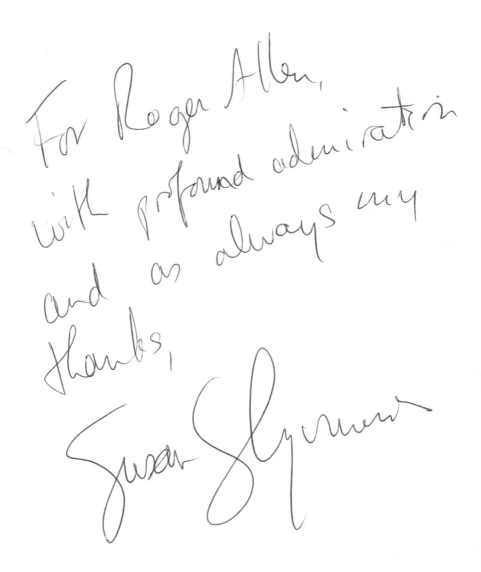

PENNSYLVANIA STUDIES IN HUMAN RIGHTS

Bert B. Lockwood, Series Editor

A complete list of books in the series is available from the publisher.

The Performance of Human Rights in Morocco

Susan Slyomovics

PENN

University of Pennsylvania Press
Philadelphia

Publication of this volume was assisted by a grant from the Graham Foundation for Advanced Studies in the Fine Arts.

Printed in the United States of America on acid-free paper

10 9 8 7 6 5 4 3 2 1

Published by
University of Pennsylvania Press
Philadelphia, Pennsylvania 19104-4011

Library of Congress Cataloging-in-Publication Data

Slyomovics, Susan.
The performance of human rights in Morocco / Susan Slyomovics.
p. cm.—(Pennsylvania studies in human rights)
ISBN 0-8122-3858-3 (cloth : alk. paper); ISBN 0-8122-1904-X (pbk. : alk. paper)
Includes bibliographical references and index.
1. Human rights—Morocco. I. Title. II. Series.
JC599.M8 S58 2005
323'.0964 22—pcc *2004058841*

For Nadjib and Sandy Berber

Contents

Transliteration Note

For transliteration of Modern Standard Arabic, I follow the American Library Association-Library of Congress system with these exceptions: (1) Moroccan place names are in accepted English form (Fez, Meknes, Marrakesh, etc.) and (2) personal names of contemporary Moroccans follow established French-language based transcriptions discussed in Chapter 4 (e.g., Salah El Ouadie, not Ṣalāḥ al-Wadīʿ). Also, unlike the ALA-LC system the *alif maqṣūrah* is romanized the same as the long vowel ā (rule 6a) and the prime is not used (rule 21).

Colloquial Moroccan Arabic dialect is transliterated according to the system established by *Zeitschrift für arabische Linguistik* (*Journal of Arabic Linguistics*). For words that appear in both Modern Standard Arabic and Moroccan Colloquial Arabic form and are usually transliterated according to French transcription (e.g., candle as *shamʿah* or *chemaa* respectively), Modern Standard Arabic spelling is preferred.

Introduction

Public space in Morocco—the places where people congregate, debate, exchange ideas, protest, hold court, and mourn—is in the process of opening to those whose speech narrates the story of the struggle for human rights. Individual experiences that were once unspeakable—torture and prison—are now appearing as personal testimony, performance, and poetry. Sion Assidon, arrested in 1972 and condemned to fifteen years in prison for publishing leaflets and newspapers, sent letters and photographs describing conditions from Kenitra Central Prison, the preeminent Moroccan prison for political prisoners:

Perhaps you have heard about a political prisoner who died here in the prison of Rabat on 25th December 1978. His name: Zeid Ibrahim. Age: about 50. Zeid was kidnapped by the secret Moroccan police in Algeria and secretly transported into Morocco. He remained in the house of torture (Derb Moulay Cherif—Casablanca) more than four years until August 1978 and was deferred to "justice" (military tribunal of Rabat), accused of "attempts against state security." After four years torture and secret prison, Zeid arrived to the prison of Rabat in a very bad situation. He was very ill, probably cardiac. For a long time it was very difficult for him to obtain a consultation with the physician of the prison. However the physician was not able to ascertain the illness. On Christmas night Zeid had a fit. By night, there is no physician or male nurse in prison. And the staff may not open the doors of the cells. In spite of this the other political prisoners succeeded to convince the night staff to call for an ambulance. But when the staff opened the cell, Zeid was dead.

Who is responsible for the death? The kidnappers, the tormentors, the attorney general who put Zeid in prison in spite of his illness? The director of the prison who neglected to examine Zeid carefully, the stupid regulation which forbids opening cells by night, the criminal negligence of the direction of the prison who leaves 1000 prisoners by night without any medical assistance? Zeid is not the first political prisoner who died by calculated negligence. Ahmed Ben Moussa Brihich in Kenitra and Saida Menebhi in Casablanca in 1977. Five other prisoners in Meknes 1976. Another in Fez in 1975. I let you conclude.[1]

Assidon's correspondence to Amnesty International Group 30 of San Francisco, written in English, is an epistolary example of personal testimony that publicized and physically conveyed difficult information and knowledge to an audience abroad. An exemplary medium of actual and symbolic exchange among groups inside and outside Morocco is the letter: the letter smuggled from prison, the letter asking pardon from the king (*risālat al-ʿafw*), the open letter addressed to the Moroccan government and to the conscience of the outside world, the letter-writing campaign to amass support, and the massive correspondence between external support groups and the incarcerated Moroccan prisoner of conscience.

An archive of letters fleshes out aspects of Moroccan history during the postcolonial era: individual human voices narrate in personal writings key notions about human rights, the public sphere, and prison reform. To describe those post-independence years, Moroccans assign the names *zaman al-raṣāṣ* and *al-sanawāt al-sawdāʾ* in Arabic, in Moroccan Arabic *liyyām l'kḥla* (in French, *les années de plomb* and *les années noires*): "the years of lead,"[2] phrases evoking an era of grayness and lead bullets, and "the black years," the times of fear and repression, and *les années sombres*, the gloomy years of forcible disappearances, farcical mass political trials, and long prison sentences for large numbers of people who from a variety of political positions voiced opposition to the regime and became prisoners of conscience. Since Morocco's independence from France in 1956, thousands from the student and intellectual communities—of every political persuasion, Marxist, Islamist, nationalist, Sahrawi, feminist, Amazigh/Berber activist—were arrested, held incommunicado at various sites, tortured, and tried en masse in waves of political trials for "plotting against the state." Artistic expression—articles, books, magazines, broadsides, graffiti, and cartoons—comprised most of the evidence of their "crimes." Sentences ranged from a few months to the death penalty.

In Morocco, a community of human rights activists, many of them survivors of forcible disappearance, torture, and mass political trials, has long endeavored to reconstruct this hidden face of postcolonial history and to account for what truly happened, despite perpetrators' attempts to remove both material evidence and human witnesses. As with other projects in which a state appears to declare war against its own citizens, the attempt to analyze such an historical past tests the limits of our ability to portray such experiences. In 1996 while in Tangier, I came upon an article, "Du jamais lu" (Never before read) by Aziz El Ouadie (political prisoner, 1974–84).[3] A full page of the Moroccan francophone newspaper, *Libération*, was devoted to chronicling clandestine cartoons and writings from two journals, *al-Sāḥah* (courtyard) and *al-Ṭarīf* (sympathetic one), produced in Kenitra Central Prison:

> To look at and to say what one sees. To say and to see, even if it comes from behind the unbearable power of cement walls. Words only have weight when they come from the heart, when they are sincere testimony, alive, a cry that comes from the inside. Without the ear and the voice, nothing whatsoever. Life no longer has meaning. Because to be silent in the face of injustice is to forget the struggles, all those battles for this ideal and this passion that give meaning to existence. It is to forget the reason why men and women are isolated from the world behind the unbearable cement walls.[4]

During two research trips in 1996 and 1997, funded by grants from the American Institute of Maghribi Studies (AIMS), I was introduced to a community of human rights activists composed of the students, poets, novelists, and artists who had been imprisoned together. An unusual discursive formation has emerged from my interviews that links authors, writing, political detention, and torture: prisoners' guilt was based on their imaginative and political writings, torture was applied to elicit written confessions, and finally, a large body of writing was produced during decades of incarceration.

My original 1996 and 1997 Moroccan fieldwork project was to examine the literature and art of writers imprisoned and tortured. One motive for inflicting physical pain, literary critic Elaine Scarry argues in *The Body in Pain*, is to destroy the voice that would express torture in language, thereby eliminating any representations by the victim.[5] By embracing questions of language and the difficulties of telling the story, Moroccan literature written in prison takes as its subject the overtly political insistence of witnessing. Drawing explicitly on Palestinian *iltizām* or "commitment" literature, such works belong to an "engaged" literature of testament and commitment that has shaped literary themes throughout the Arabic-speaking world in particular.[6] Terms to characterize writing emerging from political and social extremity occur in Carolyn Forché's anthology on the poetry of witness where in 1993 she proposes a third space for poems that do not belong purely to the realm of the political or the personal; instead, they are part of what Forché calls a "social" arena which she defines as "a place of resistance and struggle, where books are published, poems read, and protest disseminated. It is the sphere in which claims against the political order are made in the name of justice."[7] It is noteworthy that Forché's formulation of an *engagé* poetry of witness overlaps with another concept, one owed to Palestinian writer and critic Ghassan Kanafani. As early as 1966, he had employed the term *adab al-muqāwamah* (resistance literature).[8] Kanafani emphasizes what was particular to the Arab writer composing under a state of cultural, political, and personal siege, which he defines as the gap between literature produced by authors living safely in exile versus writers living under occupation or in prison. For Kanafani, a seminal influence on this group of Moroccan authors, the personal, the political, and Forché's sense of the "social" space are inseparable from precise questions of geographical location and historical time. Where do you live? For whom do you write? When and under what circumstances did you write? Which prison "published" your writing? What was the manner of your torture or death?[9]

In the Arabic-speaking world, one early and influential example of prison literature is the Qur'anic story of Joseph, similar to the Joseph story found in the biblical text of Genesis 39: 1–23. In the Qur'an, Joseph is brought to Egypt as a slave and sold. When Joseph rebuffs attempts at seduction by his master's wife, she threatens him with prison: "If he does not do my bidding, he shall certainly be cast into prison and what is more be in the company of the vilest!" Joseph's reply of "Lord, prison is more to my liking than that to which they invite me" resounds through the centuries as a key statement, especially for Morocco's Islamist political prisoners, about political and literary obligations to their readership. Even though Joseph is vindicated, his innocence is of no moment; in some sense he is guilty of having exposed the master's wife as sinful and the master retaliates: "then it occurred to the men . . . (that it was best) to imprison him for a time."[10] That Joseph languishes in prison despite proven innocent exemplifies the universal plight of the righteous prisoner of conscience.

Much classical Arabic poetry in the premodern period was composed about prison.[11] In tandem with the rise of the novel in the Arab world in the twentieth century, narratives about prison, political detention and torture proliferate. Mohamed Choukri's *al-Khubz al-ḥāfī* (literally, barefoot bread), subtitled an "autobiographical novel" (*sīrah dhātīyah riwāʾīyah*), chronicles the protagonist's life from conditions of extreme poverty in Tangier to imprisonment for petty alcohol and sex-related offenses. Illiterate, Choukri is forced to leave his thumbprint on a confession authored by the police. Prison alters his life. He begins to learn the alphabet, instructed by famous lines of anti-colonialist poetry penned by the Tunisian Abū al-Qāsim al-Shābbī: "If someday the people decide to live, fate must bend to that desire / There will be no more night when the chains have broken."[12] At the end of Choukri's account, the reader discovers that the book in hand is the material outcome of the plot: the attempt to reveal the truth about poverty and prison through literary efforts. Written in literary Arabic, Choukri's book was banned in Morocco until 1999.[13] A first publication in 1973 was Paul Bowles's English translation, *For Bread Alone*, followed by Tahar Ben Jelloun's French translation, *Le pain nu*, in 1980.

A continuous production of writing by Moroccan political prisoners has long been disseminated in France in French during the post-independence decades (1956 to the present). Francophone writers not only documented human rights abuses (as did many international human rights organizations publishing in various languages) but, more importantly, they also produced best-selling works on the subject. The circuitous transnational and translated routes of certain artistic products (and their confusing, changeable book titles) would return home to Morocco only after the death of King Hassan II in 1999 and the enthronement of his son and heir, King Muhammad VI. Abdelaziz Mouride, for example, a political detainee in 1974–84, laboriously smuggled his cartoon book out of prison page by page, exposing the horrific conditions under Morocco's repressive police state. Originally written with Arabic titles and speech balloons, it was published pseudonymously in France in 1982 as *Fī ʿaḥshāʾ baladī* (In the bowels of my country) and subtitled "On Political Prison in Morocco." A French version by noted poet, translator, and writer Abdellatif Laabi, Mouride's fellow inmate in Kenitra Central Prison, appeared simultaneously with the equivalent French title, *Dans les entrailles de mon pays*. Its publication impossible to imagine under Hassan II, Mouride's greatly revised work was finally published in French almost twenty years later on March 2000 as *On affame bien les rats!* (They starve rats, don't they?) by a transnational Paris-Casablanca publishing house.[14] Abdellatif Laabi's own searing novel of his arrest, torture and imprisonment, published in Paris in 1982, was made available in Morocco only in 2000, thanks to Casablanca's Éditions Eddif and financial support from the French embassy in Morocco. Laabi's 1982 title, *Les chemins des ordalie*, literally, "the ways of ordeal," more approximately, perhaps, "trial by fire," would become its Moroccan subtitle, superseded by *Le fou d'espoir* (A fool for hope). Laabi's book is a rare example: translated into English but published in 1989 by Readers International under the unfortunately unmarketable, all too foreign title (at least to Americans), *Rue de Retour* (Street of return). In 1992, an exposé of Tazmamart, the notorious secret prison, was published in France by Christine Daure-Serfaty, the French wife of Abraham Serfaty, one of Morocco's longest-serving political prisoners—but it was only translated and published during Morocco's post-Hassan II era in daily serialized excerpts beginning 21 December 1999 by *al-Munaẓẓamah*, the Arabic-language newspaper of the OADP (Organization of Democratic and Popular Action), an official political party.

This series of novels, memoirs, and oral histories about Morocco's human rights abuses—by French and Moroccans, by authors in and out of jail, in French and in Arabic, published by French-Moroccan transnational companies or circulating clandestinely—represents the long, tortuous, and complicated cultural and political exchanges that have taken place between France and its former North African colonies. The contrasting histories of prison writing in Arabic and French (with attention to Morocco's other literatures in Amazigh/Berber and Spanish) challenge conventional political, linguistic, and literary relationships. In many instances, the choice to publish in any of Morocco's languages is governed by histories of repression. Throughout this study, places and dates of publication appear as one aspect of lapses that exist between the act of creation, the ability to write, and the freedom to publish. Consequently, prisoners' narratives are embedded in, correspond to, and transfigure Moroccan society and history.

Chapter Outlines

I had turned to the analysis of prison writings because of the pervasive climate of fear and police surveillance, censorship, and self-censorship that characterized the thirty-eight-year rule (1961–99) of Hassan II. Funded by a Fulbright research award and also an AIMS grant (1999–2000), I arrived a week after the death of Hassan II, the accession to the throne of his son and heir, Muhammad VI, and a day after the new king's first throne speech, televised to his subjects, confirming his commitment to establish the rule of law, and to safeguard human rights, individual and collective liberties, and a constitutional monarchy. Chapter 1 begins with a review of the Moroccan legal system. Changes in the law are discussed in relation to events of the 1990s in which a different Morocco seemed willing to begin addressing the state's acknowledged crimes against its own citizens: illegal detention, forcible disappearance, and torture.

What it means to be "disappeared" is addressed in Chapter 2. Who does it, to whom, how, when, and where in Morocco, and does this practice continue? In the Moroccan context, incarceration became a formative experience that served to forge a growing national will to human rights consciousness. "Where, after all, do universal human rights begin?" questions Eleanor Roosevelt during her last speech to the United Nations. She answered: "In small places, close to home—so close and so small that they cannot be seen on any maps of the world. Yet they are the world of the individual person; the neighborhood he lives in; the school or college he attends; the factory, farm or office where he works."[15] Indeed, human rights activists emphasize that the Moroccan state, in effect, has criminalized all manifestations of political activity and thought—acts such as writing tracts, meetings, and demonstrations, whether national demonstrations or local school discussion groups. Political imprisonment in Morocco is thus linked with a wide range of views emerging from *any* act deemed political by the regime. Chapter 2 analyzes the phenomenon of disappearance, while Chapter 3 describes the sites of secret detention and prison. Chapter 4 takes the ritual of the mock trial as a point of departure to consider the 1981 Casablanca uprising, thereby including stories by those imprisoned, killed, or disappeared who were not politically involved. Chapter 5, on women political prisoners and their testimony, and Chapter 6, on Islamist political prisoners, present the history and works of imprisoned Moroccan poets and writers to exemplify the themes of writing during political incarceration and the ways in which prison writing, as a critical and analytical weapon developed by dissidents, underpins current human rights political activism.[16] The role of the family, especially the mothers, concludes Chapter 5. Topics such as expressing the experience of torture, disappearance, and prison indicate the importance of performance in social and political life at the same time as this study focuses on the special role artists and ritual play in public truth-telling and in the construction of civil society.

The Performance of Human Rights

Performance has many meanings. Key questions about the performance of human rights include the social, political, economic, and institutional indicators that permit quantifying and comparing human rights performance transnationally and regionally. In sum, how are countries ranked in terms of performance of human rights? As with any rating system, individual country standings are contested by a variety of interested parties. Reports in the 1980s issued by the United States Department of State, for example, were questioned in *Critique*, the review of human rights country reports by the Watch Committees (Americas Watch/Asia Watch/Helsinki Watch) and the Lawyers Committee for Human Rights (U.S. Lawyers Guild). The evaluations were described as

> misleading, factually inaccurate and occasionally absurd . . . tak[ing] a . . . cavalier approach to torture. The State Department notes that while a number of "Moroccan *political* organizations (emphasis added) have alleged mistreatment of detainees, "there was not, however, a clear nationwide pattern to such charges." The report goes on to stress, "there is no indication that such treatment was ordered by the government." In fact, torture has long been practiced by the Moroccan armed forces, it occurs throughout the country and there is more than ample evidence that it has been ordered by the government.[17]

While reports filed by individuals or organizations inside and outside a country assessing the nation's performance on a human rights ratings scale offer opposing conclusions, observers from a variety of vantage points agree that the absence of torture and disappearance, freedom from repression, and freedom of expression paint clear pictures of praiseworthy human rights situations. At issue is evidence for a pattern of abuse and what such a pattern implies; mistreatment and torture are discernable only when part of a pattern. Actions that are recurring and countable, the management model of performance, conclusively amount to government instigation.[18]

When viewed by the folklorist, anthropologist, and verbal artist, the expression, "the performance of human rights," has added interpretive value. Pattern and repetition, necessary for quantification procedures, are equally hallmarks, according to Deborah Kapchan's definition, for culture-based qualitative approaches to performance:

> Performances are esthetic practices—patterns of behavior, ways of speaking, manners of bodily comportment—whose repetitions situate actors in time and space, structuring individual and group identities. Insofar as performances are based on repetitions, whether lines learned, gestures imitated, or discourses reiterated, they are generic means of tradition making. Indeed, performance genres play an essential (and essentializing) role in the mediation and creation of social communities, whether organized around bonds of nationalism, ethnicity, class status, and gender. Yet performances provide an intricate counterpoint to the unconscious practices of everyday life insofar as they are stylistically marked expressions of otherness, lifting the level of habitual behavior and entering an alternate, often ritualized or ludic, interpretative "frame" wherein different rules apply.[19]

Using Kapchan's definition, let us consider entrenched patterns of torture and disappearance as but one indicator of the performance of human rights. In the Moroccan case, consistent, numbing everyday practices point objectively, verifiably, and quantitatively to the lack of human rights. At the same time, a theory of "performance" permits deeper analyses and applications. Performance also occurs during sports, rituals, civic events, political rallies, and popular entertainments as well as what are conventionally called the performing arts—theater, dance, music, storytelling, and more. These performances are part of a wide range of heightened, esthetic expressions: performance and "to perform is to carry something into effect—whether it be a story, an identity, an artistic artifact, a historical memory, or an ethnography."[20] Such cultural expressions are the subject of scholarly analysis when performances so defined are framed as discrete occasions with a beginning and an end. Woven into this study are performances in Morocco—the practices, discourses, events, occasions, and cultural behavior associated with enacting human rights onto the public arena. The many ways in which everyday life can be viewed as performances of human rights come through in the ceremonies and activities that are at the heart of this study: funerals, eulogies, mock trials, vigils and sit-ins, political rallies, conferences, public testimony and witnessing, storytelling, poetry recitals, and letter-writing campaigns.

Translating concepts about performance to Morocco raises questions about Western scholarly projects, terms, and goals when applied to Moroccan sociocultural contexts. The works of folklorist and anthropologist Deborah Kapchan and Moroccan theater critic Abdelkrim Berrechid identify for Moroccan performance the centrality of the *ḥalqah*:

> The word *halqa* delimits both a physical and a symbolic space: literally meaning a link in a chain, the *halqa* is defined by a circular assembly of people surrounding a performer in a public setting, usually in a marketplace or at a city gate, spaces of threshold and transition. The interdependence between performer and audience is implicit in the word *halqa*; neither exists without the other, making all who are present coparticipants in the performative event. . . . Often associated with tellers of episodic tales, praise singers, snake charmers, and clowns, the *halqa* is also populated by clergy (*fqaha*) who write charms, by clairvoyants, and by herbalists who sell homemade remedies using elaborate oratory. Their performances are characterized by license, humor, and symbolic inversion.[21]

The *ḥalqah* as a space of Moroccan performance—indeed, Berrechid insists it is the most authentic space—conforms to the long and flourishing tradition of vernacular performing arts throughout the Arab world in which public space seems to enlarge powerfully its reach and scope due to the presence of those who speak well.[22] While the ḥalqah in its simplest linguistic use is a physical space, it is one that must be formed by a circle of humans. They may be the traditional storytellers, such as bards, poets, singers, religious orators, praise-singers, and puppeteers.[23] Even when they are not, tellers are influenced by the spoken arts of the traditional storyteller.

An example of the ways in which aspects of performance tell us about the status of speaking in relation to political action is the life and work of Driss Benzekri, who has conducted extensive research on victims of torture in Morocco. Benzekri was a political prisoner (1974–91) from the outlawed Marxist-Leninist group Ilā al-Amām. Moroccan Marxist groups in the 1970s were divided into Group Alif (A) and Group Bāʾ (B) as a result of a split in 1972. Ilā al-Amām began as Group Alif (A), which emerged from the Moroccan Communist Party and was headed by Abraham Serfaty. Group B further divided into "23 March Movement" and Li-nakhduma al-shaʿb (To serve the people).[24] Benzekri completed advanced university degrees in Amazigh/Berber linguistics and oral poetry and studied Moroccan law while in prison.[25] He is unusually positioned as a human rights investigator, a victim of torture, and a scholar trained in traditional theories of orality as well as contemporary approaches to human rights testimony and witnessing. When first interviewed in 1997, he was secretary-general of al-Munaẓẓamah al-Maghribiyah li-Ḥuqūq al-Insān (known also by its French initials, OMDH, Organisation Marocaine des Droits de l'Homme), a nonpartisan human rights monitoring group. Then, OMDH researchers were in the midst of documenting widespread torture and forcible disappearance in the Middle Atlas Mountains, Benzekri's home region, following large-scale rural antigovernment uprisings that had taken place more than twenty-five years earlier, in 1973.[26] Given the passage of time, decades of fear and silence, and questions about victims' memories, Benzekri thoughtfully articulates an additional framework that relates Moroccan conceptions about verbal performance with the associated problem of writing down spoken testimony about torture:

> In writings by people who have been tortured, it's true, they have many scruples in speaking about it. It is not at all easy to testify (*témoigner*) about torture, let's say about personal testimony that speaks about their sufferings and talks about their emotions. One can talk about it orally but in writings, people cannot express it. Usually, they express it in an emotional manner in poetry and one must know the biography of the person to understand that this is about the agonies of torture, or its consequences, or formulations that express the problems and are in relation to torture. There are testimonies of this genre, but this problem is classic and known: the fact of incapacity or powerlessness or refusal to exteriorize.[27]

Benzekri's statement—that one can talk about torture orally but not express it in writing—pleads for a consideration of the ways in which literature, especially poetry, confronts torture. So oblique and condensed are the tortured poet's versifying techniques that Benzekri cautions readers to know the writer's personal history. In essence, one can potentially read torture into a poetic text, but this reading relies on knowledge extraneous to the creative text. Even speaking about torture for Benzekri's group of Marxist-Leninists was repressed, in no small part because the very process of having been tortured is stubbornly and horrifically fused to the victim's "performance" under torture:

> It is especially so for this group [of Marxist-Leninists] which was politicized, which was implicated in a very difficult conflict with the political power and with its police representatives. Torture was something taboo. This caused many problems among us. One of the fundamental writings for Marxists, and those in the extreme left in general, is that when they are arrested, those that meet again after prison, after the arrest, is to conduct what is called an evaluation of the performances (*l'évaluation des performances*) of each one. Each one is judged according to the capacity to resist torture. The capacity to not confess. These were things that were of the spirit of the times. They were important parameters.

Evoked is a nuanced redefinition of performance in which political prisoners measure themselves by their silence under torture and by subsequent oral evaluation of their behavior, in itself a performative rite of self-criticism about performance. Salah El Ouadie (Marxist political prisoner, 1974–84), notes the paradoxical nature of silence during secret detention, where he was both beaten to speak under torture and beaten to remain silent, as prisoners were forced to lie blindfolded and immobilized between torture sessions. To retain silence, he repeated to himself the phrase *anā muthḥākim fī afkārī* (El Ouadie's French translation, *je suis maître de mes pensées*), I master my thoughts. To speak about torture, El Ouadie avers, is torture.[28] Benzekri notes the extraordinary powerful conflation of silences, those taken on and those imposed on the idealized political activist. Psychic and physical humiliations, no less than the silence enjoined on the militant revolutionary, continue to bar disclosure and confession, first to the torturers (when this was possible) and currently to disallow public testimony about past abuses:

> I understand why people cannot speak about this directly. I imagine that even if, for example, we suggested as a subject for debate, an analysis of torture, its mechanisms, and all, people would not be capable of writing in a precise fashion. Of

course, we were all aware that torture was used as a means for repression, a method of punishment because many torture sessions were gratuitous. I myself was tortured as soon as I was arrested, all those first weeks in January. But seven months later they called me in the middle of the night with dogs attacking me, things like that. True there were small items of information to verify but also a sort of humiliation. They wanted absolutely, it was necessary that those in the opposition know that they were less than nothing, that they were destroyed. Thus it is a difficult process. Even more, people do talk about visible physical aspects: there was something broken, an attack, cigarette burns, the bottom of the feet wounded. But the psychic and psychological aspect, no one talks about it or analyzes it. Are the reasons only because of the consequences of torture or also imprisonment, isolation, all this life. . . . As for me, I ask myself if I am truly normal psychologically because I live always with a prison cell in my head.[29]

The muffled, secretive nature of prison and disappearance is in many ways opposed to the qualities that make for verbal performance in the public domain. Transmitting social and public knowledge and memory calls for breaking the silences. Many cannot or will not do so. This book focuses on the public performance strategies in which many Moroccans can and do go about insuring the rallying cry of the Moroccan human rights movement: *ḥattā lā yatakarraru hādhā* (in French, *plus jamais ça*), never this again. How do contemporary Moroccans think creatively about multiple processes of what legal scholar Paul Schiff Berman terms "the idea of alternative assertions of jurisdiction"?[30] These may be in the form of mock trials regarding past atrocities, indemnity hearings, actual transnational human rights trials in official courts, and demands for truth commissions. In the foreground are what people do and the places where they gather (notably the prison, the gravesite, the underground cell, the urban riot); the slogans, graffiti, and tracts they disseminate; and the collective actions undertaken (pilgrimages, conferences, and demonstrations). By analyzing changing repertories of public protest and dissidence, the outlines for postcolonial transformations of Morocco are charted.

Chapter 1
Law and Custom

Morocco has been ruled by the Alawite dynasty since the seventeenth century, a lineage disrupted for forty-four years between 1912 and 1956 by French colonial rule known as the "Protectorate." Muhammad V, the first king of independent postcolonial Morocco, was the grandson of the precolonial Moroccan sultan, Moulay Hassan, and the nephew of the last two sultans before the French era. The monarchy reinstated in Morocco in 1956 was not historically inevitable; rather, the fact of the king's restoration relied on complex political and social forces that propelled Muhammad V, exiled by the French, into the symbol for the Moroccan nation during the struggle for independence.[1] Muhammad V ruled from independence in 1956 until his death in 1961, succeeded by his son Hassan II, king from 1961 to 1999. While there has been dynastic continuity from the pre-Protectorate sultanate to modern times, the path from colony to nation has forced each country subjected to French colonization to confront change and renovation. A challenge for each Moroccan monarch has been the postcolonial legal system.

The current monarch (since 1999), Muhammad VI, son of Hassan II and grandson of Muhammad V, is the third ruler since independence. After the death of Hassan II on 23 July 1999, the first speech from the throne by Muhammad VI signaled a commitment to establish the rule of law and to safeguard human rights.[2] Morocco's projects to reorganize its judicial and police systems go hand in hand with a national response to create governmental and educational organs, for example, an indemnity commission, a center in Casablanca to rehabilitate victims of torture, and revamped school curricula, intended to address a past history of abuse. To investigate how society is constructed after periods of authoritarian rule, this chapter describes decades of changes in the national legal system before turning to the government's initial chosen avenue of redress, an Indemnity Commission, proposed by Moroccan authorities in contrast to remedies promoted by the regime's victims.

Garde à vue

In Morocco, many instances of state-instigated disappearance depended directly on the existing legal system, in particular on the Code of Penal Procedure (CPP), a compilation of rules governing police investigations, prosecution, remedies to the law, and evidence.[3] Procedures that set no limits to police power—*al-iʿtiqāl al-iḥtiyāṭī* in Arabic and *garde à vue* in French—point to an absence of a body of fundamental laws to protect the basic rights of defendants. A literal translation of the older French term unites *garde* meaning "to detain" with the component *à vue* to mean "closely observed" or "kept in sight." In practice, garde à vue refers to the period during which the suspect spends in detention while a police inquiry is undertaken, but before he or she is charged with a crime and brought to trial. In Morocco under the reign of Hassan II, garde à vue had been effectively reversed from a person "kept in sight" to one "out of sight," as the monarchy within a newly created post-independence political context maintained colonial legal mechanisms that were repressive, arbitrary, and undemocratic. Garde à vue—how it has been practiced and the changes in these laws—recounts formally and legally the history of the treatment of political prisoners in Morocco.[4]

An understanding of garde à vue based on its procedures is central to torture, disappearance, and political imprisonment in Morocco. To achieve the balance between individuals formally accused of a crime and their government, the rights to which defendants are entitled are safeguarded. Specific garde à vue procedures govern how a person is to be treated by the authorities from the moment of detention by police for a crime allegedly committed. This initial encounter between the accused and the police has been called the "seismograph" or "bellwether"[5] of how a state respects its citizens' rights because justice at this moment is a matter of just procedure. The absence of fair procedures signals the opportunity for abuses.

English-language human rights reports routinely gloss garde à vue as incommunicado detention.[6] The translation itself defines an inherently illegal procedure according to Anglo-American procedures: to be held incommunicado circumvents provisions of *habeas corpus* (Latin phrase for "you should have the body," shortened from the phrase *habeas corpus ad subjuciendum* meaning "you should have the body to be subjected to examination"). Habeas corpus stipulates that detention is to be acknowledged and that a detainee is to appear before a court in order to assess the lawfulness of the detention. What must be disclosed are the charges against the detainee, punishment, if any, and when the detainee is to be released. If the imprisonment is invalid, a detainee is to be released immediately.[7] The earliest appearance of a version of habeas corpus in England is said to have been when men jailed during the reign of Henry VII (1486–1509) were freed by invoking an already existing law that describes a set of procedures to ensure a speedy judicial inquiry and trial. The Habeas Corpus Act of 1679 was passed after a London merchant was unable to secure bail easily after being jailed on the charge of making subversive speeches.[8] The first example during Henry VII's reign highlights the ways habeas corpus provisions protected English citizens from an abusive royal power while the second case of a London merchant links habeas corpus directly to the protection of free speech. Habeas corpus addresses the legality of detention; habeas corpus presumes neither the guilt nor innocence of those held in custody. Habeas corpus is, nonetheless, a procedure important to a fair trial because it ensures that a citizen cannot be held secretly and without reason by the authorities; habeas corpus is "the great remedy of the citizen or subject against arbitrary and illegal imprisonment; it is the mode by which the judicial power speedily and effectually protects the personal liberty of every individual, and repels the injustice of unconstitutional laws and despotic governors."[9]

Current Moroccan law does not provide for habeas corpus; garde à vue governs practices during the pretrial period. Abdelaziz Nouaydi, professor of constitutional law at Mohamed V University in Rabat, neatly summarizes the legal circularity and police insularity built into any garde à vue detention:

> The officers of the judicial police (*police judiciaire*) can hold persons in custody in police stations in three situations: in the case of a flagrant offence; during the preliminary investigation and when implementing a judicial order to carry out an investigation.
>
> Two conditions are required to hold persons in garde à vue detention: the presumed offence must be punishable by imprisonment and the necessity of investigation must require the detention. But it is the police officers who estimate that necessity![10]

The Moroccan police act both as investigator and as judge presuming the crime while imagining, indeed foreshadowing, the eventuality of criminal charges and while preemptively acting on a punishment that might be meted out.

During the first years of independence from France, 1956–59, Morocco's penal procedure, including the procedures governing garde à vue, reflected an inheritance from the former French Protectorate, as do many provisions of the Moroccan Penal Code and Code of Penal Procedure.[11] Under Abdallah Ibrahim, who served briefly as prime minister during the winter of 1959–60, a new Code of Penal Procedure was enacted. Ibrahim's political party, Union Nationale des Forces Populaires (UNFP), a stream within the Moroccan left, advanced changes in the law long pursued during the country's fight for independence from the French. Two years after Morocco's 1956 independence from France, a new procedure was instated such that the accused could not be held by the police in garde à vue for more than 96 hours; this procedure remained in force for four years. In 1962, a year after Crown Prince Moulay Hassan was proclaimed King Hassan II of Morocco, a *dahir* (royal decree) of 9 November 1962, with articles 76, 82, and 154, extended garde à vue to 144 hours or six days. Deemed especially dangerous were cases involving political prisoners accused of "threats to the security of the state" (*atteintes à la sûreté de l'État*) where garde à vue could be doubled to twelve days and, according to some Moroccan legal experts, construed as a period of unlimited duration.[12] In fact, renewed extensions of incommunicado detention were meted out routinely to political opponents, whose ill-treatment was publicized and deplored annually in Amnesty International reports on Morocco.[13] Thirty years later, a 1992 revision of the Code of Penal Procedure reverted to the pre-1962 provisions for garde à vue, a historical step backward that paradoxically signaled a landmark reform correcting three decades of human rights violations.

Moroccan law permits garde à vue for a maximum of 48 hours, renewable once to 96 hours. In state security cases, garde à vue is 96 hours, renewable once to a total of 192 hours. Authorities responsible for the detention are obligated to inform family members immediately. Although judicial oversight and accountability are mandated by law, in practice such guarantees are all too often ignored because, as documented in subsequent chapters, detainees are often never seen again. Moreover, since the events of 11 September 2001 and the passage of the U.S.A. Patriot Act, Morocco has increased the amount of time spent in garde à vue as part of new global antiterrorist legislation initiatives. In the 1990s, laws were revised to reconsider the relationship between the rights of individuals and the requirements of national security. Like a pendulum swinging back into the position of curtailing freedoms, powered this time by American policies and directives, Morocco reinstated lengthier detention periods. Detainees may be held in custody for 144 hours (six days), twice renewable, each time for

96 hours (four days), for a total of fourteen days. In reality, suspects have been detained indefinitely. Following bomb attacks on 16 May 2003 in Casablanca that claimed the lives of forty-five people, the government is accused of holding between 2,000 and 5,000 people allegedly with ties to Islamist groups in garde à vue in the name of national security.[14]

Enforced disappearance ignores the concept of habeas corpus. So crucial is habeas corpus that the United Nations has proposed to turn the habeas corpus provision into a right that cannot be suspended. Indeed the right to acknowledgment and trial has been laid down in the International Covenant on Civil and Political Rights (article 9). If a writ of habeas corpus is granted, there is more certainty about the whereabouts of the detainee and the chances of disappearance are reduced. In the absence of habeas corpus, for example during the period of garde à vue, torture occurs when Moroccan defendants are denied access to counsel while interrogated. Under garde à vue, police and security forces have long been accustomed to indefinite precharge access to detainees. In practice this means that routinely lawyers for political detainees are not informed of the date of arrest; hence no one can monitor compliance with even officially permitted garde à vue detention limits.

The use of garde à vue leads too often to the government, especially police officials, presuming the guilt of the detained. The presumption of the guilt of persons already in police custody propels a police investigation that in turn leads to proving officially their guilt. Compounding such a powerful burden of presumed guilt by de facto imprisonment are the written results from the police inquiry (*procès-verbal*) presented as primary proof to a judge as part of Morocco's rules of evidence. Mohiedine Amzazi, law professor and author of a lengthy section in the *International Encyclopaedia of Law* describing an idealized Moroccan criminal law system, concedes that judicial presumption of innocence is flouted. Amzazi maintains that "the burden of proof . . . based on the presumption of innocence . . . is on the prosecution . . . [and] the accused does not have to prove his innocence; he is acquitted unless he has been proven guilty." Amzazi notes a Moroccan exception in article 291 of the Moroccan Code of Criminal Procedure:

> Official statements (*procès verbaux*) or reports drawn up by officers of the *police judiciaire* [criminal investigation department] and the *gendarmerie* to record misdemeanors and contraventions are deemed true unless there is proof to the contrary.[15]

Amzazi acknowledges: "this requirement of proof to the contrary constitutes a reversal of the burden of proof, thus departing from the principle of the presumption of innocence. The procès-verbal is also deemed authentic unless there is a plea of forgery or identification of handwriting."[16] An accusation of forgery calls into question police procedures and authorship. Formal features of a report, for example, the date and exact hour of arrest, are frequently falsified to mask prolonged secret detention. Moreover, the report is a genre of authoritative writing, an essay by the police that locates a political detainee in his or her specific historical and juridical context of presumed criminality. The imbalance of power between written police document and oral testimony by detainees produces circumstances in which

> it must be remembered that the procès-verbal is conceived and executed by the investigator. Certainly the facts are related by the victim, a witness or interested party but their agency, their construction, their sequence are performed by the investigator. Is it possible, in this context, to pretend to a faultless objectivity?[17]

Taken to be true and valid, police reports promote police practices and procedures relying on and leading to conviction.

Each day, in accord with Moroccan law, judicial police officers are required to submit a list of those in garde à vue. Names and dates of arrest are presented to the public prosecutor as the principal way to monitor the system of detention, since Moroccan law does not allow lawyers' visits to detainees during garde à vue. The public prosecutor's office may have jurisdiction in matters pertaining to lists based on police paperwork; it has no control over police methods of inquiry and interrogation. The detainee disappears bureaucratically, procedurally, and legally as a name that cannot be found on any lists, and as a victim of torture held in unknown places. At each stage during detention and garde à vue, the likelihood of disappearance or torture, or both, is amplified for the detainee as the outcome of processes that permit free rein, in practice though not in the legal codes, to police, guards, and officials of the Ministry of Interior. Although Moroccan law penalizes abuses by agents of authority, sanctions are not deterrents when fines are negligible: 100 to 500 dirhams (U.S. $10 to 50), for example, for not listing or incorrectly listing detainees.[18] France, the source for Moroccan garde à vue, has slowly changed its garde à vue laws to align with normative European practices. In 1999, nonetheless, the European Court of Human Rights condemned members of the French police for acts of torture perpetrated on a Moroccan-Dutch national during garde à vue.[19] As part of a project to strengthen the *présomption d'innocence*, the French government considered proposals, such as allowing lawyers to be present immediately on arrest (as opposed to the current practice of at the twentieth hour of garde à vue), or that only suspects, not witnesses, may be held in garde à vue.[20] Garde à vue remains a dark zone ruled by the police, unruly and unpoliced as long as there is no adequate judicial and civilian supervision.

Distinguished from garde à vue in Moroccan penal procedure is preventive detention (or remand in custody), supposedly "an exceptional measure,"[21] although it too slides easily into incommunicado detention. The accused remains in jail from the preliminary investigation until a final judgment occurs. Ordered by an investigating judge, preventive detention is also contrary to Morocco's stated presumption of innocence. Detention periods may be as long as two months, renewable to a full year.[22] While Moroccan law provides for a limited system of bail, it is rarely employed, because the system for determining guarantee of payment is so unreliable that extended and unwarranted detentions are the rule rather than the exception:

> another possibility was added to put the accused in jail: when he or she does not offer sufficient guarantees to appear before the court. The article [76, CPP] leaves the public prosecutor unlimited freedom to evaluate these guarantees. So the public prosecutor can put an accused in jail, arguing that he offers no sufficient guarantees to appear before the court, even if there is no flagrant offence and even if the offence is not punished by jail and the person offers guarantees.[23]

The nature of the Moroccan approach to criminal procedure—the inquisitorial system—serves to reinforce bureaucratic attitudes that presume the guilt of the accused. There are two principal modes of criminal procedure. The common law, also known as the accusatorial system, found in England, the United States, and most English-speaking countries, is in contrast to the civil law, or inquisitorial system, of the European continent:

> In the traditional inquisitorial model, a theoretically neutral judicial officer conducts the criminal investigation and a judge (or panel of judges), who has full access to the investigation (dossier), determines guilt or innocence. The trial is a relatively brief and informal affair conducted by a presiding judge without a jury; the accused does not necessarily have the right not to testify and neither counsel has much of a role, if the defendant even has a counsel . . . the behavior of the police and the conduct of judicial proceedings are governed by a more or less detailed code of criminal procedure.[24]

The inquisitorial and civil law system that prevails in Morocco, first installed during French colonialism, is exemplified by the preparatory phase of a trial in which "the procedure is secret, written, and non-adversarial."[25] Disadvantages of the inquisitorial court system for Moroccan political detainees are obvious and numerous. According to law, non-adversarial pretrial investigations should have been conducted by judicial officers and examining magistrates employing all the resources of the regime to gather evidence. The state, supposedly neutral and acting in the best interests of all parties, instead actively prosecuted and persecuted detainees who voiced opposition. In the case of political detainees, the state broadened the definition of a crime. Fatna El Bouih, a Moroccan political prisoner, succinctly denounces the politically insecure Moroccan government that grants too wide latitude to police and judges: "Torture as part of a thorough search was permitted because we were *hors la loi* (outlaws). We were condemned before we were even judged, we were considered already guilty. It was not for what I did but what I wrote: I threw tracts but I never threw bombs."[26] El Bouih's comments highlight the impossibility of separating contemporary Moroccan police and penal procedures from the fact of politically motivated enforced disappearance and the widespread use of torture.

One definition of political prisoners proposed by Abderrahman Benameur, political prisoner, lawyer, and activist with the Moroccan Association for Human Rights, links political imprisonment with nonauthorized views emerging from any "political" act, where "political acts" as interpreted by the state tarred so vast a group of activists as to constitute an absence of any semblance of judicial neutrality:

> Detention for political and union offences is not a contingent fact in contemporary Moroccan history, nor purely a series of provisional measures required by particular circumstances, nor a kind of extortion on the part of certain officials exercising the authority conferred by their job. On the contrary, detention for crimes of opinion, political and union activity is a method constantly used to destroy non-official opinion.[27]

The state, in effect, has criminalized all manifestations of political activity and thought that promote *l'opinion non-officielle*: political acts such as writing tracts, holding meetings, and demonstrating.

Casablanca-based human rights lawyer Mohamed Karam pinpoints another aspect of retrogade legal changes, one he notes that emerged after Hassan II's ascent to the throne in 1961; by 1963, the phenomenon of large-scale mass political trials was initiated and the year 1973 marks a further change in the history of Morocco's human rights abuses: the moving of the main torture center at Dar El Mokri in Rabat to Casablanca's Derb Moulay

Cherif (cf. Chapter 3).[28] From the victim's point of view the change of city and venue is irrelevant to the horror endured under torture. The transfer to Derb Moulay Cherif, however, marks the advent of mass secret detention and the space to torture large numbers of individuals.

By 1973, all the constituent elements for widespread abuse were in place: the criminalization of political opinion, arrest without warrant, detention without reason, unlimited extensions of time spent in garde à vue or preventive detention, the creation of secret prisons, and the institutionalization of torture. While the long and difficult legal struggle to respond to human rights violations was never abandoned throughout Morocco's *sanawāt al-raṣāṣ*, this study of remedies for victims of human rights violations begins in 1990.[29]

Indemnities

What brought about change? Mohamed Karam indicates that 1989 was a turning point but only after decades of internal and external pressures. The lengthy struggle by Moroccan human rights organizations and activists was coupled with outside forces, such as the power of the international press. Demands for respect for human rights coincided with the fall of the Soviet Union. Morocco's role as a pro-Western ally, as opposed to neighboring Algeria's alignment with the Soviet Union, became geo-politically irrelevant. Morocco, no longer shielded from scrutiny about domestic violations, was forced to accede to changes, among them the practice of human rights.[30]

The 1990s was a decade of change in Moroccan law and procedure. On 8 March 1990, Hassan II created al-Majlis al-Istishārī li-Ḥuqūq al-Insān (Advisory Committee on Human Rights, ACHR) avowedly modeled on a similar 1984 French institution.[31] In 1993 a new Ministry of Human Rights was formed; on 21 June (though not in force until publication on 16 December 1996 in the *Bulletin Officiel*), Morocco ratified the United Nations Convention Against Torture. Finally, in 1998, the Ministry of Justice and the prison administration implemented a law that made autopsies routine for any death that occurs in detention.[32]

The year 1998 brought more activity by the government concerning human rights reforms that seem to have complemented Morocco's newly elected 1997 government of "alternance" (rotation of prime ministers). On 9 October 1998, a speech by Hassan II directed again that all human rights cases should be resolved within six months. In ACHR meetings to discuss the "disappeared" file on 28 September 1998 and again on 15 October, the ACHR and its president, Driss Dahak, issued a press release establishing a list of 112 people: 56 persons were declared dead with no accompanying information, the others described as disappeared in unknown situations, either living abroad or in Morocco, or presumed dead. While these figures were absurdly low, the ACHR memorandum confirmed official recognition by the state of the fact of forcible disappearance.

The 1990 ACHR memorandum describing the procedures, mandate, and membership of the Indemnity Commission was widely criticized by the Moroccan community of victims and human rights activists, two groups with overlapping memberships. For example, victims filing requests for indemnities had no right to appeal decisions or pursue civil court actions. Most outrageously, in a 28 September 1998 memorandum to Hassan II, the ACHR granted immunity to torturers and to all those responsible for a state apparatus of secret detention centers, incommunicado detention, unfair trials, and the systematic practice of torture in police stations and prisons:

> The servants of the Cherifian throne, members of the ACHR, and following what you, Majesty, are known for concerning your unbounded forgiveness, beseech Your Majesty to shed Your kind forgiveness on all those who were fool enough to commit, help, or participate in a crime and threatened the security of the state, and whatever may have resulted in the concerned authorities' reactions or auxiliaries in order to protect and secure state security. This is just to execute Your Majesty's obeyed order, to close what is left of the pending human rights files.[33]

This memorandum posits that political prisoners are considered responsible for, if not instigators of, the very repressive state and police practices used against them. Torturers and their victims, according to the ACHR formulation, both share an equal culpability.

On 17 August 1999, a few weeks after the death of Hassan II, his son Muhammad VI ordered the ACHR to activate an independent Indemnity Commission with a mandate to expire at midnight 31 December 1999, for the purposes of indemnifying former victims "who suffered moral or physical prejudice as a result of enforced disappearance or arbitrary detention."[34] The official name of the Moroccan Indemnity Commission is Hayʾat al-Taḥkīm al-Mustaqillah lil-Taʿwīḍ al-Mutarattib ʿan al-Ḍararīn al-Māddī wa-al-Maʿnawī li-Ḍaḥāyā wa-Aṣḥāb al-Ḥuqūq mi-man Taʿaraḍū lil-Ikhtiṭāf wa-al-Iʿtiqāl al-Taʿassufī (Independent Arbitration Commission for Indemnities Caused by Moral and Material Damages to Victims and to Those Who Suffered Disappearance and Arbitrary Imprisonment).[35]

The first months of the new king's reign, the last six months of 1999, were filled with events dramatizing the past history of human rights abuses and the importance of international human rights cases for Morocco. Moroccan newspapers had given wide coverage to the year-long events following the 16 October 1998 arrest in London of General Augusto Pinochet, Chilean military junta leader (1973–1990) and his possible extradition to Spain for the crimes of genocide, torture, and forcible disappearances committed during his rule. Inspired by the "Pinochet Precedent,"[36] a legal tactic to pursue tyrants through foreign courts, Mohammed El Battiui, a student activist arrested and tortured in the 1983 Oujda University riots protesting huge price increases in basic foods, filed a case against the man deemed responsible for, and the symbol of, the Moroccan regime's human rights abuses, former minister of the interior Driss Basri, fired by the new king on 9 November 1999. After his removal from a position he had held since 1979, Basri, now stripped of his immunity, was accused by El Battiui, now a Belgian resident, of "crimes against humanity" on 16 November 1999 at the Tribunal of First Instance in Brussels. El Battiui's file includes descriptions of incommunicado detention as well as innocent family members held hostage in jail and subjected to weeks of torture.[37] Moroccan authorities drew on familiar explanations of state security to justify the possibility that the state might have overreacted in the treatment of political prisoners, who were "fool enough to commit, help and participate in a crime" that is defined, ironically, by the Moroccan state to comprehend dissent according to laws carried over intact from the French colonial period.

Post-independence Moroccan civil and penal codes remain French-inspired, with the important exception of personal status laws. Personal status deals with family law defined, for example, as birth, marriages, death, inheritance, and divorce.[38] For most of the twentieth century, first under French colonization and subsequently in independent Morocco, Islamic law could be said to live primarily in personal status law (called the code of personal status—in French, *code de statut personnel* and in Arabic, *mudawwanat al-aḥwāl al-shakhsīyah*) under the authority of Islamic courts. The complex heritage of the current Moroccan legal system embraces an uneasy mix of some, but not all, laws practiced in France at a particular historical moment, along with decrees and military emergency laws enacted by French colonial authorities to preserve French hegemony over Morocco. Examples carried over intact and "Moroccanized" are codes governing what was known as *libertés publiques* both in France and under the French Protectorate (translated into Arabic as *al-ḥurriyāt al-ʿāmmah*) and becoming in independent Morocco the laws governing the right to organize, to assemble, and to a free press. French laws were as restrictive after independence as before and frequently more punitive; the dahir (decree) of 26 July 1939 promulgated under the French Protectorate, for example, which mandated prison terms for making, distributing, or selling tracts "de nature à troubler l'ordre, la tranquillité ou la sécurité" (to disturb order, tranquility, or security) continues to be enforced by the Moroccan regime to repress demonstrations and publications. From 1963 to 1990, the legal strategy to prosecute student, labor, and political organizations and activists employed inherited French colonial laws and produced the majority of victims to whom the Indemnity Commission must pay reparations.[39] When laws declaring the person of the king and the royal family sacred were enacted, a new category of crime and attendant punishments added more names to the growing list of prisoners of conscience in postcolonial Morocco.[40] Muhammad VI has made no public criticism of his father (in fact, Moroccan law prohibits any form of negative commentary about members of the royal family, present and past). Indeed, the primary example of immunity (defined as a barrier to any kind of prosecution) can be found in the Moroccan constitution: "The person of the King shall be sacred and inviolable."[41] Many accused of "offenses against the monarch" were also subjected to illegal detention and torture and sought redress through the Indemnity Commission.

The Moroccan Indemnity Commission officially recognizes the status of *ḍaḥāyā* (victims). Inadvertently, commission reports produce a radically different Moroccan historiography, one that acknowledges repression beginning the first year of Morocco's independence. An example of human rights abuses as central to past history is the speech by Abdelaziz Benzakour, head of the ACHR working group to human rights organizations, to the International Federation of Human Rights in which reparations and indemnities are contextualized according to a new chronology of events, one that characterizes forty-five years of Moroccan government violations:

> It is worth noting here that [indemnity] requests refer in particular to events from the following years: 1956 (post-independence); 1963 (so-called "Complot" or plot trial); 1969 (so-called "Marrakesh" trial); 1972 (Skhirat); 1972 (Airplane); 1973 (Moulay Bouazza/Khenifra); 1976–80 (Laayoune, Agdz, Kalaat M'Gouna); 1981 (Casablanca strikes); 1984 (strikes in the north); 1990 (Fez strikes); 1999 (Laayoune), in addition to multiple cases of detention even in Algeria and the Tindouf camps as well as during the Protectorate era without speaking about numerous cases of de-

tention in matters having no obvious connection with any political, union, or organizational activity and some others that strictly have no connection with disappearance or detention.[42]

Previously, Moroccan history has been constructed through a variety of approaches, for example, centuries of the Islamicization of the Maghreb, or the era of French colonialism met by Moroccan nationalism and resistance, and more recently, the impact of economic and political integration into contemporary global networks. Benzakour's list, despite its many omissions, is an extraordinary recasting of historical reporting. Based on victims' written testimonies, the "hidden history"[43] of systematic bureaucratic and judicial violations is enumerated year by year. Details from each testimony and indemnity file, including depositions objecting to indemnification, add historical facts. The chronology of repression advanced by the Indemnity Commission according to topics treated prominently in oral testimony and written literature sketch a hidden history becoming public history. Readers of these documents share the experience of a bewildering array of facts newly exposed and debated about Morocco's past in response to developments in writing and righting human rights abuses.

Precedents

The effect of indemnities on torture survivors and the pursuit, or refusal, of reparation are part of a growing literature in human rights legal studies, with Holocaust survivors an obvious, much-studied group.[44] Morocco's Indemnity Commission requested the deposition of written dossiers based primarily on victims' own oral testimony. The commission began with indemnities (*taʿwīḍ*); the usual truth commission first deliberates and then offers indemnities. Indemnity as conceived by ACHR gives evidence of acknowledging an official policy of illegal state practices: compensation means something compensable occurred. If human rights violations are presented only in material terms for indemnification, then acknowledging an indemnification claim becomes a way, perhaps the only way, for victims to be recognized. In Morocco, there were no public hearings, no attempts to provide the nation with an account of the past, and blanket amnesties were part of the creation of the Indemnity Commission. Functionaries in power despite much negative newspaper coverage include Youssfi Kaddour, a high civil servant and known chief torturer at Derb Moulay Cherif, and Mahmoud Archane, former police officer and torturer at the Rabat Commisariat, who was a member of Parliament until his defeat in the 27 September 2002 elections.[45] No one has been tried. Crimes by government officials and functionaries are considered not proven. In the case of Morocco, human rights abuses are subject to a statute of limitation of twenty years and international instruments of human rights, though ratified, were not in force until recently.[46]

When the commission's allotted existence of less than six months expired on 31 December 1999, more than 6,000 indemnity applications had been filed. Reactions to the royal inquiry by a vast community of Moroccan victims—not only political prisoners of every location and persuasion (e.g., Marxist, feminist, Sahrawis, Islamist, Amazigh/Berber nationalists) but also bystanders, forcibly disappeared during frequent police round-ups—are many and varied; this chapter, however, focuses upon responses by former Moroccan political prisoners living in Morocco, as opposed to others who chose exile. What are the difficulties in accurately describing any event when corroborating police or governmental documentation is denied and absent? What are the meanings and consequences of gestures made by a government to its formerly persecuted citizens? Finally, what is the genealogy of the Moroccan indemnification program—Nuremberg? Islamic *sharīʿah* law? Customary Berber tribal law? French civil codes?

Truth and Reparation

Human rights violations evoke several national responses: create a governmental organ intended to record the truth about past history; declare an amnesty, prosecute those responsible, or do both; arrange indemnities for the victims and their dependents by means of official rehabilitation and material compensation. The creation of a Moroccan Indemnity Commission owes much to the unprecedented legal history of the Nuremberg war crimes trials and German redress programs to victims of Nazi persecution in the aftermath of World War II. The eventual fate of material goods and assets of destroyed European Jewry presented complex problems of heirless personal property and communal property owned by eradicated Jewish communities. Because a defeated Germany was the cause of the disappearance and death of Jewish owners, one impetus for formulating laws and administrative practices was to handle the disposition of assets such that they should not revert, as was customary, to the benefit of the state, namely Germany.

Assets estimated at $14 billion would otherwise go to enrich Germany. Historian Ronald Zweig summarizes the dilemma of postwar Jewry facing the daunting tasks, both moral and organizational, to press claims:

> How could Jews negotiate with Germans so soon after the crematoria and the gas chambers of Hitler's Third Reich? What recompense was possible for the murder of six million people and the destruction of communities hundreds of years old? How was it possible to estimate the value of individual and communal Jewish material assets, which the Germans had plundered between 1933 and 1945?[47]

The postwar Federal Republic of Germany nonetheless took responsibility for meeting material claims by Jews in a widely publicized speech by Chancellor Conrad Adenauer addressed to the German parliament on 27 September 1951:

> Unspeakable crimes have been committed in the name of the German people calling for moral and material indemnity, both with regard to the individual harm done to Jews and to the Jewish property for which no legitimate individual claimants still exist. . . . The Federal government is prepared, jointly with representatives of Jewry and the State of Israel, which has admitted so many stateless Jewish fugitives, to bring about a solution of the material indemnity problem, thus easing the way to the spiritual settlement of infinite suffering.

A year later, on 10 September 1952, the Federal Republic of Germany signed Protocol No. 1 "to enact laws that would compensate Jewish victims of Nazi persecution directly" and Protocol No. 2 that would "provide funds for the relief, rehabilitation and resettlement of Jewish victims of Nazi persecution," both confirmed and partially extended as a result of the unification of East and West Germany in 1990.[48] Policies enacted were based on sincere government apologies and the principles of restitution, indemnification, and reparations: restitution as the restoration of actual individual assets, indemnification as compensatory payments, while reparations were the collective payments made by one state to another, in this case to the Jewish people and eventually to the State of Israel after its establishment in 1948. German reparations were called *Wiedergutmachung*—literally, making good again. Ways to gauge the weight of reparations in the case of Germany were based on a government that admitted to harm committed in the name of Germany and that sought to atone for past injustices. Germany has created the largest sustained redress program amounting to more than $60 billion in payments, a landmark process that set into motion a global legal transformation in how abuses by a state may be evaluated. In legal discourse, the absence of governmental atonement and apology is assumed to signal that a more common legal category is operating, one in which parties agree to a settlement: one side pays without acknowledging or apologizing for violating any laws and the other side, the aggrieved party, receives a cash award. No liability is implied or assumed.[49]

Reviewing current international reparation protocols, Patricia Hayner defines the terminological terrain:

> *Reparations* is a general term that . . . include[s] *restitution, compensation, rehabilitation, satisfaction,* and *guarantees of non-repetition.* Restitution aims to reestablish to the extent possible the situation that existed before the violation took lace; compensation relates to any economically assessable damage resulting from the violations; rehabilitation includes legal, medical, psychological and other care; while satisfaction and guarantees of nonrepetition relate to measures to acknowledge the violations and prevent their recurrence in the future.[50]

Hayner maintains that programs that mix redress practices, as did the German government, work best for the victims. She compares Chile's 1997 reparations program with an earlier 1994 Argentine program, each resulting from respective truth and reconciliation commissions. Chile pays for the dead and the disappeared but not the larger numbers of survivors of torture and illegal imprisonment, while Argentina has extended reparations to all. Truth commissions formed in Haiti, El Salvador, and South Africa recommended inclusive financial reparations, but neither Haiti nor El Salvador were financially able to implement the payments.[51] Though reparations were never paid in many cases, compensation to victims and their families became linked to deterring the repetition of abuses, especially the prevention of torture, in the wake of three pathbreaking reports in the 1990s presented to the United Nations Commission on Human Rights.[52]

The Chilean National Commission on Truth and Reconciliation, formed in 1990, extensively documented violations but had no authority to judge those responsible. In Argentina, the National Commission on Disappeared Persons (CONADEP), established in 1983, published its findings in *Nunca más* (Never again), listing almost 9,000 unsolved disappearances, with charts of secret detention centers; these findings resulted in more than 1,000 cases presented to Argentine civilian courts. The South African Truth Commission of 1996, chaired by Bishop Desmond Tutu, created subgroups to promote national reconciliation: a Committee on Violations of Human Rights to identify victims and review compensation proposals, a Committee on Amnesty to grant amnesty or indemnities, and a Committee on Compensation and Rehabilitation to provide victims of violations of human rights with a public forum to narrate what befell them. South African victims of serious violations of human rights have the right to file a request for compensation. In South Africa, the policy was to grant amnesty when information was fully disclosed about political acts, the latter defined as acts committed by a political organization or a member of the security troops within the framework of obligations and authorities.[53]

Al-Muntadā al-Maghribī min Ajl al-Haqīqah wa-al-Insāf (Moroccan Forum for Truth and Equity)

The response to politically negotiated indemnification for an entire population, mandated by Muhammad VI in the form of the Indemnity Commission, was immediate. Groups of former political prisoners and human rights activists called an open meeting in Casablanca on 10 October 1999. At the Touria Sekkat Social Center in Maarif, more than 300 people were present in support of a provisional national committee comprised entirely of what the Indemnity Commission designated as *ḍaḥāyā wa-aṣḥāb al-ḥuqūq mi-man taʿaraḍū lil-ikhtiṭāf wa-al-iʿtiqāl al-taʿassufī* (victims and those who suffered disappearance and arbitrary imprisonment). On 17 October, at the Casablanca union headquarters of the Confédération démocratique du travail (CDT), a reunion was held for members of the Union Nationale des Forces Populaires (UNFP), who were arrested, collectively brought to trial for "plotting against the king" in 1971, and tried under the name "Group 193, 1971 Marrakesh trials." Approximately a hundred people were present, self-described as farmers and workers active in the Union Nationale des Forces Populaires, and as the first political prisoner group formed in response to mass government arrests to break the power of an opposition political party.[54] Organizers were the children of the detainees, notably Fatna Afid, the daughter of M'barek Bensalem Afid, who articulated the goals of the meeting: to determine the number of victims, to force a government acknowledgment and apology, to seek reparations, and to bring torturers to trial. Elderly men rose and demanded why speak out and to whom, noting that they had never before talked about their torture. Names of those responsible at Derb Moulay Cherif were uttered for the first time without fear in the company of fellow detainees. One speaker proclaimed: "This is our country, no longer the time of colonization, and it is our right to have our torturer, Abdelmalek Hamiani, tried." Long-term strategies were articulated to collect information from family and political networks and to encourage the production of victim *shahādah* (testimony).[55]

On 27–28 November 1999, a two-day conference lead to the formation of al-Muntadā al-Maghribī min Ajl al-Ḥaqīqah wa-al-Inṣāf (Moroccan Forum for Truth and Equity, henceforth al-Muntadā) and the election for three-year terms of a thirteen-member executive committee whose very composition, ten men and three women, is a microcosm of the postcolonial history of mass political trials and forcible disappearances: Driss Benzekri, president (political prisoner 1974–91, 1970s Marxist-Leninist group Ilā al-Amām); Salah El-Ouadie, vice-president (political prisoner 1974–84, 1970s Marxist-Leninist group "23 March Movement"); Khadija Rouissi, secretary general (member of the Committee for the Families of the Disappeared and sister of Abdelhak Rouissi, union activist forcibly disappeared in 1964); Abdelhak Moussadak, vice-secretary general (political prisoner 1985–94, 1980s Marxist-Leninist Group 26 Ilā al-Amām); Mostefa Meftah, treasurer (political prisoner 1974–84, 1970s Marxist-Leninist group "23 March Movement"); Ahmed Haou vice-treasurer (political prisoner 1984–1998, 1980s Islamist Group of 71); Abdullah Zrikem (political prisoner 1974–84, 1970s Marxist-Leninist group "23 March Movement"); Nezha Bernoussi (political prisoner 1985–91, 1980s Marxist-Leninist Group 26 Ilā al-Amām); Abdellah El Manouzi (member of the Committee for the Families of the Disappeared and brother of Houcine El Manouzi, activist forcibly disappeared in 1974); Fatna Afid (daughter of Mbarek Bensalem Afid, political prisoner, 1971–74, Group 1971 Marrakesh trials); and Hassan Mutiq (Sahrawi political prisoner, 1977–82, Group Meknes).

Driss Benzekri, al-Muntadā's first president, was among the last political prisoners from an outlawed Marxist-Leninst group, Ilā al-Amām, to remain incarcerated in Kenitra Central Prison; he was amnestied in 1991. After his release, Benzekri traveled to England, where he obtained the LLM in International Human Rights Law from the Department of Law, University of Sussex, under the supervision of the eminent human rights scholar Nigel S. Rodley; Benzekri's dissertation, "The Status of International Law in the Moroccan Legal System: Domestic Applicability and the Attitudes of National Courts," analyzes the complex and myriad ways in which Moroccan constitutional law evades or ignores international human rights law. As part of his indictment of the Moroccan legal system, Benzekri points out the existence of a subservient, incompetent, and corrupt judiciary:

> The national courts failed, until now, to contribute to the recent development of international human rights culture. The predominant legal culture among them

rests on the whole on a traditional and uncertain Islamic jurisprudence mixed with a selective approach to the French jurisprudence. The absence of an express and comprehensive reference to universal human rights norms is one of the salient features of that impoverished culture.[56]

In Benzekri's life and research—from clandestine leftist opposition to long-serving political prisoner to human rights advocate trained in both Moroccan law and international human rights law—a guiding principle is the acknowledgment and application of international human rights standards to Moroccan domestic law. Although Moroccan constitutions since independence in 1956, including those revised in 1962, 1970, 1972, 1992, and 1996, routinely declare the state's commitment to international law, a clear assertion appears only in the preamble to the 1992 constitution, where the issue of compliance by Moroccan constitutional law is forthrightly addressed:

Paragraph 3: Aware of the necessity of setting in action within the framework of international organizations of which it is an active and energetic member, the Kingdom of Morocco subscribes to the principles, rights, and obligations resulting from the charters of the aforesaid organizations and reaffirms its attachment to the human rights as they are universally recognized.[57]

Benzekri lectured publicly and at length to an overflow audience during the 1999 al-Muntadā conference about the history and legal instruments of international human rights case law relevant to indemnities. He emphasized the importance that parliamentary sessions in 1998 recently accorded to ACHR proposals that would bring domestic law in line with international human rights covenants. He pointed out the difficulties of pursuing torturers abroad through criminal law and applications of the doctrine of universal jurisdiction, which enabled a state, for example Spain, to prosecute an individual, Pinochet, for the crimes of torture and disappearance, even if the state has little or no connections to the offender, victim, or crime.[58] Instead of relying on the low probability of successfully pursuing cases in international courts, Benzekri suggested that deficiencies in the Moroccan Indemnity Commission might be analyzed productively within a framework of torts, that is, pursuing torturers for damages in civil actions rather than convicting and jailing them through the criminal courts. Tort law covers remedies for a tort, defined as a wrong inflicted regardless of intention. Such a policy could draw on important tort law rulings on indemnities in relation to human rights abuses. Examples include *Filartiga v.*

Peña-Irala, in which a Paraguayan couple brought a case in a U. S. District Court against a Paraguayan police officer for the torture and death of their son and were awarded $10 million in damages; both plaintiffs and defendant were living in the U.S.[59] Another precedent is the 1989 *Velásquez Rodríguez* case, in which the Inter-American Court of Human Rights proposed as "a principle of international . . . even a general principle of law . . . that every violation of an international obligation which results in harm creates a duty to make adequate reparation."[60] Additionally, the Inter-American Court of Human Rights held in *Velásquez Rodríguez* that an international court could determine the indemnity amount and was not bound by the internal laws of Honduras, the state that in this case was found in breach of international human rights law.

Opposition

While Latin American cases point to possible precedents for Morocco, either as civil or criminal actions, these new directions in prosecuting torturers were forged through third country actions—in England, not Chile, against Pinochet, and in the U.S., not Paraguay, against Peña-Irala. Outcomes for both criminal and civil actions are unfortunately symbolic. Because defendants are not in the country where courts and plaintiffs are located, judgments are thus difficult, if not impossible, to enforce.

Al-Muntadā proposed a range of remedies for dealing with the Moroccan disappeared and victims of torture, publicly insisting that a more extensive national process is essential, one that resembles truth and reconciliation commissions elsewhere, for example, the South African model. Additional recommendations of al-Muntadā include public rehabilitation of the victim, restitution of remains and a death certificate of a "disappeared" person for reburial, provision of monetary benefits to victims and relatives, and providing medical care, education, and shelter for all those involved. Eliciting the truth about past abuses requires cooperation from perpetrators—state officials, various police forces and ministries—none of which to date have been prepared to participate or cooperate.

Victim and family reactions, even among members of al-Muntadā, varied greatly. Despite the Esslami family claim that Mohamed Esslami, a twenty-seven-year-old doctor active in politics until he disappeared 29 November 1997, is being held incommunicado by the Moroccan secret service, Mohammed Esslami's name does not appear on the 1998 ACHR lists of 112 disappeared; the ACHR representatives maintain that the matter is too recent.[61] Houria Esslami, Mohammed Esslami's sister, cogently summarizes the point of view held by many families searching for their disappeared kin only to be informed that no human rights organization has been able to obtain information of their whereabouts. Houria opposes indemnities as they are conceived by the ACHR:

> As the family of a "disappeared," we are against the process of indemnification for those competent to stand on behalf of the dead or for the survivors. Because indemnification should be the last stage of this dossier. In the first place, it is necessary to acknowledge all the disappeared, free those still living, speak the truth about the reasons for their disappearance and incriminate those responsible. It is only at that moment that one can speak about indemnification that should be equitable and correspond to the degree to which we have suffered.[62]

Although endorsing familiar international recommendations and remedies as proposed by al-Muntadā, a number of vocal former political prisoners oppose filing any indemnity applications for various complex personal and emotional reasons. Fatna El Bouih, a woman political prisoner (1977–82), refused to request money:

> Personally, I don't want indemnities because it comes from the state. I find my indemnity elsewhere: in my activities and activism. Financial indemnities cannot make up for what I lost. I advocate for real truth and justice to be put in place for all. I personally am not greatly interested in trials. I can forgive if I know *lā yatakarraru hādhā* (never this again).[63]

Khadija, Jamal, and Muhammad, siblings of Abdelhak Rouissi, a union activist missing since 1964, were personally requested by Driss Dahak, then head of the ACHR, to file indemnity claims not only on behalf of their disappeared brother but for their own detention periods in Derb Moulay Cherif. The three refused. Instead they chose remedies available through the Moroccan courts. In Moroccan law, following French legal practice, a citizen may initiate criminal prosecutions and a civil action (*action civile*) for damages as a victim. As the first step, an investigating judge (*juge d'instruction*) must be willing to consider the case and determine that an indictment and trial is possible. According to Khadija Rouissi, no judge in Morocco has been willing to investigate the family's case for Abdelhak Rouissi, advocated since 1993 by human rights activist and lawyer Abderrahman Benameur.[64]

Abdelaziz Mouride (Marxist political detainee, 1974–84) has made

Figure 1.1. Abdelaziz Mouride, *On affame bien les rats!* 31. Cartoon on Judge Afazaz: "Today a member of the Advisory Committee on Human Rights. A minor country judge before the trial, he has known a murky ascent before becoming an authority in matters of human rights." Reprinted by permission of author.

clear in graphic terms his opposition to the corrupt and historically complicit membership of the ACHR. While incarcerated in Kenitra Central Prison in 1977–84, Mouride drew, then smuggled out of prison, a cartoon book *On affame bien les rats!* (They starve rats, don't they?).[65] In his redrawn, updated edition of the events of the notorious 1977 Casablanca trials, Mouride depicts five judges on the bench fast asleep, snoring loudly (swarms of the letter z swirl around their heads) as verdicts condemning 178 Marxist-Leninist prisoners of conscience to decades in jail are pronounced (Figure 1.1).[66] The tribunal president during Mouride's trial was Mohammed Afazaz, for whom Mouride's cartoon book offers as a biography: "today a member of the Advisory Committee on Human Rights. A minor country judge before the trial, he has known a murky ascent before becoming an authority in matters of human rights."[67]

The Moroccan Indemnity Commission also stands accused of disregarding the case of the Sahrawis. Only 320 were amnestied from sites of secret detention by 1993. As the struggle for control of the Western Sahara is defined as an armed conflict between Morocco and the Polisario (Popular Front for the Liberation of Saguia el-Hamra and Río de Oro, which has contested Moroccan control of the Spanish Sahara since 1975), Sahrawi civilians are treated as soldiers and prisoners of war. Many Moroccan human rights activists have indicated that acts of genocide against the Saharan population perpetrated by Colonel Ahmed Dlimi in the late 1970s and 1980s included collective punishment of family groups, tribes, and entire villages.

Opposition to the Indemnity Commission also comes from Moroccan human rights lawyers who point to misuses of the legal concept *taʿwīḍ*, the Arabic term for indemnification. Compensation and payments are key terms in contract law, part of the legal vocabulary for economic disputes involving reimbursement and arbitration of damages, all of which are regulated by Morocco's codes governing obligations and contracts, and are procedures that closely conform to French contract laws. As do articles 77–106 in the Moroccan code concerning contracts, the Indemnity Commission draws on the same term, *taʿwīḍ*, and the same phrases to refer to victims, who are described as suffering "material and moral damage" (*al-ḍarar al-māddī wa-al-maʿnawī*).[68] Use of the same words does not make a shared vocabulary between the Indemnity Commission and Moroccan contractual codes; several breaches occur in the application and arbitration of *taʿwīḍ* by the ACHR. First, during *taḥkīm* (arbitration) for indemnities as defined in the Moroccan legal code, the opposing parties designate the arbiter or arbiters. Instead, under ACHR, members of the Indemnity Commission are state-appointed, and the state, therefore, occupies simultaneously the positions of judge and interested party. Second, final judgments in indemnity suits under Moroccan legal code must follow Moroccan civil code procedures as set out in articles 306–327, in which arbitration cases must be reviewed and controlled by the president of the Tribunal of First Instance to ensure their legality with respect to possibilities of recourse. Under ACHR, there is neither judicial control nor oversight for any Indemnity Commission ruling. Third, article 12 of the ACHR indemnity protocols requires that all applications include a signed statement that the victim will accept the indemnity amount assigned by the commission and waive recourse to subsequent civil court actions.[69] Those who do file with ACHR automatically forfeit the right to appeal, a right that should be upheld in Morocco following international norms.

Victims and legal experts have denounced the Moroccan Indemnity Commission from a variety of legal, moral, and emotional quarters: indemnities cannot recompense torture, there should be no impunity for the perpetrators, the process is illegal and secret, and the administrators are complicit with the government's past abuses. By focusing on the ways in which the ACHR substitutes the human rights category "victim," for the civil law category "litigant," the problems of current Moroccan indemnity laws frame cogent, internal Moroccan objections within a specific historical context—not only the content of indemnification but also the tactics, processes, and strategies of Moroccan authorities to indemnify and reproduce structurally the same erasure of already existing laws that was so successfully accomplished as a primary strategy of French colonialism. Just as the project of French colonialism in Morocco was to marginalize, if not eliminate, both sharīʿah (Islamic law) and Berber customary law (*ʿurf* in Arabic, *izref* in Tamazight), so too does the Indemnity Commission deliberately fail to include substantively the three legal systems of indemnification that play or have played a crucial role legally and historically in regard to Moroccan reparation, namely, (1) the evolving international norms and practices that began at Nuremberg and continue through to contemporary national truth commissions; (2) laws regulating damages and indemnities according to the Moroccan civil code currently in force; and (3) ʿurf and sharīʿah provisions that deal with damages and reparations articulated in both systems under the general rubric of *diyah* (blood money).

While the deficiencies of the Moroccan Indemnity Commission in regard to points one and two have been elucidated, the relationship to Islamic (and implicitly to precolonial Berber) practices is brought to the fore due to the commission's own formulations. The Moroccan government took pains to endow the Indemnity Commission with Islamic moral origins, even though "enforced disappearance" and "arbitrary detention" are derived from the vocabulary of international human rights:

> The issue of enforced disappearance and arbitrary detention is on its way to a final solution after the file has been closed, and after the Committee [ACHR] complied with the royal instructions addressed to the members in the October 1998 speech, and respected the set period of six months. The issue is about the task of the board of arbitration regarding the award of compensation to those entitled to it. As a result of the wise policy of the late King Hassan II, the state was able to heal its wounds by resorting to the Islamic rule "neither harm nor injustice."[70]

From the arrival of Islam to North Africa in the ninth century until French colonization in the nineteenth century, the Maghreb region followed the Maliki school, one of four Sunni schools of sharīʿah (Islamic law) attributed to the Imām Mālik bin Anas (c. 712–795 C.E.). "To avoid harm and injustice to others" (*lā ḍarar wa-lā ḍirār*),[71] a leading principle of the Maliki school of law, is evoked by Moroccan authorities as the moral source that underpins the right to reparation. In the best of all possible worlds, we might agree with legal scholar Abdullahi An-Naʿim, who maintains that a recognition of the Islamic dimension of society as a meaningful cultural tradition could legitimate international human rights standards and implementation in the Arab-Islamic world. Maliki law, for example, through laws of inheritance, recognizes burdens to families when a husband disappears, although the waiting time of seventy to eighty years is greater than those in current laws governing disappearance.[72] Moreover, An-Naʿim hopes that "existing inconsistencies between the norms of a given culture, on the one hand, and internationally recognized standards of human rights, on the other, can . . . and . . . should be overcome and resolved."[73] Unfortunately, other than dispensing funds to several thousand victims, the practices of the Indemnity Commission hardly comply with international human rights norms for reparation in the *Filartiga v. Peña-Irala* and *Velásquez Rodríguez* cases. From the perspective of sharīʿah, is the Indemnity Commission neither harmful nor unjust? Is the quotation from Islamic rules, "neither harm nor injustice," symbolic window-dressing to emphasize that political institutions under the monarchy are to be rendered legitimate in Moroccan eyes by creating an Islamic pedigree?[74] To answer these questions, it is pertinent to consider the ways in which Islamic law and Berber customary law, as practiced in precolonial and colonial Morocco, conceived of violations in relation to the right to restitution, reparation and compensation, despite difficulties in recreating actual historical practice.

ʿUrf and Sharīʿah

French colonial policy followed the classic tactics of *diviser pour regner* (divide and rule)[75] by pitting the "good Berber," who inhabited the mountains, was democratic, not really Islamicized, and governed by customary law, against the "bad Arab,"[76] resident of the plains, submissive to the central government and the sultan (the *makhzen*), and a follower of sharīʿah. French officers and ethnographers, fascinated by what they called customary Berber law, produced a vast literature on the subject, some of which attempted to highlight Berber particularity in the precolonial, pre-French period by eliminating from their accounts the interpenetration of Islamic law into most of Berber life.[77] After ten centuries of Islamic law, scholars conjecture that the local customary laws of the indigenous Berber tribes, while respected up to a point, were integrated into sharīʿah with some Berber practices deemed exceptions and unacceptable in Islamic law, e.g., disinheriting females and trial by collective tribal oaths.[78] Between 1914 and 1933, as part of the French pacification program, a policy to divide Arabs and Berbers racially and juridically was pursued: tribes were categorized as either *tribus de coutumes*, subject to Berber customary law, or *tribus de makhzen*, subject to the central authority and sharīʿah; these arbitrary designations affected a third of the Moroccan population.[79] In practice, however, the French recognized Berber customary law only in certain restricted civil matters; Berbers and Arabs were bound by criminal law as defined over the decades by French colonial authorities through decrees (dahirs) supposedly emanating from the puppet sultan but actually issued by the current French Resident General.

Within the complex colonial framework of competing legal systems, hierarchically ordered and unequally applied, there were, however, Islamic and Berber laws on *diyah* (blood money), dealing with reparation and restitution. As an example of French approaches to the subject of diyah, in 1928, Georges Surdon authored a description of the sanction system of the Imazighen/Berbers by dividing Berber punishments according to prevailing French penal code categories: involuntary manslaughter called for compensation in the form of traditional rules governing diyah; voluntary manslaughter led to the perpetrator's flight or the victim family's vengeance; physical injury called for fines set by the tribe—indemnities for adultery, fines for rape paid to the parents or to the tribe, and a variety of prices fixed to compensate acts of stealing and arson.[80] On the eve of Moroccan independence, Jacques Berque, who studied the Seksawa Berber of the High Atlas mountains, concluded that ʿurf was based on sharīʿah, that Berber customary law was a subset of Islamic law, and, therefore, regarding punishments and blood money, the intent was not private vengeance but the restoration of public order and social accord achieved primarily through reparations in the form of money, food, and livestock.[81] Thus, it appears that although Islamic law had largely absorbed Berber customary law by the time of the Protectorate, under French colonialism both systems were shunted aside and replaced. Not only French legal codes, but lessons from the colonial French capacity to efface vibrant, existing legal systems were carried over intact into post-independence Morocco and exemplified by the

Indemnity Commission's erasure of both existing international and domestic Moroccan law on indemnification and arbitration.

Apology

Legal scholar Martha Minow suggests occasions for symbolic reparation to begin the work of repairing the past, ideally exemplified by the persuasive power of an official apology: "Official apologies can correct a public record, afford public acknowledgment of a violation, assign responsibility, and reassert the moral baseline to define violations of basic norms." Minow notes, however, the limited force and appeal of words only:

> [Official apologies] are less good at warranting any promise about the future, given the shifts in officeholders. Unless accompanied by a direct and immediate actions (such as payments of compensation) that manifest responsibility for the violation, the official apology may seem superficial, insincere, or meaningless.[82]

Malika Oufkir and her family, disappeared for over eighteen years, emphasize the importance of government apologies that go hand in hand with government indemnification. Although the Oufkir family produced an inventory of their despoiled belongings and property to Moroccan lawyers, Oufkir reports in her 1999 book that she is still waiting for restitution.[83] Now residing in France, she has stated publicly: "If the government says 'we are sorry you are victims,' then we can come back to our country.[84]

The Moroccan combination of paying indemnities to victims while absolving the guilty redirects our focus to the case of post-war West Germany. Chancellor Konrad Adenauer, who launched the German reparation program, began his new government in 1949, as German historian Norbert Frei notes, by dismantling the Allied denazification programs for Nazi-era crimes: "Its price was living memory . . . [society] pardoned, as it were, itself," as the majority of West Germans were determined to "overcome" by forgetting everything to do with Nazi past.[85] Amnesty programs for those guilty of serious crimes were created and restitution laws reintegrated hundreds of thousands of Nazi party members into their former jobs and professions, including many from the Gestapo and SS who would then be called by the post-war German government "those damaged by denazification"; Frei calls this "a policy for the past (*Vergangenheitspolitik*) whose failings would stamp the new state's spirit over many decades," suggesting that

Germans were acknowledging that the entirety of German society could not be disentangled from complicity in Nazi crimes.[86]

Despite more than fifty years of German payments, it is not yet possible to gauge the extent of suffering caused by Germany's postwar self-pardoning (Frei's concept) and its effect on its victims, or on subsequent generations. As in the Moroccan terms *ṭayy al-safḥah*, there are many advantages to "turning the page" on state crimes—the necessity to retain large numbers of trained civil servants, the impossibility of dismantling a complicit army and police force, the need to ensure a stable government as these institutions progress toward economic and political reform—all of these reasons is advanced by Morocco's ruling elite.

In Morocco, victims are forced to face, indeed they encounter on a daily basis, perpetrators of torture and forcible disappearance in place as judges, governors, bureaucrats, lawyers, military personnel, and police officers. Aziz El Ouadie (Marxist-Leninist political prisoner, 1974–84) ran into his torturer, Bettache, known to him by the nickname al-Fasi, in a Casablanca store; El Ouadie reports that he cried in rage.[87] In 1994, Abdennaceur Bnouhachem, forcibly disappeared to the secret detention sites of Agdz and Kalaat M'Gouna (1976–1985), heard the name of his torturer, Allal El-Ouazi, when both were standing in line at a Rabat government office. Bnouhachem recounts that he introduced himself in order to find out reasons for his kidnapping and torture. El-Ouazi turned pale and blurted, "you're still alive!" El-Ouazi claimed that Bnouhachem's name was listed as a follower of Colonel Ahmed Dlimi, who had attempted a coup d'état against Hassan II. In fact, Bnouhachem belonged to groups opposing Dlimi.[88] In 2002, Islamist political prisoner Hasan Elhasni Alaoui recognized his torturer, Mohamed Legnoufi, when both were repairing cars in a Casablanca garage. Alaoui reports Legnoufi's story:

> I was a teacher. I wanted to improve my situation so I took the police test. They sent me to the brigade of torturers. Once they brought a member of my own family to Derb Moulay Cherif. I tortured him even worse. Why? Because with the other torturers present, I had to do it, otherwise they would report me. So, understand, I was forced to do it to you.[89]

By June 2000, al-Muntadā had established a standard form to be sent to all who suffered from arbitrary repression or to those competent to write on behalf of the dead, the disappeared or any others unable to write themselves. Al-Muntadā's legal recommendations for prevention of abuses include ratification of international treaties, an automated and publicly accessible database on detentions, and the inclusion of human rights education at all levels of schooling from primary to university. Morocco is to become a state under rule of law with parallel secret police services either disbanded or placed under parliamentary control. According to Driss Benzekri, al-Muntadā's first president, what characterizes the Moroccan approach, compared to international efforts, is that so far it is the most underdeveloped and the least serious. Unlike Chad or South Africa, Morocco has not changed regimes; in Morocco, a regime is attempting to transform itself from the inside, trying to become democratic yet retaining control, a process that is reflected in the regime's approach to human rights. Benzekri believes the difficulties began when Hassan II created the ACHR as a non-independent body with no clear mandate or procedures.[90] The powerful and conflicting Moroccan taboos of impunity and accountability for acts by a police state (the government acts with impunity and cannot be held accountable) overcome "turning the page" without recognizing state crimes.

What Benzekri and al-Muntadā have asked for is the establishment of a commission of inquiry with powers of investigation to attach necessary official archives or police documents and to summon witnesses, in other words, with legal powers and authority of the judiciary. Al-Muntadā members envision their actions within a larger framework. They employ political and legal discourses that are performance-oriented; by relying on participatory structures, audience-speaker interactions, the role of the public human rights lecture as a genre, and the status of speech as social action, the community of the disappeared and of political prisoners creates novel dimensions of performance, auguring what many hope will prove to be a new era (*ʿahd jadīd*). Although immediate goals are to rehabilitate the disappeared and the victims of oppression with recognition or money and jobs, they seek to rehabilitate not just individuals but all of Moroccan society by abolishing a culture of fear and victimization in order to produce confidence in society and secure the human rights with which to build a new state. Victims' responses to the fact of indemnities are framed by performances in the public sphere—conferences, sit-ins, vigils, rallies, public testimonies, funeral eulogies, and commemorative days—that invite critical reflection on the ways in which performance plays a role in wider socio-political contexts. Such performances are social practices deeply connected to Moroccan history and current attempts to uncover, write, and revise that past. To sustain the notion that the social life of human beings can be viewed through performance, accounts of specific Moroccan legal and prison practices allow us to reconstruct mechanisms of abuse, with some attention to complex underlying social and political causes and contexts, against which communal cultural enactments are composed.

Chapter 2
Disappearance

In Morocco, what does it mean to be disappeared? Who does it, to whom, how, when, and where? Does being disappeared continue to occur? Much of the story of forcible disappearance in Morocco is told about the past from the perspective of the present, particularly by what has become public since 1999. Neither the death of Hassan II that year nor the enthronement of Muhammad VI constitutes a regime change according to which paradigms of law and governance are drastically altered; rather, the emergence of the disappeared happened because political and cultural changes that took root over decades flourish and encourage the narration of human rights abuses. The humanity of the disappeared is kept alive through performance, storytelling, and writing: contemporary letters, reports, bulletins, and communiqués, many dating from the 1970s onward, create a human rights archive that sustains and informs knowledge about disappearance in Morocco.

Language

To designate someone as "disappeared," if only on the printed page, new grammatical forms, notations, and distinct writing styles have evolved in many languages. The body of the "disappeared person," for example, lies between quotation marks. Amnesty International places the term between inverted commas (suggesting irony?) perhaps more to emphasize that the person has not truly disappeared because the government knows the victim's whereabouts but such knowledge is cruelly denied to the rest of us. Not only written references to an actual person but also to the act of enforced disappearance revises syntax. Grammatically, the verb "to disappear" in English and Moroccan Arabic has taken on an additional causative sense in order to denote transitively "to make someone to disappear." So ubiquitous have these new uses for "disappear" become that most authors currently dispense with quotation marks to describe the contemporary practice of eliminating political opponents discursively and physically.

The French word *un disparu* is employed in francophone contexts for a person who has been forcibly disappeared. Official Arabic-language human rights terms, as used in United Nations documents, are *al-ikhtifāʾ* (disappearance), *al-ikhtifāʾ al-qasrī* (forcible disappearance), *al-ikhtifāʾ ghayr al-ṭawʿī* (involuntary disappearance), *al-ikhtiṭāf* (kidnapping), and *al-iʿtiqāl al-taʿassūfī* (arbitrary detention). The Moroccan Arabic verb *ghabber*, as uttered most frequently in the phrase *Ḥasan ghabbru*, means "Hassan forcibly disappeared him" and permits the following macabre causative and transitive conjugation: *ghabbrūh* (they disappeared him), *ghabberhum* (he disappeared them), *ghabberha* (he disappeared her), *nghabbrik* (I will disappear you), and so on according to context. Literally and letter by letter, the Arabic triconsonantal root *gh-b-r* denotes "someone or something covered over" as well as "the act of being turned to dust," a case in which a semantic field links enforced disappearance to one of its gruesome outcomes, the dead missing body disintegrating beneath the sands, perhaps part of a mass grave.

The war of words between victims and government authorities rages as ferociously as any battle over territories. In its contemporary human rights forms, contrasting Moroccan terminologies are best considered beginning in 1990, when Hassan II issued a *dahir* (royal decree) that created al-Majlis al-Istishārī li-Huqūq al-Insān (Advisory Committee on Human Rights, ACHR). Although the ACHR was first charged with missions to investigate preventive detention and the situation in Moroccan prisons, and press announcements about these projects were issued, little was accomplished until April 1998, when Prime Minister Abderrahmane Youssefi revived the case of those disappeared before parliament. Based on meetings held 20 April, 28 September, and 13 October, a controversial ACHR memorandum emerged. Those missing were referred to as *mā yusammā bi-al-mukhtafīn* (the so-called disappeared) and an absurdly low total of 112 persons were listed: 56 *mutawaffūn* (deceased), 44 *maṣīruhum majhūl* (their fate unknown), although acknowledging that 18 are *al-ikhtifāʾ fī ẓurūf ghāmiḍah* (disappeared under mysterious circumstances), and 12 alive and living in Morocco or abroad.[1]

Government statistics and terminology exacerbated differences between the victims of disappearance and those in authority. The government caused people to disappear. The government created categories of disappearance disputed by victims. Thus the government does not acknowledge the true numbers in its various categories and that its figures for the disappeared are but a subset of the total number of victims. Naima, the sister of Omar El Ouassouli, who disappeared in 1983 but is listed as living abroad, states:

When we heard Dahhak drily reading his list in the form of numbers, we were flabbergasted. They told us that he was abroad. It seems we have a brother in France but they don't know where he is. When my mother heard the news, she nearly went crazy. She has suffered in anticipation. What does it mean abroad: the sea, the land, the sky, the moon or Mercury?[2]

Moroccan authorities echo their Argentine counterparts. In an act of "uncanny sadism" to cover up the political violence unleashed on their own population between 1976 and 1983 during the era known as the "dirty war," the Argentine military's denial took the form of declarations "that the persons reported as missing were living in voluntary exile in Europe or Latin America."[3] Because a number of those disappeared reappeared, as if miraculously, in both Argentina and Morocco, the cruelty of no bodies and cynical insistence upon lives lived normally elsewhere compounded the grief of many families as they waited long years with emotions suspended between terror and hope.

Recognizing the difficulty of legally defining disappearance, British jurist Nigel S. Rodley circumvents the problem by declaring:

that causing disappearance is a form of torture. . . . All the legal consequences of torture would be the same for disappearances since they would be one and the same thing. . . . We may not be able to specify what amounts to refusal to acknowledge detention or length of time that has to elapse, but we know a disappearance when we see it.[4]

Rodley's allusion to pornography is apt: disagreements over what is obscene and offensive ensure that no consensus or precise definition is likely, as when U.S. Supreme Court Justice Potter Stewart concluded that the French film, *Les amants* (The lovers), was not pornographic: "I shall not today further attempt to define the kinds of material [pornography] . . . but I know it when I see it."[5] Stewart's remark highlights the necessity of seeing in order to make judgments. Rodley's appropriation of Potter's well-known phrase means that we see an act of enforced disappearance precisely when we no longer see the disappeared person. Given that terms for disappearance are translated into Arabic, one of the official UN languages, the distance between an existing international vocabulary for the disappeared and the Moroccan "so-called disappeared" confirms Rodley's notion: the Moroccan authorities do not see the disappeared, and they conclude, therefore, that there are no disappeared Moroccans. If there is a term, once the circumstance has a name, then a history, a literature will develop and remedies can be sought. Those who use UN terminology are victims of human rights abuses or their representative associations. The Moroccan government, in contrast, has produced its own set of terminology.

At the international level, in 1992 a Working Group on Enforced or Involuntary Disappearances (WGEID) established by the United Nations Commission on Human Rights defined disappearance as a process in which

> persons are arrested, detained, or abducted or otherwise deprived of their liberty by officials of different branches or levels of Government, or by organized groups or private individuals acting on their behalf, or with the support, direct or indirect, consent or acquiescence of the Government, followed by a refusal to disclose the fate or whereabouts of the person concerned or a refusal to acknowledge the deprivation of their liberty, which places such persons outside the protection of the law.[6]

Enforced disappearance is recognized as a crime against humanity by a number of international conventions, organizations, and courts.[7] In 1994, Argentina became the first state to recognize a family's legal right to transform the status of a missing member from "disappeared with the presumption of death" to "forcibly disappeared" and to request a "certificate of disappearance," a document that does not foreclose the possibility that that one day the missing person may return.[8] In Morocco, since 1960, laws enabling families to declare the death of one of its members exist in the form of the dahir of 10 August 1960, but could not be invoked for a judicial certificate of decease for a disappeared person, because article 3 places the burden of proof on the petitioner to present the actual place of death or disposition of remains.[9]

Documenting

Using testimony to document disappearance and absence is not always successful. Courts and lawyers prefer to deal with texts and documents generated by witnesses but less so with deeper levels of feelings and the experience of everyday life. The paradox of "seeing" someone who has been disappeared is to acknowledge publicly a network of terror that has produced the nothingness of absence, and to proclaim fearlessly the no-longer-being-there of loved ones. The testimony of absence raises problems of context and memory, of first-hand versus second-hand witness, and of witness versus hearsay: how are the people arbitrarily disappeared, killed, tortured, and detained to be numbered?[10] A haunting essay by novelist Annie Dillard conjectures:

anyone's family and friends compose a group invisible, at whose loss the world will not blink. Two million children die a year from diarrhea, and 800,000 from measles. Do we blink? Stalin starved 7 million Ukrainians in one year, Pol Pot killed 1 million Cambodians . . . shall this go on? . . . How about what journalists call "compassion fatigue"? Reality fatigue? At what limit for you do other individuals blur? Vanish? How old are you?[11]

Mind-numbing statistics of the Holocaust as well as the recent genocidal histories of Cambodian and Rwanda set ghastly standards for the number of victims of human rights abuses. A major difficulty for Moroccans is to uncover the lineaments of a different kind of depopulation and population, not only the numbers of disappeared but also those terrorized by direct and indirect means into silence. Morocco has produced subtle gradations of disappearance. There are those who disappeared and never reappeared, and to this day it is not certain if they are alive or dead. Others disappeared, reappeared to be judged, were liberated, and then redisappeared. Important leaders and activists, such as Mehdi Ben Barka in 1965 and Houcine El Manouzi in 1974, were kidnapped abroad in front of witnesses and disappeared. Interviewed at age ninety in 1999, Ali El Manouzi, father of Houcine, concludes that his son's disappearance is the price paid by his family for their proud genealogy of resistance:

Here it has been almost thirty years that we hope for a sign of life from Houcine, our eldest son, who disappeared in the beginning of the 1970s. It was when Morocco was shaken by coups d'état, uprisings, and a barbaric repression. I myself, my seven brothers, and my seven sons were in the resistance against injustice and repression. We fought to improve our lot, to have the right to free expression, the right to work freely, and to go wherever we want. It was a hard fight, one that has not yet ended. Not even when we fought for independence that we obtained in 1956. We quickly learned that the liberty for which we fought was not given. We have paid a high price. My brother Brahim was executed because as commander in the army he participated in an attempt against the king. My son Houcine is perhaps dead these past thirty years without us being able to bury him in the family circle. All the men in the family have, at least once, most of us more often, seen the inside of a prison cell. Where one feels only, because for entire weeks or months we were chained and blindfolded. I myself, my brother Abdallah, and my son-in-law Houcine ben Mohammed have deep scars on our arms between wrist and elbow due to the iron wires with which our arms were attached for long months. They became infected wounds and we carry forever these scars on our hands and our souls.[12]

Some who disappeared have returned; the price to reinhabit the world of the living is silence, silence from the victim and silence from his or her extended family. Most disappeared never reappear. Even modest attempts by families to locate missing members expose family members to charges of political subversion. Family members and neighbors of the disappeared become targets of disappearance. Sion Assidon recounts that after he escaped from a prison hospital on 13 October 1979, more than 25,000 Moroccan policemen were mobilized throughout the country to blockade borders from Oujda to the Sahara and all roads leading to major cities, and that the families of the escapees and hospital personnel were tortured for information, the houses of anyone who had ever visited a prisoner were placed under police surveillance, and police sweeps netted disparate groups of the usual suspects, such as bearded Moroccans, drug dealers and known delinquents.[13] The family of Mohamed Nadrani, a disappeared student (1976–85), also passed through Derb Moulay Cherif: Ahmed Nadrani, brother of Mohamed, for three months (December 1975 to mid-April 1987), joined by their father and another younger brother.[14] In the summer of 1983 in response to antimonarchy graffiti painted in the town of Mohammedia, police arrested, tortured, and eventually released 80 high school students before sending 30 to Derb Moulay Cherif. An entire town was paralyzed with fear.[15] On 25 October 1985, Amina Boukhalkhal arrived at the Casablanca apartment of her fiancé, Brahma Moustapha, who had been arrested earlier for membership in Ilā al-Amām. Police intercepted her and forced her and other random visitors to lie blindfolded on the floor. The apartment was ransacked and tapes and books confiscated. She was held five days in Derb Moulay Cherif and threatened with rearrest were she to speak about her illegal detention.[16] To calculate the total of Moroccans who experienced the sequence of arrest and torture—be the result disappearance, release, or trial and prison—consider the following conservative hypothesis: for every known political prisoner, add five to account for friends, family, neighbors, and random passers-by.

Moroccan victims and human rights organizations dispute Moroccan government disappearance figures. How does one ascertain the veracity of numbers when the perpetrators, the world of "violence workers," reconstruct numbers and descriptions of torture relying, for example, on a rare instance of a Moroccan policeman's confessions?[17] Beginning in 2001, Ahmed Boukhari, a former secret service agent, began granting interviews to French and Moroccan newspapers detailing a world of secret detention centers, torture, and disappearances during the decades of the 1950s, 1960s, and 1970s. In his book, *Le secret*, published in France in 2002, he writes:

> I chose to speak. For a long time I wanted to burst out with the truth, reveal the techniques of the Moroccan secret service, tell about the kidnappings and disappearances. In 1972 already, I was in Paris intending to shout out the truth. Then I became afraid. For myself, but mainly for my family. Repression swept heavily over Morocco and I gave up having my voice heard. In 1983, a new stay in France. But the time had not yet come to open sensitive files. It was necessary to wait. It was difficult for me to reveal all, I had kept the secret so long.[18]

Boukhari admits to his own roles as both accomplice and witness to the 20 October 1965 kidnapping of Mehdi Ben Barka, Morocco's exiled charismatic opposition leader, in front of the Brasserie Lipp in Paris, an operation that is reported to have involved the French authorities, assorted French gangsters, the French and Moroccan secret services, Israel's Mossad and the U.S. Central Intelligence Agency (CIA)—a lethal cocktail of operatives representing those most committed to upholding Hassan II's regime.[19] Boukhari narrated the removal of Ben Barka's body from Paris to Dar El Mokri, a secret torture center in Rabat, and the disposal of Ben Barka's body with the help of "Colonel Martin," a CIA man in Morocco, who promoted the usage of a stainless-steel tank filled with acid, its efficacy proven during the reign of Muhammad Reza Shah of Iran (1941–79), to dissolve all physical evidence of a human body.[20]

Ben Barka is the most notorious symbol of Morocco's ongoing difficulties with kidnapping and disappearance. While Ben Barka's case continues to roil relations domestically and internationally, it is Boukhari's estimates of hundreds of forcible disappearances and thousands of kidnappings that stuns: a total of some 13,500—approximately 350 people each year between 1960 and 1973, to which are added sizeable increases during years of specific political upheavals in which plots against the throne were to have taken place, for example, 5,000 kidnappings in 1963 (only two of whom, Boukhari notes, ever appeared before any judge) and more than 2,500 between 1969–70, and 6,000 in 1973 following an uprising in the Middle Atlas mountain region.[21]

Boukhari's estimates are based on the years 1960–73; missing are statistics before and after his working life in the secret police that might double or triple his number of 13,500. Any attempt to count confronts contested interpretations of Morocco's history: when do *les années de plomb* (the years of lead) and *al-sanawāt al-sawdā'* (the black years) begin or end? Muhammad El Atlas counts immediately after independence in 1956, when Muhammad V ascended the throne only to disarm, disperse, or destroy the various independent and competing resistance groups and armies to which El Atlas belonged.[22] For the Riffians of the northern Moroccan zone, marginalization and impoverishment deepened with the December 1958-February 1959 uprisings quelled by an army of 15,000 men lead by Crown Prince Moulay Hasan (later King Hassan II) and General Mohamed Oufkir, both held responsible for napalmed villages, unknown numbers killed (estimates are between two and eight thousand),[23] many arrested and the property of notables confiscated.[24] Riffians call these years *assouggas n'ouedhra* (in Tarifit Berber, the year they went up the mountain; in French, *l'année de la montagne*).[25]

For journalist Jamal Berraoui, the Paris 1965 kidnapping of Morocco's most famous disappeared leader, Mehdi Ben Barka, marks the beginning: "The Ben Barka affair initiated a black era in Morocco. Between 1965 and 1985 thousands of Moroccans suffered torture and arbitrary detention. The entire society was frozen with fear."[26] For Khadija Rouissi, member of the Committee of the Families of the Disappeared, *al-sanawāt al-sawdā'* began when her brother Abdelhak Rouissi, a trade union activist, disappeared on 4 October 1964 and continues through decades of her family's harassment—her own and her brothers' tortured passage through Casablanca's Derb Moulay Cherif—and it will not end until her brother Abdelhak's fate is revealed:

> Abdelhak remains alive among us, just as he has and will forever these past thirty-five years. If Abdelhak is dead, we demand that his remains be returned to us, my family refuses all indemnities until the truth is established, and those responsible for his kidnapping be brought to justice and judged for crimes they have committed.[27]

Were exact numbers known and the missing accounted for, how does one measure the range of people affected? Political prisoners, for example, were officially recognized but only after they emerged from months or years of enforced disappearance in secret detention centers. Are they to be counted as the formerly disappeared or the "so-called disappeared"? For those who will never reappear, how does one measure absence? Boukhari's confessional book, for example, tells the fate of those who died between 1963 and 1970 while disappeared in Dar El Mokri: "In case of decease, the cadavers, packed up in a black sack, were thrown either into a common grave or into individual holes dug in a corner of the park. Other remains, ballasted with a weight attached to the feet, were thrown into the sea from high cliffs along the Atlantic, others were buried at night far from Rabat in the region of Ain Aouda."[28]

Argentina also sent disappeared to watery graves. Only in 1995 did a retired Argentine navy captain, Adolfo Francisco Scilingo, attempt to justify to the public his role in throwing hundreds of bodies from military planes into the Atlantic Ocean. As with Boukhari's confession about tortured Moroccan bodies decomposing in the Atlantic Ocean, the reaction of authorities was disconcertingly similar: Scilingo in Argentina and Boukhari in Morocco were arrested by their governments in 1995 and 2001, respectively, and each charged with passing bad checks.[29] Boukhari, after serving a three-month reduced sentence, was released in mid-November 2001, still deprived of his passport and, thus, missed his rendezvous with a French judge appointed to revisit the case. Latin American dictatorships presented a terminology and set of practices that brought the category of *los desaparacidos* to the world's attention; Boukhari tells us the nameless Moroccan experience proves these grisly practices need not have precise wording in order to take place.

Categories

Mehdi Ben Barka is the most famous example of a disappeared political figure for whom no body has been found, no government information provided, and no resolution yet available. In contrast, another Advisory Committee on Human Rights (ACHR) category, *lam yaʿūdū mukhtaṭafīn* (those who are no longer disappeared), indeterminate in number, history, and content, and roundly criticized by Moroccan victims' associations, are those forcibly disappeared, arbitrarily detained, never tried in any court, but eventually liberated.[30] A double negation of status—a person once missing but absent no longer—calls into question the fate of thousands whose disappearances were "temporary" but did not result in prison or death; victims were tortured then released without trial.

On 12 October 1999, in response to the ACHR list of 112 disappeared, the Bnouhachem Group protested that their names once again did not ap-

Figure 2.1. Kalaat M'Gouna Prison, March 2000. Photo by author.

pear on any lists. Five students "forming a single group, a family," namely Abdennaceur Bnouhachem, Mohamed Errahoui, Abderrahman Kounsi, Driss Lahrizi, and Mohamed Nadrani, were kidnapped on 12 April 1976 and tortured in a Rabat secret detention center for over a year before their transfer to the prisons of Agdz and Kalaat M'Gouna (Figure 2.1).[31] They were released in 1985 as arbitrarily as they were disappeared nine years previously. Just as they were told in prison, "Your names are not on any list. You are here to die," so too did Moroccan ACHR authorities erase their disappearance. In both cases the phrase "the person's name is not on any list," seemed lifted from prison administrators as they answered the families and officials of an Amnesty International campaign who tried to gather information.[32] A booklet of their nine-year travails, with text and paintings by Mohammed Nadrani, the artist of the group, produced a new and heartfelt benediction on behalf of the disappeared from the community of human rights workers: "may your name be on our lists."[33]

For Nadrani, the struggle to remain alive and sane after spending years blindfolded and manacled or in solitary confinement meant that he asked himself daily the questions: "Will there be anyone left to testify, to scream to the world, about all these horrors?"[34] Nadrani's techniques for survival, repeated by many victims, are also part of the struggle to be present, accounted for, and counted. As he recalls toxic liquids forced down the throat under the water torture, Nadrani counts out the faces of his friends who he believes speak to him in the accents of poetry, and quotes verses to himself by another political prisoner, the poet Abdellatif Laabi, while urging himself to recite during the worst beatings, "Hold fast comrade" (*Tiens bon camarade*):

Not the first, not the last
Before and after
I thought of others
With the same thick pain
Cut through with dizziness
And I called out:
Hold fast, comrade
Your first steps in the barbarous night
Your heart suspended
A large stone in your throat
And bleeding in your guts
The anguish of not being human
The immense solitude
And this terrible scream
That passes through walls
To go out again from the chest
Hold fast comrade
I know the exact ten steps
Turning in wait
I know the language of the walls
Suffering summed up and dated.[35]

Nadrani reports that he sings to himself these well-known verses during torture sessions, a sustained attempt by a person in pain to borrow a specific literary representation. Laabi's poem is centrally concerned with Nadrani's own experience as he is living it at that moment: remember the time, dates, and places. What Nadrani and his fellow prisoner Abdennaceur Bnouhachem recall is the assault on writing and language by secret service agents who greeted them upon their arrival in the prison at Kalaat M'Gouna with words confirming that their kidnapping, secret detention, and tortures would endure undocumented: "We won't write our reports on paper but we will write them on your skin" (*innā lā naktubu al-taqārīr ʿalā al-waraq, wa-lākin naktubuhā ʿalā al-jild*).[36] To translate the wounds of police tortures inflicted on the flesh into writing, newspaper articles, and communiqués, the Bnouhachem Group members continue to disseminate the data concerning their own disappearances, they declare to the ACHR that the disappeared number is considerably higher, and they include biographical information about other detainees, for example the young male students who joined them at the torture complex and became known as the Group Complex.[37] Because of the Bnouhachem Group's testimony, the list of the disappeared grows. Without the detailed collective memories of groups that disappeared then reappeared—who, when, and where, and how many died with them or crossed their paths—the existence of hundreds of Sahrawis in extended families held in secret prisons is unverifiable.[38] The Bnouhachem Group members unfortunately are unable to confirm whether those who remained in secret detention after their own release in 1984 are alive or dead, only that they passed each other, vowed to remember names and dates in the netherworld of the undocumented, and returned to compile the lists.[39]

Kinship

Forcible disappearance cut a wide swath through the student and intellectual populations in urban areas. But as a Moroccan phenomenon, disappearance is contagion. It is a form of collective punishment that first engulfs the disappeared person, then is visited upon relatives, visitors, friends, and perhaps the neighborhood and the clan at large. Entire families, even the larger tribal lineage, disappeared based solely on kinship association with declared political opponents of the regime. A sensational disappearance befell the Oufkir family.

Malika Oufkir is the eldest daughter of General Mohamed Oufkir, the brutal and much-feared minister of the interior for Hassan II. Brought into the palace at age five by Muhammad V (the first king of independent Morocco and Hassan II's father) and raised at the royal court, Oufkir begins *Stolen Lives: Twenty Years in a Desert Jail*, her book about her family's disappearance, with wondrous tales of seraglio life in a North African palace. In August 1972, her father's failed attempt to overthrow the king brought an abrupt end to nineteen-year-old Malika's storybook youth. The palace announced General Oufkir's suicide and his wife and six children disappeared, not to be seen or mentioned again for years. Describing the moments they were taken away, Malika writes:

Where were we going? I had no idea. We were traveling at night. . . . I didn't know what to think any more. Was I right to fear the worst? Was my father really dead? . . . I didn't understand. But was there anything to understand? We were entering the realm of the irrational, the arbitrary. This was a country where they locked up young children for their father's crimes. We were entering the world of insanity (103). . . . But what could we do? We were so powerless and alone, so utterly dependent on the monarch's whims. (129)

The Oufkir family spent fifteen years of deprivation and maltreatment in various secret prisons, most often in solitary confinement. In 1987, family members staged a dramatic escape by tunneling out of their secret desert prison to enjoy only five days of freedom, during which Malika revisited her family house in Rabat only to find "a wasteland . . . Hassan II had ordered the house to be razed to the ground. It no longer existed, just as we no longer existed. Through this brutal act he had obliterated us" (213). Their family abode destroyed, their names not uttered for twenty years, and their existence known but to their torturers, such was the disappearance of an entire family exacted by royal will. Captured and kept under house arrest an additional four years, the Oufkirs were finally released in 1991 but prohibited from leaving Morocco, joining legions of disappeared Moroccans who " 'reappeared' one day, without any rhyme or reason."[40] The Oufkirs' return received enormous media coverage in Europe. For audiences in France, where Oufkir's book was first published to great acclaim in 1999 under the title *La prisonnière*, these dramatic Moroccan events and personages come with a certain familiarity and context—given France's history as Morocco's former colonial master, France's long-term economic, military, and academic interest in the region, the importance of Morocco's own francophone political and intellectual elite, and the transMediterranean character of France's large North African population. In 1996, Maria Oufkir, Malika's youngest sister, fled the country on a boat to Spain, another highly-publicized escape that attracted international attention and finally secured the Oufkirs' freedom to travel abroad.

To describe her reappearance among the living, Myriam Oufkir, imprisoned with her sister Malika, chooses poetry:

Like a bird whose nest has just been destroyed
Like a child who loses his mother's hand
In a street scuffle
Like a coffin in a vast cemetery
Like a flower with no leaves or perfume
Like an angel driven from paradise

Like someone condemned to death who loses herself in the noise of nothingness
For long and precious minutes to contemplate the finger caressing the trigger.
Woman oppressed, I announce my return.[41]

Malika Oufkir has authored her condemnations as core texts around which to build a new national literary history and communal identity. Despite the bloody family drama of her father, a towering figure in Franco-Moroccan military and political history, who built a system of secret prisons and torture centers—only to have it consume his own family—Oufkir's personal and family struggle is deeply political and patriotic, and she understands her media blitz, book publication, and tours as part of a strategic campaign for democracy and the rule of law in Morocco:

Because even in telling the truth of the past, I still love my country. That's why I can't understand some people who make [a] confusion between a past and the present. It's not easy to witness the truth but I'm sure that many of us through their witness are going to build their country more than destroy it.[42]

Malika Oufkir's memoirs exemplify a return by the disappeared to the attention of the Moroccan public and world via international publication networks and a return to examining a regime's repression during the waning days of one ruler's reign, Hassan II. The publication of Oufkir's book in the last years of Hassan II's reign was seemingly possible under the shield of a French venue.[43] Morocco's quest for documentation about the past, for the actual bodies of the disappeared and for the names of the torturers is an elaborate and frustrating process, filled with confusion and moral complexity. In a television interview in 2001 with Oukfir, American television personality Oprah Winfrey asks: "When you were released he [Hassan II] was still alive. Did you want to say something to him? Was there something you wanted to say?" Indeed, Oukfir's response reflects both the difficulty of extracting meaning from mass torture and arbitrary imprisonment, and at the same time the necessity of testifying to it:

Yes. Maybe I think I told him everything I want to tell him through the book. The first thing—the most important thing—it's to tell him the truth, because nobody in his life was allowed to tell him really who he was. And the second thing maybe the only question, why?[44]

Tazmamart

What happens when abject fear in a terrorized population conceals accuracy in numbers and intensity of loss? Many of the "temporarily" disappeared still fear to count themselves, perhaps accepting the lesson that they serve as an example, while others refuse to declare their past for a variety of reasons. Women who were abducted, tortured, and raped fear social stigma or repercussions to their own families; many women interviewed discounted their own experiences, asserting theirs should never be compared to a brother, father, son, or husband's sufferings.

In a series of newspapers interviews in the spring 2000, Abdennaceur Bnouhachem attempts to answer why he and other students, none markedly active politically, were singled out for disappearance: "I believe that they wanted to present to the Moroccan people an example in order to intimidate and create a situation of fear and alarm to the point that no Moroccan would think of political or union opposition.[45] Bnouhachem uses the Arabic words *irhāb*, *khawf*, and *halaʿ* to describe a pervasive Moroccan political and social climate of government intimidation, terror, and fear in the face of anything resembling *niḍāl* (political activism). Abdelaziz Mouride's terms are the normalization of *thaqāfah dyal khawf* (a culture of fear) during which time the politics of amnesia took over; few were willing to pronounce, for example, the name of a place called "Tazmamart."[46] The subjective experience of fear, inspired by the objective existence of sites such as Tazmamart prison, encompassed an entire population to create a context that forced many Moroccans into silence and complicity. Anthropologist Abdellah Hammoudi meditates on the conundrum of his generation of Moroccans, the first educated elite created in the new era of post-independence Morocco:

> We were to fit the slot of the respected, learned, privileged elite, but the disciplining of our minds and bodies was effected through that fit as well as through coercion and privilege itself. How did that control prove to be so successful? Is there a way to speak about it, to speak to it, to talk back at it? Many militants in the political parties and the unions sacrificed their careers and lives to shake the shackles of that control.[47]

Although many Moroccans perceived political militants and activists as isolated figures, resented and feared individuals who demonstrated courage against the regime or cynically and realistically made intellectual accommodations to state terror, opposition to the power of the Moroccan state by Moroccans was and is widespread and implacable. Nonetheless, varying degrees of coercion and privilege produced a culture of fear and terror, effectively so for any society facing state strategies where disappearance is endemic:

> The basic characteristics of cultures of terror is that these are societies where "order" (more precisely, the order of stratification or social inequality) and the politicoeconomic status quo can only be maintained by the permanent, massive, and systematic use of violence and intimidation by the state as a means of political control. A culture of terror is an institutionalized system of permanent intimidation of the masses or subordinated communities by the elite, characterized by the use of torture and disappearances and other forms of extra-judicial "death squad" killings as standard practice. A culture of terror established "collective fear" as a brutal means of social control. In such a system, there is an ever present threat of repression, torture, and ultimately, death for anyone who is actively critical of the politicoeconomic status quo. . . . When fear becomes a way of life . . . a culture of terror has emerged.[48]

Tazmamart, a French-built military barracks converted to a secret detention center, is located in the remote regions of southern Morocco. It is the extreme case for state terror, the example against which all other Moroccan disappearances are measured. Stories about the disappeared soldiers confined at Tazmamart for eighteen years are inseparable from who tells them and for what motive. To Moroccans, Tazmamart stands for the most abject disappearance; that its location is known and that it is now called by name, Tazmamart, also signals that it is acceptable, even appropriate, for all the stories of what happened during the "years of lead" to enter the public arena.

In 1971, a group of military officers and soldiers failed to oust Hassan II during an attempted coup at Skhirat palace near the capital. Coup leaders were summarily executed; 61 men, tried and sentenced to prison terms ranging from one year to life, were incarcerated in Kenitra Central Prison. A second failed coup, known as the Boeing Royal Affair because the attempted regicide was to occur while the king was in his private plane, followed in 1972. Fifty-eight men from the two coups were kidnapped from Kenitra Central Prison in 1973 and disappeared until 1991. The first to pinpoint their whereabouts to the outside world was one of the missing officers, Mohammed Raiss of the Skhirat coup, whose death sentence was commuted to life imprisonment. Raiss smuggled a letter to his wife, Khadija Chaoui, dated September 1973, a month after his disappearance from Kenitra Central Prison: "I am writing to you from Tazmamart between Ksar Souk (Rachidia) and Midelt. I am imprisoned night and day in a dark and humid narrow cell. Here, everything is forbidden including the sun and clean air. I never thought I would be transported by plane like a package: blindfolded and handcuffed."[49] Raiss's home for the next eighteen years was Block 1, Cell Number 14:

The guards left Block 1 at 10 in the morning. We were alone, I decided finally to inspect my new abode where henceforth I would govern alone, as absolute master. I began by groping like a blind man swinging my arms first in front, then laterally to touch anything. My cell was approximately three meters long and two meters wide, all of it in reinforced concrete, without windows, only seventeen small holes perforating the wall, onto an interior corridor, itself always dark except during food distribution. There was also a hole in the ceiling; there must have been a double roof because no light passed through, except when the sun was at its zenith, a moment when pale light timidly infiltrated. A cement slab one meter long and sixty centimeters high on which were placed two old used covers were to serve us as the bed. There was no mattress, no insulation, no pillow. In the left corner a small hole served for the toilet. I exerted myself to find a switch or faucet, but in vain. The floor was covered with plaster rubbish. The cement was still fresh and humid. My hand felt a plastic pitcher of five liters filled with water. This would be my daily ration. Nearby was a small mess-tin for food.[50]

By 1980 the prisoners of Tazmamart succeeded in conveying brief messages and information by means of letters circulated to prisoner families, Moroccan political parties, and associations, notably the Moroccan Association for Human Rights (AMDH, founded in 1979),[51] and carried to international groups. Newsletters of the France-based Comité de la lutte contre la répression au Maroc (Committee of Struggle Against Repression in Morocco) regularly published queries or clandestine letters that made their way out of Morocco. One letter, dated 5 August 1980, was reprinted anonymously in 1982; its author would be identified much later as Abdelatif Belkbir, originally sentenced to four years of prison:

We were shut in individually not to leave ever again. They are four square meter cells without air and without light. They are nauseating: badly built toilets and without toilet chains located in a corner. There is no window. A hole in the ceiling lets pale light filter in; a poor reflection, there is a double ceiling of corrugated iron, that lets us distinguish between continuous gloom and nighttime. True furnaces in summer, they transform into cold rooms in winter (eight months). Furnishings are reduced to a pitcher, a plate, a deformed plastic pot. Two covers filled with mites, spread on a mattress of stone make up the bedding of the prisoners who share bedbugs and roaches who are masters of the place. Scorpions proliferate. Snakes come sometimes to chase rats in the corridor to the great amusement of the jailers armed with sticks "the infamous wardens of hell" who feast their eyes on these macabre spectacles.[52]

The book credited with bringing the story of Tazmamart to international attention was Gilles Perrault's 1990 *Notre ami le roi* (Our friend the king), while interest in the subject was sustained abroad by Christine

Daure-Serfaty's *Tazmamart, une prison de la mort au Maroc* (Tazmamart, a prison of death in Morocco). Prisoners' own accounts and subsequent translations of testimony awaited their 1991 release as well as improvements in Morocco's human rights climate.[53] Beginning in the fall of 1999 during Ramadan, the memoirs of Mohammed Raiss were serialized in the Arabic-language newspaper *Ittiḥād Ishtirākī*, reputedly increasing daily circulation to half a million readers. Each morning it was possible to walk the length of Boulevard Bourgogne, my Casablanca neighborhood's main street, and meditate on the extraordinary spectacle of readers avid for information about Tazmamart. In cafes lining the street, identical newspaper pages were unfolded and held aloft to the same pages by row upon row of Moroccans that stretched for several miles. Raiss's book, originally written in French, was published in Morocco in 2001 in Arabic translation and followed a year later by the French text. On 21 December 1999, excerpts from Daure-Serfaty's 1992 French-language book were translated into Arabic and serialized in the weekly *al-Munaẓẓamah*, newspaper of the left political party, OADP (Organization of Democratic and Popular Action). In 2001, Ahmed Marzouki, originally sentenced to five years, released his published testimony, *Tazmamart, cellule 10* (Tazmamart, Cell 10). Composed once he was free in keeping with a collective oath by the prisoners that survivors must testify publicly, it was written in French and published simultaneously in Morocco and France.[54] Marzouki's work is an ethnographic account of more than six thousand days in secret detention, a chronicle of everyday life viewed from Cell 10, with a soldier's keen eye for observation and whose literary force comes from the relentless accumulation of detail. A novel about Tazmamart, *Cette aveuglante absence de lumière*, by Tahar Ben Jelloun, based on interviews with a survivor, Aziz Binebine, was published in France in 2001. It was swiftly followed in 2002 by an English translation, *This Blinding Absence of Light*, the only volume from the Tazmamart writings with a wider transnational reach.

Books by Ahmed Marzouki and Tahar Ben Jelloun appeared simultaneously, occasioning invidious comparison and furious debate. Ben Jelloun, a well-known francophone Moroccan writer and long-time resident of France, daringly writes as a Tazmamart prisoner for novelistic purposes, composing his work entirely as the interior monologue of a hallucinating, apostrophizing, and imprisoned self:

> Faith is not fear, I told myself. Suicide is not a solution. An ordeal is not a challenge. Resistance is a duty, not an obligation. Keeping one's dignity is an absolute neces-

sity. That's it dignity is what I—what we—have left. Each of us does what we can to preserve his dignity. That is my mission. To remain on my feet, be a man, never a wretch, a dishrag, a mistake. I would never condemn those who cannot bear what is inflicted on them, who end by breaking under torture and letting themselves die. I have learned never to judge people.[55]

Ben Jelloun's novel was respectfully reviewed for English-language audiences. Its reception in France and Morocco met with vitriol; Ben Jelloun was judged harshly—"one was immured, the other never murmured."[56] Accused of cowardice for never employing his considerable novelistic skills during the "years of lead," Ben Jelloun pointedly notes that, with one brave exception[57] no Moroccan politician had ever raised the question of Tazmamart in Parliament: "I was afraid. I didn't want to confront Hassan II. I wanted to be able to come home."[58] Ben Jelloun was quickly embroiled in a secondary dispute about his project's genesis with Aziz Binebine, his Tazmamart prison informant. Binebine claims Ben Jelloun harassed him into speaking about his memories, whereas Ben Jelloun insists that the approach to narrate came from Binebine. A more equitable financial settlement between the disputing parties calmed matters, though opening possibilities for mockery and self-castigation, a task immediately taken up by Moroccan writer Abdelhak Serhane, whose short story is a soliloquy by the dog of Tazmamart, in actuality the pet of the Tazmamart prisoners made famous in their writings:

Fuck you with this idiotic leitmotiv! As I've said I was condemned and incarcerated in Tazmamart and all you can tell me is "Go back further into your past!" Do you even know where Tazmamart is? Yes, that's it. It seems the place was leveled. It doesn't exist any more. But it still exists in my memory, in the memory of other prisoners and especially in the nation's memory. Forget! Forget what! Eighteen years of a life interrupted! Eighteen years of physical and moral tortures. And all the consequences! And all who remained there! Forget? As if it were easy to forget all those scars in the body and in the mind. What a mistake! I am the only political prisoner bitch on earth and you continue to drive me crazy with your nonsense. Did you ever deal with an animal that went through imprisonment in a secret place? Do you realize how lucky you are to have me as a patient? Do you realize the importance of the privileged moments that I grant you? Do you know that I could have sold the rights of this story to a big publisher?[59]

Serhane, masked behind the bitch of Tazmamart, concludes that all Moroccans are dogs for doing nothing to prevent the existence of this site.

Were it possible to cast aside momentarily the distracting battle over the role of complicit intellectuals in general and in particular, Ben Jelloun's character—was he a coward, a protégé of Hassan II, an opportunist?—what is increasingly at stake for writers, novelists, and ethnographers of Morocco's "years of lead" are multiple ways to give voice to a variety of victims and survivors, and to locate possibilities for telling the story that emerges from the details of actual physical spaces at Tazmamart. Prisoners were placed arbitrarily in two separate groups, and housed in either Block 1 or 2. They could communicate easily within their respective buildings, less so between blocks. Only a few soldiers survived Block 2—among them Bouchaib Skiba, originally condemned to three years, Achour Ghani, to a life sentence, and Abdelaziz Daoudi and Aziz Binebine, to ten years—while the majority of survivors were from Block 1, for example, the authors Marzouki and Raiss. Why the discrepancy in the number of survivors between blocks? Is there a connection between Binebine of Block 2, whose traumatic memories were given over to and appropriated by Ben Jelloun, and Raiss and Marzouki, who witness on their own behalf in their own voice?

Some conjecture that the two blocks were sited differently on the terrain, with Block 2 subjected to harsher environmental extremes and inclement weather. Christine Daure-Serfaty offers one analysis of Block 1's survival success that takes into account the presence of M'barek Touil, sentenced to 20 years. As the husband of an American citizen, his treatment differed, permitting brief excursions outside the cell, food, medicines, and letters that were shared with fellow prisoners, and an astonishing 1985 visit from an American ambassador to Tazmamart: "Chance was a fact: Block 1 contained men who succeeded in establishing links to the outside. Materially they had more money, some money, they could obtain the small things necessary to survive. Morally, they felt less abandoned."[60] Abdallah Aagaou, an aviator picked up in random sweeps of the military after the attempted overthrow, resided in Block 1. He believes that the answer to any numerical discrepancy in survival rates between the two buildings lies in the art of storytelling. Although innocent of any coup activities, Aagaou was condemned to occupy Cell 5 facing Marzouki's Cell 10. Interviewed in Casablanca, he describes group resistance through coordinated and deliberate acts of imagination. He recalls years of scheduled tale-telling sessions carefully assigned among the prisoners, who could not see one another yet heard each other narrate for eighteen years. They spun out hours of film plots, street-by-street promenades through Paris, descriptions of lovemaking and women's bodies, endless rewrites of *A Thousand and One Nights*. Each man was Sheherazade, observes Aagaou, each in turn contributing to the special Friday noon narrative sessions reserved for elaborate descriptions of cooking the traditional couscous meal. Aagaou proposes tale-telling as an effective act of resistance, one that consciously sought to replicate the public space of the ḥalqah and the traditional storyteller.[61] Raiss also speculates about Block 1's strengths, and concludes that his fellow detainees' storytelling prowess evoked for him the legendary hero Sindbad of the Arabian Nights.[62]

The story of what happened in Tazmamart, eighteen years of disappearance in the worst incarceration conditions in the kingdom, is no longer disputed. The greater challenge, however, remains for Morocco, where the publication of Ahmed Marzouki's book to great acclaim in French in France did not spare him persistent police persecution in his own country. Since Marzouki's release in 1991, he was deprived of a passport—a common strategy to convert an entire country into a prison—until 2001, ten years after his release, to accommodate demands for book tours abroad. Marzouki concludes his memoirs with accounts of repeated post-prison summonses (understood as police interrogations) and stresses the ways in which he and his family are harassed, notably his shocking second kidnapping in 1995 when police detained him secretly for heated discussions about his manuscript's contents.

Beginning in 1995, Tazmamart survivors were accorded a monthly pension of 5,000 dirhams by the government of Hassan II. In April 2000, to mark the Moroccan visit of Mary Robinson, then United Nations High Commissioner for Human Rights, Muhammad VI bestowed additional one-time, lump sum payments of two million dirhams or more.[63] As much as the soldiers of Tazmamart have snared the literary limelight as victims of horrific disappearance, another category of victims, the families of those killed or wounded during the 1971 coup d'état, by soldiers such as Mohammed Raiss, have also raised their voices in the form of litigation and newspaper publicity.

Mohamed Ziane, a lawyer and former minister of human rights, promotes the cause of indemnification for members of the association of victims and families of Skhirat, with approximately 1,036 killed or wounded during the first and second failed palace coups. The Tazmamart survivors, who were tried and convicted after the two failed coups only to disappear, in Ziane's arguments are guilty of "crimes against humanity." He draws on international human rights law to categorize them as armed soldiers who fired murderously and with intent on an unarmed crowd during the failed coups.[64]

In 2003, Abdelatif Belkbir's wife, Rabéa Bennouna, published her memoirs, *Tazmamart côté femme: Témoignage* (Tazmamart, the woman's side: Testimony) describing the route her husband's letter took to her and then abroad to publication in France, detailing decades of surveillance and interrogations endured as government authorities attempted to control information about the disappeared soldiers. Caught in endless bureaucratic nightmares because she could not prove Belkbir was dead or alive, Bennouna describes the nefarious ways government harassment prevented her from obtaining basic documents such as a passport or her son's diploma, each a document requiring a husband's signature:

> Tazmamart governed their thoughts, their decisions, their actions in society. Even were they to distance themselves from this cursed name, the latter imposed itself on them, towards and against everything. A generation lost that a country turned into a dead-end. A generation traumatized that passed on to its descendents paranoia about everything that touches relations with the state. . . . Mankind can take on anything except injustice. The family can put up with anything except the unknown fate of its own members. The state can take on anything, put up with anything.[65]

As book follows book (testimonies, memoirs, and novelizations of disappearance), the cumulative effect of amassing disclosures of victim experiences has led to public and collective acknowledgments. A muted royal admission, evidenced by indemnification, attempts to set legal and financial limits. Indemnities, disputes about right to indemnification, human rights reports, international letter-writing campaigns, and court cases have become crucial to acts of describing past abuses. Their importance lies in the capacity to circumscribe and contain disappearance according to transparent and transnational protocols and vocabularies. In contrast, the controversy surrounding the merits of Ben Jelloun's novel versus Marzouki's eyewitness testimony has not been exhausted to this day, surely because both works are literary and ethnographic responses to the task of modifying the ways in which the past is to be remembered.[66] Ben Jelloun's voice is perceived as bifurcated, starkly embodying an as-yet unacceptable gap between writer, written testimony, and lived experience, in comparison to Marzouki and Raiss, who belong to the long line of activist prison authors compelled to write and lecture about one topic, their subjective experiences of disappearance. For the moment, Marzouki pens the question found in the ultimate sentence of his book. He asks: "Will we change this country one day?"[67]

Performances

On 7 October 2000, al-Muntadā assembled more than a thousand people to join what they called in French a *pèlerinage* and in Arabic *ziyārah* (pilgrimage) to the site of Tazmamart. Among the participants who experienced forcible disappearance and undertook the long bus trip to the remote southern region were Aziz Binebine, Ahmed Marzouki, and Malika Oufkir. On the level plain facing the entrance to the prison, pilgrims held photographs of the disappeared, lit candles, and scattered rose petals on the land. Government permits restricted pilgrims to the area surrounding Tazmamart.

Moroccans traditionally conduct pilgrimages; the term is commonly applied to visiting recognized Muslim saints' shrines. Many benefits derive from visits to well-known sites, specifically attaining a state approaching *barakah* (grace) or the holiness of blessed virtue that may come through direct physical contact with sacralized places. Shrines must be entered. At such times, petitioners and pilgrims may leave objects at a saint's grave to secure a related protection or they may circumambulate sacred sites and request the return of something or someone missing. An offering of candles, money or oil is also called ziyārah. To be present, to rub and to kiss sections of the interior, and to make recitations are customary practices.[68]

When the ziyārah reached Tazmamart, visitors were not permitted to enter the prison barracks that were impregnable, being a circuit of unbreachable walls topped with barbed wire.[69] A lone guard peering over the wall is said to have told the crowd: "I swear there is no longer anyone inside," a statement that unleashed weeks of nightmares for Fatna El Bouih, a political prisoner and victim of years of disappearance who joined the pilgrimage.[70] The guard's presence and government refusals to permit entrance to the visitors gave the lie to the guard's statement, turning confirmation into a threat. The built environment of Tazmamart is cruelly imbued with the ideas of political authoritarianism. Government authorities and policies that control access to places such as Tazmamart are willing to stand aside for the ephemeral performance of pilgrimage to sites of secret detention. Such performances as yet do not alter the site, although participants are profoundly affected by the journey and performance. The Tazmamart pilgrimage momentarily created the form of the ḥalqah, the newly created and redefined circles of exterior civic space where human rights speeches are articulated. But pilgrims could not enter what they thought was their destination. That space is policed inside the perimeter, rigidly circumscribed to exterior surface performances in front of the prison structure. By not allowing people to penetrate inside Tazmamart, in a sense the prison has been made to disappear, one more way to make disappearance continue.

Chapter 3
Prison

Debía tener barrotes en el corazón
quién primero pensó
en la carcél.

He must have had shackles
On his heart,
Who thought of building
The first prison.
—Mustapha Kamal (political prisoner, 1974–84)

When will it ever be written on Arab prison doors: it is forbidden to enter unless accompanied by ideas.
—Dahbi Machrouhi (political prisoner, 1985–91)

Torture, according to Article I of the "Declaration on the Protection of All Persons from Torture and Other Cruel, Inhuman or Degrading Treatment or Punishment" adopted by the United Nations on 9 December 1975, is

> any act by which severe pain and suffering, whether physical or mental, is intentionally inflicted by or at the instigation of a public official on a person for such purposes as obtaining from him or a third person information or a confession, punishing him for an act he has committed, or intimidating him or other persons.[1]

Two places—Kenitra Central Prison, Morocco's preeminent penitentiary to house political prisoners, and Derb Moulay Cherif, a secret detention center in Casablanca where many were forcibly disappeared—are Moroccan stories. How does writing work when the subject is the memory of torture? How may the writer translate past experience of torture into a present experience for listeners and readers?

Figure 3.1. Aerial photograph of Kenitra Central Prison, 1949–50. Institut Géographique National, France, MTC 1949–50 (NI 29-XVII-1d/2/-81).

Kenitra Central Prison

How is and was the kingdom of the incarcerated organized? Kenitra Central Prison continues to house political prisoners—the current population of Islamist political prisoners has replaced the leftists and Sahrawis of the 1970s and 1980s waves of repression. Reconstructing its lineaments and footprint from above is provided by a bird's-eye view in a 1950 French aerial photo (Figure 3.1). Its interior is reconstructed, described, and viewed by combin-

Figure 3.2. Interior courtyard of Kenitra Central Prison, circa 1980. Clandestine prison photograph.

ing selections from an extensive Moroccan prison literature paired with paintings and drawings produced in Moroccan prisons.

Artwork and photographs of political prisoners depicts the prison interior barred to spectator-visitors (Figure 3.2). One set of black-and white ink drawings by Abdelaziz Mouride (Marxist political prisoner, 1974–84), are the pages from his cartoon book. Mouride imagines the high walls, a massive barrier barring all knowledge of the prison's inner workings, as if

Figure 3.3. Drawing of Kenitra Central Prison walls. Abdelaziz Mouride, *Fī aḥshā' balādī* (Paris: n.p., 1982), 61, back. Reprinted by permission of author.

standing outside and viewing the external wall and tower that confront the passerby (Figure 3.3).[2] His depiction shows no trace of humanity. A painter and poet imprisoned with Mouride for ten years, Hassan El Bou, meditates upon the fact and effect of prison walls:

> The essential thing is the walls, the high walls of protection behind which falling into line are courtyards and buildings and another wall, much lower, and white, that hems in the entire base of the hill on which the fortress is perched. The essential thing is the young men deprived of liberty, separated from the river, the ocean, spring flowers, the scents of mint and semolina, work, music and holidays. There they may live as they feel like, provided that the rest of the kingdom's subjects are protected from them by this *cordon sanitaire* of strong stones."[3]

Sketches by political prisoners map the interior arrangement (Figure 3.4).[4] The photograph shows that Block A1 contains individual prisoner cells along a corridor; these cells are for political prisoners (Figure 3.5). A turn in the corridor takes you past the warden's office and leads to Block A2, whose row of single windows from one set of cells overlooks a courtyard surrounded by a wall that separates maximum security prisoners from

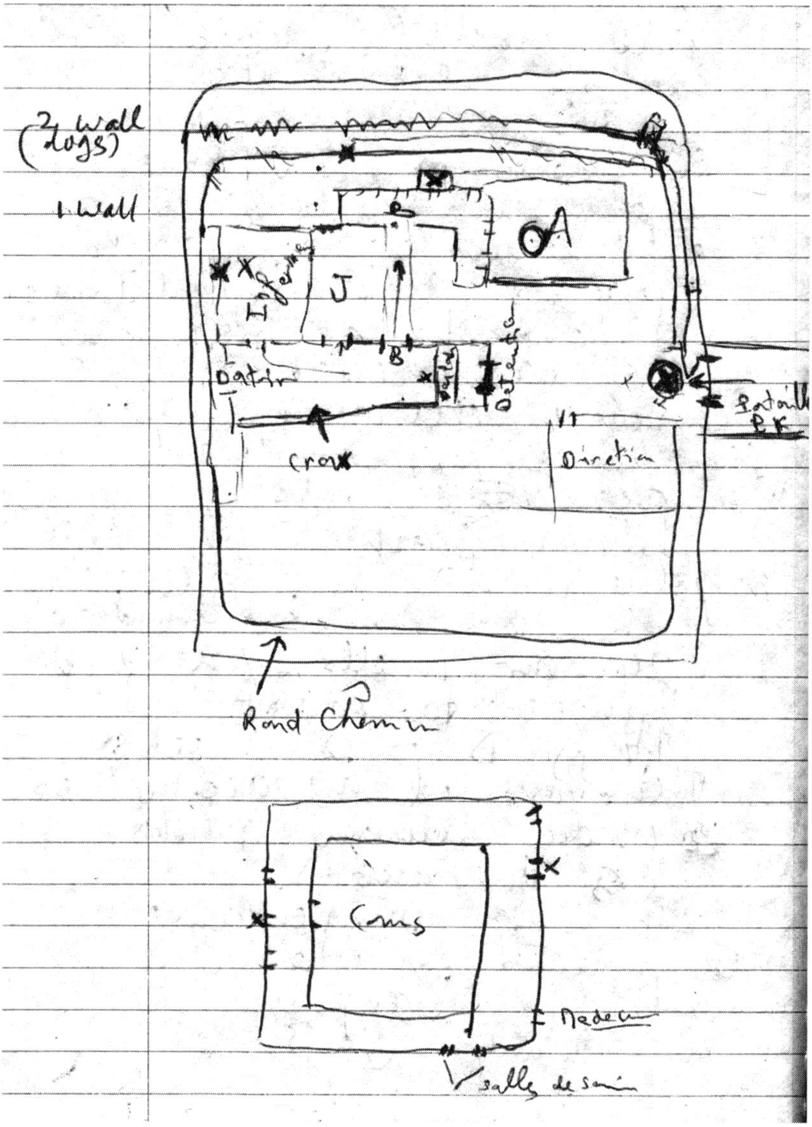

Figure 3.4. Sketch of Kenitra prison interior by Ahmed Haou. Reprinted by permission of author.

Figure 3.5. Political prisoner, Block A1, Kenitra Central Prison, circa 1980. Clandestine prison photograph.

death row prisoners. Inside the courtyard a structure served as a meeting point for prisoner confabulations and organizational activities after prisoners successfully used hunger strikes to win extensive outdoor courtyard time. The structure was called Lalla Chafia and touching its column and base would be one way to invoke a hoped for communal peace and cooperation among the prisoners (Figure 3.6). Driss Bouissef Rekab's novel *À*

Figure 3.6. Inner courtyard with the shrine of Lalla Chafia, Kenitra Central Prison. Clandestine prison photograph.

l'ombre de Lalla Chafia was written and published while he was still in Kenitra Prison:

We held our general meeting (*assemblée générale*) except for rainy days close to Lalla Chafia, which translated into European Christian culture, gives something like Our Lady the Healer (Notre-Dame-Guérriseuse). It was a thick column in the form of a parallelepiped hardly more than a meter in height, with an overhanging sort of capital. It was situated about the middle of courtyard A1. Next to it was a pretty apricot tree, a peach tree, and a young avocado tree which we pulled out and replaced with a garden and other trees in 1983. . . . The optimists, before the beginning of debates, would place five fingers of their right hand on the capital, embrace it and pray: Our beautiful Lalla Chafia, may God bless your family, you who know calm and serenity, make it so that this general assembly will be calm and serene and that the comrades don't lose their temper. Amen.[5]

Abdallah Zaazaa (political prisoner, 1974–89), offers an etiological narrative about the Lalla Chafia fountain's origins that Zaazaa reports from the chief prison warden, Abdullah Lakhsassi, himself a prisoner in Kenitra during the French Protectorate as a member of an anticolonial resistance group. Zaazaa, a self-proclaimed republican and antimonarchist, repeats the warden's tale:

In 1957–58, Muhammad V went to Kenitra Central Prison to visit prisoners incarcerated by the French but not released by Moroccans accompanied by his youngest daughter born in Madagascar. She pissed in the corner of the courtyard. It became sacred so they built a fountain.[6]

Zaazaa notes that a difference of twenty-three years separated his wave of 1970s Marxist political prisoners from the warden's, with no sign of identification between their common fates of dissidence. Nonetheless, invocations by prisoners at a site marked by royal urination also offered prisoners rituals and meeting places whose etiological narrative was sufficiently complex and sardonic.

Not the exterior courtyard but the interior world is the focus of Abdellatif Derkaoui's series of oil paintings about the cell bars of Kenitra Prison; he writes:

I strongly desire to give appearance to the reality of torture by means of painterly expression, a vast and fertile domain that requires much energy and materials. It is a world that demands to be seen in the light of day, though certain paintings are already in my imagination. I hope to realize them as soon as I complete an initial series on the influence of bars on the detainee's psyche. This is about painting all possible aspects of prison bars and deepening this technique by going as far as possible."[7]

Prison bars and cell ceilings, the boundaries of a prisoner's world, become for political prisoner Abdellatif Laabi "a silent, secret dialogue . . . an integral part of life like the ritual of eating and that of roll-call":

Every evening after the door had been closed, you automatically turned to this dialogue, as others might, after work, go and sit on the terrace of a café to look at passers-by. The ceiling was a second ocean for you. But unlike the sky it offered nothing to you to view. . . . The sun never appeared there nor the stars. But it was an ocean all the same. It was you who gave it life. . . . And this passive ocean turned out to be the best possible screen for allowing you to imagine as much as you wanted so that you could assure yourself that your mind still had the power to create. . . . You had already erased the shock of doors brutally slammed in your face. Ceilings [and bars] are made to be passed through.[8]

Derb Moulay Cherif

Writers when they are former political prisoners confront the lack of official documents to provide any facts about one of the principal torture factories,

Derb Moulay Cherif. The metaphor of the past of political prisoners as writing and indeed an emphasis on the materiality and artifactuality of the physical page in a vast book readable, visible, and legible to an entire nation, owes much to the famous speech by Hassan II on the occasion of the Youth Festival Day of 8 July 1994:

> We have therefore decided to turn definitively the page on what is called "political prisoners" . . . I intend that this situation will be definitively clarified in order to put an end, on the one hand, to a situation of embarrassment and doubt inside the country and to tendentious criticisms by ill-willed people or enemies abroad. In this way Moroccans will be sincere and credible when they affirm that Morocco has the rule of law [French, *état de droit*; Arabic, *dawlat al-qānūn*], that their words are corroborated by acts.[9]

According to al-Muntadā al-Maghribī min Ajl al-Ḥaqīqah wa-al-Inṣāf (Moroccan Forum for Truth and Equity), "to turn the page" as the late king pronounced, the page on which presumably are inscribed the names of the forcibly disappeared, if not the history of Moroccan repression, can only occur at the end of a process. Al-Muntadā's banner, displayed 27–28 November 1999 at the Cultural Center of Maarif in Casablanca, narrates its proposed themes: "No to forgetting, no to a spirit of revenge, yes to truth, yes to steps that restore justice and permit the page to be truly turned" (Figure 3.7).[10] Those missing, dead, and disappeared are envisioned as part of a vast archive of dossiers, pages and pages not yet made available to those most concerned to read them. Juridical and moral conditions must precede any attempt to turn these pages according to the poet Salah El Ouadie (political prisoner, 1974–84), and first vice-president of al-Muntadā, who said to a journalist:[11]

> "If your path should cross that of your torturer, what would you say to him?" Salah El Ouadie: "If he can look me in the eyes, I would say, quite simply, that as long as he remains with impunity at his job, the page cannot be turned."[12]

The page cannot be turned unless it is rewritten, read, known, widely disseminated, and whole in all its details:

> To turn the page, yes, but how to turn it before reading it well, and fully assimilating its contents?[13]

The names of the torturers, officials, judges, police officers and prison wardens, in fact the responsibility of an entire state apparatus, must also be

Figure 3.7. Banner of al-Muntadā: "No to forgetting, no to a spirit of revenge, yes to truth, yes to steps that restore justice and permit the page to be truly turned." Left to right: photograph of Mehdi Ben Barka, Driss Benzekri, Mohamed Hajjar, Hassan Saib, Salah El Ouadie, Abdelkader Zeroual, El-Ghnimi Belhaj, photograph of Saida Menebhi. Photo by author.

inscribed on these pages with their victims. Only then can the page be closed and a new blank one be opened. Salah El Ouadie reaffirmed the conditions to close the files:

> When the last victim willingly accepts to close the file, at that moment we can say that the page has been turned. What is remarkable today is that there are people who do not want to read the page, when it must be read. There are even those who want to tear out the page. Rather, it is necessary to save the page, because what will also be written on this page is the way in which we deal with this problem. It will be a page of our history.[14]

El Ouadie's account of his past takes the form of a novel. *Al-ʿArīs* ("The Bridegroom") is the misnomer nickname that El Ouadie's torturers assigned to him when they kidnapped him as he was leaving a wedding party. Dressed in tuxedo and bow tie, El Ouadie was forcibly disappeared into Derb Moulay Cherif. El Ouadie writes the novel as a sequence of clandestine letters from Derb Moulay Cherif to his mother, to the outside world from memory—because he had no pen or paper—and from the memory of torture in 1976 to publication with great acclaim in 1998, and translation into French in 2001, as *Le marié: Candide au pays de la torture* (The groom: Candide in the country of torture). *Al-ʿArīs* provides the immediacy that comes from employing the most intimate and local medium of counter-discourse, the letter written ostensibly for the eyes of the recipient only. El Ouadie sets the scene for the ensuing stream of letters, addressed to his mother but avidly read and disseminated to Arabic-language readers, by acknowledging that although she will never receive them he is "writing" them through willed acts of memory under dangerous conditions. As El Ouadie recounts his travails to his mother, his voice is one of Candide-like innocence. He will be tossed into a corner to be replaced by another political prisoner whose screams under torture pierce the dark cells and his consciousness. The author is forced to relive a torture session, this time, however, concentrating on what he has heard the police say as opposed to the pain he experienced, thereby permitting him to draw a series of parallels: the first one, equating the treatment of man to that of beasts, he rejects, while the second, between his individual plight and the degradation of the Moroccan population, he embraces:

Letter 1:[15]

Dear Mother:

I am writing you a letter you will never receive. I will write it in my memory because I lack pen and paper—how wretched a privation. I have many reasons to convince you that writing you now would be a grave imprudence even had I the means. I do not want—were I discovered, God forbid—to spend the night under a rain of abuse, of curses and gross insults, of beatings and random blows to my neck as if planned among them. I have already received today my share of offerings by the faithful who watch over our repose in this unique refuge. We eat, sleep, drink, keep silent, scream, bide our time, we cradle our hopes, praise God that we are still alive breathing the air of our country, and that our swollen bodies occupy space therein. When a well-trained prison guard arrives to call one of us ceremoniously for a high-level encounter with the agents that watch over our repose and those of our peers, he jumps for joy from his bed, leaves smartly in order not to miss the opportunity. Between you and me, how much time does it take an ordinary citizen to meet an official? Generally one year or two but here—long life to them—never is anyone left to wait. Personally, barely had I entered between their walls then I was given cast-off khaki, manacles, even more, they bestowed on me some black fabric whose use I did not immediately grasp, but finally, later, it protected my eyes from a light bulb illuminated day and night so they could follow all our movements. This I understood later. When they finished dressing me, somewhat energetically, they pronounced a number and said: "This is how we call you. When you hear it, say 'present.'" I said: "So be it." One of them smashed his fist into me: "Do not speak, dog, except when we order you to talk." I almost said, "Amen" but for a merciful God who restrained me. I will be silent now, Mother, they are coming shouting and I don't want to be surprised in the act . . .

Letter 2

Having conferred on me my own personal number, they put me in a humid place, and barely settled in, I heard one of them bellowing. Only then did I become aware that silence covered the place. I asked myself why silence on the one hand and yelling on the other. I had no leisure to answer the question. I felt a fist on my neck and a hand of iron grabbing me by my khaki shirt collar and lifting me into emptiness. The voice screamed at me: "Why didn't you answer the roll-call?" I slid on my shoes like slippers to gain time, grasping instinctively that to take time and lace them up could bring upon me severe reprisals. I marched hurriedly after the voice sincerely trying to make him understand that I was not yet accustomed to my number, but he was not the least convinced by my words rather he considered them nonsense. I was offended by this. I do not permit anyone to doubt what I say especially if the skeptic is a citizen with this degree of energetic force.

This citizen grabbed and pulled me by my handcuffs causing me pain. I was aware of entering a room, I believe by the door, because the citizen with the voice only lifted me when I was inside, where he was joined by other voices, other hands and feet that insulted, cursed, hit, smashed and kicked. Finally they attached me to a pole, with my face and stomach down; their chief said to me: "Your nose to the ground." I thought to myself, "Good heavens, he is right," despite this small observation which is that my nose was in cold cement, when they lifted the pole into the emptiness, as it happened, it, me, and all my weight carried by my handcuffs and my feet tied with a rope, and it was there, dear Mother, to speak truthfully, I understood I was being tortured. I said to myself, "Be a man," and I started to howl. You know how silent I am, how I hate noise, but the torture was intense. They interrogated me between one slap and another and strokes of the whip about names, concepts, and big words, So-and-so, Such-and-such, democracy, socialism, classes, citizens, countries, revolution. Then they brought an engine that hummed and maneuvered it near my skull and I in the situation I could see nothing. I believed at first that this affair concerned an enormous fly. But the story of a fly took wing when they placed the apparatus on my skull, my neck, my limbs, and I felt a shock and jolt travel through my entire body. I suddenly remembered that I knew this jolt from childhood, the day I was electrically shocked while playing; I remembered how you took me in your arms when I came in tears looking for you. Here was electricity being installed in my body long before reaching the countryside and the villages, even though I made no request to anyone. How can the government plead a lack of means—here they distribute electricity so generously without payment? I was brought out of my meditations by insults. Because they began to insult my father, you also, my descendants and my origins, saying my father was a big thief and you a big p . . . , not surprising I should be like you, I and my brothers, and that we would be extirpated (What is extirpate?), that I should be a man and speak the truth, neither more nor less. (Here they are returning to spit, threaten, yell, trailing behind them noise and the smell of tobacco. There is one who screams and has no fear of anyone: "Speak, who led you astray? Speak or I'll . . . motherf. . . .")

Letter 3

Mother,

They asked me, while I was in the air, to tell the truth and I replied as soon as they stopped hitting me: "It is not required to beat me for me to tell the truth. Lower me and I'll tell you." So they became quiet and I understood they believed me because they lowered me. The strangest thing, Mother, is that when they released me I could no longer feel my body. For the first time in my life I felt that I was a mere thought, that is all, without a body, and all this was as a result of an excess of pain. Two of them started pushing me while yelling, "Jump, jump, to make the blood circulate." And little by little, I was no longer a thought. After, they sat me down so I could speak the truth. I began to speak with some pride because these citizens were hanging on my lips in quest of knowledge. I said, "The people are poor, most children do not go to school, liberties are oppressed, and our country, after years of independence, is still—" I could not complete the sentence; they threw themselves on me all at once. Very curious. They find someone who tells them the truth, freely, and they repay him in this way. Curse them! Thus they continued to repay me each time they called my number until I began to think that my lying would avoid torture. I said to myself, "Next time I will lie to them, perhaps this decision will solve my problem." For this reason, I prepared in my head what I would say: "The people are rolling in comfort, all children are learning and even learning the love of Morocco, with liberty for all, and our country, after years of independence—" But this time too, they suddenly threw themselves on me and began to hit me, whip me, and say gross words about you and my father. This time even my paternal uncles, my paternal and maternal aunts did not escape their insults. I said to myself stretching out to rest after torture, "This is payment for liars." I had repeated these sentences in my mind to the point of almost believing. (I will sleep now, my body is completely desiccated after this round and only a kind of moaning emerges from my mouth. Here is what remains of me: a hoarse grunting from my mouth and heavy breathing from my nose).

Letter 4

After they finished whipping me, Mother, they threw me, as I told you before, into a smelly and very humid corner. The reason for this, as I understood subsequently, is because the sun never enters here. I lay down to rest; one would say I was carrying heavy stones on my shoulders. I remembered the slaves who long ago built the Pyramids and I compared my fatigue to theirs. I wanted to reflect on the differences between these two fatigues but for the first time my skull hurt when thinking. For the time, I set all this aside and began to feel my head. I found my hair shaggy and solidified in many places. I said to myself, "What is this?" I began scratching something hard, it was blood that flowed from head wounds. Here I understood what one of them said during my torture session: "Hit him in the head so as not to injure the skin." I thought they were speaking about sheep. I understood instantly that the sheep in question was me and I understood suddenly why they suspended me. Consider the confusion in their brains between a sheep and a human being. Perhaps they do not see why we should enjoy human rights because they take us for sheep. Ah, I get it. We must convince them that we are human beings, surely then they will stop beating and whipping us and cursing our fathers and mothers. . . .

Letter 5

I took it upon myself to enlighten their thoughts and I called one of them. He took me by the handcuffs and pulled me. I let him do it because he still took me for a sheep. I came to their chief who sneered and said, "You have become reasonable? You have something to say?" His words surprised me. I thought, "Perhaps he understood what I am about to say," which encouraged me and I began to speak. Hardly had I begun to explain the manifest difference between sheep and human beings, in particular, the horns, the tail and the walk on all fours, that the same blows, the same curses about my parents and entire family fell on me. So I said to myself while tasting the truncheon, "Are you more intelligent than the state? If the state tells you something there can only be sufficient reason." The beating continued as they yelled at me, "You make fun of us, you ass." You see the level of their knowledge about animals. Surely you want to know how the ordeal ended. Naturally with the baton, very quickly, and I was brought to my place where they threw me once again. I neither ate nor slept that night. I swore by the Lord of the Kaaba not to take any new initiatives without thinking about it a thousand times. The silence served me well because I passed the night hearing groans from all sides around me. I understood I was not alone in this ordeal and other Moroccans were undergoing the same ignominy. This discovery encouraged me to patience and I found consolation in the age-old adage: Collective punishment is less painful. My imagination roved, I said to myself, "If this situation extended to all Moroccan citizens, the ordeal is minimized because there would be more people whipped than whippers, then the whip would become impossible, citizens could speak freely about politics and wages. The problem for me would be if the formerly whipped decide to become the whippers, whence their multiplication. As for me, I am, as you know, against the whip wherever its source.

At the novel's end, the reader learns that a fellow political prisoner has mailed the twenty-six letters from Derb Moulay Cherif only after the author's death. This is fiction. The truth is that Salah El Ouadie is very much alive. He continues to publish poems and articles.

Abdelaziz Mouride's cartoon book about his experience of torture in Derb Moulay Cherif parallels El Ouadie's innocent injured voice, but with the sardonic overlay that caricature encourages. Mouride approaches his material from the victim's point of view, but as if desiring to provide torturers with a teaching manual for the most efficacious techniques. The top frame (Figure 3.8) depicts the prisoner's body contorted in the "parrot," a device for torturers to beat the soles of the feet and simultaneously force liquids down the victim's throat. Mouride's accompanying text forces the reader to engage the violent images of torture: "After an exchange of courtesies, the place for serious things." About the "airplane" torture, in which a victim's hands and feet are bound behind to a pole, Mouride helpfully concludes "that there is nothing better to stretch the muscles and on occasion to develop the voice"; pictures of the blindfolded victim whipped are described as a "light massage."[16] Caught in the terrible machinery of torture, El Ouadie and Mouride play the perplexed citizens come to remonstrate with torturers as if it were possible to converse and joke with them as reasonable human beings.

Kāna wa-akhawātuhā

If the past of the tortured is a page of history, surely the writing of history demands accuracy, chronology, significance, and interpretation. To what genre does Abdelkader Chaoui's book, *Kāna wa-akhawātuhā*, belong?[17]

After studying philosophy and Arabic literature at the University of Rabat, Chaoui, originally from Bab Taza near Tetouan, taught Arabic in Casablanca until his arrest on 13 November 1974 while teaching at Lycée Moulay Ismail. He was arrested for belonging to the Marxist-Leninist "23 March" movement. *Kāna wa-akhawātuha* was written during the early 1980s and published in 1986 while he was incarcerated in Kenitra Central Prison. A first edition of 5,000 sold 1,000 copies within a week before the title was seized and forbidden by the authorities. A second edition was issued December 1999 with 5,000 copies printed, but to test the possibility of censorship only 1,000 were released on the market—*une opération militante* (an activist action), said Chaoui.[18] While in Kenitra Prison, Chaoui and Driss Bouissef Rekab, a fellow *frontiste* (member of a Marxist-Leninist group) who had also completed a manuscript in French about his prison experience—*À l'ombre de Lalla Chafia*, published in Paris by Harmattan in 1989—undertook to translate each other's works: Chaoui translating Bouis-

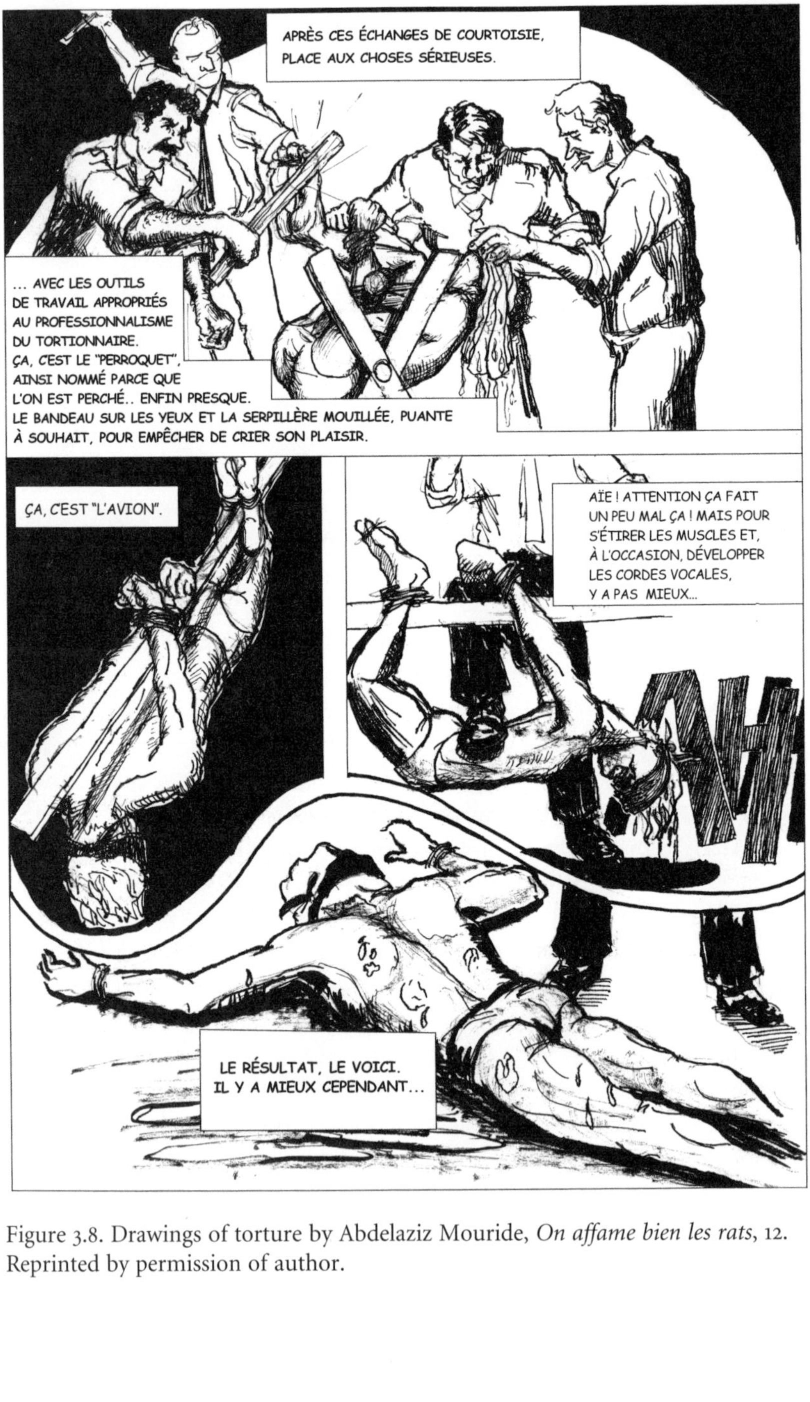

Figure 3.8. Drawings of torture by Abdelaziz Mouride, *On affame bien les rats*, 12. Reprinted by permission of author.

sef Rekab from French to Arabic and Bouissef Rekab translating Chaoui from Arabic to French.[19] Chaoui also solicited reviews from his fellow prisoners and appended them to the published work. Unusually, author, translator, subjects, critics, and readers were all together for years in one confined space, Kenitra Central Prison, a situation described by Chaoui as *une marmite chaude* (a hot pressure-cooker).[20]

Chaoui's book is a literary chronicle of his prison years. He calls *Kāna wa-akhawātuha* an autobiography, but one that is a collective autobiography in which he recounts the life of a community, *la tribu des incarcérés* (the tribe of the incarcerated). He mixes genres and voices. He recasts trial accounts furnished with notes of the famous 1977 Casablanca trial of *frontistes* (trial notes provided by Assia El Ouadie, a sister of two political prisoners); the reader also comes across fragments of contemporary newspapers and radio broadcasts. Figure 3.9 is an example of Chaoui's work, his sketch of Derb Moulay Cherif where he spent more than nine months.

Vertical and horizontal lines, room numbers, and Arabic letters delineate this infamous place that remains to this day a secret site, the interior unseen except by guards and prisoners, an underground place whose inhabitants were forced to spend their days, when not subject to torture, in immobility and silence, hands manacled and eyes blindfolded. Chaoui's sketch gives the appearance of the real, of a place that can be seen and known, even viewed from above, hence drawn. In fact it is imagined because Chaoui could never really see Derb Moulay Cherif with the precision that such a footprint of a building assumes. Like the blind man he was forced to become, he sensed the place and tried to figure out its dimensions as he was dragged from corridor to room to torture chamber, sometimes surreptitiously lifting his head to see below the blindfold but always holding his head at an angle so that vision could search below the black blindfold to describe and memorize the lineaments of the world where he found himself. The sketch is simply drawn and effective. It is immediately comprehensible to any reader's eye.[21] In contrast, the Arabic text surrounding the sketch is a flood of words without punctuation, and in Bouissef Rekab-Chaoui's collaborative French translation,[22] without sentences and capitalization, thereby not including the normal reference points of clarity for the printed page. Chaoui is standing against a wall, unwashed and stinking, his hands manacled behind his back. An urgent and clear prose style expresses the disintegration of his world and mimics the destruction of language and coherent thought. While hearing the screams of the tortured, he addresses in a relentless stream of consciousness an *inta* (you) that is at the same time himself, the reader, and the unhearing world outside, as if he is also speaking to memory itself:

Then they left you and it was about 11 o'clock in the morning you were terrified you shuddered no you swayed like the Moroccan flag finding yourself between one wall and another wall as if you were the third side wiped-out, emaciated distended frail your hands dangling behind your back a smell coming out of you emanating from you a smell gushing from your guts how then involuntarily because of your wait did your body melt and did a fire evaporate inside you and your blood you are not weary you are worried, somber no but say to your self in this place

الركن (ج) ثم انصرفوا عنك وكانت الساعة حوالي[1] 11 صباحا أنت مرعوب
وتهتز بل وتخفق كالعلم المغربي تقع بين الحائط والحائط وكأنك لهما الضلع
الثالث المنهوك والمنهوش والمنفوش والمغشوش ويداك مرميتان وراءك
ورائحة منك تفوح منك تفوح رائحة العرق الباطني فكيف ذاب جسمك في
غفلة وترقب وهل تتبخر الحرائق في ذاتك ودمك لست متعبا إنك مهموم
ومغموم بل قل لنفسك في هذا المكان

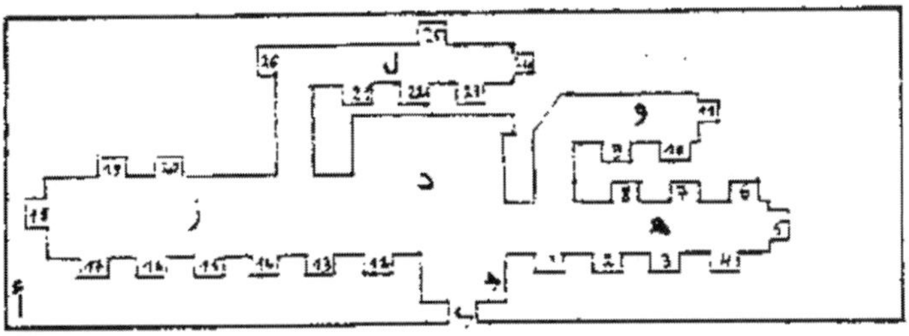

من الركن (ج) ما لهذا الصعق يا هذا أيمكن أن تضيع في لحظة عهدك
بالتجبر أيمكن هذا قل والآن بالضبط تسمع صوتا جريحا يعلو في صراخ مدو
في ناحية ما فهل يخرج منك ويصل اليهم ام يخرج منهم ويصل اليك هذه
اصوات جريحة أصوات مبحوحة أصوات هادرة أصوت متقطعة المكان كله
جوقة من العذاب الأليم والتحديات والتخنوع والشتيمة والمقاومة والذل والوشاية
المكان في الواقع ضجة حامية ومرعبة وأنت ماذا تنتظر هل سيخرج الصوت

Figure 3.9. Sketch of Derb Moulay Cherif by Abdelkader Chaoui. *Kāna wa-akhawātuhā*, 21. Reprinted by permission of author.

The line ends in the middle of the page, below which is Chaoui's sketch of Derb Moulay Cherif. Chaoui will eventually locate himself in the drawing at the bottom center, standing where the Arabic letter *jīm* is drawn:

> In corner jīm that is this breakdown my friend is it possible in a moment you lose your bravery say this, is it possible exactly at this moment you hear a harrowing scream that arises somewhere does it go out from you or does it come from them these are battered screams coiled screams noisy screams jerky screams this entire place is about suffering defiance submission, injury, resistance, debasement, denunciations, the place is in reality a site of burning horrific howling you, what do you wait for? will the screams come out of your guts as it does theirs and at that moment because you know they put you in this corner for a specific reason and they left for a specific reason they ordered you to close your eyes

Chaoui's text is indifferent to closure, to conclusions, to happy endings. Random moments surface in his narrative not as a culmination of logically preceding events or even as inspiration for subsequent ones, but as a creation of anguished memory born of Chaoui's efforts to reconstruct the world of Derb Moulay Cherif by punctuating torture with memories of childhood and family. Chaoui's text reminds us that there is, and there will always be, an enormous distance between what the tortured writer remembers and what we the readers have in front of our eyes, the artifactuality of a white page covered with black print.

Writing to Exist

For Maria Charaf, whose husband Amine Tahani died under torture in Derb Moulay Cherif, "happily there is still writing / to continue to exist, as a woman."[23] In 1985 she chronicled her experience of kidnap, and her husband's torture and death, although publication was delayed due to censorship until 1997.[24]

Charaf's book tells us about her origins (she was born in Marrakesh in 1958) and education (she is a graduate of Morocco's elite engineering school, where she met her husband, Amine Tahani, a fellow engineer). Active in the leftist student movement, they were arrested at the same time during waves of police round-ups that swept through the student and intellectual milieu beginning October 1985. At Derb Moulay Cherif, she too was blindfolded and found herself among the overflow of prisoners confined in the corridors. She labels herself a third category of detainee, the rare one eventually released, unlike her husband, whose presence she sensed nearby even while he was subjected to brutal interrogation:

I have no idea about the duration of my detention: a day? A week? A month? A year? Really, I had no idea, all is so conjectural in these matters! This uncertainty caused me anguish and I began to lose all notion of time by the third day, my uncertainty was already of the order of 24 hours. So, I pulled a rather thick thread from one of the covers and I knotted it three times. From then on, each time the guard gave me my daily bread in the morning I would add a knot. That was already something won, because this mastery over time, though relative, brought me a certain calm. Amine was frequently called for interrogation, he returned from it each time held up by two guards, his head falling on his shoulder as if he had fainted. Despite these conditions, I was able to keep my morale high, refusing to think about my son, in any case he could only be in good hands. . . . Beginning 4 November, I could no longer sense the presence of Amine. I no longer heard him coughing, they no longer called his number for interrogation. Anxious, I questioned one of the guards, but he would tell me nothing. I finished by understanding that he was transferred to the hospital. I learned later that medical personnel refused to admit at first given his desperate state. Finally, they admitted him and registered him under a false name.[25]

Amine Tahani's death on 11 November 1985 left Charaf a widow and single mother to an eight-month-old son, Aymane. In 1999, despite her son's objection, Charaf filed indemnity applications on her own and his behalf. She disregarded the required form and sent two letters in which she asked for the rehabilitation of her husband's memory, judgments against those responsible for his death, and indemnification for his family. Charaf believes she is not bitter because she expressed herself in writing and her book was published in Morocco while Hassan II was still alive:

To write is a kind of therapy, indispensable to turning the page and to encounter the future with hope. Also, I am happy to be able to publish this work in my country. Thank you to all who labored so this would be possible at last.[26]

Charaf's book ends with the realization of her loss articulated in poetry, one poem dedicated to the act of writing and a second to Morocco, *Mon pays, ma rose* ("my country, my rose"): "You torture me, sometimes / But I love you even more."[27]

On Sunday 14 November 1999, the first public commemoration service—the fourteenth anniversary of the death of Amine Tahani and the twenty-fifth anniversary of the death of Abdellatif Zeroual—was held at the

Complex Anoual of Casablanca to celebrate the lives and achievements of two successive generations of young Marxist activists, united by political convictions but also by the status of each as *shahīd* (martyr) to torture. Before 1999, there were only annual private ceremonies in the families' homes, always subject to intense police surveillance. To highlight political and juridical demands that are part of contemporary public commemoration, the moderator Abdelhak Moussadak (political prisoner, 1984–91) called for trials of Derb Moulay Cherif's torturers, especially the head of operations, Youssfi Kaddour.[28] Maria Charaf and Abdelkader Zeroual, the father of Abdellatif Zeroual, had both passed through Derb Moulay Cherif, as did many family members of political prisoners. Each speaker testified to his or her personal experience, placing narratives in the context of remedies for disappearance and political imprisonment. Demands were reiterated for a Moroccan truth commission. Charaf read an Arabic translation of her book, the section on kidnapping, and Zeroual presented the audience with cogent reasons to judge perpetrators.

Why perform *al-dhikrā* (commemoration), asked Omar Jbiha (brother of Rahal Jbiha, a Marxist political prisoner who died in 1979 during a prison escape), if not with the expectation that there will be a Moroccan judgment against human rights violations? The commemoration included a recitation of a poem by Abdellatif Zeroual. While a student of philosophy at the University of Rabat, Zeroual published a poem, *Shahīd*, uncannily presaging the manner and terms of his own death as a martyr:

Here am I falling on the battlefield
I carry my heart as a red flower that sheds blood
Here am I naked crawling over dead bodies
Gathering my limbs to seize the torn banner
Fanning with my blood remnants of ashes alive
Here am I paying the price
Then bless my death, my love[29]

Two years later, Zeroual died at Derb Moulay Cherif, although the authorities recorded Zeroual's (as well as Tahani's) deaths under false names. Zeroual's name lives on as revered author of this poem, orally transmitted by prisoners through Derb Moulay Cherif. In Jaouad Mdidech's memoir, *La chambre noire ou Derb Moulay Cherif* (The black chamber or Derb Moulay Cherif), Mdidech (political prisoner, 1975–89), reproduces Zeroual's verses attesting to the power of poetry clandestinely circulated by prisoners in order to be "reverently learned by heart and hummed."[30]

Many poems created in Derb Moulay Cherif were committed to memory in the absence of pen and paper. On 23 March 1975, the date of the tenth anniversary of the 1965 Casablanca uprising, Abdelkader Chaoui recalls verses he composed while lying blindfolded and manacled in Derb Moulay Cherif. Abdelaziz Mouride, artist and fellow detainee, had secretly sculpted a human head from pieces of bread; encouraged by this artistic human presence, Chaoui dedicated verse fragments to the poet Salah El Ouadie, likewise blindfolded and manacled, who faced Chaoui in the prison corridor:[31]

When I asked who wept blood on his cheeks
While the wind drinks out of his eyelids
Tear after tear?
The question disintegrated

When I asked the writhing dancer stirred by sorrow:
How was sadness born?
The question fell apart

Because you are my sadness
That gives rest from the journey's burden
And stood on the edge of suffering,
Embracing sleeplessness

Salah El Ouadie responded immediately with a poem that he committed to paper months later after his transfer from secret detention to Casablanca Civil Prison. He smuggled the text from prison embedded in a letter to his family. The complete poem, dedicated to Chaoui, was published ten years later in 1985, a year after El Ouadie's release from prison:[32]

Light up with your eyes the darkness in my heart
Patience is exhausted by the wait
Red anemones bend from longing
In thirsty fields, they long for the light
Eyes blindfolded, hands manacled

Torture was both an individual and a collective experience in that each blindfolded prisoner heard and suffered from others' screams or forced public confessions while enduring torturers' beatings and insults. The experiences of the tortured may be put to many uses. In Derb Moulay Cherif, the state's concealment of repression was met by the oral performance of poetry; both Chaoui and El Ouadie chose to create love poetry. Human voices countered silence by breaking through into language, not in order to describe torment directly but to add new meaning and context to the tradition of Arabic-language poets who have mourned and celebrated the meeting and union (*wiṣāl*) with the beloved, as Chaoui's additional lines evoke:

Here the silent wall separates lives
Weary steps distance my meeting
Away from you, the unique one, who burns at the heart of my sleeplessness
Your distant place lodges like a guest among my desires
Like exile in prison
Like prison in exile

Poetic exchanges and dialogues in Derb Moulay Cherif did not document suffering under torture except obliquely; they sustained the belief that literature in the form of the publicly performed oral poem mattered. Twenty-five years later, Mostefa Temsamani recited Chaoui's poem, and thus amplified its reach, because he had learned it by heart as had many prisoners, and he still savored the verses *qaṭratan qaṭrah* (tear after tear).[33]

At each public event centered on human rights violations, the names, dates, and places of disappearance must be pronounced aloud as if the incantatory qualities of oral performance in the service of history might produce the desired outcome of a government investigation. All that happens in the police and prison system takes place orally. Torture becomes oral, so to speak, with no written trace or trail known or available. As a consequence, oral testimony and publicly naming martyrs have become new and important performative recourses.

Amine Tahani's life and martyr's death were memorialized in writing not only by his wife Maria Charaf but also by Abraham Serfaty. Serfaty is counted among Morocco's longest-imprisoned political detainees. He is widely known internationally for decades of opposition to the colonial French and Moroccan government during years in prison and in exile, his founding and leadership of the Marxist group Ilā al-Amām, his complex positioning as an "Arab Jew" and anti-Zionist, his co-authorship with wife Christine Daure-Serfaty of several books, and a famous article about torture dedicated to the memory of Amine Tahani.[34] "Face aux tortionnaires" (Facing torturers), written in the 1980s while Serfaty was imprisoned in Kenitra Central Prison, distills experiences of torture in Derb Moulay Cherif:

I must warn the reader: I do not write the pages that follow, where I try to describe torture, except with skepticism. The world of torture is a world so inhuman that it becomes unimaginable for common mortals, happily moreover; the fantasms of childhood, horror films might give an idea of what are these monsters with a human face, let loose to destroy the body of a man in order to tear out his soul. But this destruction of the body, this degradation in the vile, this rending of an entire being in suffering without limit, cannot be felt by means of a description that will be always, for the reader, abstract, unreal.

This is the first reason that those who have undergone torture hardly like to speak about it. A second reason, especially if one has undergone it so long and so intensely that it has penetrated your body and your being—and this reason will perhaps be understood by the reader of this text—is that to speak of it, for those who have undergone it, is as if to extirpate from oneself the vomit (*vomissure*) buried in the depths of one's body. I say buried, now, ten years later. While it is still living, and this endures for years, it is impossible to see it in front of oneself. On the contrary, one must do everything to forget these foul hours to find again the human figure after months and months of physical degradation, so that the heart no longer trembles at each sound remembering that deep voice that whispered in my ear in the depths of my torpor: "Nuhud" (get up) and I knew that it was for torture—in order to find again peace and serenity.[35]

Reporting torture and human rights abuses is a genre of writing. As Moroccan writers' works shows, the sources for writing styles are protean: cartoon, novel, biography, testimony, love poem, coming-of-age autobiography, and the list—the precise record of names, dates, places, individual biographies, description of torture techniques and effects (the latter a narrative strategy reminiscent of Amnesty International dossiers). Torture is the motivating narrative frame and oral performance is a primary mode of transmission.[36]

Pilgrimage

Who has custody of the public memory and what went on within the confines of Derb Moulay Cherif? Journalists? Researchers? Historians? Poets and novelists? Survivors and political prisoners? The Indemnity Commission? Each recreates details and images of torture through written texts. Oral testimonies, often articulated in literary Arabic, are represented rather than unmediated reality. On 4 March 2000, al-Muntadā organized a sit-in, for many a pilgrimage (*pèlerinage* in French, *ziyārah* in Arabic) at Derb Moulay Cherif. This sit-in took the form of a circle, the ḥalqah of the storyteller, and those encircling Derb Moulay Cherif telling the stories of their victimization and presenting the living presence of the human capacity to

Figure 3.10. Candlelight vigil at Derb Moulay Cherif, 4 March 2000. Holding candles are Hassan Elhasni Alaoui (political prisoner, Group 71 Islamists) and his wife Khadija Warab, a lawyer. Photo courtesy of Elhasni Alaoui family.

make explicit the will to change. Over a thousand people formed a human chain. Flowers were placed on the ground in memory of the dead, many disappeared were present in photographs and posters carried by participants, and candles lit were held aloft, then placed in rows on either side of the road leading to the entrance gates of the prison (Figures 3.10–3.13). The imagery was stark. The candles for mourning illuminated the community of human rights activists silently asking for light to be shed on the dark years and the black pages.[37] Those most wounded by torture were only permitted to encircle the place that most dramatically represents their bodily pain. From the outside the pilgrims demanded the unveiling of flagrant violations in this repression center and the converting of the site into a museum and documentation for *les années de plomb*. A circle may enclose and exorcise, but it also establishes a *cordon sanitaire* to keep people standing outside distanced from the protected inner sanctum. For now, what is within the circle remains black, unreadable, and unknowable. The great doors to Derb Moulay Cherif are barred shut, its torturers fully protected, and its archives and documentation secret.

Figure 3.11. Derb Moulay Cherif vigil. Photo by author.

Quarters

The prison in contemporary Morocco owes much to the confluence of two historical trajectories that connect punishment to larger social patterns. In nineteenth-century, precolonial Morocco, prisons were constructed as part of a *qaṣbah* (fortress complex) by powerful local chiefs, who emerged as regional mini-despots in relation to serving the interests of the *Makhzen* (central authority of the sultan). According to Mohammed Mouaquit, French colonialism seized on the emergent and partial centralization of power embodied in the chief's prison and fortress and created an efficient, centralized "French Makhzen," not only more despotic than the Moroccan sultanate but also more restrictive toward local governance.[38]

Numerous foreign travelers describe Moroccan fortresses of imprisonment in the decades before the French colonization. During a voyage to Morocco in 1890, Robert Bontine Cunninghame Graham, a socialist Member of Parliament from England, described two varieties of late nineteenth-century prisons. One site he viewed was an open courtyard in the main

Figure 3.12. Derb Moulay Cherif vigil: Khalid Bakhti (political prisoner, Group 71 Islamists) holding poster of Abdellatif Zeroual, Marxist political prisoner tortured to death at Derb Moulay Cherif. Photo by author.

square of El Jadida, a city twenty miles south of Casablanca, where an outdoor space was used as a collection area for offenders.[39] A second prison was located in Goundafi in the High Atlas Mountains. It too included the outdoor courtyard by day as in El Jadida; Graham notes, however, the evening schedule:

> At night the Kaid who had a not unnatural wish to keep his prisoners safe, lowered them one by one into a deep dry well, a mule revolving slowly round a rude kind of capstan, as with an esparto rope hitched in a bowline under their arm-pits, one by one they were lowered underneath the ground.[40]

The courtyard and the dungeon, one above and the other below ground, share features of overcrowding and mixing as places of custodial detention—too many people whose food, bodies, and bodily functions commingled promiscuously. In this crush of humanity, prisoners were never alone.

In the late 1890s other British visitors to Morocco described the state of the prisons. Donald McKenzie, a frequent visitor to Morocco, penned

Figure 3.13. Derb Moulay Cherif vigil: flowers and posters. Photo by author.

his reports to London's Howard Association, an organization founded for "the promotion of the best methods for the treatment and prevention of crime":

> A Moor may be seized at the will of the Sultan, or of a governor, and may remain all his life in prison without trial, or indeed without knowing the nature of his offence. In the prisons there is no classification; all are crowded together, ragged, hungry, unwashed, infested with vermin, with no bedding, no occupation, and heavily ironed or chained. . . . No pen had ever sufficiently described the horrors of Moorish prisons. Want of light, absence of all sanitary arrangements, filth, vermin and want of food, and even fresh water are the chief characteristics of the Moorish prisons throughout the country. Some of these are supplemented with underground dungeons where political prisoners especially are confined.[41]

William Tallack, secretary of the Howard Association, concludes that miserable conditions in prisons follow from the larger problem of generalized lawlessness endemic to this society: "A principal cause of the casualties inflicted upon so many people in Morocco is that there is scarcely any administration of justice or law in that country."[42] While British observers astutely chronicled deplorable penal conditions, their solutions, if not their initial observations, were colored by the contemporary European rush to turn as yet independent Morocco into a British or French colony. As with so many colonialist projects, colonizers believed that a European takeover would not only ameliorate internal conditions but was even vociferously called for by native Moroccans themselves: "The poor natives look to England to aid them in their difficulties. It is a great blot on civilization that a feeble and corrupt government like Morocco should defy European Powers, and be permitted to carry on a system of oppression and cruelties hardly to be equaled in Central Africa or any other part of the world."[43]

Underground imprisonment in Morocco before French colonialism in 1912 is not so different from French prison practices prior to the great penal reforms that resulted from the 1789 storming of the Bastille. One of the best-known early French prisons, Le Châtelet, located on the right bank of the Seine, was a fortress belonging to the royal governor of Paris; the north-east tower of one prison was spatially divided according to social class and financial means among

> the comfortable highest rooms, maintained for nobles who paid their own expenses of four pence a night for a bed and two pence a night for a room. On a lower level was a single room shared by prisoners of lower social status, and below this, as in English prisons, was the *fosse* or *oubliette*, into which prisoners were lowered from the floor above, although even there prisoners had to pay one penny per night for their room.[44]

French colonialism triumphed over Moroccan sovereignty. A new era, termed the Protectorate, began after the Franco-Moroccan Treaty of Fez on 30 March 1912 transferred internal jurisdiction and external prerogatives from Morocco to France. The framework for French control in Morocco was the *état de siège*, a perpetual state of emergency. First pronounced over Morocco by the resident general, Marshal Louis Lyautey, on 2 August 1914, modified 7 February 1920, and proclaimed again 1 September 1939, this state of emergency was in force for forty-two years until the end of the French Protectorate in 1956.[45] As with any colonial enterprise, Lyautey's residency depended heavily on military officers from the Services des Affaires Indigènes (SAI or the Native Affairs Service), who exercised military rule throughout the rural areas, and on French military chiefs who governed the urban areas.[46] The effective legislative mechanism to oversee Moroccans was by means of dahirs drawn up, approved, promulgated and executed by the French administration. Prison administration in Morocco was governed by a series of dahirs issued in 1915, 1927, and 1930. The year of the last comprehensive decree issued by the French to govern Moroccan prisons was 1930, and these French decrees would remain in effect in Morocco from 1930 through independence in 1956 until 1999.[47] The year 1930 marked the legal and architectural culmination of French prison administration for Morocco. The third dahir, the final one after a series of ever more elaborate directives, coincided with the 1930 opening of Kenitra Central Prison, constructed in the city of Port Lyautey to house 425 prisoners.

Port Lyautey was laid out, in fact was founded by Marshal Louis Lyautey, the French resident general, in 1912 at the mouth of the Sebou River, the progenitor stamping his own name on what was then Kenitra, a tiny settlement of 500 Moroccans, in order to create what would become colonial Morocco's most important riverine port and its second busiest port after Casablanca. Both Port Lyautey and Casablanca were colonial creations designed principally to eclipse the well-established precolonial native maritime cities and Moroccan commercial ports of Larache, Safi, and El Jadida. As many architectural historians of Morocco have noted, Lyautey's urban projects separated the *medina* (*ville indigène*, native quarter) from the colonial town (*ville nouvelle*, the new city, *ville européenne*, the European city) according to a planned system that Janet Abu-Lughod critically denounces as "urban apartheid."[48] Frequently, a third area intervened, the military area, further emphasizing Lyautey's spatial distinction between native and colonial entities. Lyautey was preoccupied with the appearance of colonized space as sites to impress Moroccans, as well as his fellow French settlers, with the Protectorate's grandiosity, power, and public theatricality. Military camps and barracks were always in front of Moroccan eyes. In Rabat, for example, along large swaths of the coastline west of the walled city were major military encampments. The European new city ensured that the intervening military area functioned as the separator between native and colonial space. The pattern in Rabat was repeated in Fez, Meknes, and Port Lyautey (Kenitra).[49]

Barracks and parade grounds intervened and mediated between colonist and native. Equally constitutive of an imposing French presence, although isolated in the distant western outskirts of Port Lyautey, Morocco's first official purposefully built edifice of maximum security incarceration, the supreme category within the French penal hierarchy, *la maison centrale*, was erected in 1930 and eventually came to be known as Kenitra Central Prison. In France and in Morocco, the category of *maison centrale*, in addition to providing maximum-security incarceration was reserved for detainees condemned to serve long prison terms, in particular the category of political prisoners. As with French-built prisons in Rabat and Casablanca, the maison centrale of Kenitra adjoins a cemetery. In his prison memoir, *Le chemin des ordalies*, Abdellatif Laabi (Marxist political prisoner, 1972–82) muses whether this conjoining of prison and cemetery is "a coincidence, a local characteristic or a universal phenomenon."[50] So close is the spatial and conceptual notion of cemetery and prison in French Morocco that the Civil Prison of Casablanca is popularly known as Ghbila (Moroccan prison slang for "cemetery").

French builders in Morocco were guided by two available models of prison architecture. From England emerged the influential 1842 Pentonville prison model, a radial design, as Michel Foucault notes, directly derived from Jeremy Bentham's Panopticon to ensure that the inmate of a cell "must never know that he is being looked at any one moment; but must be sure that he may always be so."[51] The French example of this design is the Paris prison of La Petite Roquette, designed by Hippolyte Lebas and constructed between 1826 and 1836. La Petite Roquette achieved notoriety in a French-North African colonial context when it was used to house Algerian political prisoners during the 1954–62 Algerian war of independence. Before it was demolished in 1974, it best exemplified the prison architectural form of wings radiating from a central point or rotunda from which guards could observe each cell door.[52]

A second model, adopted for Kenitra Central Prison in Port Lyautey is the telephone-pole configuration, in which multiple cellblocks are set at right angles to a long central corridor, and was consciously modeled by the French in Morocco on building principles employed for the American prison facilities at Auburn Prison in New York State. Opened in 1819,[53] Auburn Prison employed single cell construction for prisoners. The original design included sixty-one double cells, but William Britten, the first warden, turned double occupancy cells into solitary cells, believing that individually housed convicts were more effectively handled. The "Auburn system" evolved during the 1800s with a plan for inmates to work silently together during the day and return to individual cells at night. The plan included a striped suit, close cropped hair, lockstep, and harsh punishments, such as beatings and floggings. The then influential Boston Prison Discipline Society called Auburn "probably the best prison in the world . . . a model worthy of the world's imitation." Other nations sent visitors, including Alexis de Toqueville who recorded his impression of the American penal system. During a visit to Auburn Prison on 9 July 1832, he studied the Auburn system for possible export to France. Tocqueville wrote home:

"And why are these 900 collected malefactors less strong than the 30 individuals who command them? Because the keepers communicate freely with each other. Suppose for an instant, that the prisoners obtain the least facility of communication, the order is immediately the reverse," Tocqueville presciently concludes.[54] The Auburn system of enforced silence and separation spread throughout Europe in the nineteenth century. In *On the Penitentiary System in the United States and Its Application in France*, Tocqueville and Gustave de Beaumont observe: "This absolute solitude, if nothing interrupt it, is beyond the strength of man; it destroys the criminal without intermission and without pity; it does not reform, it kills."[55]

Opened and functioning as a prison by 1930, Kenitra Central remains an evocative Moroccan example of the French-built, American-influenced Auburn system. World War II and the high cost of the cellular system intervened to halt further prison construction plans for Morocco following this model. The Auburn system, influenced by models of Pennsylvania prison architecture,

> isolated the convict for long hours in his own cell to commune with his conscience. The skill of architects and builders was devoted to preventing communication between prisoners in their cells and to deprive them of any glimpse of the outside world. The sight of a hillside or distant buildings beyond the wall was believed to frustrate reform.[56]

Abraham Serfaty, incarcerated first by the French during the Protectorate as a Moroccan political prisoner in what was then called the European bloc, would return to prison to serve an additional twenty years in post-independent Morocco. Finally released in 1992, Serfaty's 1993 published *La mémoire de l'autre* described his two years of total isolation, one that echoes Toqueville's and Beaumont's observations:

> Evenings the prisoners were silenced except for prayers. Metal bedsteads were taken away and the W.C. [toilet] separated off. Most of all, [prison] construction was such that any ray of sunlight was prevented from penetrating the walls. [The prison] was built directly on the earth, separated from it by only a thin layer of cement. The humidity was extreme. They gave me four used blankets, and presented me, as a favor, with a bolster and a mat, that I had to get rid of urgently because it had become a compost heap of bed-bugs. I had the right to promenade a half hour in the morning, and a half hour in the evening, but because this was a regime of isolation, I was only permitted in the courtyard very early in the morning and at the end of the day, when the sun had passed beyond the high walls.

Isolation," Serfaty concludes, "is the most refined form of torture."[57]

The prison dahirs of 1915, 1927, and 1930 produced legislation to create the administration and construction of a penal system. A second set of decrees defined the category of political prisoner with which to populate the newly built maximum-security establishment in Port Lyautey. The dahir of 29 June 1935 mandated prison terms for demonstrations and other actions that disturbed order, peace and security, and the dahir of 26 July 1939 added sentences for making, distributing, and selling tracts *de nature à troubler l'ordre, la tranquillité ou la sécurité.*[58] These two sets of decrees put in place during the French Protectorate would provide Moroccan authorities with both the legal apparatus and the constructed carceral world to condemn and house large numbers of intellectuals and students for nonviolent crimes of opinion, a process that simultaneously and automatically designates for international human rights organizations, such as Amnesty International, the category of prisoner of conscience. Various instruments of repression—the legal system, the creation of bureaucrats and police officers, and the prison system—an entire apparatus built by the French Protectorate to oppress Moroccans was carried forward intact after independence and Moroccanized. What allowed the French to control, dispossess, and oppress Moroccans would permit Moroccans to control, dispossess, and oppress Moroccans. The judgment of writer and former political prisoner Abdellatif Laabi is apt:

> The post-colonial *ijtihad* (ijtihad being the renewal of institutions and laws) stopped short at the prison walls. It did not touch them. To be sure there were more urgent matters than the reorganization of the kingdom of the dead and the half-dead.[59]

Prisoner and jailer are locked in an unrelenting battle to shape the prison regime. From the viewpoint of the state, the discipline of the prison is incarceration, punishment, and torture. For the early Quakers, the discipline was penitence. For those incarcerated, the discipline is to retain selfhood and sanity, to analyze the workings of power and resistance, and to break free from actual confinement through the imagination. The transnational circulation of the word "penitentiary" provides a potent metaphor for the conflicting histories and present form of the Moroccan disciplinary prison regime. Penal architecture, practices, and terminology traveled—from England to America, back to the continent, especially to France, and on to North Africa as part of French colonization processes. The word "penitentiary" in both English and French comes from the word "penitence." Originally developed by American Quakers in Pennsylvania, the penitentiary was a place where criminals were to reflect on and repent for crimes, understood as sins, before returning to society. The French word, *pénitencier* (penitentiary) was assimilated into Moroccan Arabic prison slang as *bidancié* (penitentiary inmate) and the original meaning of penitentiary as a place of penitence that relied on solitary confinement was elided, though the form and content of maximum-security imprisonment was thoroughly grasped by Moroccan political prisoners. A similar transformation affected the French phrase, *maison centrale* for France's maximum-security facility. For Moroccan Arabic speakers, the word *centrale* minus "l" designates one site: Kenitra Central Prison has become *sentra*.[60] *Bidancié* and *sentra*, prisoner and prison, have been suggestively "Moroccanized."

Prisons were the darker side of the Protectorate and are the same dark side of independent Morocco. The skills of colonial-period architects continue to inform prison planning and design in Morocco, extending and multiplying carceral processes set in motion during the colonial era. Penitentiaries for political prisoners are the consequence of French and Moroccan state responses to political and social opposition; thus, for both regimes, architecture was a serviceable weapon in their war to keep political prisoners segregated and policed, and non-prisoners outside. Though haunted by their historical past, penitentiaries in Morocco—with their roles first as incubators of Moroccan nationalist resistance against the French in the colonial period then subsequently as sites for human rights dissidence against the current Moroccan monarchy—are fully intact and carrying forward their inherited, historical discourse and mission: namely, to forcibly disappear the existence of the dangerous individual, so designated by the ruling power, as part of the struggle between ruler and ruled.

Chapter 4
The Casablanca Uprising of 1981 and Its Aftermath

In the name of the first bullet fired into the chests of the Casablanca demonstrators
In the name of the first martyr fallen on Casablanca's sidewalks
In the name of small Fadwa and the innocence of children, her brothers
I touch these words . . .
A place that one could say erases the past—no, it's not at all capable of doing so—that keeps the bitter present, the reality of indifference and perhaps the reality of death in the grave of life.
It's true . . . and this hurts those who defend the word justice, but if you fight permanently, this time between life and death, you can create something from nothing.

—Hassan El Bou, political prisoner, 13 July 1981

The Beginnings of the Uprising

The French colonial presence in Casablanca is a microcosm of the ways in which France affected the postcolonial Moroccan state. Just as the French superimposed the city of Casablanca on the Moroccan landscape, so too were French laws enacted to preserve French hegemony over Morocco. A notable exception is the code of personal status (in French *code du statut personnel*, in Arabic *mudawwanat al-aḥwāl al-shakhṣīyah*) that deals with birth, marriages, death, inheritance, and divorce. Otherwise post-independence Moroccan civil and penal codes remain largely French-inspired. One example pertinent to the subject of the 1981 Casablanca uprising is the French laws governing identification cards and the family passbook. French bureaucratic controls established over the population were maintained after independence; indeed, they were carried over intact and "Moroccanized" as restrictively and frequently more punitively. In this chapter, the techniques of identification—first, over the individual body, and then the family unit—form an intersection for complex twentieth-century histories of Casablanca. How does the state, whether colonial French or postcolonial Moroccan, contain massive population increases in new urban settings created by colonization? What are the ways that identification procedures, and therefore techniques of controlling the individual body, were used to track crowds and rioters? How did the jurisdictional claims of the Islamic personal status code clash with French paper recording technologies? In the aftermath of the Casablanca events, what linked the identification system, the criminalized body, and the criminal justice system? The power of the identity card reaches beyond the police station, the courtroom, and even the grave to determine who we are, what names we give ourselves, and how we reconstruct the past of the 1981 Casablanca uprising through narrative, storytelling, and performance.

The Story of the Family ID Card

The Moroccan regime possesses an extensive administrative infrastructure to regulate unambiguously the identity of each and every one of its subjects. Morocco inherited from the French Protectorate a nineteenth-century European "culture of identification" in which the personal name is the essential component of the modern state system of identification. In France laws governing personal names (for example, the law of 1 April 1803, repealed only in 1993), restricted the French to names duly registered at birth.[1] France extended the notion of standardized names to its Arab subjects in North Africa beginning with Algeria, the first North African country invaded in 1830 and colonized. The law of 23 March 1882 on the civil status of Muslim natives in Algeria imposed the combined French systems of identity cards and patronymic surnames on all Algerian heads of households. In cases of Arab refusal to choose a fixed surname, article 5 states that French civil servants may create one of their own devising.[2] In contrast to French naming practices, precolonial North African names consist minimally of a first name followed by the father's name and the grandfather's name, but often includes a string of names representing the holder's moral, physical, or social qualities, place of birth or ancestry, and tribal affiliation or membership in religious orders. An Arab-Berber name functions as a biography, unique to the individual and, thus, disappears with his death. Moroccan anthropologist Hassan Rachik calls his naming tradition a "beautiful labyrinth," a history of names inherited from Moroccan forbears that changed every generation, pointing to the ways in which identity is never fixed by name but rather is to be sought through points of intersection with place, family migration, and even national consciousness:

> If I write imagining that [my grandfather] were speaking: "You know, identity cannot be totally inherited nor rejected totally. It is for you to construct your own identity multiplying endlessly your circles of belonging. In the matter of identity there is little to transmit from generation to generation, but much to invent individually and collectively. Identity is not a simple line linking an individual to a group whatever the foundation of the group—linguistic, religious or political. Identity is the actual connection that a biography has with other biographies and other groups. . . . Look! I did not submit to my father's name. Can you not see what a labyrinth you become entangled in wanting to reunite in one text what I have lived successively and partially? Even for a single individual, names and identities change, fall into disuse.[3]

In Algeria, the French perceived onomastic chaos and discontinuity in the Arab-Berber preference for human history embodied in a biographical approach to naming. Furthermore, French officials in Morocco queried how names could be individually assigned, genealogically arranged, alphabetized correctly, and made orthographically uniform. The proliferation of Ahmeds and Mohameds recurring from grandfather to father to son raised the possibility of a bewildering and uninformative genealogy comprising, for example, Mohamed ben Ahmed, son of Ahmed ben Mohamed, grandson of Mohamed ben Ahmed.[4]

In addition to the French standardization of names as part of the identification process, all documentation of Muslim subjects (including Arabic-language place names) was to be written not in Arabic but in French, Algeria's sole official language. To produce Arabic-language personal and place names accessible to users of the Latin alphabet, two French army interpreters attached to France's Ministry of War in Algeria were charged with fashioning a transcription protocol. With minor changes, William MacGuckin de Slane's and Charles Gabeau's 1866 transcription of Maghribi names remains in use in North Africa and France to this day.[5] North African identity was, thus, arbitrarily fixed, and transcribed for official confirmation purposes into a document of identity.

The apparatus of French state control over an individual was preceded historically by registration controls for the French family, embodied in the family passbook (in French, *livret d'identité et d'état civil*, and in Moroccan

Arabic, *kunnāsh al-taʿrīf wa-al-ḥālah al-madanīyah*). Laws creating family documentation papers for a couple and their offspring are said to have been enacted after fires set during the 1871 Paris Commune, an uprising that burned registers of civil status in the Paris region. Demonstrators targeted for destruction official buildings, such as the Palais de Justice and the Hôtel de Ville, housing birth, marriage, and death certificates. For a time, Parisians could fabricate false documents and create new identities. By 1875, however, residents of greater Paris in the Seine prefecture carried family passbooks.[6]

French laws, which presume a fixed patronymic surname and which establish identity registration for Morocco, a Protectorate headed nominally by the sultan, appeared much later than those in Algeria, incorporated into metropolitan France as provinces. In 1914, two years after the Protectorate was installed, the decree of 4 September established the administrative means to register only French nationals. In contrast, full and obligatory documentation of "native" Moroccans was not uniformly enacted until 1950, six years before independence.[7] Over decades identification documents, nonetheless, were issued in piecemeal fashion, with the earliest ones of 1925 optional and readily available only to Moroccan workers and employees in French factories and establishments.[8] That the police were in charge of issuing identity cards apparently contributed to their unpopularity and the lack of compliance, as did the two required accompanying photographs in profile and full face, as if the bearer were a wanted criminal.[9] Identification—a civil and legal practice in France to establish citizenship—was placed under police control in Morocco, emphasizing its role as a criminological practice foisted on tractable colonies to circumscribe identity without granting full citizenship. Two other factors contributed to Moroccan resistance to identification laws. The fear among the populace was that identity documents were a prelude to mass conscription. More important was the fierce opposition by the Moroccan sultan to foreign systems of registering births, marriages, and deaths; these were perceived as intrusions on Islamic control over family law.[10] Morocco's family laws follow the Maliki school of Islamic law. Not only are matters relating to women and the family regulated, but more so an ideal of the Moroccan family is conveyed through the legal system. As sociologist Mounira Charrad concludes, the "message" of Maliki family law is to "favor males and kin on the male side . . . and solidify ties within the extended patrilineal kin group."[11] While much-studied consequences of Maliki family law are weak marital ties, ease of divorce, polygamy, and unequal inheritance for women, it was also the case that traditional authority, evoked by the presence of the sultan, the nominal ruler who sits at the top of male, patriarchal kin groupings, and embodied in many ways by the right to confer names, managed to resist French control over Muslim family names until 1950. Moreover, the sultan oversaw a large indigenous bureaucracy of Muslim clerics and notaries tied to the monarchy by patronage and kinship, and authorized to register information similar to that sought by French-style identification.

The formation of a centralized, authoritarian, postcolonial Moroccan state in 1956 owes much to continuities with the bureaucratic French colonial state. Family passbooks and identity cards remain constituent elements of Moroccan sovereignty even as they are administrative formalities of civil identification that extend control over the population, a surveillance that was at its most efficient and rigorous in large urban settings. The capacity to identify criminality through records is salient to comprehending the history of repression in Morocco's largest urban agglomeration, namely Casablanca.

Casablanca, City of Dissidence

By the 1920s, rural migrants were flocking to the newly French-created industrial zones of eastern Casablanca. André Adam, eminent French historian of North Africa, believes that the word *bidonville* (the all-purpose French word for shantytown) originated in North Africa, probably in Morocco, possibly in Casablanca. Adam conjectures that both the French *bidonville* and its Moroccan Arabic homologue *qaryan*, meaning shantytown, arose in Casablanca. Bidonville derives from *bidon*, the gasoline can recycled to wall and roof urban shanties with flattened-out discarded petrol tins. To explain qaryan, he notes that Moroccan workers attached to an electrical factory, called Centrale Thermique, constructed a nearby shantytown on a quarry, an area that became known in French as Carrières Centrales (*carrière*, French for quarry and *centrale* after the factory), which was altered in Moroccan Arabic from *carrière* to *qaryan*, a uniquely Casablancan term that came to designate new shantytowns, not necessarily built on quarries, but sprouting throughout the industrialized coastal region.[12]

From the beginning of the French Protectorate era over Morocco, officially initiated in 1912, master plans produced by the French colonial administration for Moroccan city spaces repeatedly depict the same configuration: a *cordon sanitaire* (literally a sanitary line or belt) created to separate colonial French from Moroccan native space, with the industrial zones (surrounded by shantytowns) relegated to the periphery. The preferred structure of cordon sanitaire was usually the wall surrounding the medina, the native Arab-Muslim urban quarter, whose separation was reinforced by an added greenbelt that served twin purposes: to contain the native area while distinguishing it spatially from a new and expanding European city (*la ville nouvelle, la ville européenne*). This was also accomplished by including vast and forbidding army barracks, speedily erected, that underpinned the colonizer's power through architectural arrangements. Due to the tiny size of Casablanca's unimportant medina and the uncontrolled European settlement abutting its walls, instead a French-built major thoroughfare through the city—the Place de France—came to serve as an equivalent physical and social barrier of the cordon sanitaire between the unequal worlds and lives of the colonizer and the colonized.[13] Casablanca, designated the economic powerhouse of the colonial enterprise, was the birthplace of a new, French-created city with a large and exponentially growing working class that swiftly replaced in economic importance the precolonial urban and commercial centers of Meknes, Fez, Salé, Tetouan, and Rabat.[14]

The very processes that created shantytowns to service the factories and that were set in motion by French colonialism—for example, French rural land seizures dispossessing peasants and French wars of pacification against Berber tribes that sent entire clans to the urban zones—were also decried by French urban planners. In 1834, the population of Casablanca was 800 inhabitants. By 1913, the first years of colonization, it attained 12,000, and a mere seven years later rose to 111,000 people (46 percent Moroccan Muslims, 16 percent Moroccan Jews, 23 percent French nationals and 15 percent diverse foreign nationals).[15] French planners were quick to point out the intertwined evils of an urban health menace and the existence of dangerous classes in the shantytowns. Such French fears were sources for their partial solution to Casablanca's lack of affordable housing; destroy the shantytowns and build planned worker agglomerations as model cities for the natives (*une cité ouvrière pour indigènes*). Although projects began as early as the 1930s, only after World War II did the arrival of Michel Ecochard, French master planner, focus urban construction on Casablanca. He set in motion massive building programs of mass-produced workers housing adjacent to industrial zones, what he termed a *trame sanitaire*, a sanitary or healthy architectural framework, to accommodate the influx of rural migrants transformed into a low-paid urban proletariat, and forced to inhabit minimal standard living quarters. Ecochard describes his plans to "retake" (*reprendre*) Casablanca by building single-story, one-room dwellings:

On the infrastructure of future quarters, where the major streets, the open spaces, the secondary roads, and the public building areas areas have been reserved [we shall ordain the] creation of a *trame sanitaire* (with streets, water lines, and sewers). In this *trame sanitaire* will be hard-surfaced building (*en dur*) as well as provisional structures (*nuwalas* in Arabic and *baraques* in French) produced by the inhabitants . . . the basic element of this *trame sanitaire* is the minimum housing cell, established after research and experimentation, at 8 meter by 8 meter and containing two habitable rooms with obligatory orientation toward the south or the east, a W.C., a kitchen, the unit turned around the courtyard. . . . The actual density of this trame is 350 inhabitants per hectare.[16]

A contrasting evocation of the same inhabited space is by the shantytown's native son and poet, Abdallah Zrika, born into Carrières Centrales in 1953, raised in the bidonville of Ben M'sik, and imprisoned 1980–82 for his political poetry.[17] Zrika favorably compares his carceral conditions to the slums, where even Ecochard's panacea of the eight by eight meter cell was rarely the norm:

In spite of all its horrors, I found prison better than Ben Msik. What can you say when the cell is better than the hut in which you live? What dictionary must you use to express that? And who are you? . . . The absence of toilets. This is what I would like to begin with. By these excrements piled up all over the place (everything piles up here) and that nobody wants to look at. They look at them surreptitiously when they pass by. For their humanity is spread out there. Their shame. Their words are there. Their innermost self. The non-existence of toilets is your own non-existence. Or your non-existence more than your existence. . . . The absence of toilets. This is where I want to begin and end. People who creep about at night so they will not be seen and who throw out their excrements. Be careful not to trip and fall. No one must see you carry your debasement in your hands, your ugly humanity in a chamberpot.[18]

In 1950 French historian Robert Montagne observed interiors in the Casablancan qaryan. He singled out what he called telltale signs of "parasitic" (*parasitaire*) modernity. Montagne based his conclusions on the presence of objects that revealed an acculturation to Western habits, if not a debased mimetic relation to the European model, while inadvertently describing the processes that went into maintaining and disciplining a colonial people on the level of everyday life:

Several observations suffice to convince us of the tight connection that exists between proletarian agglomerations and the European city. On entering a barraka, one is often struck by the presence of an object unknown until now whose significance is evident: the alarm-clock that is enthroned in a good place in the foyer like the new master of family life. At its signal, the man arises from sleep and like a Westerner rushes out to work. From six o'clock in the morning, one can see in the neighborhoods around Ben M'Sik thousands of bicycles sweeping down the slopes bringing the *zoufriats* to their distant factories.[19]

To designate the new denizen of Ecochard's framed housing cell who emerges at dawn to the factory abetted by the alarm clock and the bicycle, Montagne called on a new Casablancan idiom, *zoufriat*, to match the modern Casablanca worker. The French *les ouvriers* (workers), transformed as *zoufriats*, was restricted in local parlance to the large population of unmarried male laborers.[20] Thus, the French shaped the megalopolis of Casablanca by creating industrial zones, the Moroccan proletariat, vast tracts of uniform housing with "modernized" domestic interiors, and even the descriptive vocabulary, but never did they envision Casablanca as catalyst for and bitter battleground of the Moroccan struggle for independence from France. Especially after 1953, urban clandestine groups formed, of which the Black Hand, the Black Star, and the Black Crescent (the latter grouping formed from the outlawed Moroccan Communist Party) were the most deadly, all united loosely in a resistance movement supervised by nationalist leaders. Operating from the Carrières Centrales and Ben M'sik were the first generation of Casablanca city-dwellers to become *mujāhidīn*: freedom fighters to the Moroccans, terrorists to the French.[21] In December 1952, what is considered the first shantytown uprising of the Carrières Centrales was set off by the assassination in Tunis of Ferhat Hached, the Tunisian union leader, a death with reverberations throughout the colonized Arab world.[22] Five thousand inhabitants of the Carrières Centrales attacked police stations and stores leading to hundreds of Moroccan deaths at the hands of French security forces. Between September 1953 and September 1955 there were 2,276 "incidents"—assassinations, arson, sabotage, and bombings—claiming more lives on both sides.[23]

Under the French, the Carrières Centrales and its surrounding districts were, and in postcolonial Morocco are, politicized sites, places where the nationalist urban working class actively engage in union activities and political organizing. Despite Moroccan government plans promoting decentralization and regional industrial development outside Casablanca, the city's role as the nation's economic hub was greatly reinforced in the three decades after independence. By 1981, twenty-five years after independence, the population of Casablanca attained at least three million, a significant portion of residents inhabiting Casablanca's poorer quarters of Carrières Centrales, Ben M'sik, Roches Noires, Place Sraghna, Sidi Bernoussi, and Sbata. These were core, industrialized zones in Casablanca dating from the Protectorate; they suffered the highest numbers of those wounded, arrested, or killed. After the 1981 strike, unconfirmed statistics by French monitoring groups reported 450 people on trial and, of the dead, one-third were children believed buried in anonymous mass graves dug by Moroccan army conscripts.[24]

The Riot and a Brief History of the 1981 Uprising

Bread riots and food protests are not mere "rebellions of the belly," argues Edward P. Thompson's classic study, but best viewed as a "highly complex form of direct popular action, disciplined and with clear objectives."[25] Thompson's formulations about the eighteenth-century English crowd offer one description of North Africa where large-scale twentieth-century, urban, antigovernment revolts play out his concept of a "moral economy of protest." These uprisings are examples of power and resistance in which the strategies and language of justice articulated by protesters are dynamic evidence of social assertion in the Arab world. Bread riots continue to occur throughout the Arab world, and as evidence of social claims for greater equity, scholars point to specific acts by crowds that target cars, banks, and wealthy neighborhoods for destruction as symbols of economic injustice.[26]

A 1981 popular uprising in Casablanca, against a Moroccan state perceived to be authoritarian and corrupt, outwardly took the form of a bread riot. Terms to describe what happened make clear that naming the event positions the speaker. Vocabulary in Arabic and French includes *émeutes du pain* (bread riots), *iḍrābāt* and *grèves* (strikes), *intifāḍah* and *soulèvement* (the former a later, deliberate rewriting of Casablanca according to the term for the 1987 Palestinian "uprising"), *tamarrud, insurrection*, and *révoltes* (revolts, rebellion) along with official attempts to understate the crisis by resorting to *aḥdāth* and *événements* (events, incidents).

In the twentieth century, many events in Casablanca merited the designation of revolt. The Protectorate years are framed chronologically by significant riots in Casablanca: the first as early as 1907, when the French desecrated the Casablanca Muslim cemetery while constructing a railway track led to the first uprising against the incursions of colonialism; in the decade of independence, in 1952 and 1955, inhabitants of Casablanca erupted in anticolonial riots. In postcolonial Morocco, the uprising of 23 March 1965, a response to government decrees to reform and restrict educational opportunities, catalyzed generations of Moroccan youth to embark on political careers defined by implacable opposition to the central authorities.[27]

In 1981 Casablanca, although protesters demonstrated to maintain subsidies on staple goods (and contemporary journalists labeled the events "bread riots"), demands to the government encompassed the right to education, affordable housing, and employment opportunities. Political scientist Larbi Sadiki advances the radical argument that North African riots are central, not marginal, to the process of democratization,[28] as does Moroccan historian Mostefa Bouaziz, who points to the historical necessity for Moroccan mass mobilizations embodied in bread riots. Strikers were not politically naïve, Bouaziz maintains, and they willingly sacrificed themselves for the cause of political and social change, anticipating severe reprisals. Bouaziz proposes that Casablanca strikers represent "the consecration of a martyr's behavior, a symbol of determination, faith, and courage and the abnegation of self that procures respect and popularity for the leader and his organization."[29] By applying an exalted religiopolitical perspective to activities of the Moroccan unions, Bouaziz depicts self-sacrificing martyrs whose leadership and rank-and-file were, nonetheless, politically astute, intimately allied to powerful political parties, and well organized.

The 1981 Casablanca uprising is said to have begun on 28 May, triggered by a brief article in official government newspapers that announced major price increases. Mandated by International Monetary Fund debt repayment schedules, the price increases affected basic foodstuffs. The price notice was so imperceptible and laconically phrased that Hassan Bazwi, then secretary general of the Moroccan Labor Union (UMT, Union marocaine du travail), one of Morocco's three trade unions, would later recall in his memoirs that the publication of price increases—butter 76 percent, sugar 45 percent, oil 28 percent, milk 14 percent—appeared "clandestine."[30] The union calculated that by 1981 standards of a minimum monthly wage of 500 dirhams, a family subsisting exclusively on sardines, bread, tea, and sugar needed 300 dirhams per month to sustain the diet, leaving 200 dirhams for transportation from distant shantytowns to work in the city center.[31] To protest higher costs of food staples, the UMT called a strike (*iḍrāb*) on 18 June. By Friday, 19 June, joined by the rival union Confédération démocratique du travail (CDT), the UMT demanded the abolition of all price increases and declared a second general strike for the following day. Immediate government responses were to force small business and garage station owners to remain open or face sixteen-month prison sentences and loss of licenses should they join the strike. While the majority of urban transport workers observed work stoppages, on Saturday morning, 20 June, demonstrators stopped buses traveling in the poor neighborhoods, shut down the main highways, overturned cars, pillaged banks, and broke shop windows in the city center. That same day the Moroccan army with snipers, tanks, and helicopters advanced on the city of Casablanca.

As with naming the event, so too in dispute are the numbers the Moroccan police and soldiers wounded, killed, arrested, and caused to disappear, primarily in the Casablanca region but also in other cities where demonstrations and strikes had spread.[32] The authorities reported 66 dead and 110 wounded. Hassan II announced in a palace press conference that the events in Casablanca concerned merely 2,000 demonstrators arrested and, thus, were not serious.[33] Opposition parties provided figures of 637 killed and thousands wounded, primarily among the young and poor urban population.[34] More than 200 political and union leaders were arrested in Casablanca and other large cities.[35] Among them was Mohamed Karam, a distinguished human rights lawyer and, in 1981, the Casablanca-based secretary general of the Union Socialiste des Forces Populaires (the party allied to CDT, the union that called the strike). Karam had previous experiences with the regime's illegal processes of arbitrary arrest (the authorities targeted the executive bureau of his political party), trumped up reports (police witnesses accused Karam of directing the riots and even throwing stones), and two years in Casablanca Civil Prison without trial before his amnesty in May 1983 (Figure 4.1).[36]

Unconfirmed estimates are 5,000 people picked up throughout the country in *laraf*, the Moroccan Arabic revoicing of *la rafle*, the French word for "roundup." "Mahmoud," described as a twenty-two-year-old participant by France's *Le Monde* newspaper, was cited as an eyewitness to the military incursions that he described as the "martyrdom" of demonstrators armed only with stones:

> Around noon, the army relieved the police and immediately began shooting on us. Certain demonstrators were completely overexcited and advanced toward the soldiers, rocks in their hands, yelling: "Kill us, kill us." We thought they wanted to commit suicide. So the army opened fire with rifles and machine-guns. It was incredibly violent. . . . One of my friends, fourteen years old, took a bullet in the head and his brain literally exploded in front of my eyes. The confrontations lasted until

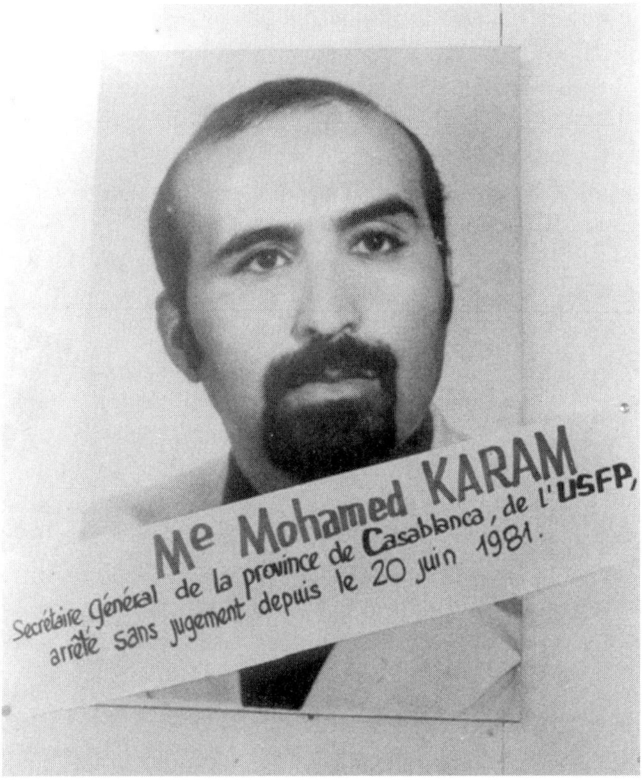

Figure 4.1. Poster to free Mohamed Karam, illegally detained even two years after the Casablanca uprising. Courtesy of Mohamed Karam.

21:00. All night tanks patrolled the neighborhood and police cars with mounted microphones that passed and passed again in the streets ordered people to bring the authorities their wounded relatives and friends as well as the corpses of those killed in the demonstrations.[37]

In his speech to the nation immediately after the 1981 Casablanca events, Hassan II characterized those detained as both "recidivists" and peasants, the latter the deleterious outcome of a massive rural population influx into Casablanca by those possessing neither urban connections nor urbanity:

People from the countryside who were attached to their neighborhood by nothing whatsoever. . . . Which were the neighborhoods that were the theater of incidents?

Not one of these neighborhoods was truly Casablancan. Is it imaginable, for example, that an inhabitant of Derb Ghallef would set on fire a store in his neighborhood, one that he saw born and grow up as did his parents. . . . The riot concerns those neighborhoods where is to be found measures contrary to the dignity of Islam and that we have allowed to be constructed."[38]

The royal disdain for certain Casablanca subjects is evident in the king's use of the French word *récidiviste* in the context of an Arabic-language speech. The French word emerges from nineteenth-century scientific preoccupations with the criminal personality type linked to physiognomy in general, and in particular to specific facial or cranial characteristics.[39] Complex systems of identification involving photography and fingerprinting were developed in France to tie the criminal body of the récidiviste to archives and records. When such histories and technologies of identification are conveyed from France to overseas colonies, they are allied to pseudoscientific notions of inferior heredity: French colonial officers believed that Berbers were good and Arabs bad (as discussed in chapter one), while the Moroccan king applied a similar logic of criminal identification to peasants in urban settings. According to this view, the uprising is not due to adverse social conditions in need of social cures; the Moroccan judicial and police focus was the application of the law on repeat offenders defined as an urban criminal underclass drawn from an unredeemable peasantry. It comes as no surprise that techniques to contain the uprising sought to target and label a social pathology of dangerous persons, and then to remove them from society. To implement this scenario were the identification card, the mass grave, and the prison.

The Aftermath: Political Trials and Mock Trial

Accounts of the 1981 Casablanca uprising offered in this chapter provide multiple frames to describe the complex modalities of power relationships available to and exercised by unions, unemployed urban youth, and innocent bystanders caught up in the crisis. A wide range of responses to repression emerged from the city of Casablanca. What happened to the union leadership has been the subject of much historiography and memoirs, whereas chronicles about actors not affiliated with unions are less known. Moreover, in the post-Hassan II era, stories about the Casablanca riots are inseparable from memories of past state violence. When victims tell their stories in the year 2000 after an interval of nineteen years, the uprising becomes symbolically central to reclaiming the past. For many Casablancans, that past is heroic, dissident, and rebellious; for others, the random quality and arbitrary consequences forever darken lives ruined by personal and pecuniary losses. The ways in which narrators' complex memories of dissidence and rebellion, sorrow and mourning have come to light in newly opened public spaces of Casablanca constitute enactments of the struggle for meaning. These new performance venues and novel rituals tell the unfolding human rights story of Morocco.

The aftermath of the Casablanca "bread riots" of May and June 1981 is one example of the multiple ways in which official history is undergoing revision when told by victims and survivors. Nineteen years elapsed before al-Muntadā, as one declared objective to research the past, organized a first public commemoration (*dhikrā*) in the form of a mock trial. Why a mock trial? Answers to this question emerge from the role of the law courts in creating the category of political prisoner and the urgency to produce counterhistories to Moroccan political trials.

The life and work of Abderrahim Berrada, a well-known defense lawyer for Moroccan political prisoners, is instructive in this regard. While in France in 1957–66, he studied law, journalism, and psychology. He returned to Casablanca to mount landmark legal defenses on behalf of political prisoners during the decades of the "years of lead" characterized by hundreds of mass political trials that burdened Morocco's court system. Berrada advocates a primary line of defense outside the courtroom and in the public arena noting possibilities for complementary political performances, such as sit-ins, demonstrations, and speeches to the media. Berrada claims inspiration from Jacques Vergès, lawyer for members of the Algerian political leadership tried in French courts, as France pursued both legal and military exactions against the Algerian independence movement.[40]

De la stratégie judiciaire, published in 1968, outlines Vergès's approach to political trials by setting up two opposing kinds of cases categorized by the attitude of the accused: during *le procès de connivance* (complicit trial), the individual acquiesces, and following Vergès's terms, is "in dialogue" with his judges, accepting them as embodiments of the state and arbiters of the law; in contrast, during *le procès de rupture* (ruptured or broken trial), the accused refuses to recognize the judicial apparatus.[41] Referring to the case of George Dimitrov, a Bulgarian Communist accused by Hermann Göring of setting the Reichstag ablaze on 27 February 1933, Vergès demonstrates a nascent example of the "ruptured" trial because acquittal was secondary to demolishing in court accusations by a Nazi-dominated juridical and political apparatus. Rupturing a trial was accomplished successfully when lawyers highlighted Dimitrov and his fellow detainees' political ideas and ideals both inside and outside the courtroom, a tactic that generated massive international support, which in turn led to their eventual liberation.[42] Although Vergès provides no details, a countertrial of Adolf Hitler for "crimes against civilization" organized in London garnered much adverse criticism for the German court and forced it to account for accusations publicized effectively abroad.[43] The London events took the form of a mock trial, a tactic legal scholar Paul Schiff Berman analyzes as the production of alternative histories in the form of "non-state assertions of jurisdiction [that] may sometime take the guise of more formal legal proceedings."[44]

Vergès, however, castigates Dimitrov's lawyers because they did not pursue such tactics to their logical limits. Dimitrov did not base his legal battles in challenges to the *right* of a German tribunal, even a Nazi one, to judge him, unlike the FLN (Algerian National Liberation Front) trials in which Vergès would gain fame. In the trial of Djamila Bouhired, a member of the Algerian resistance who charged French officers with torture in 1957, Vergès perceives the logical endpoint to the ruptured trial: no dialogue between opposing parties was possible for Algerians facing French judges. Instead, legal strategies included vocal denunciations of the French colonial administrative system, the French army, and, ultimately, the French right to rule Algeria in the form of accusations of "crimes of colonialism." Courtroom tactics called for reparation to Algerian victims of torture, who exemplified the pervasive French practice of arbitrary detention and enforced disappearance, along with a worldwide campaign in support of a war against colonialism, even as that entailed reciprocal Algerian acts of violence on French soil.[45]

For Algerian lawyers under French colonialism, and subsequently for Moroccan defense lawyers under postcolonial repression, strategies for the legal offense transformed the courtroom into a theater of political struggle and a battlefield for public opinion. Vergès's tactics, embraced by Berrada and a cadre of North African human rights lawyers, were in many ways an inevitable alternative, perhaps the only corrective, to rampant state suborning of judicial processes from the pretrial period to tribunals closed to the public, witnesses silenced in the courtroom, and a muzzled press in the national arena. Lawyers and political prisoners were forced to produce countertestimony outside the courts in order to unmask the farcical nature of the state's legal discourse. Actual trials became historic trials, trials about history that narrated a different account and generated a vast literature about the Moroccan past. Far-reaching consequences to the regime's political trials were not only international censure but also an increase in literary production about the law by Moroccans who came under court jurisdictions. Since actual Moroccan political trials recounted neither "official history" nor dissident narratives, the question arises who would retell the past of uprisings and political trials, when, and how?

In the absence of written documentation, the gap between what happened in the past and how to tell it in the present presents formidable problems for storytellers and witnesses. The courtroom affords one solution. Trials provide a venue in which versions of the story are articulated then judged. Once political trials were rigged. When testifying during the performance of the mock trial all that was omitted in the 1981 mockery of a trial, for example specific formal features of a genuine trial, may provide a new basis for considered judgment. While the 1981 Casablanca trials were secret and hasty but written, the al-Muntadā-initiated mock trial is public, and human voices oppose established documentation. A mock trial, therefore, is an opportunity for victims to reproduce trial techniques, such as testimony never voiced in Moroccan courtrooms, and to take on roles denied as prosecutor and witness, judge and jury. A mock trial enjoins victims, publicly and painfully, to articulate their stories. As victims they invert, and in this sense they "mock," the structure of a trial by transforming themselves from the persecuted into the persecutors. Their inversion and putative mocking of a trial, nonetheless, illumine emotional and moral forces at work for Casablancans still marked by the 1981 events. During al-Muntadā's mock trial, no representatives of the state are present; witnesses, thus, are neither examined nor cross-questioned. The focus rests narrowly yet powerfully on the story each victim relates, a narrative whose purpose is to judge a regime that implicated everyone—perpetrators, victims, and in the Casablanca uprising, a significant number of bystanders.

The gathering to commemorate what is currently called the Casablanca *intifāḍah* was held on 18 June 2000 in the Complex Anoual, a cultural center in the heart of the city. Inside the main auditorium, chairs were arranged in a square with a center space left prominently unoccupied. Two elected leaders from al-Muntadā, Salah El Ouadie and Abdelhak Moussadak (themselves former political prisoners), acted as moderators and questioners and were seated on the side facing the hall's entrance. Witnesses were ranged in rows that formed the right and left sides of the square. Audience members surrounded the central actors on all four sides providing a close approximation of what was deliberately configured to recreate the space of

Figure 4.2. Commemoration of the 1981 Casablanca uprising, 19 June 2000. Abdelhak Moussadak, al-Muntadā organizer, holds a victim's photograph. Photo by author.

a tribunal. Al-Muntadā's interlocutors performed the role of lawyers, while listeners to the victims' testimony were put in the physical and moral position of judges in a conventional courtroom. Taped to the walls and pillars were photographs of individuals. As the public testimony unfolded, witnesses' words and gestures pointing to photographs of the dead constituted the sole primary evidence with which to indict the regime for violent reprisals against its citizens (Figure 4.2).

Shahādāt (Testimonies)

To remember the prisoners and memorialize those buried in unknown graves, the mock trial encouraged public testimony from victims and their families belonging to two hitherto silent groups. The first speaker, Lakbir Dadi, for example, had never before spoken of his loss. He was introduced as a father whose two children died by asphyxiation while confined, along with an overflow crowd of arrested, to the military barracks of Ain Harrouda:

Salām ʿalaykum. I am Dadi Lakbir. That day I was with my children in the house. At 15:00 I heard knocking at the door, they broke down the door. I was with my three children. They took us and they separated me from my [two] children, they put me in one room and the children in another. At midnight they opened the room and they took out forty people and they laid them out on the ground. When I saw my [two] children among them, they made me go out and stay far away from them, they took me with my youngest child in another direction and we passed the night. Since that time I have never seen my children again. They transferred me and my youngest child to Ain Harrouda and there they separated me from my son. I was brought in front of the tribunal, then spent ten days in the [Casablanca] Civil Prison of Ghbila. Then I was brought to the Court of Appeals, Penal Chamber and my friends found me a lawyer. I kept screaming [during the trial] where are my two children? Where are my two children? Finally the tribunal declared me innocent and I was freed. At that time they had written on my file [as the charge] that I had killed a Christian [European]. Since that time I have never seen my children. It is now nineteen years. This is what happened to me. I was in my house. I saw no demonstrations. I saw nothing at all until they entered my house and took us. I still carry those scars, the oldest was born in 1961, the second in 1965, and the youngest in 1967.[46]

Dadi does refer to his sons by name, but because both were killed in the military barracks, their names, unlike those of subsequent victim families who testify, appeared on Moroccan government and French monitoring-organization lists: Mohamed and Abdelhaq Dadi, profession: high school students. In July 1981, Paris lawyer Jean-Pierre Mignard, sent to Casablanca by international human rights organizations, returned to report a situation in which an unknown number of children killed by bullets was deposited in mass graves, prison conditions were such that many arrested died by asphyxiation, and minors were not subject to trial but held in police custody and "auctioned off" (*ventes aux enchères*) to parents until payments as high as 3,000 dirhams were extorted.[47] Dadi's testimony also attests to the multiple roles played by the military both in targeting bystanders on the streets and in killing detainees concentrated in army camps. To emphasize the random nature of the authorities' use of round-ups and trumped-up trials, Dadi was initially held accountable for the demise of the lone European, Alexandre Cuquel, stoned to death in his car by crowds occupying the main Casablanca-Rabat highway that circles the bidonvilles.[48]

The second speaker, Azzedine Achab, was formerly a photographer. Arrested with his camera and equipment, he was released and then rearrested when confiscated films were developed. His photographs were used as evidence of his guilt during the trials and he was sentenced to seven years in prison:[49]

Around Kriaa [market], Derb Foqqara, Hay Bouchentouf, Place Sraghna, buses were burned, cars and motorcycles torched, there were demonstrations, banners. The Auxiliary Forces (*al-qūwāt al-musāʿidah*) struck with bludgeons, children demonstrating threw stones, lots of photos. Kriaa was surrounded by the army. I took all the photos that were very moving, published by the press. The photos presented against me in court were those I took on motorcycle.

Several women stood up, each in turn replacing Achab in the "witness seat." They introduced themselves by the names of their slain children: the mother of Jamal Misyou, the mother of Hafid, and the sister of the martyr, Fatima Ouaddak. Their narratives are brief, cautiously describing an unnamed "they," as in "they made him go dead." For the bereaved women, the pain of officially-instigated disappearances strikes listeners in the telling detail of the white car, the familiar and feared security forces' vans that transported their offspring away forever:

My son died in the strike (*iḍrāb*). They opened the door. He went out and never returned. He was the sixth brother, eighteen years old. I never saw him. They came, they made him go out and they took him. I never saw him again. I don't know his grave. They made him go out from my house, they made him go out dead. Ah, my son went out and he never returned. This is what happened.

My son Hafid had gone to visit his grandmother and when he was returning to see me they shot him near the Kriaa market. I have not seen him up to now, I don't know where is his grave. They took him away in a car and asked me to bring in the family identity card. They took him away in a white car, that's the story (*hādhā huwa al-klām*).

I am the sister of the martyr Fatima Ouaddak, there she is in front of you [weeping, she points to a photo on the wall]. That girl went out only to bring back her brother from the front door of the house. My brother was two years old. He went down the stairs and outside, she followed him to bring him back to the house. They fired a bullet at her, she was hit inside the hallway, she fell. We took her in. The boys began screaming. My father brought her to the district where they said: "We can do nothing for this girl, take her back." They took her back to the house, put her down, they called out to her, she said: leave me, leave, then she died, she was fourteen years old. They came, my mother asked for time to wash her and wrap her in a shroud. They refused. They said: Don't talk, we will take her and that's all. They took her away. The army took her away. Derb Bouchentouf, Street 11, number 9.

The microphone passes to the sister and brother-in-law of Rabiaa Rizki and Said Rizki, residents of Derb Mabrouka; Rabiaa Rizki died and Said Rizki survived:

Each June 20th we live in mourning (*naʿish al-ḥidād*) because we lost two. At the time I was ten years old, my sister fourteen. We were at home when we heard the news of the strike. Then my sister went out in front of the door and a bullet hit her, they had fired on her. The bullet touched her directly in the heart. When my brother saw that it touched her, he went to her and he too was hit by a bullet. It is only by God's mercy that he is still alive. He bled for two days at home, then we took him to the hospital and he was operated on. As for my sister, she lost her life the instant the bullet hit her. She died in the arms of our brother-in-law who will give his testimony (*shahādah*) and recount how my sister died.

The brother-in-law's story:

Salam aleykum. For these people, we beg God to pardon us and them and have mercy on them. We went out the door, we were seated, we saw a man take bullets from his pocket, and aim at people, and anyone was shot, he aimed right and left, a bullet passed three fingers from my head. When I went to take the girl who was shot, he aimed at me, I took her. As soon as we entered the house, she gave up her life (*aslamat al-rūḥ*). The corpse stayed in the house Saturday, Sunday, Monday it began to emit a terrible smell. An ambulance was passing and I signaled it, it stopped, and they asked what there was. I said: "A girl was killed, tell us by God what are we to do?" They came accompanied by the three agents from the Sīmī [CIMI: Compagnie d'intervention mobile interurbaine], an agent came in with me, another stayed in front of the door, and a third outside the house. He examined her, then he said: Yes, she is one of ours." They brought a stretcher and took her away. As for the other child, they said to bring him to Soufi hospital, where they took him away and operated. We were forbidden to see him. When he was healed he was brought to the Maarif police station, then to the emergency room of Averroes Hospital where he was examined, then he was brought to Ghbila [Casablanca] Civil Prison. At that time he was studying. Now he does not wish to live in Morocco, he resides currently in Europe where he married a foreigner and has two children. Now we beg God to pardon us and them and have mercy on them.

Corpses with bullet wounds are in the custody of the authorities. "Yes, she is one of ours"—is the chilling phrase uttered by a mysterious government agent who appears in their homes to view their child's bullet-ridden body. "The Makhzen (central authority) will bury him," another official peremptorily declares. Wounds are considered self-evident proof of guilt as a rioter by government authorities. Whenever feasible, bodies were whisked away from the family abode and also from hospitals, barracks, and morgues. To complete the job of eliminating individuals shot during the uprising, the state, licensed to establish identification mechanisms, also confiscated identity documents as an effective way to enforce government versions of the events in Casablanca.

The next two women's testimonies describe the battle surrounding paperwork that took place between the families of dead children and the bureaucracy. In both cases, corpses and their identifying documentation were removed under duress:

Here is my son whom you see [points to a photo of a boy taped to the wall]. He is eight years old. I have two sons and one daughter. I kept them at home throughout that day. At 18:00 the street was empty in Derb Shorfa, the Sultan neighborhood. My son went out in front of the house and a bullet hit him in the intestines. I took him to the hospital. When we arrived they took him away while I cried and they threw us out. The doctor took him, my son gave up his life in the doctor's arms, even though his intestines came out of his stomach, he was still alive. The next morning, the district chief (*qā'id al-dā'irah*) demanded to see us. He took our family ID card and promised to return it to us later. The child stayed in the hospital and they said to us: "We will let him out today, we will let him out tomorrow. Finally the district chief said to us that an order had come from Rabat, that no one was to take the child and that the Makhzen would bury him, "Get out of here and on your way." The family ID card is still at the district office. We had another one made up after we had another child. It has only the names of the [living] children, it is not a family ID card. My son, up to now, I never saw him again, I never saw his grave.

It was my brother-in-law who worked and spent for the family. That day, my mother-in-law waited his return from work. At that moment the children in the neighborhood ran to us and said: "Sister Marrakchia, your son has been killed." We went out and we found him on the corner stretched out dead on the ground. We brought him to the house with the neighborhood youth. They took him way from us. They took him away with his papers. He was coming from work, he was the sole provider of the family. They demanded that we give them the family ID card . . . they never gave it back. We had another made up. Until today we have never registered his death. His poor mother is a victim of age, with a heart condition, diabetes. She lives a pitiful existence. We want to know his grave. She always says that her son has no grave, that they are without news. At the time he was twenty years old. Derb Foqqara, Street 12, number 18.

James Scott proposes the concept of a "legible people," a metaphor for the emergence of writing as central to the creation of nationhood and to modern forms of national control.[50] People come to legibility, can be "read," when they are under the official scrutiny of paperwork, files, dossiers, archives, records, and identity documents. A family passbook, for example, routinely inscribes the organization of family life by marking dates of death. For parents, the pain of their dead and missing children is deflected to inaccuracies in the family records that list only living children. Where can the bereaved read about their children's existence, if not their fates? The powerful Moroccan human rights metaphor of the nation's past history as a blank page has long been articulated in opposition to government demands "to turn the page" (*ṭayy al-ṣafḥah*) on past abuses. To the act of chronicling Moroccan history are added the voices of grieving families mourning the missing page of a reissued family passbook intended to reconstitute a family despite absent members.

Obtaining a Moroccan family passbook, required of all household heads, ensures an endless process of administrative harassment. Yet, without this document, one has no official existence.[51] At the best of times, to amend any part of recorded vital statistics requires complex interactions between powerless residents of poor neighborhoods and the formal administrative institutions. Ordinary requests for elementary school enrollment, certificates of employment, applications for public welfare, or passports depend on the ability of the head of household to produce correct papers documenting the family's official existence. As an example, one witness during the mock trial, a victim's sister, recounts the travails of the family of Hassan Hantri, a passerby shot as he returned home, and what happened when his family refused government efforts to record his killing as a natural death:

> I am the sister of the martyr Hassan Hantri. That day my brother was working, he returned from his job, we didn't know there was a strike until people came to tell us my brother was hit by a bullet. The bullet hit him in the forehead, went out the head and into the wall. We all went out, we, my mother . . . I put my hand on his head, his brains fell into my hands. We brought him into the house and he gave up his soul around 5 in the afternoon. He was hit around 4:30 in the afternoon. My poor mother and my father refused to give over his body to the police. When they wanted to bury him themselves they were directed to district, they threatened them and said: if you don't speak we will finish you and we will make you follow your son." Then they were directed to the police station to request authorization for the burial. Then the police commissioner Hassouni threatened my father, saying if you don't go we will make you follow your son. My father returned home crying. He said: "I can do nothing for my son." His corpse stayed with us from Saturday until Monday at 5 in the afternoon. Then soldiers came into the house pointing their weapons at us to frighten us, and in effect we were afraid. They asked for a blanket, we gave it to them along with what they had they covered my brother, carried him to the police van, and threw him like a fly. We said to each other, that's it, it's finished, we can do nothing." We closed the door behind us and we cleaned the house of blood. We've done nothing about it until now. We knocked on every door to register his death in the family ID card. Everywhere we went we were told that "we were doing politics. It is impossible to expunge him from the family passbook: If you wish to do so, bring us proof from 12 witnesses that he died a natural death." We refused. We told them that our brother died from bullets and we will say forever that he died from bullets.

> I want to say one thing that continues to hurt the heart—that is we want to know his grave, even if it's a hole where they put him. We want to know this hole, go there, sit next to it and weep in order to unburden our grief. We want to mourn our brother, to finish our mourning at least and to say that we have mourned our brother. He was not only a brother to us, but also a father, our mother, our aunt. My parents waited for him to grow up to help alleviate familial burdens. Certainly we called him our father, our mother. There is no power and no force except in God. The name is Hassan Hantri, Derb Bouchentouf, Street 69, number 36.

Morocco's laws pertaining to identity cards were twisted to allow for the elimination of individuals and to enforce silence about this elimination. While identity cards are routinely used to match names with the unidentified dead, in Casablanca the link between a unique physical body and its record was severed. The result was a blanket process of criminalization that covered victims, families, and urban neighborhoods. Inevitably, criminality would also stain the reputation of the authorities. It is not too easy to eradicate an individual's paperwork without suborning complex bureaucratic networks of hospital, police, and prison records. During the mock trial, the violence of state coercion is temporarily counteracted by the creation of free public space to support a community of victims who testify because they are in search of explanations and redress. They had been subjected to unjust application of their country's codes that extended the domain of social control over the living and especially the dead. The state owns the family passbook that Moroccans carry. And the state can make the passbook say what it wants it to say even as this does violence to families and demoralizes the population.

The Unknown Grave

To this day, many do not know the whereabouts of the victims' graves. The identity card photograph is all that remains. Alphonse Bertillon, the French police clerk credited in 1872 with the invention of the standard frontal and profile shot to identify récidivistes, called identity photographs *portraits parlés* (speaking likenesses).[52] The identity card photograph coincided and was in complicity with the advent of French colonialism: the year 1912 not only began the era of the French Protectorate but also introduced to Morocco the French police service, the prison system, and an attached anthropometric section (*service anthropométrique*).[53] Anthropometry deployed photographs and written descriptions to establish extensive physiognomic portraits of criminals. As the work of Michel Foucault attests, the birth of the prison and police photography in the 1840s are central to issues of modern disciplinary power that call for isolation, the imposition and recording of individualized names, supervision, and surveillance.[54]

Artifacts born of colonial control and postcolonial repression are transformed into memory devices, the traces of remembrance with which to conjure the dead and missing. The photograph, regardless of its provenance, proves a child's existence. During the mock trial, the identity card photograph is an object that can be referred to and pointed at, the sole evidence to anchor the presence of the disappeared, as families grapple with endings to mock trial narratives. No one, especially the bereaved families, consider the photograph to be remotely related to the reality of their missing children. The picture is all that remains.

Identity card portraits enlarged and pasted on the wall look out and speak to the audience, underlining the import of the witnesses' last sentences. They testify to the presence of visual likeness in the absence of the physical body: "They came, they made him go out and they took him. I never saw him again. I don't know his grave. They made him go out from my house. They made him go out dead. Ah, my son went out and he never returned. This is what happened." "My son, up to now, I never saw him again, I never saw his grave." "I want to say one thing that continues to hurt the heart—that is we want to know his grave, even if it's a hole where they put him. We want to know this hole, go there, sit next to it and weep in order to unburden our grief. We want to mourn our brother, to finish our mourning at least and to say that we have mourned our brother." The right of relatives to bury their dead is recognized crossculturally, even legally.[55] In Morocco, complex funeral rites are prescribed both communally and familially. They begin at death with the command to wash, dress, and shroud the body, and then to lament and pray over it. Family and friends bear the corpse to the cemetery, and prayers are offered at the gravesite. A long period of mourning ensues with specific ceremonial gatherings, for example, to mark the fortieth day and the year anniversary of the death. Traditionally, if a person is killed, the family cannot be released from their mourning until revenge has been taken or an indemnity paid (for tribal Moroccans, the mechanism of reparation for a member killed was blood money, cf. Chapter 1). For the deceased and for the bereaved, it is considered among life's gravest misfortunes to be deprived of the observance of mourning rituals such as a funeral, and obligatory visits to and care of the grave. The loss of the ability to express mourning conventionally and individually no less than the uncertainty whether family members are in fact dead carries with it immeasurable grief and trauma.

As early as December 1981, the bulletin published in France by the Comité de lutte contre la répression au Maroc produced a hand-drawn map locating two mass graves in the Ben M'sik bidonville quarter of Casablanca, subsection Hay Al-Farah between the Boulevard Ibn Tachfine and the Route des Ouled Ziane. Unnamed sources placed the mass graves precisely in an unbuilt area adjacent to the confluence of Casablanca's separate Jewish, Christian, and Muslim cemeteries.[56] The mass grave is itself a scene of crimes as well as an archive of evidence against perpetrators.[57] The police sweep, the arbitrary round-up, mass arrests, killings, enforced disappearances, and unmarked graves are brutal and cruel abuses. Adding to these offenses is the state's unwillingness to acknowledge that those who died and those imprisoned were not, in fact, criminals.

Aftermath: Prison

States have mechanisms for dealing with civic disturbance, most commonly, a sequence of arrest and trial with the possibility of imprisonment. Morocco's prisons, divided according to length of prison sentences, accommodated the Casablanca influx: those sentenced to more than ten years were sent to Kenitra Central Prison, up to ten years to Essaouira Prison, and up to five years to Adir Prison.[58] In the aftermath of the 1981 uprising, approximately 8,000 people were arrested. As al-Muntadā's mock trial unfolded, witnesses who suffered silently and mourned in private family settings for the disappeared were followed by victims of the apparatus of criminal justice. The mock trial format presents an obvious counternarrative, one method to right the wrongs of formal legal proceedings in which the police, the courts, and the prisons managed the dangerous chaos of an uprising by fabricating criminal identities. Two women testified, Fatiha Hamoussi on behalf of her absent father and Fatima Rabia speaking about her son, present but handicapped, and gesturing to surrounding audience members who formed a section of detainees:

My name is Fatiha Hamoussi, born in 1976 here in Casablanca. My father was arrested when I was five, I am the oldest of four. My father's name is Si Larbi Ben Miloudi Hamoussi, born 1940, profession before his arrest, a worker. He was given ten years imprisonment and ten years exile from Casablanca. My father was arrested during the uprising (*intifāḍah*) of June 20, 1981 leaving behind him a family of five people without a provider. He was arrested in the house, they beat him up on his face in front of our eyes, with clubs and weapons, and they broke his leg. They took him fainted to the district of Bernoussi. They held him where he saw people dying victims of asphyxiation next to him in that cemetery they called a cell. After we went looking for him in the district headquarters, we were told that he died as a result of his wounds. Immediately our house went into mourning, we received condolences from the neighbors. Sometime afterward, we learned he was still alive and he was in the Essaouira Civil Prison ill with various sicknesses from the prisoners, tuberculosis. He was not treated or transferred near the family to alleviate his sufferings. We suffered all sorts of annoyances from the prison authorities beginning with the director, Baalouane. My father spent four years of punishment then he was transferred to Adir Prison where he completed his sentence and suffered many health problems. We also suffered, traveling hundreds of miles to visit him. . . . I am Fatiha Hamoussi, 24 years old, unemployed and responsible for the entire family, no comment. I demand that justice and equity be rendered. I salute al-Muntadā and all those forces that work toward that bring the truth to light.

I am Fatima Rabia, mother. The son is in front of you, handicapped, without health. When they took him away we searched everywhere for months. We were directed to Ain Harrouda, the police station, until we learned that he was in the Civil Prison according to a go-between, a prison guard. When we asked to visit him we were thrown out. He was tired, in a pitiful state. According to what he told us he was beaten. The blood flowed from his ears and nose. There you see him in front of you. He suffers from mental instability. I visited him during the three years that he spent in Adir Prison. Here is a group of friends who were together in prison. They know him. They watched him lose his reason. He does nothing. He doesn't work. Derb Bouchentouf, street 62, number 13.

This woman in front of me. She too, her son, born in 1961. They made him go out, with his two brothers and his father. They released the father and two brothers. They took him with my son and he spent three years in Adir. They mistreated them. They mistreated us until we meet each other before God and may each receive his rights.

Al-Muntadā representatives conclude the afternoon with poetry readings and discussions about the struggle for human rights in Morocco. As they stand before the audience, behind them loom oversize portraits of Morocco's royal family, whose visual presence is mandatory for all public places.[59] Portraits of Muhammad VI are obscured by al-Muntadā's banner draped across the back hall: "ḍaḥāyā intifāḍat 20 Yūnyū al-majīd wa-ʿāʾilātuhum yuṭalibūna bi-al-kashf ʿan kull asmāʾ al-shuhadāʾ wa-taslīm rufātihim ilā ḍawīhim" (victims of the celebrated 20 June uprising and their families demand an investigation of all the martyrs' names and the handing over of bodies to their kin).

The performance staged by al-Muntadā was both a mock trial and a memorialization, events suggesting that to depend after many years on witnesses, who have no legal recourse, and their memory is a substitute for power and reinscribes their powerlessness. Speakers and listeners are drawn from the same community. Yet the Casablancans' oral testimony precisely and lucidly concentrates on the acts of the perpetrators and less so on their own immeasurable suffering. In so doing, they reenact the reverence accorded by both Western and Islamic law to the human voice in the act of witnessing.[60] Justice is equated with the search for lists of names, identification documents linked to the physical body, and their location in Casablanca. The mock trial is also a political trial, if only because statistical estimates are transformed into human beings. When performed as a public spectacle, a mock trial deploys legal forms and discourse to remedy past wrongs of the Moroccan courts and laws. Witnesses are physically present while absent perpetrators and hidden government actions are constructed through word and image, testimony and photography.[61]

The Aftermath According to Jamal Lakouis: "How to Become a Political Prisoner in Spite of Oneself"

Jamal Lakouis attended the mock trial but chose not to speak. He proposed an interview among a group of friends, one in which questions and corroborative information could take place.[62] Lakouis, a Casablanca native, began his story on 20 January 1981, when he was a twenty-three-year-old accounting student who stepped outside his parent's home to smoke a cigarette with friends. His large family was indoors, involved in wedding preparations for an older sister:

> I was outdoors with my friends. It began to heat up. Before there were small groups here and there, the police, what one calls the forces of order, intervened to scatter people with dogs and tear gas. We were young and it was like following a film, a film that we couldn't tear ourselves away from. If you see a shocking film, with events, suspense, you cannot give it up, you hope to see the film and how events work out.
>
> I was smoking a cigarette, just like this. And a rain of bullets came out of nowhere. Without being aware, after three or four hits, I realized I was wounded. I felt a shock to my head and I held my head thinking that I was wounded in the head. Suddenly I saw my leg gushing blood. I asked myself: Was I wounded in the head or the leg? Because when I wanted to walk or run or flee, I fell. I got up and crawled home 50 meters away. I tried to run because I thought the police were chasing me, because everybody was in shock, everyone was afraid and running every-

where. I opened the door and fell into the house. My parents, everyone began screaming. I think I fainted or was semiconscious because I couldn't follow events completely. There was blood everywhere, they tried to do something but couldn't because the wound was too serious. Some said take him to the hospital, others said no, they'll arrest him there. The blood flowed. An intern who was a neighbor came and tried to do something. He couldn't. He said you have only one solution. I said, what? You must go to the hospital or you will die. There is too much blood loss and nothing can be done." Finally, they decided to bring me to the hospital. An ambulance came. They said to bring you we need an authorization, or something, in any case they wouldn't bring me, whether this was on purpose or not. Someone from our house brought a car, they took me to the emergency room of Ibn Rochd, I went in and they registered me.

Lakouis's story foreshadows the unhappy outcome as he narrates the cruel family dilemma: to risk bringing him to the authorities' attention by a hospital visit or watch him bleed to death. Lakouis was finally brought in the evening to Ibn Rochd Hospital, where he fainted when his wound was treated without anesthesia. His fate unfolded, Lakouis notes, as if he were the spectator watching himself in a film or a dream.

I woke up, and as soon as they finished I thought I could leave. There were two uniformed policemen and two in civilian clothes who intervened and said, "This man, he stays here, he is blocked." They moved me to a large ward with the other wounded. I knew what would happen. I stayed there calmly. Everyone said we would be given the death penalty. I was arrested Saturday, Sunday, Monday, Tuesday, and Wednesday evening taken to the central police station where I stayed all night. In the morning they made a report. Questions asked were name, parent's name, address, that's all. They wrote what they wanted without asking questions. Were you or were you not involved in the riots, was not asked. When they finished the report, I asked if I could read it. They cursed me, hit me when I asked if I could read what I was supposed to sign and I said I wouldn't sign anything I hadn't read. They began hitting me again. They brought me to the basement. They beat me one two three times, I was forced to sign. They pushed down on the wound to hurt me, I couldn't take the pain any more. I signed and spent the night there.

The next day I appeared before the procureur de roi. They had written that I was in the riots, I fought the police, I destroyed I don't know what. They asked me did you do this? I said, no I didn't, here's what happened to me. They gave me another paper to sign. I signed. They brought me to Casablanca Civil Prison. We were welcomed with curses, beatings, our heads shaved, and we were 150 people in one room, 50 square meters, quarter 5, called "la paille" [straw]. We slept like sardines in a can. When a signal was given, we all fell to the ground otherwise you had to stand.

Monday morning we were brought to court. There was no family participation, lawyers came but I hadn't hired one. Judgment was handed out around nine in the evening, they were sentencing up to 20 years, from 5 to 20 years. Two women were given 5 years. I was given 15 years plus 10 years forbidding residence in Casablanca. About thirty of us were sentenced that same day. I thought I was dreaming, I kept saying, no, this cannot be true.

At every stage, the regime's actions to record are accompanied by violence. A police report is concocted and Lakouis is forced to sign without reading. Despite vociferous denials, each signed form conducts him inexorably from hospital to police station to courtroom to jail and finally, consigns him to Morocco's penitentiary for political prisoners. Lakouis was one of twenty Casablanca residents arbitrarily arrested, condemned to more than ten years of prison, and transferred to serve sentences in the maximum-security confines of Kenitra Central Prison. At first he was placed in Casablanca Civil Prison, along with 150 detainees crowded into a single room approximately 500 square feet in size in Quartier Paille, built by the French Protectorate to house convicts engaged in forced labor with straw (*paille*): "We called it a box of sardines. To sleep, it was necessary for a signal to be given and we all had to fall down at the same time, otherwise you ended up standing on someone else." Then Lakouis and other so-called rioters were dispersed among the regular prison population in Kenitra. Somehow the Casablancans stayed in touch, coming into contact with what Lakouis describes as a "cohabitation" between leftists and Islamists political prisoners: each group maintained their respective positions and principles yet all united around the goal of the right to political prisoner status. Abraham Serfaty, Mohamed Srifi, Mustapha Temsamani, and others from the Marxist-Leninist group imprisoned in Kenitra since the 1977 Casablanca political trials urged Lakouis to organize his group of detainees. It took five years of clandestine meetings before they made claims to the prison administration demanding political prisoner status. Unlike the leftists and Islamists, Lakouis states, because his group never existed outside prison walls, effecting a coherent internal prison organization was difficult. Pure chance brought together what became known as the "Group of June 81." Among their first actions in prison were organized group hunger strikes undertaken in 1982 and 1984:

An individual hunger strike could never be done. You would be massacred, beaten. Prison was severer then, you could never say, "I demand my rights." The word "right," you never had the right to pronounce there. In 1984 I tried to return to my studies. The group around Serfaty gave me books and urged me to return to studying.

In contrast to support summoned on behalf of leftists and Islamist political prisoners, Amnesty International and local human rights groups did not adopt the cause of the Casablanca Group of June 1981. Classified by the state as common criminals, both the authorities and the opposition were in agreement not to accord prisoner of conscience status. First, the Casablancans lacked any political organization or recognizable party affiliation outside in the world before their arrests; they were united by their neighborhood address in Casablanca. Second, their wounds were proof positive of violent acts, if not intentions, even by those who considered themselves in opposition to the regime and supporters of the strike. Mohamed Srifi (Marxist political prisoner, 1974–91), proposes class differences at play within the human rights community: the Casablancans were not intellectuals or cultivated dissidents quick to take up the pen and write a poem or book.[63] Despite minimal outside support, Lakouis describes his rising political consciousness:

> At the instant I contacted the Serfaty group, it was at that moment that I began to recognize how I was a political prisoner without knowing why. Because I did not participate in any riot. In fact, I did nothing. I was wounded and all, but. They thought I was a political prisoner because the objective of the riot and the strike was what? It was political. People demanded their rights, the right to live because those were the drought years. There was a crisis, a difficult life for the Moroccan people, especially the poorer masses. The riot didn't just come like that! There was a reason. What was the reason? The Moroccan people needed a little bit of liberty, but they called it a bread riot, *intifāḍat al-khubz.*

By 1984, waves of government arrests targeted political opponents from leftists to the Islamists, a shift that increased the political prisoner population of Kenitra. Over the years, close ties and deep friendships developed between Lakouis's group and the Islamists, who were generationally closer as most pursued studies while together in the "Jīm" section of the prison. By 1989, although conditions in prison had improved, the Casablanca group joined a general prison strike called throughout Morocco in December 1990 and again in 1991 to mark International Human Rights Day. In 1993, three years before he completed his fifteen-year sentence, Lakouis was amnestied, having served all twelve years in Kenitra Central Prison. As with many of the political prisoners, he completed a law degree while in prison.

Prison transformed Lakouis. A literate and educated member among the detainees of the Casablanca 1981 uprising, Lakouis was the first to appreciate political prisoner status, and thereby organize the collection of random suspects of round-ups into the Casablanca "Group of June 1981." He was the obvious leader to negotiate with prison administrators and to initiate contacts inside and outside Kenitra, seek alliances with disparate factions of the political prisoner population, and perform the carceral practices of the hunger strike and the law degree. Lakouis and his group of Casablancan innocent bystanders were no longer alone, outside of and against a well-established structure of power well understood by political prisoners according to which an entire country is construed as a prison. It is remarkable that the model of Morocco as a giant penitentiary, grasped by Lakouis within prison, gave him two options: to be oppressed or to resist. "In spite of himself," Lakouis took on the identity and role of the militant, combative, legally-trained, hunger-striking political prisoner: "We took the road of struggle (*le chemin de la lutte*) in order to have our rights, it wasn't easy, it wasn't automatic, it was after a long road."

Outside the prison walls, immediate consequences of the 1981 Casablanca uprising were the intensification of government control. In the weeks and months after the uprising, families of Moroccan political prisoners attested to nightly police round-ups, extensive police presence, and surveillance on every street and in the universities.[64] On 27 July 1981, the Moroccan Parliament hastily adopted a plan to reorganize administratively the city of Casablanca. Five regions (in French *préfectures* and in Arabic *muqāṭaʿah*) were carved out, each one allowing for increases in the number of police stations. Planning policies shifted from ineffectual attempts at restructuring existing shantytowns to resettlement projects aimed at reducing the population to those able to buy apartments built on the same sites; neither policy was sufficiently successful other than to highlight what Abdellah Lehzam, scholar of urban Morocco notes: "what characterizes the state (*le pouvoir*) in Morocco is its capacity to control directly local space."[65]

Chapter 5

Rānī nimḥik: *Women and Testimony*

Rānī nimḥik (I will erase you) is the brutal phrase uttered by Youssfi Kaddour, named as chief torturer by Fatna El Bouih in her account of disappearance and prison:

> Feelings of exile were powerful. When the police chief said, I will erase you, I said to myself, this is the reality, I was erased from the country's map. No one knows where I am. I have no existence except in the memory of my relatives and even these will be exhausted after they search and put me among the lost and dead.[1]

Despite knowing she had disappeared somewhere into Morocco, El Bouih first experiences her abduction in familiar categories of displacement and exile, a sensation intensified by her torturer's words to efface her from the record, the written page, the very map of her country. She alone knows she is being held in her own country; no one else but her captors knows her whereabouts. Kaddour's reference to obliterating his victim takes up the "lexicon of terror,"[2] part of a torturer's paradigmatic working vocabulary repeated in so many places that human rights instruments were created in the 1970s and 1980s as if to respond specifically to Kaddour's threats. To eliminate El Bouih's place in the world, not unlike disappeared political prisoners elsewhere assigned numbers as one effective technique to undermine individual identity, Moroccan women political opponents were given different names:

> "Here, you never see the sky. If you lift up your blindfold, I erase you. If you speak, I cut out your tongue. Take her away to be educated." That man was the *mʿallem*, the "teacher" Youssfi Kaddour.
>
> I couldn't believe I was in front of the man in charge, the chief himself, the teacher, the government authority. My God, were these the men in power in my country? They gave me a number and a name: "From now on you're name is Rashid." "You cannot move or speak unless you hear your name, which is 'Rashid.'" It was the beginning of the destruction of my identity. My kidnapping and my arbi-

trary imprisonment, and now it was the turn of my femininity in making me into a man. For them I was a man called Rashid.[3]

El Bouih was regendered a man by her torturers. So central is the theme of a woman forced to become a man that her book, *Ḥadīth al-ʿatamah* (a literal English translation, "Talk of Darkness"), was published in French under the title, *Une femme nommée Rachid* ("A woman called Rashid"). A fellow detainee, Widad Bouab, was renamed Ḥamīd: "Guards represented a separate category of humanity. One day one of them said to his colleague: 'You see these girls (*fatayāt*) that want to enter the world of politics and to perform men's jobs (*an yaqumna bi-aʿmāl al-rijāl*). Select . . . for them men's names.' In this way they chose a man's name for each one of us."[4] When a guard handcuffed El Bouih as she was being transported to trial, she asked why she was being treated differently from the nonpolitical women prisoners. Her prison guard replied: "For me you are not a woman. You are a man. Women are in the harem."[5] Seventeen years after her disappearance, Latifa Jbabdi writes in her published testimony: "To hide the feminine presence inside detention they called us by masculine names. They called me Saʿīd or Ṭawīl [the tall one] or the Doukkali. Only during interrogation was my name feminized to summon me as the Coach or La Pasionaria."[6] Jbabdi, Bouab, and El Bouih doubly disappear: first as activists, then as female voices in the political sphere. Calling women political prisoners by men's names did not deter the more commonplace insults and violations directed specifically at women. When arrested in her house, for example, El Bouih was called a whore, and in the police station she witnessed as routine police behavior the rape of arrested prostitutes.

Fatna is not Rashid. Her prison memoirs are part of another story, one that assumes the development of a rapidly expanding, post-independence Moroccan educational system admitting lower middle-class and rural women to the ranks of an educated intellectual elite. Fatna El Bouih was born on 10 July 1955 in Benahmed, a village in Settat province. In 1971 her academic achievements entitled her to a boarder's scholarship at Lycée Chawqi, a prestigious girls' high school in Casablanca, where she became active in the national union of high school students (Syndicat national des lycéens). She was arrested for the first time as a leader of the 24 January 1974 high school student strike. The students protested the closing of the UNEM (Union nationale des étudiants marocains, National Union of Moroccan Students) and the lack of decent education and facilities for high school students. El Bouih was detained overnight at the Maarif police station in Casablanca. Immediately upon her release she courageously spoke publicly, at age eighteen, writing and publicizing her ordeal in the newspaper.[7] Her violators did not forget the widespread publicity and sympathy generated by her extraordinary testimony. When she was detained a second time,

> I was met by an important official who appeared very angry and very knowledgeable about me. "You are the anarchist leader, you led us a merry dance at the Chawqi High School. That play comes to an end here: here you are no longer the famous anarchist, here the skies are not cloudy because of Fatna the oppressed." He was alluding to slogans shouted by fellow students during my arbitrary imprisonment when I was a student at the Chawqi High School and to the solidarity campaign that enveloped all Morocco.[8]

After her second arrest, she disappeared from 17 May to November 1977 into Derb Moulay Cherif with five other women activists, namely Latifa Jbabdi, Widad Bouab, Khadija Boukhari, Maria Ezzaouini, and Nguia Boudaa. Transferred to Meknes Prison, the women political prisoners were held from 1977 to 1979 without trial. In 1979, El Bouih helped to organize a hunger strike to establish her group's status as political detainees:

> It was inevitable that we undertake violence against ourselves. It was inevitable that we prefer death to these conditions forced on us. It was inevitable that we charge those responsible with our imprisonment. . . . Negotiations only began at the end of the second week when a committee composed of the prison director, some bureaucrats from the prison administration and the ministry of justice, and the prisoners' representatives. The hours of negotiations, to which I participated as a representative, made me suffer, demanding of me, in addition to concentration, exceptional strength to plunge into hazardous battle in order to wrest our written demands. . . . We won the battle. Even though we didn't end up with the status of political prisoners, we were treated as such. . . . It was a necessary step to build new relations and to evolve different treatments in the struggle to conceive new laws on behalf of political prisoners.[9]

Three years after her arrest El Bouih was finally sentenced by the Rabat court in 1980 to five years in prison for "conspiring against the security of the state," for membership in the illegal Marxist "23 March movement" and for distributing political tracts and posters. She completed her sentence (1980–82) at Kenitra Civil Prison, during which time she also earned her *licence* (bachelor's degree) in sociology (Figure 5.1).

Added to political repression, El Bouih reports, is a repression specific to women: "Torture, interrogations, wounds, cries, and moans. . . . We used

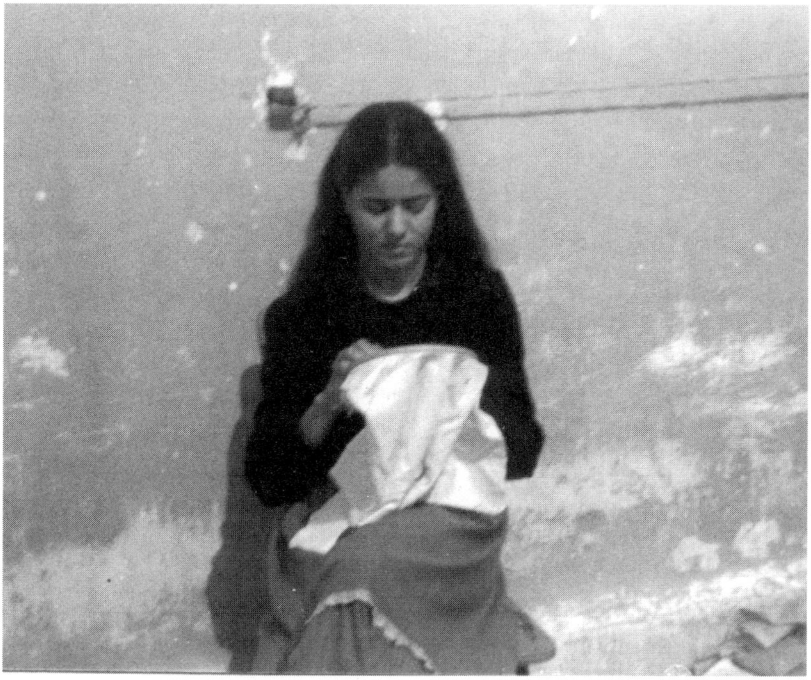

Figure 5.1. Fatna El Bouih, courtyard of Kenitra Civil Prison, circa 1980. Clandestine prison photograph.

to suffer a great deal, we women, for example during our period, because we couldn't change."[10] Widad Bouab, who shared time and space with El Bouih in Derb Moulay Cherif, maintains that long delays in delivering sanitary napkins to the women prisoners were deliberate prison policy.[11] Allowing the women to soil themselves with their menstrual blood was a part of a system of humiliations and worse, specific to women detainees, that included being treated as prostitutes, forced nakedness, rape threats, and rape: "I was blindfolded, hands manacled behind me, and thrown into a van with no place to sit. I vomited, I had my period and bled heavily, I was bathed in blood. Fortunately I was wearing black pants . . . I wore red and black for seven months, a red sweater and black pants—the red and the black."[12] Notwithstanding the increasing access of Moroccan women to education and political activism after independence, a woman's participation in the public sphere provokes powerful social alliances centering around gender, in which Moroccan protagonists usually at odds with each other seem to collude: male comrades unwilling to include wives, sisters, and mothers in clandestine oppositional networks were matched by the persecution of authoritarian governments ferociously eliminating all opposition, both male and female, yet reserving specific apparatuses of control over women who transgress against taboos.

While in prison El Bouih kept a diary framing her writings from the beginning as testimonial. Her narratives have appeared intermittently as newspaper articles. In the post-Hassan II era, she testified on television and in public venues that she regained her name after seven months enforced disappearance when her group of women political prisoners were brought through the subterranean maze beneath the Casablanca tribunal ("a place not of justice but of underground corridors," El Bouih says) and briefly relieved of their blindfolds to face a preliminary inquiry by the investigating magistrate:

> It was before the judge that I retook my name. For seven months I was called Rashid and number 45. I was so happy, you cannot imagine because at last there was someone who called me by my name. He was the first. Are you called Fatna, he said. I said, yes, yes, I swear it's true and he couldn't understand why I swore I was called Fatna El Bouih because during seven months I did not have the right to this name.[13]

El Bouih relates her entry into official judicial interrogation and legal criminal procedures, however delayed and suborned, to the moment when she can reclaim her female name and her "lost femininity."[14] Minus her blindfold and enunciating her correct name, she finds that vision and individual identity were simultaneously restored, as were the spaces and peoples with her in secret detention:

> [When my blindfold was removed] I couldn't raise my eyes. We always looked with our eyes lowered. I couldn't look up. I was very touched when we were in the corridors [of the Casablanca tribunal], they removed the men's blindfolds. I found the men were so handsome as if I had never seen a man. It was an extraordinary effect when you take off a blindfold and you see a face. It was the first time I had seen the faces of the women who were with me. We were six. We began to hug each other, to know each other. True, we had spent seven months together but seven months in total silence, with writing on the body.[15]

El Bouih dates the first women's revolt in secret detention to the moment when a guard attempted to rape one of the women prisoners after following her to the toilet: "It was a memorable night: the walls of that prison heard in its history the first voices of protest, and most amazing, women's voices."[16] All were blindfolded, manacled, and forced to lie still in complete silence; yet somehow the woman under attack was able to raise an alarm:

> It was our first revolt in Derb Moulay Cherif center, the first voices raised besides the screams of men and women undergoing torture, it was the first cry of denunciation of a particular injustice, sexual harassment. We screamed loudly around three o'clock in the morning during Ramadan, we screamed loudly and we thought they would kill us. We screamed that he was assaulting us, that we were women, it shouldn't be allowed, it was an injustice. Everyone talked, Latifa [Jbabdi] began, and then it was me. She was terrified but we said we had to do it. We held a demonstration, we insulted them, we were women and we were there but we wouldn't be made to accept it. The next day they conducted an inquiry. They hit us and humiliated us to shut us up. But the next day, their superiors came, the commanders, even with our eyes blindfolded there were ways to see. We saw by their shoes, boots, fabrics that they wore that they were high-ranking officials who questioned us while we were blindfolded and they said they would punish them.[17]

In the diabolical world of secret detention at Derb Moulay Cherif, where strict codes of silence reigned except for the screams of the tortured and the utterances of forced confessions, El Bouih proudly describes a women's "demonstration." No matter that they expressed themselves solely by screams and words while blindfolded and immobilized and that they paid physically for transgressing the imposed silence. The women still recall their triumph of reaffirmed gender, dignity, and identity. For that moment, prison officials conducted a perversion of a formal inquiry with the result that the torturers and prison officials acquiesced to limiting their atrocities: abduction and mental and physical torture were routine, but in the fall of 1978, for those women political prisoners acting together, there was a temporary respite from threats of rape.

Given the clandestine lives led by the political opposition, the six women detained together, known as the Meknes Group, would not have met each other. Neither Widad Bouab nor Maria Ezzaouini, arrested within days of each other in Marrakesh, considered herself a political activist. (Widad's fiancé was Maria's brother). In contrast, Fatna El Bouih and Khadija Boukhari, arrested together, were members of the illegal Marxist 23 March movement. Absent from the world and not visible to each other, how did they become acquainted, how did they come to know and trust each other sufficiently to stage a collective revolt against rape? Although deprived of speech, they discovered new modes of communication:

I knew the women through different ways. We created the means to contact each other, we wrote on our bodies with our fingers. We had no ink, no pens, our eyes blindfolded, you lie here, and with a little light through the sides of the blindfold like this, we recounted films, we told all, who are you, who am I, what are you doing here, why were you arrested, what did they do to you, what kind of interrogation, were you hit? We were in camp beds, you lie down or sit up eating on your knees, always blindfolded. I don't think we talked about food though there was no variety in our menu. We wrote on the back, the hand, when a cop was looking at you, you wrote on the thigh but with extraordinary finesse. These were fingers transformed into pens. I can describe to you now the small street where Nguia lived, the bakery, the grocery store of Goulimime because we had lots of time. Besides torture, we had nothing to do, nothing to occupy ourselves. We spoke, we spoke at night time because we had the light on us all the time. It was extraordinary. I know Latifa [Jbabdi], her sisters, brothers, the closets in her house, her history, everything. Widad [Bouab] also because each one transmitted to the next one. Widad has such and such a history because we were lying next to each other and we couldn't change positions. I was always next to Latifa and Khadija and I transmitted. That's how we became acquainted.[18]

To see around the blindfold and to write the experiences of women political prisoners, El Bouih considers logical forms of resistance. In her memoirs, she distills her French and Moroccan Arabic spoken interviews into the poetic cadences of literary Arabic. In so doing she returns to the act of writing on paper her letters once traced on other women's bodies. Bodily transmission begets writing because speaking is forbidden. Literary theorists of Arabic literature long have noted and discussed the complexity of linguistic registers governing oral and written Arabic, for example, differences between what is written and the varieties of spoken Arabic dialects and Amazigh/Berber languages in Morocco. Women political prisoners not only produced new narratives of resistance but their experience of political detention also discovered, if not created, corporeal Arabic. Each of their writing forms—chronological, corporeal, testimonial, and published book—mirror and reinforce techniques of female survival. El Bouih's prison memoir, composed in literary Arabic, describes a mass of reclining women's bodies, thigh against thigh, hidden hands communicating information secretly, telegraphing worlds left behind, but most of all clandestinely "extending bridges" to build personal and political relationships via that most intimate of human contact, the consolation of touch on flesh:

I succeeded in coming close to my comrades despite harsh guarding and continuous surveillance. I extended bridges between them and me. We became acquainted with each other in silence and darkness as words [speech] were forbidden under the watchful controlling eyes of the guards. Our fingers dexterously and warily began to write on our ribs, tales and stories, events and jokes. Fingers were transformed to pens, sides of chests to pages. In these stolen moments, life was reduced to gestures and signs that we alone understood and that we alone created.[19]

If the women's bodies were the locus of pain and physical destruction during sessions of torture, then the delicate embrace by gentle fingers conveying stories and physical solidarity serves to remake their bodies as sites of resistance. Torture scars the body as does the loss of language itself. If it is possible to imagine that a political prisoner and her society may one day be free and even be healed, as El Bouih does, surely it took concrete form when the flesh of punished women's bodies became an unbounded canvas on which to communicate dreams, private worlds, and public hopes in writing.[20] Believing that "writing is a form of deliverance," El Bouih exploits the literary uses and power of language armed with intellectual humanism and belief in the efficacy of language. Her experience of Derb Moulay Cherif is filtered through the purifying vocabulary of affirmation and hope. As a survivor of Morocco's torture and prison centers, her testimony underscores the triumph of defiance and resistance precisely because she never relinquishes her original political goals. In public testimonials, El Bouih confirms:

Detention established [literally, anchored] in me even more a love for my fellow human beings and the desire that justice rule. It confirmed and made me comforted with my convictions, it supported them for even more powerful reasons. I became stronger as time pressed inexorably on.[21]

Shared Space

The place of women's incarceration for decades is a triangular cell located in the women's section of Casablanca Civil Prison. The triangular cell housed the small numbers of women political prisoners of Morocco's leftist movements from 1976 until 1991. The space of this oddly shaped cell and its relation to the female body loom large in women's prison experiences and narratives. Before entering the prison triangle reserved for female prisoners, they recount strip-searching processes during which they were forced to undress completely and to bend forward and cough repeatedly ensuring nothing was hidden in the vagina. El Bouih remembers the women's shared mystification about the meaning of this strange prison ritual as she and Latifa Jbabdi concluded that perhaps this was the authorities' way to determine whether a girl was a virgin.[22]

Only when transferred to Casablanca Civil Prison after seven months in Derb Moulay Cherif and a brief encounter with a Moroccan judge did El Bouih and her women comrades reemerge to the world's attention. El Bouih describes the triangular cell that she shared with Latifa Jbabdi for twenty days:

> The prison cell was dark and small with a tiny window at the top. We learned after our stay there that this was the cell that sheltered our comrades: Fatima Okacha, Rabia Ftouh, and the martyr Saida Menebhi, the women of the political group that preceded us.
>
> We searched for their traces in this cell, on the walls, in the confusion of voices that came within our hearing, but to no avail. The tie between the outside world and us disappeared. The prison cell was dark and small. All that we owned within were some *kwash* (military blankets) to cover and to sleep on. No clothes, no cleanliness, nothing, nothing . . . walls, the faucet, Latifa and I, the sound of keys, the sound of women prisoners emanating from cells that never quieted until late at night.
>
> Once again I was forced to hear without seeing because the cell was locked all day, its doors opened only twice a day for a few minutes to go out to the courtyard. Ten minutes was the time limit. From behind the walls, where existence was long and filled the whole day, I learned a new lexicon: *labbel* (*l'appel*) roll call, *lafūy* (*la fouille*) the search, stand at attention, *laklas* (*la grâce*) at ease, words that mean specific movements inside prison.[23]

Fatna El Bouih and Latifa Jbabdi were shut into the triangular cell after three women political prisoners—Saida Menebhi, Fatima Okacha, and Rabia Ftouh—were moved to Avicenne Hospital toward the end of the 1977 hunger strike. Rabia Ftouh was one of the early women political prisoners who inhabited the triangular cell. There she was incarcerated with three other women arrested with her on 23 January 1976 in Tangier as part of police round-ups of leftists. Eventually, the three women and a fourth, Pierra di Maggio, a European sympathizer, were released by December 1976, although Ftouh remained. Added to Rabia Ftouh's cell were Fatima Okacha and Saida Menebhi, two women from the Casablanca group of Marxists. They lived together through 1977, the year of the small hunger strike in January to claim their rights as political prisoners, another short strike in March, and the long, deadly strike of November.

The triangular cell also housed Saadia Kabil, who was part of the last wave of women political prisoners to inhabit this space (Figure 5.2). Kabil

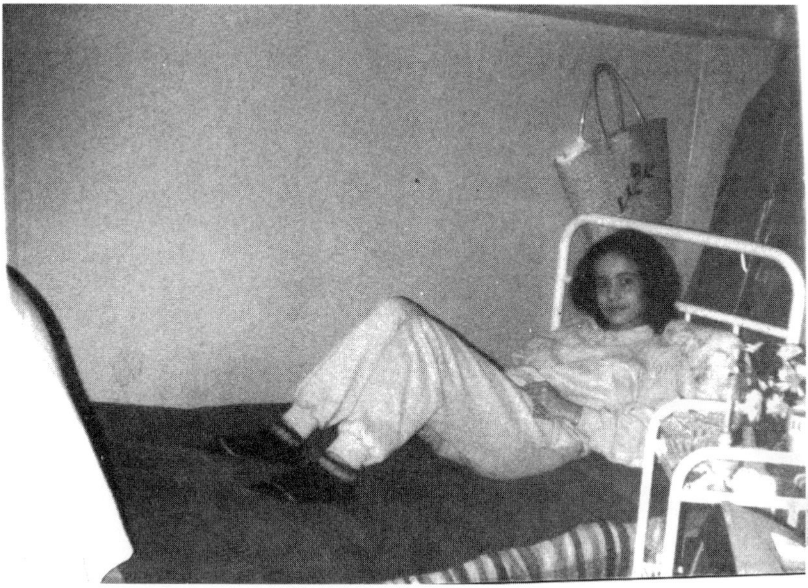

Figure 5.2. Saadia Kabil in the women's triangular cell, Casablanca Civil Prison, circa 1986. Clandestine prison photograph.

was disappeared on 6 November 1985 as part of arrests targeting the Marxists and spent twenty days in Derb Moulay Cherif. With her was Nezha Bernoussi,[24] also a member of the illegal Marxist organization Ilā al-Amām, and Maria Charaf, wife of Amine Tahani who died at the hands of the torturers of Derb Moulay Cherif. Kabil reports:

> They put us in a cell and gave us three blankets. I had nightmares that night because the cell—[in comparison to] Derb Moulay Cherif was large, even though I had my eyes closed it was spacious [Kabil laughs]. The cell was too tiny and, moreover it had a triangular form. It was not a square, it was another view of space, and as soon as I looked in one direction, I felt sick in this triangular space. We spent a lot of time trying to arrange our blankets, in which direction would we place the blankets—two on the ground and the third as a sheet. It was in the month of November, so cold that year, and we didn't sleep all night.[25]

High in a small secondary wall close to the ceiling was the single window, always closed and unreachable, that Kabil emphasizes in her drawing, that separates the cell floor plan from its ceiling with the blank space of the page (Figure 5.3). Two doors—one with bars and a second steel-plated—

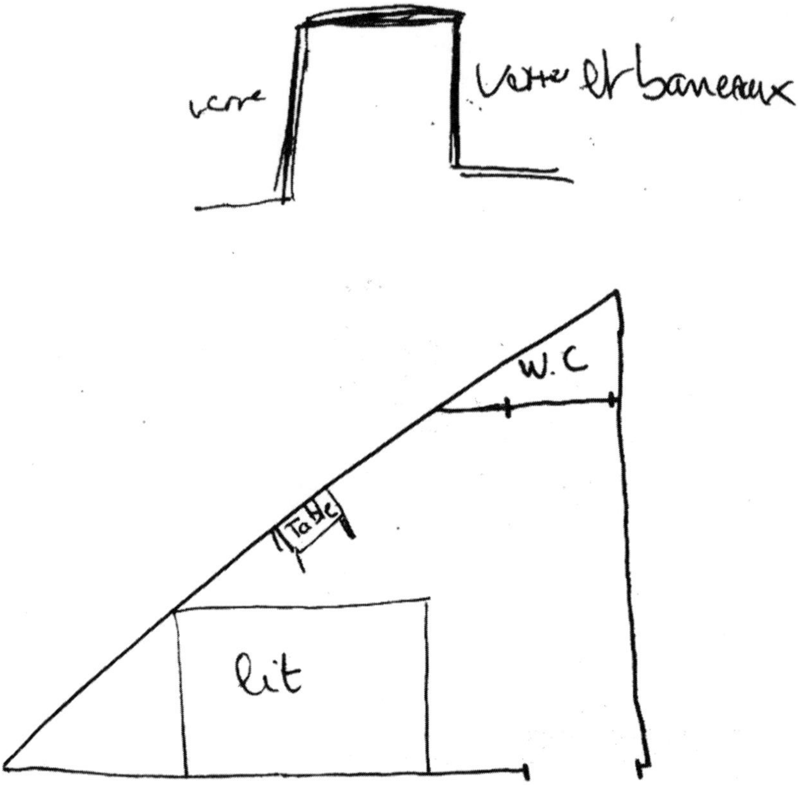

Figure 5.3. Sketch of triangular cell by Saadia Kabil. Reprinted by permission of author.

enclosed the prisoner's world. Opposite the barred door was a wall, all that could be seen of the corridor that opened on to other cells. Beyond the loss of familiar spatial sense experienced by those incarcerated and deprived of links to the outside, Kabil's spatial disorientation was exacerbated by the cell's form and perspective: the window, and the ability to receive or regulate light, was beyond the reach of human hands.

Prison guards informed Kabil that hers was the same cell that formerly housed Saida Menebhi, Rabia Ftouh, and Fatima Okacha, the early wave of female political prisoners from Marxist groups. When Kabil traveled to Kenitra Prison to take her law school examinations, she met Rabia Ftouh and Fatima Okacha, released in 1980, visiting their still incarcerated spouses. "Where are you, was it that triangular cell on the left?" they asked Kabil. Yes, but Kabil and Bernoussi remained together a brief two months until the end of their trial on 26 February. Kabil was alone in the triangular cell for the next six years.

Other Pages

"What does one do if the page is black?" asks Fatna El Bouih, in reference to the famous royal desire "to turn the page on the issue of political prisoners":

> If the page is black, it must first be grasped, read and written. Writing is a form of deliverance. Many women underwent torture, were victims of injustice, and suffered in silence and misunderstanding. Many young women, many innocent women throughout Morocco appear on the list of victims but dare not speak, testify, or write about what they endured.[26]

El Bouih spoke these words during a *shahādah* or *témoignage* (testimony) delivered for commemoration rites on the fortieth day *(arbaʿīn)* after the death of Ahmed Jaouhar, a former political prisoner. Oral testimony is an integral part of political performances that commemorate the all too numerous anniversaries of the state's misdeeds: the anniversaries of the death by torture or prison hunger strike endured by Morocco's pantheon of martyred political activists such as Amine Tahani, Saida Menebhi, Rahal Jbiha, and Abdellatif Zeroual.

El Bouih believes it important to speak publicly about the torture of women and to have this treatment recorded on the blank page upon which writing is now being placed. After five years of imprisonment and twenty years of silence, El Bouih began in 1994 to interview other former political prisoners:

> Their names are Rabéa, Fatima, Saida, Khadija, Widad, Maria, Fatna, Nguia, Hayat, Amina, Nezha, Saadia, Latifa. They were kidnapped, tortured, and only appeared in court after long months for some, years for others, in secret detention at Derb Moulay Cherif. The court condemned them to five or more years for conspiracy against the security of the state, belonging to illegal clandestine organizations, disseminating forbidden publications, etc.[27]

To transcribe oral testimony, whether that of El Bouih or other women prisoners, calls for reflection, description, and interpretation. Often testimony proceeds chronologically and concludes with the experience of liberation and freedom for the victims of repression. Individual female suffering is transformed into an exemplary expression of history corrected and rewritten, and the authenticity of the female voice is affirmed: "Women proved their courage and resistance in the face of torture, of multiple forms of torture. They lived stirring experiences, also very difficult ones, that they surmounted with courage and dignity."[28] As a voice for women detainees, El Bouih believes that neither her words nor her writings are purely autobiographical. She narrates her individual history but at the same time situates what she says and writes as part of a collective endeavor. To account for the experiences of generations of Moroccan women as voiceless and powerless, as well as the particularity of the lives of educated women like herself, she constructs a first-person narrator (what critic Doris Summer calls "the testimonials' collective self"[29]) to stand for the collective experience of her intellectual and activist women comrades, many too traumatized to tell their stories. El Bouih's prison memoirs thus include her experiences and extend to collective experiences. To her own chapters are added oral histories by two other women political prisoners from the same Meknes Group, Widad Bouab and Latifa Jbabdi, drawn from articles first published in the newspaper *Ittiḥād Ishtirākī* in 1994.[30] The impression of a collective authorship and the origins of one's own writing in collecting other women's oral histories—because a sense of shame at first impedes writing about oneself—clearly point to the imposition of powerful restraints shaped by history and gender. These restrictions also raise parallel questions concerning formal criteria to determine genre: when and where did she write? Who published it? When and where was it performed? How does El Bouih's work connect with the circumstances of her text's history?

These specific writing and interviewing strategies, El Bouih points out, are a consequence of her own years of fear and shame, the complex emotions unleashed by a woman's acts of writing and speaking testimony. Consequently, El Bouih first interviewed other women prisoners because she felt overtaken by *'ār* (shame, *honte*) she experienced as a woman to speak, to write, and to present herself as a public voice. The necessity of beginning with oral history, of immersing herself in other women's tales, is tied to El Bouih's acknowledgment that in the Moroccan context her main writings published after 1999 actually preceded her oral testimony and her sense of freedom to speak out publicly. On a literary level, however, both the written and the oral have their source in her ability to listen while encouraging other women to talk about their lives:

Beginning in 1995 and until now, I volunteer weekly at a Centre d'Ecoute et d'Orientation Juridique et Psychique des Femmes Battues in Casablanca's l'Hermitage neighborhood. It is the first such place in Morocco, a reception center for battered women where they are listened to and helped. We open a file and prepare documents for lawyers and psychiatrists on a case by case effort. I specialize in *istimāʿ* or *l'écoute* which I prefer. I can make women talk. Remember that the model for all Moroccan females is the woman who lowers her eyes, never raises her voice, whose tongue "does not go out of her mouth," as in a Moroccan proverb "al-fum al-mesdūd ma -dduxlu debbāna" (into a closed mouth no fly can enter). Girls are raised with: "-ṣṣamt ḥekmah u-mennu tfarraq leḥkāyem" (silence is wisdom and from it comes even greater wisdom). It is part of my society, this was the way I, my colleagues, and friends were raised and I revolted against this situation. In my own case, I was interviewed in 1994 by Malika Malek for Moroccan television. A half hour interview about my experiences as a former political prisoner was cut and only two minutes broadcasted. So I began writing about other women political prisoners and their amazing courage that should be part of Moroccan history. At first, I could not write about myself because that was *ḥshumah* (disgrace).[31]

El Bouih's work as an intake investigator at a Casalanca battered women's shelter is dramatically and structurally similar to her oral history projects to collect political prisoner testimony. She listens, she draws words from others, and she employs life histories and testimonials to effective political advocacy use on behalf of women, the poor and the imprisoned by transforming personal narratives from abstract statistics to immediate personalities, often embodied in her own spoken public testimonies. "I make the page turn by turning others' pages," observes El Bouih.[32]

Shahādah

El Bouih characterizes her work as pure shahādah (in French, she uses the word *témoignage*).[33] In Morocco since the 1970s, the Arabic word *shahādah* has come to express what is defined as *testimonio* in Latin American literature:

The word *testimonio* translates literally as testimony, as in the act of testifying or bearing witness in a legal and religious sense. That connotation is important because it distinguishes *testimonio* from simply recorded participant narrative, as in the case of "oral history." In oral history it is the intentionality of the *recorder*—usually a social scientist—that is dominant and the resulting text is in some sense "data." In *testimonio,* by contrast it is the intentionality of the *narrator* that is paramount. The situation of narration in testimonio has to involve an urgency to communicate, a problem of repression, poverty, subalternity, imprisonment, struggle for survival, and so on, implicated in the act of narration itself. The position of the reader of *testimonio* is akin to that of a jury member in a courtroom. Unlike the novel, *testimonio* promises by definition to be primarily concerned with sincerity rather than literariness.[34]

Encyclopedia definitions of shahādah encompass a range of meanings from simply being present to seeing events, to witnessing, and to testifying orally, a continuum that unfolds semantically and experientially with greater intensity and purpose:

(1) To be present (somewhere), as opposed to *ghaba* "to be absent"; whence (2) to see with one's own eyes, be witness (of an event); whence (3) to bear witness (to what one has seen); whence (4) attest, certify something.[35]

In *fiqh* (Islamic jurisprudence), shahādah refers both to the form and content of witnessing. Formally, it is a public performance whose juridical and social consequences are far-reaching precisely because they are legally binding. The character and authority of the witness, therefore, as well as the content of the testimony, must be adjudged just and truthful.[36]

To testify is to relay what happened using the representational means of speech and language. It is El Bouih's task as contemporary witness and victim to speak and to be heard, notwithstanding that legally and through the court system, she notes, Moroccan women do not count as witnesses (*témoigner juridiquement*) equal to men. The relevant verses from the Qur'an 2: 282 on the gendered nature of testimony are: "Get two witnesses out of your own men, and if there are not two men, then a man and two women." Because medieval Muslim jurists attached such great juridical weight to shahādah as opposed to non-legal, non-binding acts of *riwāyah* (narration) and *fatwah* (opinion), legal scholar Mohammad Fadel maintains that application of the rule "two women equals one man" is interpreted to mean shahādah alone. Furthermore, Fadel notes

in issues of fact dealing exclusively with the female body, the testimony of two female witnesses uncorroborated by a male witness is enough to win the claim. Significantly, the testimony of women is admitted in these cases because they involve facts to which men are not privy.[37]

Moroccan human rights discourse extends the legally binding, political term shahādah outside the court to public space and beyond male-female inequities to gender-neutral acts of narration by men and women. Nonetheless, shahādah is a performance-based mode deployed to express female suffering publicly. It shares with medieval jurisprudence both the primacy of the female body as the salient fact that elicits witnessing and the corroborative social aspects of giving testimony by more than one victim.

Sheherazade

As an example of the collective testimonial self, El Bouih began her 2001 American speaking tour intentionally identifying her life experience with national and universal struggles for human rights: "I do not speak only in my name, but also in the name of thousands of Moroccans before me, victims of this wound, and for those who remain so to this day throughout the world, at the very moment when we meet here in safety." When addressing a non-Arab, English-speaking public, El Bouih calls upon her audience to rethink female stereotypes of the Arab-Muslim world by explicitly invoking its most famous storyteller who so charmed her royal spouse with endless tales that she talked her way out of death and into his heart:

> Listen to the voice of the south wind, the south as the voices of peoples and social movements of liberation, the voices of women, the south as Morocco. A new voice comes from the harem, a new voice, a new harem, a new Sheherazade, who emerges from silence to go beyond history to where women are deprived of all power, to dig to the bottom of this harem to change the current of history. Sheherazade has spoken and a miracle has been produced.[38]

Again Sheherazade is reconfigured, this time by Moroccan women writers to represent the survivor who tells the story of her human rights victimization with fresh details repeatedly and publicly. The content of her trauma, endured longer than a thousand and one nights, and the form of nested interlocking narratives from the medieval Arabic text strongly parallel the vicissitudes of women political opponents and their multiple kidnappings, tortures, and travels through the vast and uncharted territory of Morocco's prison system. The survivor's tales magically convert her listeners into witnesses, and in so doing she may perhaps begin the work of healing herself, other women sufferers who are encouraged to break their silences, and the larger social community that her narrative reaches. To tell and to write the story repeatedly is a therapeutic measure for El Bouih, underpinned by her work on documenting prison conditions through site visits and reports (as a founding member with Youssef Maddad, her husband, of the Moroccan Observatory of Prisons) and as a volunteer in a shelter for single mothers.[39]

Moroccan sociologist Fatema Mernissi evokes Sheherazade as a liberator for the Muslim world, as a political heroine who keeps a tyrant at bay through the power of her intellect and wordplay, and as the truth-telling taleteller and hence the standard bearer par excellence for the human rights movement.[40] Sheherazade's plight in this recasting is less purely female and becomes universalized as the fate of the powerless, the imprisoned, and the disappeared.

Abdellatif Laabi acknowledges Sheherazade as an inspiration for his 1982 French-language novel and memoir of prison and torture. Laabi describes a compelling Sheherazade: "She who was the greatest storyteller (*romancière*) of your traditional culture was only so because she lived permanently under the oriental sword of Damocles. 'You write or you are killed'. . . . You will know that this is the voice of history speaking. It refers to one of its most brutal laws: all silence is death by default."[41] Furthermore, this tale that must be retold is elastically accommodating to the listener's level of understanding: Laabi frames a seemingly traditional folktale according to details from the real life story of a valiant Moroccan heroine. The reader eavesdrops on Laabi's bedtime story to his young daughter after he has been released from years of prison. He begins with the customary "once upon a time in a country by the sea of shadows there lived a little girl called Saida," but the ending, his daughter points out plaintively, is not cheerful.

A mere child, Saida confronts the tyrant, his magician adviser, and a host of spies for the right to the sun's rays. She is imprisoned and there chooses death by refusing food and toys. Word spreads of Saida's death; many come to protest and to watch the strange apparition of a second sun in the sky: "The spies picked three children and took them away. The next day they came and took three more children. And so, each day. But every day three more children replaced those who had disappeared. Each day three more children joined the others to see the coming together of the small sun and the large one which got bigger and redder than an ordinary sun."[42] Laabi invents no happy ending and overturns the folktale's narrative expectations. For Moroccan readers, his is a thinly disguised tale that refers to real events during an actual prison hunger strike in which Saida Menebhi, conceived as the latter-day Sheherazade, transforms the relationship between author and audience, when she too chronicles in poems and letters the topic of her physical deterioration up to a few weeks before her death in a mass hunger strike while claiming the right to the status of political prisoner.[43]

Saida Menebhi, the heroine of Laabi's folktale, has become a potent symbol of female activism and martyrdom (Figure 5.4). Before her death at age twenty-five, she produced poetry, taught English, and was active in Moroccan student and union movements while adhering to the Marxist movement Ilā al-Amām. Forcibly disappeared in January 1976, she was condemned to seven years in prison during the January-February 1977 Casablanca trial of 138 Marxist-Leninists. Her last poem, dated 10 November 1977, was composed during the first days of the hunger strike that claimed her life on 11 December 1977:

The watchdogs arrived in number
To seize everything from us
And even the prison walls
Which belong to them
Were even more grim
The women wept
Secretly
We kept our smiles
We kept steadfast
And faced pain
As we knew
That to be in prison was not the problem
It was about going *forward*[44]

Political activism, prison time, writing and public testimony: the physical, emotional and psychological risks of this sequence of events are great. Lurking homophonously in the background as part of the triconsonantal Arabic root *sh-h-d* from which is also formed the word shahādah (testimony), is *shahīdah*, whose meaning extends to the "woman martyr." The testifying woman political prisoner and the female martyr are historically and symbolically conjoined in the life and death of Saida Menebhi, the Moroccan woman prisoner of conscience. The space of her imprisonment, a triangular cell, and the manner of her death, the prison hunger strike, have become emblematic expressions for female physical suffering. At the same time, Menebhi's poetry and writings are enlisted as discursive weapons for the invisible history of Moroccan women's political opposition that took place in the spaces of prison.

Menebhi's poems, letters, and an unfinished essay (on prostitution in Morocco) were published in Paris in 1978, the year after her death; in 2000,

Figure 5.4. Banner of Saida Menebhi, Rabat Women's March, March 2000. Photo by author.

a Moroccan edition was printed for which Mohamed Belmejdoub, a Marxist political prisoner, authored a preface. Belmejdoub considers the ways in which Menebhi's death, which made her a symbol for progressive feminist causes, recasts the relevance of her political poetry after a quarter of a century:

> Beyond Marxism-Leninism, etc., the message of Saida ("modernist" poetry abhors all messages), was this: in the face of oppression and tyranny, when silence became the law and cowardice a virtue, we were always right to revolt, we were always right to express ourselves, we were always right to say: "No!" Is this really poetic? Is this good politics? . . . Beyond Marxism, Leninism, class struggles, the democratic national revolution . . . the language of her times, in sum, the message of Saida is that man—the human being, man or woman—is, must be, the first and last reference, the measure of all, the supreme value. All the rest is literature![45]

If all the rest is literature, then after their prison release, in 1980 and 1982 respectively, Latifa Jbabdi and Fatna El Bouih turned to literary endeavors about women as one way to continue their political activism without incurring the brutal attentions of the regime. Jbabdi co-founded a monthly Arabic newspaper, *Thamāniyah Mārs* (8 March), named for International Women's Day. The first front-page editorial gave prominence to the task of listening to women's voices, understood as an expression of historical experiences lived by ordinary women. Subsequent issues contain expansive oral histories and interviews with heroines of the Moroccan independence movement, essays by contemporary experts on women's issues, a variety of international feminist texts translated into Arabic, and memorials to prominent activist women.[46] The December 1983 and December 1984 issues, for example, commemorated the life and death of Saida Menebhi and brought to the Moroccan reading public Arabic translations of poetry originally written in French. Menebhi's poetry, her death during a hunger strike, and the places of her incarceration have come to represent a critical reckoning with women's participation in political struggles, especially female activism that leads to imprisonment and death. Latifa Jbabdi and Fatna El Bouih exemplify the 1970s and 1980s wave of Marxist political prisoners for whom incarceration forged links with the plight of women in Morocco. El Bouih confesses:

> It must be said that my feminist consciousness was only awakened in me in prison. I was the politician, the activist, the militant, I believed women's situation would change with my country's situation. I was wrong.[47]

The importance of the triangular cell for those who inhabited it and those who would learn about its existence remains inseparable from the death of Saida Menebhi. The link has been effectively made between Saida's struggles for political prisoner status as a woman inside the prison and the rights of all citizens outside the prison. Women political prisoners continued political organization even as they resumed professions as writers, educators, lawyers, and engineers. They emerged from prison advocating human dignity and gender equity; Latifa Jbabdi and Fatna El Bouih were prominent in the 1993 campaign to collect three million women's signatures for a petition to align Morocco's family laws with international standards governing the rights of women and children. According to Fatna El Bouih, for a generation of Moroccans, prison may well prove the nurturing ground, if not the birthplace, for the fight for human rights:

> To die is preferable than to live deprived of rights and dignity. It is the cry of the citizen that destabilizes the theater of the archaic ones that monopolize politics up to now. You will find this *cri-message* in all the literature written by the generation of the 1970s that marched through the prisons.[48]

Belles Lettres

What El Bouih writes is not autobiography; neither is it a novel, she insists. The novel that effectively presents arguments for the doubly marginalized role of Moroccan activist women is *ʿĀm al-fīl* (Year of the elephant). While narrating the story of 18 November 1956, the day of Morocco's independence from France, Moroccan writer Leila Abouzeid proposes a reassessment of women's euphoric celebrations. Zohra, the protoganist, dismissively recalls in the 1980s the heady moments some thirty years earlier when Morocco celebrated its independence from France: "Someone said we were leaving for Rabat. We boarded a bus, Roukia sitting on the engine head waving a flag and shouting slogans all the way to Rabat. Later, when I reminded her, she smiled and said 'We were crazy.'" Elsewhere in Abouzeid's novel, Zohra laments: "Everyone forgets. The nation itself forgets."[49]

Indeed, Abouzeid dedicates *Year of the Elephant* to all the Zahras and "to all those women and men who put their lives in danger for the sake of Morocco and did not expect to be rewarded or thanked for it," thereby signaling her authorial intent to narrate women's unofficial history during Morocco's struggle for independence notwithstanding the current disillusioned spirit of "we were crazy" and "everyone forgets."[50] Using fictional characters to document a background of social injustice, double standards, and oppression during the decades Moroccans lived under the Protectorate, Abouzeid charts the loss of legal rights and the retrograde return to earlier and traditional social conditions experienced by women after independence. Zahra not only acts as part of the glorious resistance *then* but also narrates her devalued role *now*. Both Abouzeid the author and Zohra the protagonist specifically evoke Sheherazade, the masterful narrator who tells her story and survives another day.

In contrast, El Bouih and Jbabdi's accounts of women consist of an interdisciplinary approach that draws on social history and oral interviews.[51] Women tellers and witnesses construct a text against a backdrop of sociocultural, historical, linguistic, and literary traditions in which both interviewer and informant strive to recuperate, to write, and to document. Especially significant for understanding these narratives are the ways in which gender and societal position define what is considered to be authoritative discourse. Indeed, Mikhail Bakhtin shows that hierarchies are intrinsic to language, but then so are authoritative voices; the authoritative is a "prior discourse," one upheld by a combined political, legal, and moral authority that will inevitably dominate public performance.[52] When the dominant voice is male, the assumption is that any countercommentary becomes the domain of female: an authoritative male projects the correct, official history challenged by a reactive female voice.[53]

Scholars in anthropology and history have expanded the study of colonial peoples and of women as active role-players in social theory and practice. The use of ephemeral political tracts, oral histories, newspaper accounts, and human rights reports to construct the histories of Moroccan women political prisoners exposes the complexities surrounding Moroccan society, culture and the position of women. Women are associated with a domestic, oral history rather than a written, political history. As with any binary opposition, this model is only partially true because much of Moroccan history awaits transcription of oral narratives from interviews into a written mode of publication that is at the heart of El Bouih and Jbabdi's writing projects. Their need to encourage and success at encouraging others to remember and allowing them to speak have given El Bouih and Jbabdi permission to narrate stories in unconventional ways.

By examining gender relations and writing within the Moroccan context, women are viewed rooted in dynamic, historical processes: they shape and are shaped by the state and specific state institutions. At the same time, a study of Moroccan women, politics, and the prison system in the post-independence period contributes to the general, ongoing project in anthropology and history: what are the anthropological and ethnohistorical ways to evaluate the historical resurrection of women, when much of the materials for the study of women prisoners has emerged largely as a result of the encounter between a repressive Moroccan state and women who testify to having been repressed and tortured?

Al-Munāḍilah

The organizations and institutions in Morocco directed to human rights were established and staffed by men. Let it be said that foremost among the pioneers of human rights are the mothers, sisters, and wives who advocated on behalf of imprisoned family members.[54] The less-known history of Moroccan mothers bears striking similarities to the well-documented Argentine movement of the Mothers of the Plaza de Mayo.[55] Both groups exploited cultural and religious expectations about motherhood, enlisting a disparate array of male authority figures—politicians, judges, prison guards, and policemen—to locate missing children. Are you not a parent too, the Moroccan mothers pleaded? Layla Chaouni, whose husband Mostefa Slimani was imprisoned for Marxist political activity (1974–79), recalls that the presence of mothers gave legitimacy to public protests because they were not young women and, therefore, were not perceived as a political movement.[56] The white kerchief, famously the headgear of bereaved Argentine mothers, has become in North Africa an ensemble with matching shirt. Khadija Rouissi, sister of Abdelhak Rouissi (disappeared since 1964), wears a white shirt patterned with the words *disparus* and *al-mukhtaṭafūn*, "those disappeared" in French and Arabic respectively (Figure 5.5). Rouissi was introduced to the act of wearing clothes to publicize her brother's disappearance by Nacéra Dutour, whose son's disappearance led to Dutour's heading Algeria's organization of the families of the disappeared.[57]

According to Kamal Lahbib (Marxist political prisoner, 1972–77), families of political prisoners and those disappeared represent continuity with the symbol of civic disobedience, Antigone, who invokes the right to disobey a ruler as the duty of every citizen.[58] In Sophocles' play, Antigone defies Creon, ruler of Thebes, after he forbids the burial of her brother, Polynices, deemed a traitor. Antigone declares: "I shall bury him! It is honorable for me to do this and die. I am his own and I shall lie with him who is my

Figure 5.5. Khadija Rouissi dressed on behalf of the disappeared, Rabat Women's March, March 2000. Photo by author.

own, having committed a crime that is holy."[59] The right to burial, the rights of families to the bodies of their dead, and by extension over the disappeared and the tortured, supersede royal injunctions or presumptions of criminality.[60] Antigone, like the Moroccan mothers, set forth divinely-inspired morality sustained by blood ties in order to lay claim to the corpses.

Kinship leads to conflicting responsibilities. The moral duty to bury one's dead is interpreted by authoritarian regimes as a shared right, one not exclusively the purview of the families. This leads to the practice of governments assigning collective responsibility (and collective punishment) for the actions and beliefs of individual kin members to an entire family, clan, or tribe. An example is Evelyne Serfaty, sister of prominent Moroccan opposition leader Abraham Serfaty. She is the author of perhaps the earliest text of a Moroccan woman's testimony about her torture. In a form of hostage-taking routinely practiced, Evelyne was arrested because she was kin to Abraham Serfaty, and because he chose clandestine political life to escape the 1970s government crackdowns aimed at eradicating the leftist organization Ilā al-Amām, founded by him.[61] Evelyne published her experiences in the 1973 Paris edition of *Souffles*, after publication by the original Moroccan journal *Souffles/Anfās* was suspended in 1972 and its editor Abdellatif Laabi imprisoned. Written in the form of a diary that begins 26 September 1972, the date Evelyne Serfaty disappeared in Rabat, she describes what it means to be at the mercy of the secret police—electric shock, beatings, suspension on a pole, threats against her elderly parents. Released on 4 October, she is able by 16 October to pen a narrative of events:

> I am in a state to be able to write this *récit*. When I arrived home, and this was after nine days of detention, I had a blue face and neck, legs and feet and equally blue, a deep wound on the right leg, the forearms and chest covered with hematomas. The doctors that examined me can testify to this. As of this day, I can wear shoes but if I walk more than a half hour, my feet swell and become painful. I suffered all this only because I am the sister of my brother. The police did not wish to admit that I knew nothing. As if anguish about his fate is not enough! My brother's son, my nephew, cannot leave Morocco to live with his mother in Paris. In spite of all his attempts, the Moroccan authorities refuse him his passport.[62]

Evelyne Serfaty's stubborn silences, the bravery of the tortured, is lauded in Abdellatif Laabi's poem "Tu parles ou on te tue":[63]

> "Talk or we'll kill you"
> They killed you Evelyne
> You didn't talk

With three simple sentences
without Coryphaeus
without choir
without theater or spectators
without intervention or absence of the gods
There it is
the tragedy
"Talk or we'll kill you"
They killed you Evelyne
You hadn't talked
Who
Where
Why
Who are you
Why should this concern us
And why can't your death
stay anonymous
why can't it be the subject
of a family prayer
that is buried
in the same vault of forgetting
once tears are shed.

The resilience of women family members derives from the capacity to remain silent and endure torture. Not even a woman's ignorance about her family members' political activities spared her mistreatment by authorities. The refusal to give any information about loved ones, often construed as the passive silence of women, instead masks courage based on love rather than political commitment.

The year 1977 saw major political and legal confrontations between Morocco's illegal Marxist groups and government authorities. The 1977 sit-in at the al-Sunnah Mosque in Rabat, undertaken by mothers, wives, and sisters related to the Marxist political prisoners, is considered the first emergence into public space by families of political prisoners. Fatima Mouride's participation in the mothers' actions was incorporated into the comic book produced by her son Abdelaziz Mouride. In interviews decades later, he remembers his mother's devotion and her transformation from an illiterate woman, who rarely left her house until the disappearance and subsequent imprisonment of two of her sons, Jaafar Mouride in Meknes serving three years, and Abdelaziz in Kenitra for twenty. Each week, Mouride recalls, his mother left home at four in the morning, walked long distances to the nearest bus station laden with two heavy baskets of food, rode a three-hour intercity bus to Kenitra Central Prison for her fifteen-minute visit with Abdelaziz, and departed for Meknes, a four-hour bus ride, to provide Jaafar with the second basket of food, before returning to Casablanca.[64] To comprehend his mother's journey from passive and fatalistic acceptance of her sons' fate to ferocious militant, Abdelaziz chronicles the Marxist political prisoners' emergence from years of enforced disappearance, his own in Derb Moulay Cherif in 1974–76, to their reappearance at Casablanca Civil Prison in preparation for trials. After a nine-month wait to be tried, prisoners launched a hunger strike that served as a catalyst for families to unite and demonstrate in the streets around the prison, actions met with arrests and beatings (Figure 5.6).

The 1977 mothers' protests were responses to prison hunger strikes. In the prison novel *Kāna wa-akhawātuhā*, author Abdelkader Chaoui describes the strike from the inmate's viewpoint. Chaoui returns to his cell to endure hunger and solitude while musing about his mother's political acts in the form of a stream of consciousness triggered by his wife's visit to the prison asking for a divorce:

> (your mother begs an imperturable column at the al-Sunnah Mosque for god to liberate you, amen, god is above all and paradise is at the foot of the mothers. A group of older women went on a strike by prayer and desperate occupied the place. It was the time of tears, tears flowing from every corner, mixed with sad sighs that echoed, weighed down from the angles of the great mosque, the imam did not appear and the faithful did not come, the eyes of the police did not rest, the families made a noisy, humanitarian demonstration. In Rabat they did not know that here we were twisted by hunger. The strike that day was in its twentieth day, a hunger strike exactly in its twentieth day. An unknown journey, a tenacity that accumulates and grows. There is the body's fatigue. November's cold in the chest. Hot water mixed with sugar and bitterness flows down throats. Your intestines growl. Do you want that your mother seek refuge crazily in god begging that he will sow in your heart patches of steadfastness and perseverance. Your mother participates in a rebellious gathering that prays begs harasses protests resists demands and "people are taking their siestas or are indifferent"[65]

It is the twentieth day of the hunger strike. Chaoui's ramblings foreshadow the fate of Saida Menebhi, who dies participating in the same hunger strike. Prison authorities refuse the families entry, notes Chaoui, by citing a law forbidding visits during strikes:

> Repeat this while filling your dry mouth and recalling the era of defiance. Your compassionate mother, her compassionate mother, all of their mothers. Women resembling gypsies, rather they were gypsies who knocked on every door, stood in

Figure 5.6. The 1977 women's strike in al-Sunnah Mosque, Rabat. Drawing by Abdelaziz Mouride, *On affame bien les rats!* 54. Reprinted by permission of author.

front of every office screamed after filling their breasts with anger and sacrifice. We want the lives of our sons . . . It is the twentieth day, this day. Water is in your mouth and your throat is dry. You will be given a rainy day, god willing to quench you just as your mother desires. When? And will there be the downpour? Your mother who is there prays to the pillar along with the other mothers. The minaret is silent, the muezzin confused, and policemen now control the unsettled signs around the mosque[66]

Saida Menebhi's death on the thirtieth day of the hunger strike marked the point after which the mothers agree that they no longer feared police and government retribution. What fear could compare with the horror of a child's death?

Beginning in 1983, fewer Marxists but more Islamists became objects of the regime's repression. However ideologically different, the travails of the families were the same. One Sunday night in August 1983, secret police knocked on the door of the Bouabid home in the city of Mohammedia, forced Abdessamad and Noureddine Bouabid into an unmarked car, and departed. Their mother, Zoubida Bouabid, did not see or hear from them for six months until she met her sons during the Casablanca trial of Group 71, Islamists (Figure 5.7):

They kidnapped them, and then I went out into the street. When their father wanted to drive the car from the garage on to the street, he couldn't do it because of fear. When the car came out of the garage, I began to smash my head against the wall, against the garage. People gathered around me and I began to cry and scream, why were my children kidnapped? My children are good, well brought up, committed no crime, their behavior excellent.[67]

Parents set off to various police stations where they reported lies, deliberate misinformation, insults and demands for bribes. Money given to police and jailers was pocketed and food eaten, although both items were intended for their imprisoned sons. Zoubida recounts:

At that moment I saw a vision in my sleep (*ra'aytu ra'āya fī manām*). A woman said to me to alert the mothers that their children would appear and asked me to make henna and to tell them to make themselves beautiful with henna and to hoist the flags. I told them about the vision. A beautiful woman, I see her always in my dreams, the same age as I am, elegantly dressed, wearing a caftan. She said, "Do not forget, make yourself up with henna." For the trial, because I was very sad, I cried all the time, I was bleeding. I soaked my hands in the henna. I hoisted one flag. She told me to raise two flags and I had only done one. She told me to tell the other mothers and that the children would appear. I told the other mothers. I told them

Figure 5.7. Zoubida Bouabid, Mohammedia, interview, 29 May 2000. Photo by author.

that I put on henna and raised the flags because a woman had told me to do this. I told them that this woman had informed me that the children would appear and to make sure to tell them. When I saw that I would embrace Abdessamad, I told the mothers. When the vision came true, they were astonished and they said the vision was true. When my sons went to the toilets accompanied by the CIMI [Compagnie d'intervention mobile interurbaine], I put myself in their path and I took them both in my arms. The mothers said, "Look, she saw them in her vision and now she sees them in reality." I was the first mother that embraced her sons. When I saw them, I ran to them.

Zoubida transformed herself into a *munāḍilah* (militant).[68] Her dreams endured the long years of her two sons' imprisonment: Noureddine appears to her dressed in his red sports outfit showing torture marks on his body while Abdessamad faints during beatings.

Subsequent to their children's arrests, a group of thirty mothers met while investigating where detainees were secretly held. Families began to share information and resources as they made the rounds of police stations, ministers' offices, Casablanca's Derb Moulay Cherif, and courthouses:

With the trial our fight and our activities began. When we went to Rabat they told us that the director general of prisons was not there, the minister of justice was busy, so we sat in front of the door of the ministers in the heat of the sun, hungry and thirsty. Armed police of CIMI encircled us and said to disperse or they would arrest and make us join our children. . . . Among us were courageous mothers and those who were frightened.

Frequently the mothers were arrested and packed into vans for interrogations before release. When hunger strikes were called inside the prisons, family networks activated outside ensured that there would be public demonstrations. Decades of prisoners' demands and communiqués were passed to the mothers during prison visits and smuggled outside hidden between their breasts.

In Rabat, they brought police cars. They asked us how we got together. They addressed me first. They put us in these cars, three or four people. The cars had no windows. An officer sat near me . . . and asked me how we got together. Who brought you together? Was there someone who brought you together? I said to him: "Prison brought us together. We met at the prison, we made a rendezvous to go to Rabat." They said, no, there is someone who is organizing you and bringing you together. Tell us who it is. We answered, there was no one. You have arrested all the sons, there is no one who directs us or organizes us. We get together by ourselves and travel together to Rabat. . . . We organized by ourselves. When the police asked me this same question I gave them the same answer. No one. There was only the families, the brothers, the sisters, especially those who were educated and God was with us. Commissioner Tabet threatened the mothers: Who organized you, there is an organization that unites and directs you. They answered: "Prison brought us together." Thabet said: Next time we will make you follow your children [into prison]. The mother of Misbah answered: "Whoever dies today, doesn't wait for tomorrow. When our children were arrested we had no more future." She said that we want to die now. As for me, when someone gets me angry and says the same thing, I answer: I want to be near my children and make them soup. We demand to be near them. . . . I was so proud of them, thank God, I was so proud.

To this day, Zoubida speaks with great pride of her children, exemplified by their achievements in examinations and the awarding of university degrees while in prison:

At that time, neighbors avoided us out of fear because we were the family of political prisoners. And when they passed exams and obtained diplomas, the neighbors exclaimed how could they study and succeed under these circumstances in prison. . . . I let out the *zaghradah* (ululation) on the occasion of their diplomas. A prison guard told me to stop whistling. I said to him: "I'm not whistling, I'm ululating and the children sang this song:

Ululate, O my mother
O mother of revolutionaries
Until birds hear you in the tree
My country is filled with the free."

Parental and children's roles were reversed, with the imprisoned sons providing instruction in political activism and religious belief. These generational upheavals were reinforced by officials, bureaucrats and police personnel long accustomed to addressing the mothers, many of whom were illiterate or elderly or both, as children, specifically as misbehaving children in relation to the nation's father, Hassan II of Morocco, referred to as Sīdnā, "our master":

They said: You came to Rabat to sow disorder. Go and tell your sons to ask for pardon (*ʿafw*) from Sīdnā, who does not accept what you do. It is shameful. The press publishes abroad what you divulge, you dishonor Sīdnā; he does not accept the shame that you do. We told them: Our sons are victims of injustice, why should they ask for pardon? They were unjustly arrested at a young age, seventeen, eighteen, twenty years old.

The mothers of the Islamist prisoners traveled regularly from their homes in Casablanca and Mohammedia to meet in the capital, where they demonstrated, importuned, and delivered prisoner correspondence to the Director of Prisons, various political party leaders, Moroccan and foreign press representatives, the head of the Advisory Committee on Human Rights, and the minister of justice:

They told us that the minister of justice [Moulay Mustapha El Alaoui] was in a meeting and we could not see him, so we lay in wait for his arrival, then I put myself in front of the route of his car and placed my hands on the car. I motioned with my hands and yelled: Our children, our children. Then he motioned to the chauffeur, and a CIMI police officer said to me: He cleans his car, you put your hands on it, you make it dirty, you leave marks on it. I said to him: I am not dirty, my hands have performed their ablutions and have been raised in praise of God, I prayed, I'm in a state of ablution, and you say to me that I put my hands on the car and dirty it. My hands are clean. At last the minister of justice said: Bring her in. I gave him a letter. His head of staff was mean, he never admitted us, never had pity on us, and everyone was afraid of him. I alone leaned against the bus stop sign during the heat, the sun burning my face, without food, waiting for the minister's arrival in order to jump on his car.

Zoubida Bouabid claims that she owes her original activism to men; nonetheless, she explicitly identifies the movement of the mothers as a source for a new political and religious consciousness:

The families called me "Mother Zoubida the militant." I said to them: "Let me go in front, I have two sons in prison. I would be at the head." In the end, I vanquished my fear. I no longer felt any fear. . . . I learned a lot. I was married at fourteen, I came to this house, I grew up with my children. I didn't know anything. Thank God, now I have learned a lot of things. They taught me how to do the prayers.

Al-munāḍilāt illumine new facets of testimony which can be used to constitute a community of witness that embraces those disappeared and imprisoned. Families did so, first, as physical conduits for written communications between prison and the outside world. Al-munāḍilāt devised hiding places, for example, material secreted on their own bodies or baked inside bread or a couscous platter or stuffed into hollow basket handles. Al-munāḍilāt indefatigably pressured authorities, staged demonstrations, collected evidence about their children's whereabouts, maintained direct contact with local and international human rights organizations. Frequently, al-munāḍilāt too were forced into the role of witnesses to events, corroborating the wrongs of prison beatings, deprivations, and tortures to their children and to themselves, as interested parties, the injuries and corruption of Morocco's judicial apparatus. The ways in which al-munāḍilāt keep alive the memory of the disappeared and act as witnesses by never forgetting wrongs inflicted on prisoners directly address the origins of a culture of human rights activism in Morocco pragmatically and humanely.

Chapter 6
Islamist Political Prisoners

"The Power of the Powerless," the legendary 1978 essay written by Czech dissident Vaclav Havel while he was a political prisoner, raises an important question about oppositional movements within the Soviet bloc; the same question is true for Moroccan political prisoners: "Why, in conditions where a widespread and arbitrary abuse of power is the rule, is there such a general and spontaneous acceptance of the principle of legality?" Although this "principle of legality," enshrined in various international covenants and instruments such as the Universal Declaration of Human Rights, is enunciated publicly and frequently, Havel notes, it remains under abusive rule an implicit, never discussed, universally agreed upon given.[1] The principle of legality as it is found within the institutional structures of human rights associations and from the perspective of *al-muʿtaqalūn al-Islāmīyūn* (Islamist detainees) (Figure 6.1) is the focus of this chapter.[2]

Groups

Members of the Islamist Group 71 and Group 26—names based on the number of those arrested and ultimately tried—trace their origins to the movement al-Shabībah al-Islāmīyah (French, Jeunesse islamique; English, Islamic Youth). Al-Shabībah al-Islāmīyah was founded in 1969–70 by Abdelkrim Moti, a nationalist and union activist once affiliated with the leftist Moroccan political party, the National Union of Popular Forces (Union Nationale des Forces Populaires, UNFP) and the Moroccan Union of Workers (Union marocaine du travail, UMT). In 1975, when Moti was implicated in the assassination of a well-known leftist journalist, Omar Benjelloun, he chose exile and clandestine political life abroad.[3]

Within Moti's movement in Morocco, a complicated series of splits ensued and breakaway groups formed, due in part to fierce disagreements about whether followers ought to participate legally in Moroccan political

Figure 6.1. Abdessamad Bouabid (Islamist political prisoner, 1983–93) speaking in Oukacha Prison, Casablanca, 18 May 1993. Banner: "Islamist prisoners celebrate their liberation after ten years." Clandestine prison photo.

life or instead bring about political change through clandestine revolutionary activities. The first scission took place in 1977, initiated by six people (referred to as *sudāsīyīn*, Group of Six), who swiftly disappeared from the scene. A second 1978 scission would eventually yield several government-recognized legal associations. The first, a group of young students in Casablanca and Rabat, formed an organization known by 1983–84 as al-Ikhtiyār al-Islāmī (Islamic Option). Emerging from a later break-up process that took place between 1992 and 1996, two more associations coalesced by 1998, both advocating constitutional and political reforms: Mohammed Marouani heads al-Ḥarakah min Ajl al-Ummah (Movement for the Nation) and its newspaper, *al-Naba*ʾ (Information) and Amine Reggala heads al-Badīl al-Ḥaḍarī (Civilized Alternative) and its newspaper, *al-Jisr* (Bridge). A third split in 1981, called "the big scission," yielded more groups, each of which chose the arena of legitimate political action. Abdelilah Benkirane created al-Jamāʿah al-Islāmīyah (Islamic Community) in 1982–84, which changed its name in 1992 to al-Islāḥ wa-al-Tajdīd (Reform and Renewal). Countering a history of two decades of splintering, in 1996 Benkirane's group joined forces with Rābiṭat al-Mustaqbal al-Islāmī (Association for an Islamic Future) to become al-Islāḥ wa-al-Tawḥīd (Reform and Unity), involved in nonpolitical social and cultural activities and, eventually, as part of a coalition with the Mouvement Populaire Démocratique et Constitutionnel (MPDC), emerged as a political party, al-ʿAdālah wa-al-Tanmiyah (Justice and Development). No longer excluded from participation in Morocco's system of political parties and legislative elections, from 1999 on an Islamist parliamentary bloc headed by Moustapha Ramid controlled 14 of 325 seats in parliament, a number that increased to 42 seats after the 27 September 2002 legislative elections.

Many shabibistes—the Franco-Moroccan name for followers of al-Shabībah—refused to form political parties and engage in public and parliamentary debate. After the 1975 exile of Moti and the many schisms up to 1981 that depleted movement membership, those that chose to remain clandestine and within al-Shabībah al-Islāmīyah provided much of the Islamist political prisoner population. Between 1981 and 1983, al-Shabībah al-Islāmīyah advocated revolution. Using a strategy to confuse the authorities by appearing to be more numerous than their actual numbers, they signed their actions with a variety of organizational names and thereby forced observers to query: who was behind these new names, where did they come from, and how were they related to Abdelkarim Moti's movement? Real membership numbers were small. Adherents were organized into three main "factions" (*faṣīlah*), the designation for various subgroupings of al-Shabībah al-Islāmīyah: Faction al-Jihād, Katībat Badr, and al-Mujāhidīn.

Faction al-Jihād, consisting of students drawn from Mohammedia and Casablanca neighborhoods such as Sidi Bernoussi and Ain Sebaa, called for revolution, but did not engage in violence. Members were arrested in 1983 and formed the majority of Group 71 (trial of 31 July 1984).[4] Three months before their arrest, the Faction al-Jihād broke away from the parent al-Shabībah al-Islāmīyah, accusing the leadership of authoritarian practices and lack of democracy. The majority were high school students who felt duped by the party line that maintained Moroccans were awaiting a signal by Islamists for a general uprising when in fact they, the student Islamists, were the only ones to do so.[5] Katībat Badr (Badr Squadron), caught smuggling weapons across the Moroccan-Algerian border, were arrested and tried as Group 26 (trial of 2 September 1985). A third clandestine group, also formed in 1983, was never clearly identified as either a faction (subgroup) or breakaway scission. Called al-Mudjāhidīn (holy warriors) and headed by Abdelaziz Naamani (with the newspaper, *al-Sarāya*), some would be brought to trial and classed as part of Group 71, while others were arrested several years later.[6]

Belkacem Hakimi (Islamist political prisoner, Group 26), describes the organization of al-Shabībah al-Islāmīyah as secret and hierarchical: "As for the internal structure, al-Shabībah was a totalitarian movement. There was neither dialogue nor debate in organizing anything. One acted without discussion."[7] For members of Group 26, only three people, Moustapha Oukil, Abdellah Hakimi, and Belkacem Hakimi, claimed any personal contact and involvement with Abdelkarim Moti, the exiled al-Shabībah leader, whom they encountered during one secret visit to Algeria. Indeed, according to Group 26 leader Belkacem Hakimi, many condemned during the trials of Islamists had no connection with al-Shabībah or with any Islamist organizations: "They were accused of crimes they did not commit. . . . Of course, it was inconceivable for the regime to conduct a trial against only three people in an affair of arms introduction by the Islamist movement."[8] Examples of those who had no political connections to the Group 26 detainees included Said Boudiaf, seventeen years old when he was arrested in Oujda, who spent five years in prison because of the political activities of his brother, Mohammed Boudiaf. Abdellah Fahd was sentenced to twenty and served thirteen years because he was sleeping at the house of a friend who was arrested; Abderrazak Trigui, not an Islamist, was arrested while visiting a friend in a neighborhood targeted for round-ups, and served fifteen years. Random police sweeps allowed the government to swell Group 71 membership. More were added as family members were arrested and condemned to four years in prison for the crime of *ʿadam al-tablīgh* (in French, *non-révelation*), refusal to report family members' activities to the authorities.[9] Islamist participant strength is, therefore, difficult to calculate. Faction al-Jihād, for example, was divided into two wings. Each knew only members in its immediate section, with one or two chosen as contacts to other shabibiste sections. Two from the city of Mohammedia, for example, acted as liaisons between a few members from the Casablanca-Sidi Bernoussi section, replicating thereby the familiar cell system of underground movements.

Taḥaddī

Members of Group 71 declare themselves the first Moroccan Islamists arrested as nonviolent prisoners of conscience. Group histories are chronicled through interviews,[10] trial records, clandestine prison photographs, indemnity applications, and literary and artistic productions such as artwork, unpublished and published letters, and diaries. *Yawmīyāt sajīn* (A prisoner's diary) by Mohamed Hakiki is a chronicle of arrest, disappearance, trial, and prison life published beginning a year after Hakiki's amnesty in the newspaper *al-Jisr* in thirty bimonthly installments beginning in the summer of 1995 and ending in February 2000:

> This diary records the period of incarceration stretching from 20 August 1983 and ended on the evening of 21 July 1994, the date of our release, immediately after [the king's throne] speech on Youth Day in which he called for 'turning the pages of the past' (*ṭayy ṣafḥat al-māḍī*). It touches lightly on events that accompany explanation or ideas about the penal system, with a reminder (*tadhkīr*) that does not chronicle every stage; it is not similar to memoirs (*mudhakkirāt*) or autobiography, on the other hand it is a formulation, a crafting of the prisoner I was that became part of the phenomenon of political imprisonment in our country.[11]

For Group 71 of Moroccan Islamists, the 1981 Casablanca uprising and its aftermath presented the government's relations with its subjects most starkly, exemplifying the state's capacity to injure Moroccans. The Islamists' single act of public, political protest would lead to years of prison. On 20–21 June 1983, during the month of Ramadan, shabibistes in Casablanca pasted posters and painted slogans on the beach, around the town center and on highway overpasses so that words were legible to passing motorists. Calligraphy and posters, largely the work of artists Khalid Bakhti and Mohammed Hakiki, were deliberately designed to resemble election posters. Painting over the graffiti, police cordoned off the targeted areas, which were repainted by the Islamists the following day. Actions timed to commemorate the second anniversary of the Casablanca "bread riots" of 1981 were defined by participants as part of the politics of *dhikrā* (remembrance) and *taḥaddī* (defiance).

Many of the groups' slogans resembled Marxist graffiti of the 1970s, decrying the lack of democracy and justice, condemning the high cost of living, and calling for freedom of speech. Only when the banners were exhibited in court as part of their trials would specific Islamist slogans, incorporated into trial transcripts, see the light of day, for example, "If religion were installed in the country, there would be justice and human rights." Other banners called Hassan II *al-ṭāghūt*, a Qur'anic term for the "impious tyrant" (Qur'an 4: 51, 60).[12]

On 11 July 1983, Ahmed Chahid and Mustapha Marjaoui, two Casablanca shabibistes, were apprehended in the city of Mohammedia covered in red paint while applying slogans. A third, Ahmed Haou, escaped but turned himself in on 30 August after learning that his father, Muhammad Haou, had been arrested and held hostage in his son's place at the Mohammedia police station. There, Haou and the Mohammedia shabibistes were first introduced to the black room ("la chambre noire") of Mohammedia, subjected to whippings (*kravash* in Morrocan Arabic, from the French *cravache*) and the "airplane" (*ṭayyārah*) torture, in which the victim is trussed and suspended to be beaten and electroshocked) before they were taken to Derb Moulay Cherif, forcibly disappeared, and tortured while awaiting their trial more than seven months later.[13] The trajectories of interrogation and torture for Moroccan political prisoners were in many respects similar, but specific mistreatments were reserved for each group. Prison guards forced Marxists to recite the Muslim profession of faith, the shahādah. Islamists were expressly forbidden from performing ritual ablutions or praying aloud, the latter defined by their torturers as a form of communication among the prisoners. Ahmed Haou, the acknowledged leader of the Islamist political prisoners in Group 71, recalls his torturers telling him, "If we could put your God through a session of *ṭayyārah*, we would do it."[14]

Although subject to six months of torture in Derb Moulay Cherif, Mohamed Hakiki merely notes in his diary in passing that all he endured is written down in Zaynab al-Ghazali's book.[15] Hakiki directs readers to a realm of shared literary and religious discourse by referring to one of the most famous and bestselling narratives of torture and imprisonment published in the Arabic-speaking world. Zaynab al-Ghazali's prison memoir, *Ayyām min ḥayātī* (Days from my life), was first broadcast on Egyptian radio in 1976 before publication in 1977. For her membership and activities in Egypt's Muslim Brotherhood, an organization banned by the government after a Muslim Brother's failed assassination attempt against President Gamal Abdel Nasser, al-Ghazali was arrested in 1965, condemned to twenty years in prison, but released in 1971.[16] Structural features common to spiritual and hagiographic journeys anchor her narrative, in which the soul plummets within the hell of prison, is tested by physical and mental tortures, and triumphantly surmounts every calamity to bring the Islamic message to the world. Hakiki need not, perhaps could not, dwell on accounts of disappearance and torture, if only because al-Ghazali's canonical Islamist text of suffering—divided into descriptions of seven different tortures in seven different cells—vividly does so while preaching ultimate redemption and salvation.[17]

Hakiki dismisses the Moroccan Islamists' government trial as *mujarrad ʿurūḍ masraḥīyah* (mere theatrical performances).[18] During the trial, the 71 Islamist detainees were charged with plotting against the regime, the public display of illegal banners showing antimonarchy calligraphy, clandestine meetings to constitute groups deemed illegal, graffiti hostile to the state, the distribution of treasonous tracts, and the transmission of tracts overseas (notably to France) denouncing the monarchy, all violations of articles 169, 170, 174, 201, and 204 of the Moroccan penal code.[19] The government also accused the Islamists, among others, of fomenting the second bread riots of January 1984, perhaps because group members were held in incommunicado detention by August 1983, six months before those uprisings, and thus were unavailable to protest against false accusations.[20] Responding to Amnesty International queries to Islamist prisoners about their activities and the real motive for detention, Bakhti replies:

> In January 1984 many Moroccan cities knew popular riots in reaction to price increases and the loss of buying power by citizens. To avoid responsibility, the king accused Islamists and Marxists on whom he placed the responsibility for the June troubles and spoke in a speech broadcast 23 January 1984 about agents in the pay of Israel for the Marxists and of Iran for the Islamists. The question is how to explain the gesture of accusing someone detained since 1983 of responsibility for a riot dated January 1984.[21]

The January 1984 uprisings began in Marrakesh, with students protesting tuition hikes. Demonstrations spread swiftly to high schools and universities throughout the country sustained by massive popular support from the ranks of unemployed fueled by major price increases in food mandated by the International Monetary Fund. Over eighty trials for *délits d'opinion* (crimes of opinion) occurred in 1984, with approximately 5,000 people arrested and 1,600 brought to trial.[22] The arrests fell most heavily on two groups seemingly at opposite ends of the political spectrum: Islamist activists and the radical left, notably the Marxist-Leninists of the Ilā al-Amām movement, the "agitators" assigned blame by Hassan II: "Muslim fundamentalists; communists and Marxists-Leninists; and Zionist secret services."[23]

Resistance

The status of political prisoner in Morocco is not defined by law; the status is acquired according to combined pressures exerted internationally and nationally, but principally emerges as an identity definition from within groups of prisoners themselves immediately upon their incarceration. Transferred among the various prisons of Safi, Kenitra, and Ghbila, the Islamists functioned organizationally in the same manner. In interviews, they affirmed that actions were espoused collectively and by consensus: "Everyday life consisted of group solidarity that called on individual strengths to create a world inside prison in which each act was perceived and valorized as an act of resistance to a dominant political discourse, thereby pointing to the limits of political control."[24] Prisoners organized a series of committees to negotiate with the authorities, to produce bulletins sent to successive Moroccan ministers of justice and the outside world, to demand improved conditions for detainees, to arrange food distribution, and to produce a cultural life in prison.

New models of organization and activism emerged from the prison spaces. First, Islamists in prison established a governing body called *tajammuʿ al-ʿāmm* (French, *assemblée générale* or *la grande instance*). Whenever discussion and decision-making were required, the institution of tajammuʿ al-ʿāmm alone possessed the right to make decisions (based on a 51 percent quorum and three-quarters majority vote) and to delegate tasks to additional decision-making subcommittees. Most prisoners agreed that the most difficult and dangerous subcommittee was *lajnat al-ḥiwār* (dialogue committee) consisting of three or four elected representatives charged with liaison to the prison administration. At first the Safi Prison administrators refused to recognize the dialogue committee as the sole representative of the Islamist group, demanding that individual prisoners submit personal, individual requests. Prisoners refused and were beaten. Eventually the prison director capitulated, admitting the existence of the dialogue committee while retaining the right to beat its members whenever unacceptable prisoners' demands were presented. Announcements of hunger strikes, communiqués to the prison administration, the minister of justice and the outside world, as well as documents with negotiable or non-negotiable demands were also the purview of the dialogue committee. Leitmotifs throughout imprisonment were requests for transfers closer to families residing in Casablanca and Mohammedia; Safi Prison was an expensive, arduous, 600-kilometer roundtrip for family members, especially the wives, sisters, and mothers who constituted the lifeline for prisoners. Persistent demands were to better prison conditions—to provide working showers, hospital and dental visits, medicine, improved food (instead of a diet of lentils with insects and old bread), and whitewash for the cell walls. Because requests for illumination inside Safi Prison cells were denied, Abdessamad Bouabid recalls preparing for his university examinations in economics sitting on top of the toilet in a niche with a single window onto the main corridor. One bulb, the only available light source, illuminated the corridor.

Other internal committees formed from the main assembly were the medical committee, charged with making doctors' appointments and monitoring the progress of prisoners' medical cases and prescriptions; the stock committee that directed the distribution of food, in particular, an equitable division among prisoners of family contributions; and the cultural committee (*lajnah thaqāfīyah*). As did the Marxist political prisoners before them, Islamist political prisoners created a rich cultural life in detention consisting of ceremonies, religious festivals, sports activities, cultural conferences and celebrations that characterize closely-knit human societies. The cultural committee organized parties during Ramadan. Infrequently, ordinary prisoners were permitted to participate in the various activities initiated by the Islamist prisoners, such as football teams, prayer and study groups, and frequent Palestinian cultural weeks (Figures 6.2, 6.3).

Membership in subcommittees followed prescribed principles. Those heading committees were chosen only if they refused, a process according to what all interviewed described as intrinsic to Muslim principles and Islamic culture. Ahmed Haou explains:

> Whoever says he wants the responsibility, we don't accept him. If he says no, we say it is you we look for. Responsibility is never given to whoever asks for it. A saying of the Prophet is: "naḥnu lā nuwallī hādhā al-amr li-man yuṭlubuh" (nous ne demandons pas cette affaire à qui la demande). The purpose is to break natural egotist tendencies among Muslims.[25]

Exceptions to this practice were noted by invoking the figure of Joseph in the Qur'an who demanded a position because he was the most competent administrator during the years of famine. To avoid obvious problems of nonvolunteerism and nonparticipation, all prisoners were asked to recommend in writing the names of three preferred candidates for each job.

In Safi Prison, Islamists were isolated on the second floor away from both ordinary prisoners and leftist political prisoners (who were also called Group 26). Islamist political prisoners took on new roles of educating families unaccustomed to advocating for incarcerated sons. Whereas in their pre-prison lives of underground political existence they noted that someone mysterious somewhere unknown issued orders for a specific action, in

Figure 6.2. Conference on human rights and Palestine organized by Islamist political prisoners, Kenitra Central Prison, 1992. Speakers, left to right: Belkacem Hakimi, Badr Idris Ouhlal, Hassan Elhasni Alaoui, Mohamed Hakiki, and Ahmed Haou. Clandestine prison photo.

prison the essential and greatest acquisition was, according to Haou, to be independent and self-governing because they were cut off from outside contacts. The result, concludes Bouabid, was that political objectives emerged from group members in prison, prisoners responded to no external institution or organization, and therefore, for many years there was no relation to any members of other Islamist movements. Only after 1990 did Amnesty International and other human rights organizations take up their cases, based on long written exchanges with the Islamists, who recall an extensive letter-writing campaign of persuasion that they were indeed nonviolent Islamists arrested solely for their convictions.

Prison afforded time to think, study, and write. Prisoners produced clandestine prison newspapers: in Casablanca's Ghbila Prison in 1984, for example, a newspaper called *Bidanciés* (Moroccan slang for "penitentiary") and in Safi Prison in 1985—86, *Madrasat Yūsuf* (Joseph's followers). An astonishingly high number of the Islamist political prisoners, some 60 percent is cited, completed law degrees in prison or began legal studies in prison

Figure 6.3. Qur'an recitation, Kenitra Central Prison. Clandestine prison photo.

and continued after their release.[26] Others obtained degrees in history, economics, or Islamic studies.

While imprisoned the Islamists married and fathered children. After ten years (1984–94) in prison, Ahmed Haou's death sentence was commuted to life in prison, and he was transferred to Casablanca's Oukacha Prison. There he married Fatima Guarai in 1995 and became a father in 1997.[27] Photographs from their wedding album are framed by the narrow confines of the visitors' section that separates prisoners from loved ones by a grille (Figure 6.4). Haou's wedding pictures depict a festive occasion, everyone feting the newlyweds and listening to loud music, momentarily on the visitor's side, as if they could all return home freely after the celebration. Other Islamist political prisoners, such as Abdelkader Sfiri, also married in prison.

Detention

The most extreme form of resistance universally available to prisoners to establish the claim to political prisoner status has been the hunger strike.

Figure 6.4. Prison wedding of Ahmed Haou (Islamist political prisoner, 1983–98) and Fatima Guarai, Oukacha Prison, Casablanca, 1995. Courtesy of Ahmed Haou.

The efficacy of the hunger strike depends on wide media coverage, that is, the passage of individual pain into the realm of public knowledge. The hunger striker inflicts pain and deprivation as part of a willed decision. The striker instigates his or her own physical destruction as an active participant who makes of the human body a weapon and a message projected outward to the world.

Extreme prison deprivations called for extreme hunger strikes. Abderrahmane Naim, Group 26 Islamist political prisoner amnestied in 1998, remembers the first hunger strike by Islamists in Kenitra Central Prison. In 1985, he began serving his sentence in the isolated wards reserved for those sentenced to death, the infamous D Section where prisoners were allowed outside cells fifteen minutes twice daily, each prisoner allotted a different time so none could meet. Family visits were restricted to one per week for five minutes while the prisoner remained manacled.[28] Those condemned to death began a hunger strike that lasted more than forty-five days, with some, like Ahmed Haou, entering a coma on the thirty-third day resulting in forced feedings initiated in the prison hospital on the thirty-seventh day. Strikers demanded, and eventually won, the right to information, permission to continue studies, adequate medical care, longer family visits with direct contact (no grille or manacles), and edible food. To attain and retain newly acquired rights, often subject to being rescinded by prison authorities, innumerable unlimited hunger strikes took place in various Moroccan prisons. When radio, television, newspapers, and books were banned for Islamist political prisoners in Safi Prison, hunger strikes of twenty-four or seventy-two hours were undertaken. In October 1985, Islamists in solidarity with another political prisoner group, Group 26 of Marxist-Leninists imprisoned in the same Safi penitentiary, joined the leftists in a long and dangerous hunger strike, one in which three Marxist political prisoners—Moustapha Belhouari, Moulay Boubker Doureidi, and Abdelhakim El Meskini—died.[29]

Unlimited (*lā maḥdūd*) hunger strikes posed theological and spiritual problems. If one were to die as a hunger striker, would one be considered a *shahīd* (martyr)? Does sharīʿah authorize dying from a hunger strike? For many Islamist political prisoners, the inability to pursue a hunger strike to the point of death weakened its usefulness as a weapon, but there was no escaping its definition as an act of suicide, condemnable (*munkar*) and figuring among the greater sins (*kabā'ir*) leading to hell. Discussions led Group 71 members in Safi Prison to conclude that a pretext was needed to stop before jeopardizing their health, because the evident intent of authorities was to handicap political prisoners physically and mentally. The Islamists asked themselves of what use was a handicapped activist. Indeed, Islamists originally housed together in Kenitra Central Prison in 1984 before they were forcibly dispersed to other prisons[30] benefited from advice given by two earlier Kenitra hunger strike experiences. Ahmed Saad, condemned to death in 1975, pointed to Moustapha Khazar, permanently plagued with serious motor disabilities, and to Abdelmajid Khachani, who died during a strike. Driss Benzekri, of the Marxist group Ilā al-Amām (imprisoned before trials in Casablanca in 1977), counseled against hunger strikes except as a last resort and urged the avoidance of unlimited strikes so as to emerge mentally and physically intact. Beginning in 1987, Islamist political prisoners innovatively embarked on what they called *iḍrāb tanāwubī* (a rolling or successive hunger strike): a group of two to four hunger strikers would fast for twenty-four or forty-eight hours, to be replaced by another group of fasters. The unlimited hunger strike, thus, persisted as a physical condition, but instead of being attached to the suffering body of a single prisoner, the state of being on hunger strike rotated among the persons in the group.

If the prison hunger strike to the death prevented Islamists from being considered martyrs, the Moroccan state created martyrs when its courts liberally handed out death sentences that were rarely executed but did lead to years of residence on death row. Six of the members of Group 71 were condemned to death: Ahmed Chahid, Ahmed Chayeb, Ahmed Haou, Mustapha Marjaoui, Youssef Rbati Cherkaoui, and Abdelkader Sfiri. Chayeb and Chadid were condemned to death after a second trial on 4 October 1988 for attempting to escape from prison, during which time one guard was killed and three others wounded. Among members of the Islamist Group 26, there were five death sentences: Abdellah Hakimi, Bouchaib Boulboul, and Abderrahmane Naim (the three amnestied in 1998 by Hassan II), while Moustapha Oukil and Belkacem Hakimi remained incarcerated in Oukacha Prison (until amnestied by Muhammad VI in 2004). Amnesties were capriciously granted to Islamists. All were eligible because none had committed a *crime du sang* (crime of blood), a necessary condition for release from prison.

Prisoners embraced the martyrdom of being political prisoners about to die, a status that resulted from specific political convictions that were validated by the state. When that status was removed—by the reduction of a death sentence to life imprisonment—its loss was keenly felt. Belkacem Hakimi, an Islamist political prisoner serving a life sentence in Oukacha Prison, wrote in his diary on 7 March 1994:

> They say our death sentence has been commuted and perhaps this is valid for me too. I really do not know from where this wave of sadness that invades me comes. I should be happy. But it is completely the opposite. I am sad and distressed. For me the death sentence was like a crown God placed on my head that mattered greatly. Everything was so clear to me: "You are dead, they are all dead." When I was condemned to death, I was free, very free, nothing mattered. Now, how will things unfold? Will fear finally inhabit my heart? Everyone knows they will die. But a death sentence is so concrete. I sensed death. I even touched it. More than that, I dared to befriend it. But now it confirms that it is always stronger. It escapes when I thought I had it. I truly fear it will vanquish me, make me submit to become like those "flocks of the silenced." People have a perverse logic, I would say even "reversed." Some came to congratulate me. Don't they know that this death sentence was God's promise to me that I have vanquished death forever, that I would "die" a martyr? Does this promise still hold? That's what I fear most.[31]

In effect the death sentence was enlisted as the supreme example, the sign of a proffered martyrdom in the world to come while remaining a fundamental attribute of, even a paradoxical metaphor for, day-to-day resistance against the prison world and the struggle to remain human and alive.

Nature was enlisted in the fight to remain human. Ahmed Haou, who inhabited death row for ten years, writes to students in a Quebec high school:

> Dear Friends . . . I am 35 years old. I was following my studies in the faculty of law in my fourth year when I was arrested, 30 August 1983 for a simple *délit d'opinion* (crime of opinion). I have a family that never stops supporting me during these years of incarceration, above all my mother, who protests continually to authorities, whether against abuses or tortures that affect me. . . . Christine . . . who drew me a sun that is trying to neutralize the clouds. . . . For the past twelve years, I am present each morning at the contest between the clouds and the sun. Here in the city of clouds [Kenitra Central Prison], mornings the sky is gloomy; but bit by bit the sky wins the contest. As for me, each morning, I go out to be present at this combat and it is a way to resist, never give up or bend.[32]

As part of the daily life of Kenitra Central Prison, Islamist political prisoners were profoundly influenced by the presence among them and the comportment of a famous leader of one of Morocco's Sufi confraternities, a man who had been a major figure in Morocco's fight for independence against the French and a signer of Morocco's 1944 declaration of independence (*wathīqat al-istiqlā*l). Muḥammad bin al-Ḥājj al-Ṭayyib al-Idrīsi, head of the Zāwiyah Zeitouna in Fez, was imprisoned in 1981 with more than thirty other Zeitouni adepts (Figure 6.5). In the wake of the 1979 Iranian Revolution, the Moroccan regime imprisoned members of organizations considered to be under the influence of, or structured similarly to, the organization of Iranian leader Ayatollah Ruhollah Khomeini. Numerous stories circulated to sustain prisoners about al-Idrīsī's steadfast refusal to comply with prison directives. He was reported to have refused to leave his cell, an act interpreted as a protest against his incarceration. He was offered his freedom many times by prison administrators if he would sign a blank sheet on which would be written a request for a royal pardon. Although health and mind were failing, he remained steadfast in his refusals; while prison authorities preferred that he wear his own clothes, he donned the *shibānī* (prison khaki), refusing efforts to be treated differently from the other prisoners. His death in prison, conferring on him the status of "martyr" occurred on 9 January 1990 as he was approaching the age of one hundred, a mere four months before his ten-year prison sentence would have been completed.[33]

The everyday struggle to remain politically aware and free is experienced by free human beings no less than by prisoners. Although the detainee is physically confined to a particular space, Moroccans by analogy

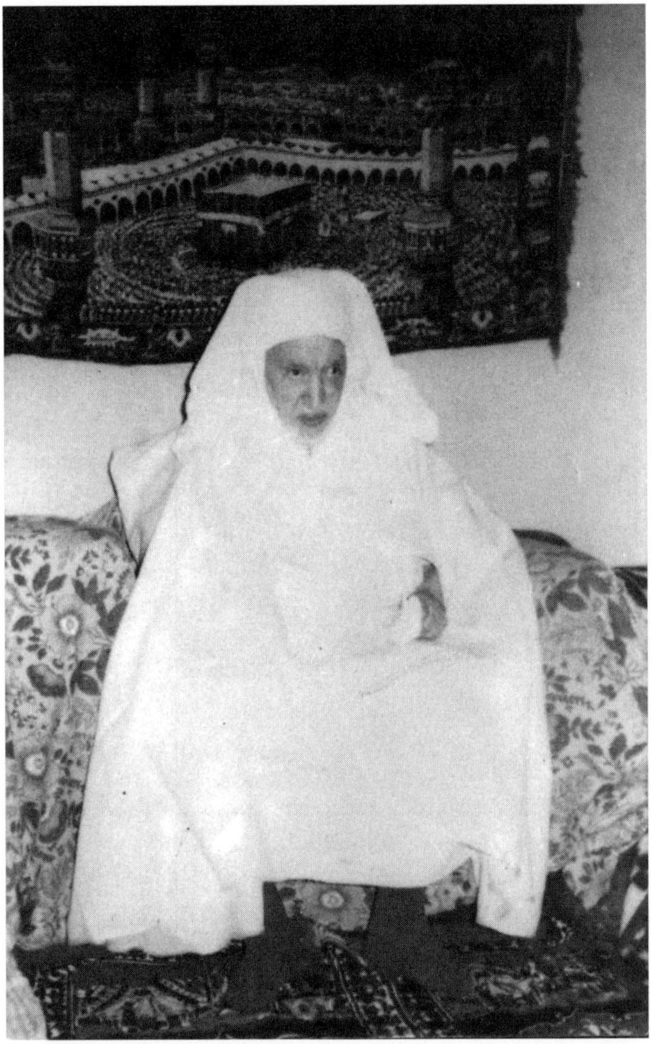

Figure 6.5. Muḥammad bin al-Ḥājj al-Ṭayyib al-Idrīsi, head of the Zāwiyah Zeitouna. Courtesy of Ahmed Haou.

frequently describe their situation as prisoners within a country whose borders form another bigger prison. The prison diaries of Abdessamad Bouabid flesh out a compound identity, what he terms "the human being/detainee," for which the slash mark is inseparable from the notion of an existence lived *derrière les murs* (behind the walls):

> Did not Pharaoh say: "I have not found you any God except for me." From that time this "Man/God" claimed for himself the rights over the feelings, thoughts and soul of his subjects for whom he created his paradise and his hell, the former for the obedient, and for the rebels such as Moses and Joseph, he set aside hell: extermination, privation, imprisonment. Doubtless prison, the machine most destructive to human beings is far from the most frightening. Once caught, the Human being/detainee is called upon to confront the whims of this infernal machine in which physical tortures and psychological war alternate. From one test to the next, and from one battle to the next, the Human being/detainee sets out towards the culminating point: the instant of exploding the frontiers that separate the two worlds: that of the prison guarded by an entire army of repression and that of everyday life, "the larger prison" in which the only difference is that in the first, the Human being/detainee is constrained by the pain of repression from leaving his cell and must return at specific moments while in the second the Human being/free is familiar with the general order, he returns home at night and closes his door at a fixed time according to various pretexts.
>
> As soon as one lives this extraordinary moment, one grasps the real meaning of liberty: that it has a subjective value before an objective being, meaning that the quest is to make the interior of one's being, of one's person, and of oneself. When one feels oneself free, it's the same whether the body is behind the walls or outside them. Liberty is to be free to believe what one wants, to think what one wants, to embrace what one thinks is just and true. The soul attains liberty when it is free, it is of little importance that the body is in prison or elsewhere, ill or healthy, the essential is to explode the frontiers and to yell at the top of one's voice to the torturer: "I am free, you can do what you want with my body, you can never break my soul." Only then does the smallness of the jailer appear, the ridiculousness of his actions, and the grandeur of the human soul that none can control.[34]

To demonstrate the depth of solidarity behind prison walls, Islamists point to the example of the letter of pardon (*risālat al-ʿafw*), the written exchange between monarch and subject that best symbolizes their unequal relations. In Morocco, the writer of a letter requesting pardon, usually a prisoner or an exile, must produce a letter in which he or she willingly concedes having embarked on the wrong path and renounces the ideas for which he or she once fought and was imprisoned. The letter by the prisoner is both written proof and symbol of a subservient abdication from political principles and further actions; it also serves to regulate dissidence inside and outside the prison walls. Families and colleagues applied pressure to all political prisoners to compose a missive addressed to Hassan II in his role as *amīr al-mu'minīn* (Commander of the Faithful), descendant of the Prophet Muhammad, requesting a royal pardon. Marxist political prisoner Abdellatif Derkaoui remembers that in 1975 he refused offers made by the Sufi Derqawa order, to which he and his family belonged, to write a letter of pardon on his behalf and thereby obtain his release from Kenitra Central Prison.[35] Pardon letters constituted a confession of wrongdoing that was culturally and juridically more powerful than those authored by the police and extracted under torture. As documents, letters requesting pardon assert the power and forgiveness of the Moroccan sovereign and were, therefore, printed for distribution in the palace-run newspaper, *Le Matin du Sahara et du Maghreb*. A pardon letter to the king signed by seven Marxist political prisoners, for example, was published in 1986.[36]

Although Islamists also sent letters requesting pardons from the king, the community of political prisoners interpreted this act in multiple ways. For those who had no connection to political movements but were randomly arrested in order to increase numbers and thus, the danger of Islamists, pleas for royal grace made sense. From an Islamic perspective, Marxists who ask for pardon were no longer Marxists, whereas a Moroccan who asks for pardon remains a Muslim because pardon is an individual decision that does not call for renouncing religious belief, only political affiliation. Moreover, because prisoners had to continue living together for years in prison, most chose to ignore requests for pardon, claimed they never discussed it among themselves and decided it was more important not to wound each other. In truth, those who requested pardon were rarely released at an earlier date.

Activism

By the late 1990s, the leftists and many Islamist political prisoners benefited from royal amnesties.[37] In early 2000, attempts were made to launch an umbrella human rights organization that would unite all Islamist associations, parliamentary parties, and political prisoners, spearheaded by members of al-Badīl al-Ḥadari.[38] In May 2000, six months after the establishment of al-Muntadā, a group of Islamist former political prisoners created another human rights organization, al-Tajammu' min Ajl Karāmat al-Insān (Assembly for Human Dignity), known by its acronym, Tamkine, which means "strengthening," "consolidation," "enablement."[39] The first nine-member Tamkine executive bureau include president Abdellah Laamari, treasurer Abdellah Belakrad, and councillor Abderrahim Rifla, members of Group 71, condemned to and served ten years in prison where they completed law degrees; vice-president Abdessamad Bouabid; secretary-general Mohammed Nabi; vice-secretary-general Abdullah Mazzi; second councillor Abdelghani Boutahar, Group 71, sentenced to life; Mohammed Hansali, condemned to twenty years; and third councillor Abderrahim Mouhtat, condemned to death three times (in 1984 in absentia with Group 71, in 1985 in absentia with Group 26, and in 1990 he was arrested and condemned to life in prison and amnestied in 1994). Despite Moroccan laws requiring nongovernmental organizations to register with both the prefecture and the tribunal, neither al-Badīl al-Ḥadarī, an organization aspiring to become a political party, nor Tamkine have been able to obtain official authorization, and like many other associations must operate on the border between illegality and self-censorship. Since 2001, Tamkine, with aspirations to serve as the human rights association for all the Islamist groups, has been inactive. Founders of Tamkine remain active members of al-Muntadā, the umbrella human rights forum for political prisoners.

The Casablanca Trial of May–June 2000

On 4 May 2000, Moustapha Oukil, an Islamist political prisoner serving a sentence of life imprisonment in Oukacha Prison, was brought to a Casablanca police station suffering from injuries sustained when a car struck him as he stood on the sidewalk in front of his apartment house in Casablanca. First Oukil, and subsequently Belkacem Hakimi and Ahmed Saad, all serving life sentences in Oukacha Prison, were charged with attempting a prison escape aided by seven guards. In a communiqué released the first day of the trial, the three political prisoners made clear their defense strategy:

> The authorities fomented a plot against us whose facts begin 4 May 2000 when Moustapha Oukil arrived at the hospital Ibn Rochd for a session of kinestherapy, he was found in a coma from which he did not awake except at the 4th district police station suffering from fractures of the right rib, serious wounds resulting from an accident of which he was a victim and only learned about later.[40]

The trial took place over a six-day period—16, 24, 31 May and 1, 5, 6 June 2000. Press coverage by the arabophone *Ittiḥād Ishtirākī* and the francophone *Libération* was virulent and unprofessional.[41] Two additional events with important political repercussions provided a backdrop to the trial: the 1989 government order that kept Sheikh Abdessalam Yassine, head of the largest Moroccan Islamist organization, al-ʿAdl wa-al-Iḥsān (Justice and Benevolence), under house arrest for eleven years was lifted, and an unlimited hunger strike began on 24 May 2000 by Islamist political prisoners in Kenitra Central Prison. Sheikh Yassine's first sortie in ten years outside his house was to pray in the local Salé mosque and his second was a failed attempt to visit Islamist political prisoners from his movement pursuing a hunger strike in Kenitra Central Prison. He was refused entry. "The parameters of political dynamics as they occur in Morocco," writes Susan Waltz are "both repression and negotiation. . . . The quality of arbitrariness frequently attached to both reprisals and measures of clemency have served to reinforce an object lesson about the king's raw power. Disjointed reprisals and unexpected amnesties throw players off balance even as they underscore the discretionary—and thus enhanced—powers of the monarch."[42] In other words, Sheikh Yassine was permitted after eleven years to leave his home, but his destinations with political purpose are curtailed.

In the 1980s the pattern of mass political trials, regardless of political affiliation, was to bar families from the tribunal—the audience consisted of secret police—prisoners were heavily guarded inside the courthouse by armed soldiers. Convictions were based on confessions obtained after months of torture at Derb Moulay Cherif; incriminating evidence was books, tracts, and posters. Lawyers were routinely forbidden access to clients; for example, when defense lawyers for the Islamists attempted to speak to their clients during the 1983 Islamist trials, Judge Rezouani threatened them with contempt of court and their lawyers with the same charges against as clients. During trials, political prisoners were permitted to answer only "yes" or "no," and severe judgments did not reflect the actual misdemeanors.[43]

The May–June 2000 trial held at the Ben M'sik-Sidi Othmane Tribunal of the First Instance in Casablanca differed substantially from the previous Islamist trials of 1984 and 1985. Lawyers during the 2000 trial repeatedly invoked the change in Morocco, pointing to the new era in which an end to the very existence of political prisoners could be foreseen. More than thirty lawyers from other Moroccan cities (Oujda, Kenitra, and Rabat) were present in court to advise and argue on behalf of the accused. Lawyers and clients were granted ample time to converse, and the courtroom overflowed with families, journalists and observers from a variety of human rights organizations.[44] Three contradictory positions were articulated by the scores of lawyers who gathered in support of the accused. One defense strategy was to support the joint political prisoner-guard contention that all were innocent, the second was to challenge the authorities to prove any attempted escape efforts—Hakimi and Saad were actually in prison the day Oukil was injured near his home—and the third was to point to the decades in which political prisoners had freely circulated for an afternoon before returning to prison, a well-known custom initiated in the early 1980s by the Marxist-Leninist political prisoners and tolerated by the authorities even during the worst of the "years of lead." Belkacem Hakimi, speaking as both the accused and a lawyer on his own behalf, gave a spirited defense of the political prisoner's right to escape. Man was born free and natural, he contended, with the right to self-defense; escape was not a horrific act, therefore, but one punishable only if the prison administration viewpoint was taken as opposed to political prisoners, wrongly and arbitrarily detained. In the end, tribunal judges condemned Oukil to two months of prison added to his existing sentence of life imprisonment, and acquitted Hakimi, Saad, and five guards. Mohamed Boulouz, responsible for guarding Oukil on the day of the accident, was sentenced to four years in prison. A second guard, Adil Souiri, had acknowledged granting permission to Oukil to visit his family on Tuesday 2 March, two days before the accident, based on instructions from his superior, Mohammed Sahih. Souiri reported during the police inquiry that when he queried his superior if Oukil could indeed depart freely, permission was given orally by the phrase "al-danya hanya," whose literal meaning—"its fine, life is easy, go ahead"—does not, ruled the judges, constitute explicit permission. Mohamed Sahih was acquitted and Souiri, the only guard to speak the truth, was condemned to four years in prison.[45] Souiri's conviction highlights the difficulties in changing and challenging Moroccan systems of prison, secret detention, and torture. Although illegal administrative directives and practices are oral and indirect, they are implicitly understood and executed. Should the chain of orally delivered commands surface, as during this trial, Moroccan courts swiftly discount their force and dismiss the consequences.

The courtroom for the 2000 Casablanca trial was packed with political prisoners, human rights activists, lawyers, and observers from various Islamist organizations and political parties. Also present was a large contingent of prison guards temporarily allied with their many former wards in support of a Moroccan prison culture that for decades permitted long-serving detainees to enjoy illegal, unacknowledged home visits. In the hallway

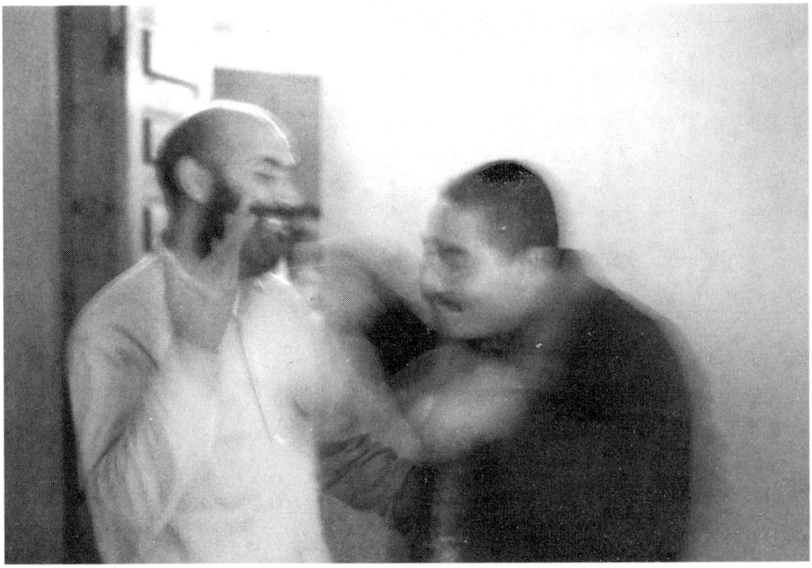

Figure 6.6. Ahmed Haou embraced by his jailer, Mostefa al-Jid, Casablanca Tribunal, May 2000. Photo by author.

of the tribunal, Ahmed Haou ran into Mostefa al-Jid, one of his jailers and torturers in Oukacha Prison. After a moment of shocked mutual recognition, al-Jid seized Haou and attempted to embrace him. While holding Haou in what seemed like a hammerlock from which Haou could not escape, al-Jid begged him repeatedly *iḍrabnī iḍrabnī* (hit me, hit me) (Figure 6.6). Haou was placed in the position of calming his former tormentor. Later Haou remembered occasions where he was beaten so severely that he lay immobilized on the floor in pools of his own blood. He said that he could forgive al-Jid for beating him because that is the culture of prison mirrored in the guards' behavior toward the inmates. Prison brutally exaggerates social relationships found in Moroccan society, observes Haou, one in which parents beat children, husbands their wives, and teachers their students. What he found hard to forgive was another episode, one that could not be pardoned by sociological analysis because it denied his individuality and humanity. After one beating, al-Jid stood triumphantly over Haou's body, and as one foot smashed into Haou's stomach, al-Jid crowed: "Now, who do you think you are?"[46]

Indemnities

The activities of the Islamist Group 71 are instructively considered in relation to victim responses to government indemnification.[47] Group 71 is the first group of Moroccan Islamists arrested and tried for nonviolent crimes of opinion. Between 1994 and 1998, the majority of Group 71 was amnestied. On 28 December 1999, three days before the deadline to file for indemnities, Group 71 collectively decided to present their individual cases. Exceptions were Abdallah Haidou, Mohamed Hakiki, and Hamid Margiche, who had no confidence in the Indemnity Commission, and Abderrahim Maknassi, too ill to file. Group 71 also decided collectively to disregard the commission format; each refused to include the necessary letter accepting the Indemnity Commission rulings without recourse to appeal, as required in articles 12 and 26. Taking the premise that truthful accounts of past criminal behavior must be aired and the guilty punished, the Islamists of Group 71 choose to act *as if* the Moroccan authorities could and would be held accountable. If the terms of debate determining how Moroccan society moves away from dictatorship are framed by indemnification plans, the Islamists are prepared to engage, even bureaucratically by filing indemnification forms, a government determined to buy off and bury the past. Each Islamist narrated the litany of arrest, torture, forcible disappearance and illegally prolonged incommunicado detention, farcical trial, absurdly long prison sentences, and physical and medical deprivations endured.

Ahmed Haou, in his capacity as vice-treasurer of al-Muntadā, participated in a meeting between members of ACHR and the al-Muntadā executive committee on 15 April 2000. At first he was informed that his arrest, eight months of torture, forced confession, farcical trial, and death sentence for writing graffiti were legal, and consequently he was not eligible for indemnities.[48] Based on interviews and copies of indemnity dossiers of the ACHR filed by Ahmed Haou, Abdessamad Bouabid, Hassan Elhasni Alaoui, and Khalid Bakhti, Group 71 chooses to embrace the universal principles of legality enshrined in human rights documents and traces their conversion to the culture of human rights via the world of prisons.[49]

"What was the manner of your torture or death?" has become a political question: the Moroccan government has attempted to contain and to manage the expressibility of individual pain, paradoxically creating an authorized story from the victims' files whose pages must then be immediately turned. The Indemnity Commission activated by the ACHR on 17 August

1999 is "charged with determining indemnification for moral and material prejudice in favor of victims and those having the right of being declared disappeared, or those who were the object of forcible disappearance."[50] Although the creation, composition, and mandate of the commission have been hotly contested and its process widely boycotted by many of the victims for whom it was created, nonetheless, like all governmental bodies of this type, it operates under the unstated assumption that the act of verbally expressing pain is a necessary prelude to the collective task of diminishing the pain. In the commission's case, the pain must also be effaced. Or, in current Moroccan terminology, this means turning the page.

The dossier to the Indemnity Commission submitted by Khalid Bakhti demonstrates what happens when the resources of writing are deemed insufficient to express the language of pain. The eye, not the voice, supplements by utilizing visual acuity to enable the victim to articulate the physiology of torture. Khalid Bakhti, born 11 November 1964, was arrested 31 August 1983 at Ain Sebaa, Casablanca, condemned to life imprisonment for "attacks on the internal security of the state," and belonged to the Group 71 (Casablanca trial, July 1984).[51] As the calligrapher and artist of the Islamist group, he was caught posting antimonarchy posters and writing graffiti and was forcibly disappeared to Derb Moulay Cherif from 31 August 1983 to 13 February 1984. Shuttled between the prisons of Ghbila and Safi, he completed a degree in history and Islamic studies. Amnestied 21 July 1994, he currently lectures on graphic arts at Casablanca's School of Fine Arts.

Bakhti narrates the familiar story of arrest, torture, forcible disappearance and illegally prolonged garde à vue, farcical trial, absurdly long prison sentences—Bakhti was condemned to life imprisonment for writing banners—and physical and medical deprivations endured including the cessation of any chemotherapy treatments for Hodgkin's disease.[52] Unusual for an indemnity file but in keeping with his talents, Bakhti's narrative is illustrated. He used the graphic software Poser to reproduce visually in three dimensions the different postures of torture. Poser provides users with the image of a marionette to manipulate at will. Bakhti's figures are blindfolded and dressed in prison khaki with the stand-in artist's model exemplifying the body in torture positions (Figure 6.7). Reading from the top left to right: (1) the detainee is forced to kneel for long periods with knees on a wooden bar and arms upraised; (2) *ṭayyārah* (the airplane); (3) the detainee must stand on one leg for hours holding a bar; middle left to right: (4) *ṭayyārah* but also known as *shabah* (in French *fantôme*), the detainee, arms tied behind the back, is hung by the hands and the feet are tied in order to

Figure 6.7. "Torture" by Khalid Bakhti, reparations dossier submitted to Idemnity Commission, 29 December 1999. Reprinted by permission of author.

receive electric shocks and beatings; (5) *falaqah*, blows to the bottom of the feet; and bottom row: forcing the prisoner to remain prone, silent, manacled, and blindfolded between torture sessions.[53]

Bakhti's testimony, framed within the constraints of a form requesting indemnity, focuses on the problem of historical responsibility: how torture is to be clearly laid at the door of the representatives of the police and judiciary. Finally, Bakhti writes his own *procès-verbal* (written testimony taken by the police), wholly different from the one he was forced to sign when blindfolded after torture sessions. This time, he is free to name perpetrators, to categorize the abuses, and to uncover the dynamics of the process that made him a victim of torture. While imposing on us a narrow angle of vision, namely the depicted physical body in the act of being punished, starved and humiliated, Bakhti's narrative produces what happened to him and the truth of his pain in his own words and with his own artistry.

More than two years after filing for indemnities, Ahmed Haou obtained from the ACHR a three-page *muqarrir taḥkīmī* (arbitration decision) dated 23 January 2003. A first page provides the indemnity date and case and file numbers; the second page summarizes facts narrated in Haou's original indemnity request. The ACHR text forthrightly includes crucial acknowledgments that Ahmed Haou merits indemnification because

> he was forcibly detained from 30 August 1983 to 13 February 1984 in the secret detention center of Derb Moulay Cherif, then to the Civil Prison based on the *procès-verbal* [written testimony] of the Direction de la surveillance du territoire [DST, or secret service] which he was forced to sign under torture, he was subjected to an unjust trial that ended 31 July 1984 and charged with attacks on the internal security of the country, condemned to death, and pardoned to life in prison in 1994 during which time he was maltreated in all the prisons whether Ghbila Civil Prison or Kenitra Central or Oukacha in Casablanca, and after his royal pardon on 13 October 1998, he was not reintegrated, he suffered loss of marriage, possibilities to work in the public sector, and he requests material and moral reparations (*jabr al-aḍrār al-māddīyah wa-al-maʿnawīyah*), medical treatments and reintegration.[54]

The ACHR and the Indemnity Commission agreed that Haou was the victim of disappearance and secret detention according to norms established nationally and internationally and, therefore, awarded the amount of 310,000 dirhams (approximately U.S. $31,000). His additional requests for reparation, restitution, and reintegration were declared to be beyond the purview of the commission (*khārijah ʿan niṭāq ikhtiṣāṣ hayʾat al-taḥkīm*). When Haou received his official paperwork and check in June 2003, he reports that he had tears in his eyes:

> The document is more important than the money, even though I need the money. It was a second liberation. For me, it was my moment of reconciliation. Fifteen years of torture and all that happened after. This is a kind of apology. At last, at last, a recognition that I was tortured and illegally tried.[55]

As of January 2003, of more than 6,000 requests for indemnification filed, the Indemnity Commission had considered 3,400 cases and settled financially 2,840, benefiting 3,700 people, and rejected 550 cases.[56] Over 9,000 additional requests were filed after the 31 December 1999 deadline.

Human Rights Work

Abdellah Laamari (Group 71), one of the defense lawyers during the May 2000 Islamist trial, explicitly points to the public connection between the fate of all political prisoners and the fight for human rights when he stated in his summation on 6 June 2000: "Political prisoners are like wood. When they start to burn, the machinery of human rights turns."[57] The fact that people who have experienced torture, bogus trials, and long years of prison for their ideas have subsequently transformed this "gift" of pain and imprisonment into committed human rights work is a somewhat astounding development that has been repeated in case after case, country after country.[58]

Beginning in the 1970s but more clearly in the 1980s, Morocco has seen the emergence of several human rights organizations and, in fact, a culture of human rights rooted in the struggles since independence to free the political prisoners who have peopled the kingdom's secret torture centers, commissariats, and tribunals. No matter where Islamist political prisoners locate themselves on the theoretical spectrum, from a movement to "Westernize" Islamists or to "Islamize" human rights discourse, their responses are practical and organizational, given that many remain incarcerated. Islamist political prisoners can participate in several social, political, and religious movements: first, as activists in an international human rights movement; second, as political prisoners belonging to an ancient crosscultural collectivity of victims of abusive regimes; and third, as Islamists participating in an Arab-Muslim Islamist movement. From the 1990s on, the Moroccan Islamist human rights movement, born during particular historical circumstances and in response to gross human rights violations, has faced a double struggle. The task is to address and educate those within their own

Islamist movements who may perceive human rights as an alien, Western, secular dogma imposed from outside to mask economic imperialism. At the same time, the Moroccan Islamist human rights movement confronts Moroccan human rights activists who often have emerged from the secular left, and some of whom may view Islamists as enemies of a universalist discourse of the rule of law promoting democracy and equal rights for women. In Morocco there is a perceived need for yet another human rights association, one that continues to campaign in support of all Islamist political prisoners.[59]

Islamist political prisoners of Group 71 and 26 are a minority among the vast population of Moroccan political prisoners, a minority among human rights associations, and a minority within the Moroccan Islamist movement. Nonetheless, they have produced a human rights discourse that is modern in spirit. It is as inclusive as possible of diverse Moroccan political trends; to take Haou's approach, what is needed is a minimum platform around which Islamists and others can unite, in effect an "overlapping consensus" about what constitutes political and legal justice, as proposed by John Rawls.[60] Haou advances reason (*ʿaql*) and the possibilities of reinterpreting juridically existing sacred law (*ijtihād*) as modalities in which to work toward changing the idea that human rights are Western notions; Islam too, he observes, has its referents. Haou translates, for example, the Arabic *banī Ādam* as "human beings" to derive the ethical and moral basis for human rights from the Quranic verse: "we have accorded dignity to human beings" (Qur'an 17:70).[61] In effect, since no single political party or bloc can achieve the rule of law, everyone is needed to solve Morocco's numerous, crushing problems. He hopes for an open, sustained internal political discourse about human rights, one rooted in Islam and Moroccan culture.[62]

No analysis is offered here of the large body of complex discourses on religion, politics, and human rights produced by either Muslim or Marxist thinkers, many of which serve as sources and reference points for Islamist political prisoners. Rather, what has been presented is the universality of the prison experience for Islamists as one contribution to a study of the unities and dissimilarities that ground a religious movement's adherence to human rights activism and, thus, the evolution of human rights in its lived context, mainly the interaction of the world of political prisoners and the Morocco they found once liberated from prison.

After 11 September 2001 and 16 May 2003

Although a few Islamist political prisoners state a preference for the possible separation of religion and the state, especially if a secular government is the alternative to what some call Islamic totalitarianism, it may be that the moods and imperatives of a mass movement are stronger and more important than the individuals involved in them. Morocco's future political organization and governance will include or possibly be controlled by the Islamist movement. Many Moroccans promote the case of Moroccan exceptionalism (*la particularité marocaine*)[63] in which the evident global resurgence of Islam will not touch Morocco with the political violence of neighboring Algeria. Two events challenge this viewpoint. The first is the 11 September 2001 attack that killed thousands of civilians in New York City's World Trade Center towers and led the U.S. Congress, forty-five days later on 26 October 2001, to pass the Uniting and Strengthening America by Providing Appropriate Tools Required to Intercept and Obstruct Terrorism Act (known as the "U.S.A. Patriot Act"). A similar event, not in magnitude but in shock value and reaction to brutality, took place in Morocco on 16 May 2003, when multiple bomb attacks in Casablanca targeting foreign and Moroccan Jewish sites killed forty-six people and also caused Morocco's parliament to enact quickly an antiterrorism law (Number 03–03) two weeks after the event.[64] In so doing, the United States and Morocco, along with other countries, make claims in regards to a global war against terrorism that places their respective nation's safety above various legal rights, or as concludes sociologist Lisa Hajjar, "the guiding principle is that absolute security is a legal right of the state."[65] The Moroccan version, according to its article 218, which is now integrated into Morocco's penal code, defines terrorism as any premeditated act, individual or collective, whose purpose is "atteinte à l'ordre public par la terreur et la violence," a phrase reminiscent of "atteinte à l'ordre publique" (attacks against public order) inherited from the French colonial era that enabled the incarceration of generations of Moroccans, but adding the new descriptors "by terror or violence." Prison terms are ten to twenty years, with life in prison for injuries and capital punishment for deaths resulting from a terrorist act. Unique to Morocco is the possibility of public apologies, acts lowering prison terms from six to two years and intended as lesser punishments for religious leaders who publicly supported Ossama Bin Laden by calling for jihad, and, thus, are liable to prosecution under new Moroccan antiterrorist laws. There are penal consequences for those supporting financial networks or contributing money to organizations deemed terrorist, and for those possessing information about terrorist crimes yet who refuse to inform authorities. Abdellah Laamari, lawyer and president of the defunct Tamkine, defended Moroccan Islamists held on terrorism charges until he himself was arrested in June 2003, tried under antiterrorism laws, jailed, and released in November 2003 when, instead of reporting, he was charged with warning an Islamist of imminent police arrest.

In Morocco, waves of arrests have targeted specific groups, primarily those belonging to organizations labeled Islamist based on the profile of perpetrators. The Moroccan government acknowledges more than a thousand people detained under antiterrorism laws, while human rights groups double and triple government numbers. Newspapers linked the United States and Morocco's antiterrorist efforts in a macabre fashion when reports announced that detainees held by the United States at Guantánamo Bay as unlawful combatants since January 2002 were transported to a Moroccan secret detention center for questioning under torture.[66] During my interviews in November and December 2003, many Moroccans note their country's lugubrious contribution to the war against terrorism, one in which the international community recognizes Moroccan expertise in torture. Others pinpoint the location of Morocco's newest specialized torture center: the basement of the building belonging to the police forces of the Compagnie d'intervention mobile interurbaine (CIMI) adjacent to a large soccer stadium in the town of Temara outside Rabat.[67]

Between 11 September 2001 and 16 May 2003, the burning question has become: who is juridically covered by the Moroccan penal code, which from its inception under French colonialism incorporated the death penalty, life imprisonment, and extended garde à vue for the crime of "attacks against the internal or external security of the state"? Because Morocco's new antiterrorism laws closely conform in their articulation and procedures to egregious practices of forcible disappearance and secret detention in the recent past, practices in fact never eradicated, the consequences of imprecise or discretionary definitions of what constitutes a "terrorist crime" or a "terrorist" pave the way for a new cycle of torture and arbitrary detention at the same time as those very same practices from Morocco's pre-1999 black years are being discussed, written down, and subject to indemnification.

Chapter 7

Ḥattā lā yatakarraru hādhā: *Never This Again*

In 1990—the year Hassan II created al-Majlis al-Istishārī li-Ḥuqūq al-Insān (Advisory Committee on Human Rights, ACHR), heralding a decade of change in Morocco's history of human rights—Driss Benzekri, a Marxist political prisoner, was serving his sixteenth and penultimate year of incarceration in Kenitra Central Prison. Twelve years later, on 10 December 2002, the fifty-fourth anniversary of the Universal Declaration of Human Rights, Muhammad VI, son and heir of Hassan II, installed Driss Benzekri as secretary-general of the newly reorganized ACHR.[1] Benzekri's personal and professional trajectory represents the movement from a culture of clandestine resistance and political imprisonment to a culture of engagement with Morocco's political and religious establishment. After his release in 1991, Benzekri completed advanced studies abroad in law and human rights, returning to Morocco to assume the secretary-generalship of the nonpartisan nongovernmental Moroccan Organization for Human Rights (OMDH). In 1999 he was elected president of al-Muntadā, the nongovernmental association for Morocco's victims of human rights abuses, a post he relinquished once appointed secretary-general of the ACHR in December 2002. Subsequent to his appointment, Benzekri announced in televised statements the government's human rights projects and plans "to adopt mechanisms in line with global standards of human rights that include civil, political, economic and social rights."[2] The content of those plans and the ways the Moroccan state takes responsibility for past violations in conformity with international laws and national norms were unveiled by the ACHR on 6 November 2003 in the form of a *tawṣiyah* (recommendation) to create Hay'at al-Inṣāf wa-al-Muṣālaḥah (Equity and Reconciliation Commission, ERC), a body to reconsider indemnities, make judgments about reparation, and investigate cases of disappearance, including locations of mass graves.[3] On 14 December 2003, Benzekri himself was

Figure 7.1. "No More of This" poster, Women's March, Rabat. Photo by author.

confirmed as head of the Equity and Reconciliation Commission, presiding over sixteen commissioners, eight drawn from the ACHR plus eight additional nationally recognized experts in law, medicine, and women's rights.[4]

Initial reactions to the second, state-mandated commission are mixed. Many who refused to file claims with the previous 1999 Indemnity Commission are reconsidering. Revised and improved ECR frameworks subordinate monetary payments of *taʿwīḍ* (indemnity) to *jabr al-aḍrār*, the more encompassing and compassionate redress measure of reparation. Item six of the new commission's mandate recommends that the government:

> pursue reparations (*jabr al-aḍrār*) for victims of forcible disappearance and arbitrary detention and to do this by presenting suggestions and recommendations concerning social reintegration (*al-idmāj al-ijtimāʿī*), psychological and medical rehabilitation (*al-taʾmīl al-nafsī wa-al-ṣiḥḥī*) for victims needing this, and to achieve solutions to administrative, professional and legal problems not yet resolved and in regards to requests concerning expropriation.[5]

Groups of human rights activists, lawyers, and former political prisoners, including many of Benzekri's former associates in organizations such as al-Muntadā and the OMDH, voice objections.[6] While promoting a spirit of cooperation with ACHR objectives to disclose the truth about past human rights violations, Morocco's various nongovernmental human rights associations intend to retain their role as independent critics of the governmental process.[7] Impunity, or the Moroccan state's disinclination to prosecute and punish perpetrators, is the point of conflict, so much so that it calls into question the disparate and distinct meanings of reparation understood by victims when confronting the state's remedies. The focus of the Equity and Reconciliation Commission, as with the Indemnity Commission previously, is primarily on real financial measures of compensation and symbolic gestures intended for victims and their families, not prosecution of those responsible. Moreover, strong opposition to the efficacy of any commission is asserted by those who point to continuities between the "black decades" of the past and contemporary government abuses. Moroccan antiterrorism laws, for example, have resulted in arrests and incommunicado detention of Islamists. Security forces operate secretly and with government protection. And retrograde laws of "attacks against the monarchy" have led to prison terms for prominent journalists whose newspaper articles investigate royal family matters.[8] In other words, even as the new commission meets and passes in review of the truths of pre-1999 brutalities, new victims are being created daily by the unchanged, untouchable legal, police, and prison apparatus.

To the charge of allowing perpetrators to go free, Benzekri advances an overarching perspective that acknowledges the stranglehold of Morocco's pervasive culture of impunity:

> Strategies must be put in place for the total eradication [of impunity]. One must also define the meaning of impunity. It is the absence of the rule of law, but

there are other forms of impunity that are not *de jure*. They do not possess legal characteristics. They are about facts. These are forms of clientelism, of public and social politics that encourage breaches, of an environment of laxity in society. It is the distrust of legal norms. We see it everywhere including disregard for the rules of the road. It is a culture that is to be fought over the long term. The ACHR does not encourage impunity. Simply as a proposed procedure, we insist that the ACHR is not meant to substitute for justice. . . .

According to the model of a truth commission [that pursues legal cases], the only ones with recourse to this legal prerogative have applied the Constitution that took measures beforehand in terms of a conflict between protagonists. For a fundamental reason, to preserve national unity, they tried to find a compromise formula where legal pursuit might eventually be made if those formerly responsible do not cooperate in the search for truth. We are not in the same situation, but I imagine as elements of proof, analyses, and reports established by the commission come to light, the state will take decisions that it considers necessary.[9]

To mark the official investiture of the ERC on 8 January 2004, Muhammad VI bestowed awards on the members of the previous 1999 Indemnity Commission and pardoned thirty-three political prisoners. These events are intimately connected. Royal pardons and the ERC function alongside normative state institutions. The king's powers of state in relation to the constitution are enunciated in the first part of article 19 of the Moroccan constitution, which lists the king's absolute prerogatives as "Commander of the Faithful" (*amir al-mu'minīn*):

(1) The King, Commander of the Faithful, Supreme representative of the nation, symbol of its unity and guarantor of the permanence and continuity of the state, ensures the observation of Islam and the constitution. He is the protector of the rights and liberties of the citizens, social groups and collectivities.

(2) He guarantees the independence of the nation and the territorial integrity of the kingdom within its authentic borders.

As a result of article 19, Morocco's constitution has been characterized, according to Driss Benzekri master's thesis, as schizophrenic and internally incoherent, an example of a modern constitution ancillary to, and subverted by, a traditional paradigm.[10] The king is above any separation of powers. As hereditary head of state, he remains the final arbiter because of his political and religious supremacy. Royal pardons effectively emphasize the raw power of the king's extraconstitutional and extrajudicial gestures. Among the political prisoners freed were Belkacem Hakimi and Mustapha Oukil of the Group 26 Islamists (see Chapter 6), both arrested in 1985, on death row from 1985 to 1994, and serving sentences of life imprisonment ended by the royal pardon. Ahmed Saad and Mustapha Khazar, accused of murdering leftist leader Omar Benjelloun in 1975, were also released after twenty-eight years in prison. The cases of incarcerated journalists who personify disputes about freedom of the press—one example is Ali Lmrabet, imprisoned for "offenses against the king"—are resolved by the king.

The Moroccan Equity and Reconciliation Commission is not the South African Truth and Reconciliation Commission. Morocco chooses to circumscribe and define an aspect of justice, one that concentrates on identifying, verifying, and reporting the process of uncovering the truth about arbitrary detention and secret torture sites. In my interviews over the years, it is uncommon to meet a Moroccan activist and his or her family who do not qualify for indemnities as victims of human rights abuses. Absurdly low numbers, for example, the few hundred initially proclaimed by the 1999 Indemnity Commission, have been superseded by a flood of dossiers arriving daily at the ACHR offices in Rabat. What appears as a minimal ERC accomplishment might well prove to be its most powerful legacy: to tabulate the enormous number of Moroccans eligible for reparations.

The hope and the plan are that such victim testimonies will become public and official, acknowledged by government reports. They are recognized as the truths of experience.[11] Consequently, the map of Moroccan torture sites and patterns of torture will be wrenched from the files according to witness testimonies and after the fact. Finally the victim's story will be believed. Reparation, restitution, and reintegration will follow. But administering justice to those who have been victimized does not entail administering justice in the form of pursuing perpetrators through the courts.[12]

Benzekri chooses not to apply for indemnities, reparation, or restitution from the commission he heads.[13] As yet he has published no record of his personal experiences of years of torture, disappearance, and imprisonment.[14] The act of creating available mechanisms for reparation, he observes, is compensation.

Candles

The image on the cover of this book is a painting by Hassan El Bou (Marxist political prisoner, 1974–89). After his release from prison, El Bou completed this watercolor in 1991, part of a new series of joyful and colorful gouaches overlaid with calligraphic flourishes. Although Kenitra Central Prison remains an obsessive theme whether he is in or out of prison, by the early 1990s El Bou had embarked on works reflecting his new hopes for Morocco. He entitles his painting *Shamʿah*, the candle (French, *la bougie*). Against a light green background, red flames burst from a red candle to form a pair of human eyes viewed as a candle in the act of becoming human or a human inflamed. El Bou observes:

It's about light, incomplete and imperfect light, light from bygone times, after my release from prison. It is related to tears of happiness and the understanding of freedom. I put in the face and a person's eyes, because it looks back at us too.[15]

The image of a candle that burns in the darkness has come to be the necessary accompaniment to nighttime vigils, demonstrations, and sit-ins in the public spaces of political activism. The candle is at once the reality and symbol of enlightenment and illumination. Peter Benenson, founder of Amnesty International, describes his organization's famous logo of a burning candle encircled by barbed wire as

the candle [that] burns not for us, but for all those whom we failed to rescue from prison, who have died in prison, who were shot on the way to prison, who were tortured, who were kidnapped, who "disappeared." That's what the candle is for . . . I have lit this candle today, in the words of Shakespeare, "against oblivion"—so that the forgotten prisoners should always be remembered.[16]

The image came to him, claims Benenson, as he thought about the famous Chinese proverb, "Better to light a candle than curse the darkness."[17] On 10 December 1961, to commemorate the thirteenth anniversary of the Universal Declaration of Human Rights, the founders of Amnesty International staged a performance with a candle as its leitmotif:

The most dramatic part of the commemoration occurred at St. Martin's in the Fields church, where Benenson had meditated on the Portuguese students about a year before. Handcuffed, with a cord linking the handcuffs, Calypso singer Cy Grant and actor Julie Christie walked solemnly into church. The amnesty candle was used to burn through the cord freeing the "prisoners." After the ceremony, former prisoners of conscience living in exile in Britain kept vigil over the candle.[18]

At occasions devoted to human rights, Moroccan activists frequently sing a *malḥūn* (a traditional song-poem in vernacular Moroccan Arabic) whose title *Shamʿah* (candle) prominently places the burning candle at center stage for Morocco's performance of human rights. Candles are present as actual objects of illumination or in song. In November 1999, a silent protest against a ceremonial government tea honoring the decades-long career of minister of the interior Driss Basri included Moroccan human rights activists lighting candles and holding signs as they surrounded the home of Prime Minister Abderrahman Youssefi. Candles lined the stage of the Hay Mohammedi Cultural Center as women testified about their disappearance and torture. Commemorative occasions to memorialize the deaths of political prisoners close with a singing of *Shamʿah.*

Shamʿah was composed by Mohamed Cherif Ben Ali, known by the name of Ould Arzine (1742–1822), a musician of Fez. In the 1970s his song, along with other examples of Morocco's rich musical heritage, was recorded and released by Jil Jilala, a musical group that was part of a wave of Moroccan musicians emerging from Casablanca's poor neighborhoods who married rock-and-roll and protest music to popular and traditional Moroccan words and rhythms.[19] *Shamʿah* opens with an interlocutor who begs the candle to answer his questions:

Why, O candle, do you weep all through the night?
What is wrong with you that you must cry every night?
Why do you spend the night as long as it is dark, giving light? What has happened to you, you who became so weak from so much crying?[20]

The poem's conceit is a candle whose "tears" of dripping wax generously serve to shed light even though copious tears are visible signs of misery. Why, the singer wonders, does the candle weep in front of friends and enemies, yet paradoxically its diminishing flame and melting shape attest to the strength of the fire within? Were the candle to possess a body or a mouth, it would write in its language and tell its story:

Complain to me without fear about what is inside you
And tell your story, I am listening to you
While I, with my story, I go beyond and add to yours

A teller and a listener, each one narrates a tale of woe. The candle is fearfully silent, although the Moroccan singer pleads for its story (*qiṣṣah*). The pain of the candle manifests itself by burning down, an act of self-immolation, while the Moroccan singer's account promises to surpass all known torments and sorrows. When the song is heard during public performances, sit-ins, and testimonials, it is as if the Moroccan candle helps to shed light on the enormity of human rights violations during the country's post-independence history by illuminating those occasions where history and memory, objective narration and witness testimony, overlap and sustain each other. The candle of the poem stands for the pain at the heart of speaking about suffering. The candle weeps, but does not, perhaps cannot speak. Its tears must be translated into words at every stage. The difficulty of recognizing and acknowledging past experiences of pain are incidentally the subjects of this study; rather the focus is on its human expression in writing, painting, and performance by those Moroccan singers and tellers who affirm that they can share, confirm, and speak on their own behalf about human rights abuses. At stake is the representation of the memory of pain and the complexities of going beyond what has been produced on behalf of all Moroccan victims by the most vocal profiled here, the activists who inhabit the coastal urban agglomeration of Casablanca-Rabat-Kenitra.

To talk about torture is to turn oneself into what poet and political prisoner Abdellatif Laabi labels a "statistician of sorrows" in *L'oeil et la nuit*, his tale of prison-like hospitals and world-destroying fires whose recurrent motifs of death and confinement yield "witness-bodies" (*le corps du témoin*) and "memory-bodies" (*mémoire-corps*) as countervailing forces to the surrounding evil.[21] Laabi's only hope is "the cry" (*le cri*), an excess of words that signals rebellion, change, finding one's voice and producing texts:

> The cry is a stampede, a rhythm to move forward. . . . The people do not move forward. It is the cry that moves forward. . . . The cry becomes an orator and shows off a large white paper on which a bloodied head will trace shame and revolt. . . . I must absolutely cry out. That will save me. Crying out, crying out until I rediscover my voice or else grab a piece of flesh and bite until it comes off.[22]

Written indemnity file applications and the oral testimonies narrated at numerous commemoration activities organized for and by the victims are available: the National Day of the Disappeared (29 October 1999), memorialized with a press conference of testimonies by the "disappeared" of Tazmamart, the Sahrawi groups, and the Bnouhachem group (Figure 7.2), followed by demonstrations in front of Parliament; the commemoration of the twenty-fifth anniversary of death under torture of Abdellatif Zeroual in the first public ceremony, 14 November 1999; on 11 December 1999, the twenty-second anniversary of the death from hunger strike of Saida Menebhi. Political prisoners believe in and have initiated innovative public performance practices to memorialize victims in celebrations, literature, museums, and school programs as part of declared objectives to seek the truth about the "years of lead" in order to "preserve the memory of the Moroc-

Figure 7.2. Torture testimony by Abdennaceur Bnouhachem, Rabat, 6 June 2000. Photo by author.

can people during more than forty years by speaking and writing about our past on the basis of the law."[23]

With this study, the crucial presence of those who speak and write back to tyranny, whether colonial imports or homegrown varieties, is respected. No encompassing historical narrative—let alone a legal one—has been articulated by Moroccans and to Moroccans to account for the "years of lead." Perhaps this is why positive changes in current Moroccan law (as well as reversals in the newer antiterrorism laws) are meaningfully, consciously, and prescriptively linked to Morocco's overcoming a history of past crimes against its citizens. The post-Hassan II world that Moroccan citizens now inhabit is made livable by new narratives, voices, and organizations. Principles of the rule of law are as yet not wholly constitutive of Moroccan legal procedure and practice, although many are "on the books." In the absence of legal remedies to overcome the repressive past, Moroccans confabulate, fabricate, and narrate coherent meanings through many discursive configurations: journalism, correspondence, memoirs, testimonials, reparation commissions, and rituals that remain open-ended and unfinished while there is no foreseeable legal closure.

Human rights groups such as al-Muntadā, the Moroccan AMDH, and the OMDH are part of a large social movement. While one purpose of this study is to translate and make known this particular historical record, it must be emphasized that all those who agreed to be interviewed and photographed because of their human rights activism do so not merely to establish what happened or even to prevent a rewriting and effacing of history. Their immediate goals are to bring those responsible to court, to create an independent truth commission, to release all incarcerated political prisoners, and to find the bodies of each disappeared.

Not all human rights activists endorse a Western-style democracy for Morocco. Favored is the concept of *inṣāf*, defined variously as equity, equality, and egalitarianism, and shared in the names of the nongovernmental victims' association, al-Muntadā al-Maghribī min Ajl al-Ḥaqīqah wa-al-Inṣāf, and the government ERC, Hay'at al-Inṣāf wa-al-Muṣālaḥah. Inṣāf resonates as both a social and religious contract to embrace equality in standards of living as well as before the law. The state is perceived as maintaining equality, even though it is unclear what kind of state could do so for all Moroccans: republican democracy? constitutional monarchy? Islamic theocracy? Proponents of a Moroccan republic or a constitutional monarchy insist that the new king and the new era will not function as a modern society trying to evolve toward democracy unless there is a public and juridical reckoning with the past. What has been accomplished so far is to put the history of repression at the center of the story of Morocco. This study ends in January 2004 as the Equity and Reconciliation Commission embarks on protocols and sets hearing dates beginning in 2004 to document this history of repression.

Despite years of violence, setbacks, and small advances in human rights, the heroic narrator that emerges is the voice of the nonviolent, stubborn dissident. The human face in Hassan El Bou's painting is the performer at the center of the tale-telling circle, the ḥalqah. Looking closely, the viewer also sees that the color relations of the Moroccan flag—a five-pointed linear green star against a solid red background—are reversed. Instead El Bou draws red lines awash in green and set against a green background, as if to suggest in painterly fashion the oppositional themes and reversals graphically expressed in his poem sent to his mother from Kenitra Central Prison:

> I blocked blows by my body, insults by my silence, humiliation by my indifference.
> I blocked ropes by my senses, isolation by my dreams, and threats by my life force.
> I blocked off the digging into my past by my youth, the rape of my innermost being by my modesty, the theft of my memory by my forgetting.
> I believed myself weak and here am I strong. I believed myself fissured with cracks and here am I whole.[24]

Notes

Introduction

1. Sion Assidon, correspondence with Deborah Kaufman, Group 30, Amnesty International, San Francisco, reproduced by written permission of Sion Assidon. I was first introduced through letters to Assidon in 1978 when I was a graduate student at Berkeley. I thank Sion Assidon and Deborah Kaufman for copies and permission to quote. Assidon was arrested for membership in Li-nakhduma al-shaʿab (in French, Servir le peuple), To Serve the People, a Marxist group. Although released from prison in 1984, he was deprived of his passport and right to travel until 1992. In the summer of 1993, Deborah Kaufman handed Assidon his letters and Amnesty International file on his first visit to San Francisco. Noteworthy examples of AI and Kaufman's efforts to publicize Assidon's case resulted in "From the Editors," *MERIP/Middle East Reports* 90 (September 1980): 2, and Hon. Tom Harkin, "A Pardon for Sion Assidon," *Congressional Record* Extensions of Remarks (23 April 1980): E 2009. Assidon is the founder of the Morocco branch of Transparency International, a nongovernmental organization that monitors corruption. See www.transparencymaroc.org.

2. The widespread Moroccan term, *les années de plomb*, echoes the Italian *anni di piombo*. Italy's "years of lead" are dated from 1969, when a bomb exploded in Milan killing 16 and injuring 84. Leftist anarchists were accused, but subsequent research assigns blame to neo-fascist groups colluding with the Italian secret services. See Paul Ginsborg, *A History of Contemporary Italy: Society and Politics, 1943–1988* (New York: Penguin, 1990), 379–87.

3. Aziz El Ouadie, "Du jamais lu: La revue du détenu," *Libération* (25–26 May 1996): 3.

4. "Le sens de la reclusion," *Libération* (25–26 May 1996): 3.

5. Elaine Scarry, *The Body in Pain: The Making and Unmaking of the World* (New York: Oxford University Press, 1985), 3.

6. Notable for disseminating Palestinian poetry in Morocco is Abdellatif Laabi, poet, novelist, political prisoner, translator, and founding editor of *Souffles/Anfās*, an influential Moroccan literary and cultural journal. See Laabi, *La poésie palestinienne de combat* (Honfleur: Oswald, 1970), and special issue number 15 of *Souffles/Anfās* on the Palestinian revolution (1969). Political prisoners Aziz and Salah El Ouadie cite prison writings by Mu'in Bseiso (Palestine), Abderrahman Munif (Saudi Arabia), and Sheriff Hetata (Egypt), interview, Casablanca, 4 August 1999.

7. Carolyn Forché, *Against Forgetting: Twentieth-Century Poetry of Witness* (New York: W.W. Norton, 1993), 31.

8. See Barbara Harlow, *Resistance Literature* (New York: Methuen, 1987), 2–3, and also Harlow, *Barred: Women, Writing, and Detention* (Middletown, Conn.: Wesleyan University Press, 1992), esp. p. 13, where Harlow argues: "'resistance literature' (*adab al-muqāwamah*) is being historically rewritten as 'prison literature' (*adab al-sujūn*)." Literary critic Hussein Kadhim traces the first use of the term "literature of resistance" to a Rome conference held 16–20 October 1961 and articulated by Jordanian writer ʿĪsā al-Nāʿūrī; see Hussein Kadhim, *The Poetics of Anti-Colonialism in the Arabic Qaṣīdah* (Leiden: Brill, 2004), viii.

9. See this theme first presented in my *The Object of Memory: Arab and Jew Narrate the Palestinian Village* (Philadelphia: University of Pennsylvania Press, 1998), 182–83.

10. Qur'an 12: 32–33, 35. English translation is Abdullah Yusuf Ali, *The Holy Quran: Text, Translation and Commentary* (New York: Hafner, 1946).

11. See Wāḍiḥ Ṣamad, *al-Sujūn wa-atharuhā fī al-adab al-ʿArabiyah* (Prison and its influence on Arabic literature)(Beirut: al-Mu'assasah al-Jāmiʿīyah lil-Dirasāt wa-al-Nashr wa-al-Tawzīʿ, 1995).

12. Mohamed Choukri, *For Bread Alone* (London: P. Owen, 1973), 126. al-Shābbī's verses, quoted by Choukri, are from "Irādat al-ḥayāh" (Desire of life), in *ʿAghāni al-ḥayāh* (Songs of life) available in the poet's *Works* (Tunis: Dār al-Maghrib al-ʿArabī, 1994), 1: 231. Selected verses also appear outside Nazareth's city hall, placed there by Palestinian poet Tawfiq Zayyad, and attest to the circulation of literary Arabic texts from North Africa to Palestine.

13. A newspaper interview with the head of Morocco's Sochepress confirms that copies could not be distributed by order of the secret service, Direction générale de la sûreté nationale (DGSN). Hassan Nejmi, head of the Union of Moroccan Writers, claims that the Ministry of Communication denies any such interdiction. See S. Afoulous, "Mais, qui a interdit Choukri?!" *L'Opinion* (19 November 1999): 6. Tahar Ben Jelloun's preface to his French translation states: "It is more serious to write about misery than to live it! Publishing in the Arab world is above all conformist and commercial. In any case [Choukri] has not found a single editor who has the courage and audacity to publish this book where the truth of experience is subversive and revolutionary. Censorship is already internalized." Mohamed Choukri, *Le pain nu* (Paris: Maspero, 1980): 9.

14. The history of Abdelaziz Mouride's cartoon book is chronicled in Ahmed R. Benchemsi, "Dessine-moi l'horreur," *Jeune Afrique/L'Intelligent* (23–29 May 2000): 34–37. It began as sheets smuggled to France published in 1981 by the Comité de lutte contre la répression au Maroc; see book publicity in "Bande dessinée," *Bulletin* 31 (April 1981): 1. The updated French-language edition is *On affame bien les rats!* (Casablanca: Tarik, 2000).

15. Quoted in Mary Ann Glendon, *A World Made New: Eleanor Roosevelt and the Universal Declaration of Human Rights* (New York: Random House, 2001), 239–40.

16. This thesis is richly developed by Harlow in *Barred.*

17. "Morocco," *Critique* (May 1985): 67–69.

18. The "political terror scale," for example, rates human rights violations (torture, disappearance, etc.) on a scale of 1 to 5, as discussed in Todd Landman, "Comparative Politics and Human Rights," *Human Rights Working Papers* 10 (2000): 1–40, available at www.du.edu/humanrights/workingpapers/papers.htm.

19. Deborah A. Kapchan, "Performance," *Journal of American Folkore* 108 (1995): 479.

20. Kapchan, "Performance," 479.

21. Kapchan, "Performance," 485–86.

22. Abdelkrim Berrechid, *Ḥudūd al-kāʿin wa-al-mumkin fī al-masraḥ al-iḥtifālī* (Boundaries of being and possibility in festive theater) (Casablanca: Dār al-Thaqāfah, 1985), 29–30, and esp. 166, where Berrechid points to traditional authentic Moroccan sources for the modern Moroccan "festive theater" derived from both the *ḥalqah* and the Sultan al-Tolbah (carnivalesque student processions held in Fez that reversed and mocked student-teacher roles).

23. See my " 'To Put One's Fingers in the Bleeding Wound': Palestinian Theatre Under Israeli Censorship," *Drama Review* (1991): 18–38.

24. Although a comprehensive history of Ilā al-Amām is lacking, relevant works about the 1970s leftist movements are Abdelkader Chaoui, *al-Yasār fī al-Maghrib, 1970–1974* (The Left in Morocco)(Rabat: Manshūrat ʿAli al-ʿAql, 1992) and Mostefa Bouaziz, "Introduction à l'étude du mouvement marxiste-leniniste marocain (1985–1974)" (DEU, Écoles des Hautes Études en Science Sociale, Paris, 1981). Information on the split is from interviews with Ahmed Herzenni (member of B but arrested before 1972 split, yet identified himself with Li-nakhduma al-shaʿb), and Hasan Semlali (arrested in 1974 as a member of "23 March Movement"), Rabat, 17 September 1999.

25. Driss Benzekri, "Poésie berbère de résistance dans les années trentes" (DEA, Université de Marseilles, Aix-en-Provence, 1987), supervised by Salem Chaker and "The Status of International Law in the Moroccan Legal System: Domestic Applicability and the Attitudes of National Courts" (LLM, University of Essex, 1997), supervised by Nigel S. Rodley.

26. The OMDH group on torture included Rabia Mardi and Muhammad Leghtas. Interviews were conducted in Khenifra (Middle Atlas) and Rachidiya, Tinghir, and Ouarzazate (High Atlas) and reported in the special issue on torture of *Al Karama* 4 (June 1999).

27. Interview with Driss Benzekri, Rabat, 17 June 1997.

28. Interview with Salah El Ouadie, Casablanca, 4 August 1999.

29. Benzekri interview, Rabat.

30. Paul Schiff Berman, "The Globalization of Jurisdiction," *University of Pennsylvania Law Review* 151 (2002): 506–12.

Chapter 1. Law and Custom

1. On the processes leading to the king's prominent role, see Hassan Rachik, *Symbole et nation* (Casablanca: Le Fennec, 2003), 96–116. Clifford Geertz famously

noted that had Morocco achieved independence during the 1930 uprisings, it would have abolished the monarchy in favor of third world secular-nationalist leaders such as Sukarno. Clifford Geertz, *Islam Observed: Religious Development in Morocco and Indonesia* (Chicago: University of Chicago Press, 1968), 80, quoted by Rachik, 96.

2. Throne speech of 30 July 1999 available at www.mincom.gov.ma/french/generalites/samajeste/mohammedVI/discours/1999/trone9 9.htm and published as "Premier discours du trône," *Le Matin du Sahara et du Maghreb* (1 August 1999): 1.

3. Three years after independence from France, Morocco enacted a new "Code of Penal Procedure" according to dahir no. 1–58–261 of 10 February 1959, published in *Bulletin Officiel* no. 2418 on 5 March 1959, and since amended. All subsequent references to Morocco's Code of Penal Procedure are from *Code de procédure pénale: Mésures transitoires en matière de procédure pénale, extradition* (Rabat: Publications de la Revue Marocaine d'Administration Locale et de Développement, 1997). All subsequent references to published decrees are from *Bulletins Officiels du Royaume du Maroc* (electronic resource), Casablanca: Artémis Conseil, CD-ROM version of *Bulletin Officiel*, based on Ed. no 10, covering 1912–2003.

4. According to Abdelaziz Nouaydi, Hassan II was moved to create the Advisory Committee on Human Rights (ACHR) in 1990 under pressure from several Amnesty International reports detailing torture practices during garde à vue detention: Abdelaziz Nouaydi, "Elite and Transition to Democracy in Morocco: The Example of the Advisory Council of Human Rights," paper presented at the Middle East Studies Association annual meeting, Washington, D.C., 16–19 November 2000.

5. Miloud Hamdouchi, *La régime juridique de l'enquête policière: Étude critique* (Casablanca: Editions Maghrébines, 1999), 11.

6. See, for example, U.S. State Department, *Morocco Report on Human Rights Practices for 1996* (released by the Bureau of Democracy, Human Rights, and Labor, 30 January 1997) and subsequent reports.

7. On habeas corpus documents, see works by Zachariah Chafee, *Documents on Fundamental Human Rights* (Cambridge, Mass.: Harvard University Press, 1951), second pamphlet, and "The Most Important Right in the Constitution," *Boston University Law Review* 32 (April 1952): 143–61.

8. Chafee, *Documents*, 306–40.

9. William Rawle, *A View of the Constitution of the United States* (Philadelphia: P.H. Nicklin, 1829), 117–19. Habeas corpus is incorporated in many Latin American legal systems, where it is called *amparo*, and also in other national legal systems (e.g., India, the Philippines, and Uzbekistan). Late twentieth-century histories of human rights abuses by Latin American regimes, such as Argentina and Chile, prove that amparo on the books does not guarantee that a person once arrested appears in any court of law.

10. Abdelaziz Nouaydi, "The Right to a Fair Trial in the Moroccan Criminal Procedure," in *The Right to a Fair Trial*, ed. David Weissbrod and Rudiger Wolfrum (Berlin: Springer, 1998), 173.

11. Hamdouchi, *La régime juridique*, 22, n. 19.

12. Mohammed-Jalal Essaid, *La présomption d'innocence* (Rabat: Éditions La Porte, 1971), 334, esp. n. 57.

13. See, for example, Amnesty International, *Report of an Amnesty Interna-*

tional Mission to the Kingdom of Morocco, 10–13 February, 1981 (London: Amnesty International Publications, 1982). Also since 1962, by common consent of political parties, the Ministry of Interior, responsible for police, prisons, and internal and external security, has been the preserve of the monarch, who is, in any event, superior to the constitution, and can suspend it, according to article 35, as happened in 1965.

14. See reports by the Fédération internationale des ligues des droits de l'Homme, available at www.fidh.org/communiq/2003.

15. See Mohieddine Amzazi, "National: Monographs: Morocco," in *International Encyclopaedia of Laws, Criminal Law*, ed. Lieven Dupont and Cyrille Fijnault (The Hague: Kluwer International, 1997), 3: 1–184, esp. the section on rules of evidence, 119–21.

16. Amzazi, 120.

17. Hamdouchi, *La régime juridique de l'enquête policière*, 51. On p. 45, nn. 76, 77, Hamdouchi notes that written police reports in the Islamic world predate fourteenth-century French procès-verbal; he cites texts concerned with the duties of the police to take down written reports by the fourteenth century Malikite judge Aḥmad ibn Yaḥyā Abū al-ʿAbbās al-Tilimsānī, called al-Wansharīsī. French translation is *Le livre de la magistrature* (Rabat: Felix Moncho 1937), 13.

18. See articles 660–662 of the Code of Penal Procedure for fine amounts. For a discussion of articles 225–32 of the Penal Code and articles 266–270 of the Code of Penal Procedure on abuses by authority, see M. A. Benseghir, "La liberté individuelle, les fonctionnaires publics et le droit penal," *Revue marocaine de droit et d'économie du développement* 29 (1993): 77–113.

19. *Case of Selmouni v. France* (Application no. 25803/94), European Court of Human Rights, 28 July 1999, available at http://hudoc.echr.coe.int/Hudoc2doc2/HEJUD/200109/Selmouni%20-%20batj.do. The court ruled that French police in the Paris-Bobigny station tortured (anal rape with a police truncheon, beatings, excessive length of detention) Ahmed Selmouni, a Moroccan of Dutch nationality accused of drug trafficking. Selmouni was awarded extensive payments for personal injury and damages.

20. Cécile Prieur, "La réforme de la garde à vue soulève l'opposition des policiers," *Le Monde* (1 March 2000): 12.

21. See article 142, Code of Penal Procedure.

22. Nouaydi, "The Right to a Fair Trial," 176.

23. Nouaydi, 178. Defendants are, however, sometimes released on their own recognizance. Under a separate code of military justice, military authorities may detain members of the military without warrants or public trial.

24. Craig M. Bradley, "Overview," in *Criminal Procedure: A Worldwide Study*, ed. Craig M. Bradley (Durham: N.C.: Carolina Academic Press, 1999), xv. Bradley describes the accusatorial or common law that "starts with a police investigation that is openly not neutral but rather, at least after it has focused on a suspect, is aimed at collecting evidence that will prove his guilt. Then an adversarial trial is held before a neutral decision maker, judge or jury, with no prior knowledge of the case, and no dossier . . . The attorneys conduct the trial, with each side attempting to convince the decision maker of the rectitude of her position" (xv).

25. Amzazi, 25.

26. Interview with Fatna El Bouih, Casablanca, 3 October 1999.

27. Benameur stresses the continuity of social and political structures rooted in the early years of independence that continue to exist within the contemporary Moroccan monarchy. See Abderrahman Benameur, "Quelques remarques sur la détention politique," *Attadamoun* 2 (February 1982): 3–4; Arabic version: Benameur, "Man huwa al-muʿtaqal al-siyāsī?" (What is a political detainee?), *al-Taḍāmun* 3 (February 1983): 8–9.

28. Interview with Mohamed Karam, Casablanca, 25 September 1999. See also Mohammed Abed al-Jabri, *Positions: Témoignages et mises en lumière* (Tetouan: Centre de Recherche et de Coordination Scientifique, 2003), 23–34. M. Abed al-Jabri's book is part of a series that recounts his testimony of historical events. Of interest is the description of his transfer during the 1963 arrests targeting members of the political party, Union Nationale des Forces Populaires (UNFP), from Derb Moulay Cherif, then a mere police station, to Rabat where the real torture center was located.

29. According to Driss Benzekri, the term "human rights" was not part of Morocco's official rhetoric until 1990; see his "The Status of International Law in the Moroccan Legal System: Domestic Applicability and the Attitudes of National Courts" (LLM, University of Essex, 1997), 7.

30. Interview with Mohamed Karam, Casablanca, 3 November 1999. For excellent histories about Morocco's human rights movement, see Susan E. Waltz, *Human Rights and Reform: Changing the Face of North African Politics* (Berkeley: University of California Press, 1995); Marguerite Rollinde, *Le mouvement marocain des droits de l'Homme: Entre consensus national et engagement citoyen* (Paris: Karthala: 2002); and Mohamed Karem, "La notion des droits de l'Homme au Maghreb" (Ph.D. dissertation, Université d'Aix-Marseille, 1991). See also Khaled Naciri, "Le droit constitutionnel marocain ou la maturation progressive d'un système évolutif," in *Les constitutions des pays arabes, colloque de Beyrouth* (Brussels: E. Bruylant, 1999), 109–26.

31. The Advisory Committee on Human Rights (ACHR) is also translated in many texts as the Consultative Council on Human Rights (CCHR). The final text is found in dahir no. 1–00–350 of 10 April 2001, published in *Bulletin Officiel* no. 4926 of 16 August 2001.

In the speech to celebrate the establishment of the ACHR, Hassan II claims the Moroccan ACHR is a copy of the French, point for point. See Mohamed-Jelal Essaid, "Le conseil consultative des droits de l'Homme: Representations des courants politiques au sein du CCDH," in *Le Maroc et les droits de l'Homme*, 409–48.

32. The Institut Médico-Légal, established in Casablanca in September 1999, became the first site to perform autopsies. Mokhtar Ghailani, "Morts suspectes," *Libération* (9 December 1999): 1, 6.

33. I thank Abdelaziz Nouaydi, professor of law, Mohamed V University, Rabat, Morocco for providing me with the English language text in his "Elite and Transformation to Democracy in Morocco: The Example of the Advisory Council of Human Rights," lecture delivered at the Middle East Studies Association 34th annual meeting, 16–19 November 2000, Orlando, Florida.

34. See "Création d'une commission d'arbitrage indépendante," *Le Matin du Sahara et du Maghreb* (17 August 1999): 1. Date of commission's expiration is the 23 Ramadan, 1420, Article 13, Internal rules (Règlement intérieur de la Commission). The first hearings began 11 November, 1999.

35. English translation from the website of the Kingdom of Morocco, Human Rights Advisory Council (not committee) prefers "Independent Arbitration Board of Compensation for the Damages Suffered by People Who Disappeared or Suffered Arbitrary Imprisonment."

36. Human Rights Watch, "The Pinochet Precedent: How Victims Can Pursue Human Rights Criminals Abroad," available at www.hrw.org/campaigns/chile98/precedent.htm.

37. I thank Mohammed El Battiui for sending me photocopies of his deposition, "Maroc: une plainte devait etre déposé," *Le Monde* (17 November, 1999): 5. In 2003, in response to international political pressure, notably by the United States, Belgium introduced modifications restricting its "law on universal competence" to Belgian citizens, which El Battiui is. El Battiui informs me that absent is "one condition: Driss Basri must be on Belgian soil to be judged," email correspondence, 10 March 2004.

38. J. Deprez, "Pérennité de l'Islam dans l'ordre juridique au Maghreb," in *Islam et politique au Maghreb*, ed. Ernest Gellner and Jean-Claude Vatin (Paris: CNRS, 1981), 315–53.

39. For the effect of the French decrees on colonial Morocco, see Paul Buttin, *Le drame du Maroc* (Paris: Editions de Cerf, 1955). Codes are available in François-Paul Blanc and Rabha Zeidguy, *Les libertés publiques en droit marocain* (Casablanca: Sochepress, 1995).

40. Article 179, Moroccan Penal Code, calls for one to five years of prison (and fines from 200 to 1,000 dirhams) for offenses against the royal family. For example, Mohamed Loukah, a teacher in Berkane, northwest Morocco, was arrested on 27 September 2002 for "offenses against the monarch" and sentenced by the Berkane Court of First Instance to one year in prison and fined 500 dirhams for claiming during the 2002 electoral campaign that Morocco was a dictatorship and calling for a "parliamentary monarchy where the king reigns but does not govern." Currently free on bail, Loukah is appealing his sentence, see "Bavure judiciaire," *Le Journal* (6–13 January 2003).

41. Kingdom of Morocco, Ministry of Communication website, "The Constitution adopted on September 13, 1996," available at www.mincom.gov.ma/english/generalities/state_st/constitution.htm.

42. Abdelaziz Benzakour, "Intervention lors du seminaire de la Fédération Internationale des Droits de l'Homme," Casablanca, 4–8 January 2001, 13 ms. pages, see p. 8. To recategorize past history is fundamental to government reparations programs. The 1995 speech of French President Jacques Chirac "acknowledg[ing] that Vichy represented the French state and supported the Nazi occupiers' 'criminal folly'" was necessary before compensating French victims. See "Kin of Nazi Victims to Be Paid: France Announces Compensation Plan," *Boston Globe* (7 September 2003): A 13.

43. Quoted from the Brazilian report on military regime torture between

1964–79: "Everywhere in the world, the issue of political repression is almost always brought to public notice by the denunciations of victims or reports written by organizations dedicated to the defense of human rights. Whether emotional or well balanced, these testimonies help reveal a hidden history," Archdiocese of São Paulo, *Torture in Brazil: A Shocking Report on the Pervasive Use of Torture by Brazilian Military Governments, 1964–1979* (Austin: University of Texas Press, 1985), 4.

44. For example, the question of what is appropriate compensation is raised by Nigel S. Rodley, "The International Legal Consequences of Torture, Extra-Legal Execution, and Disappearance," in *New Directions in Human Rights*, ed. Ellen L. Lutz, Hurst Hannum, and Kathryn L. Burke (Philadelphia: University of Pennsylvania Press, 1989), 167–94; and Libby Tata Arcel, Mi Christiansen, and Eric Roque, "Reparation for Victims of Torture: Some Definitions and Questions," *Torture* 10 (2000): 89–91. For problems on taking the Holocaust as standard and model for reparations especially in postcolonial contexts, see John Torpey, "'Making Whole What Has Been Smashed': Reflections on Reparations," *Journal of Modern History* 73 (2001): 333–58.

45. Moroccan newspapers published individual testimonies by torture victims of Archane. See, for example, Aboubakr Jamai, "Brahim Hallaoui: 'Archane m'a torturé,'" *Le Journal* (20–26 November 1999): 11. In 1999, the Moroccan Association for Human Rights (AMDH) issued a press release listing Archane's name among Morocco's known torturers. Articles by Ahmed Jaouhar, a political prisoner who names Archane as his torturer, are included in the 4–10 January 1999 issue of the Arabic-language weekly *al-Ṣaḥīfah*. They are preceded by an interview and cover story in which Archane denies all such charges. Archane, disputing the accusations, successfully sued journalist Narjis Rerhaye of the francophone daily *L'Opinion*. The Moroccan court ruled in favor of Archane and ordered Rerhaye to pay Archane one dirham (approximately 10 cents) in symbolic damages.

46. See my "A Truth Commission for Morocco," *MERIP/Middle East Reports* 218 (2001): 18–21.

47. Ronald W. Zweig, *German Reparations and the Jewish World: A History of the Claims Conference* (London: Frank Cass, 2001), 17.

48. United States Department of Justice, Foreign Claims Settlement Commission, "German Compensation for National Socialist Crimes," 6 March 1996, reprinted in Roy L. Brooks, *When Sorry Isn't Enough: The Controversy over Apologies and Reparations for Human Injustice* (New York: New York University Press, 1999), 61–67.

49. Brooks, "The Age of Apology," *When Sorry Isn't Enough*, 3–11.

50. Priscilla Hayner, *Unspeakable Truths: Facing the Challenge of Truth Commissions* (New York: Routledge, 2002), 171.

51. Hayner, 170–82.

52. In 1993, Theo van Boven's report, "The Right to Restitution, Compensation and Rehabilitation for Victims of Gross Violations of Human Rights and Fundamental Freedoms," U.N. Doc. E/CN.4/SUB.2/1993/8, followed by his "Draft Basic Principles and Guidelines on the Right to Reparation for Victims of Gross Violations of Human Rights and Humanitarian Law," U.N. Doc. E/CN.4/1997/64, discuss the obligation to pay reparation and "as a consequence of this obligation, the States

must prevent, investigate, and punish any violations of the rights recognised by the Convention." Louis Joinet's 1997 "The Question of the Impunity of Perpetrators of Human Rights Violations," principle 36, U.N. Doc. E/CN.4/SUB.2/1997/20, asserts that violations of human rights give rise to the right to reparation owed to the victim by the state, a right that forces the state to create possibilities for redress from the perpetrator. The report of Cherif Bassiouni, "Final Report of the special Rapporteur, Professor M. Cherif Bassiouni submitted in accordance with Commission resolution 1999/33," U.N. Doc. E/CN.4/2000/62, reiterates "the obligation to respect, and to see that human rights are respected imposes the obligation on States to take appropriate legislative and administrative measures in order to prevent violations (Art. 3(a) and to ensure reparation for victims (Art. 3(e)."

53. See Priscilla B. Hayner, "Fifteen Truth Commissions—1974–1994: A Comparative Study," *Human Rights Quarterly* 16 (1994): 597–655.

54. The 1971 Marrakesh trials were a legal watershed. Morocco's Supreme Court ruled that unlimited garde à vue is permitted in state security cases ("atteinte à la sûreté de l'État").

55. See M'barek Bensalem Afid, "Shahādah," in al-Muntadā, *Shahādāt ʿan al-taʿdhīb* (Testimony About Torture) (Casablanca: al-Muntadā, 2002), 11–13.

56. Driss Benzekri, "The Status of International Law in the Moroccan Legal System: Domestic Applicability and the Attitudes of National Courts" (LLM, University of Essex, 1998), 59–60.

57. Kingdom of Morocco, Ministry of Communication website, "The Constitution adopted on September 13, 1996," available at www.mincom.gov.ma/english/generalities/state_st/constitution.htm.

58. Even though Pinochet was eventually released for reasons of health, the legitimacy of universal jurisdiction and the pursuit of Pinochet were confirmed by Great Britain's House of Lords in *R v. Bow Street Metropolitan Stipendiary Magistrate and Others, ex parte Pinochet Ugarte* (1999) 2 ALL ER 97.

59. *Filartiga v. Peña-Irala*, 630 F. 2d 876 (C.A., 2d Cir. 1980). Americo Norberto Peña-Irala was discovered by the Filartiga family while he was detained in the U.S. awaiting deportation. When Peña-Irala was police chief in Asuncion, Paraguay, he was accused by the Filartiga family of torturing to death seventeen-year-old Joel Filartiga in retaliation for his father's antigovernment and political activities. Peña-Irala was tried under the Alien Tort Claims Act (ATCA), 28 U.S.C. 1350, but was deported to Paraguay before damages were collected.

60. See "Inter-American Court of Human Rights, San José, Judgment of 21 July 1989—*Velásquez Rodríguez* Case, Compensatory Damages," *Human Rights Law Journal* 11 (1990): 129.

61. Interview with Houria Esslami, Casablanca, 20 November 1999. Webpage for Mohamed Esslami: www.maghreb-ddh.sgdg.org/temoignages/esslami.html.

62. Fédération Internationale des Ligues des Droits de l'Homme (FIDH), *Rapport: Les disparitions forcées au Maroc: Répondre aux exigences de vérité et de justice* 298 (November 2000), 1–115, 9.

63. Interview with Fatna El Bouih, and "Pathways to Human Rights in Morocco," lecture delivered at the Massachusetts Institute of Technology, 13 March

2001. On Fatna El Bouih, see my "This Time I Choose When to Leave: An Interview with Fatna El Bouih," *MERIP/Middle East Reports* 218 (2001): 42–43.

64. Interview with Khadija Rouissi, Casablanca, 7 March 2000.

65. [Rahhal, pseud.], *Fī ʻaḥshāʼ baladī* (In the bowels of my country) (Paris: n.p., 1982); Abdelaziz Mouride, *On affame bien les rats!* (They starve rats, don't they?) (Paris-Casablanca: Tarik, 2000).

66. For an account of the 1977 Casablanca trial, see Comité de lutte contre la répression, *Le Maroc des procès* (Paris: Comité de lutte contre la repression, 1977).

67. Mouride, *On affame bien les rats!* 31. On Mouride and the post-Hassan II emergence of political prison writings, see my review of "Malika Oufkir, *Stolen Lives: Twenty Years in a Desert Prison*," *Boston Review of Books* (December 2001–January 2002): 53–56.

68. François-Paul Blanc and Rabha Zeidguy, *Dahir formant Code des obligations et contrats: Édition synoptique franco-arabe* (Casablanca: Sochepress, 1983), 25–37.

69. See al-Majlis al-Istishārī li-Ḥuqūq al-Insān (Advisory Committee on Human Rights), *Bayān* (Communiqué), article 12, 3.

70. Kingdom of Morocco, Ministry of Communication website, "Achievement of the Human Rights Advisory Committee in Brief," available at www.mincom.gov.ma/english/generalities/state_st/human_rights.htm.

71. For a discussion of accurate English translations, see Akel I. Kahera and Omar Benmira, "Damages in Islamic Law: Maghribi Muftis and the Built Environment," *Islamic Law and Society* 5 (1998): 131–64, and Muḥyī al-Dīn al-Nawāwī, *An-Nawawi's Forty Hadith: An Anthology of the Sayings of the Prophet Muhammad*, trans. Ezzedin Ibrahim and Denys Johnson-Davies (Beirut: Holy Koran Publishing House, 1982), 106–7: "there should be neither harming nor reciprocating harm." For English-language translations of this principle, see *Al-Muwatta of Imam Malik ibn Anas: The First Formulation of Islamic Law* (London: Kegan Paul, 1981), 307: "There is no injury nor return of injury"; and Muhammad Abu Zahrah, *The Fundamental Principles of Imam Malik's Fiqh*, see "The Ninth Source: The Principle of al-Masalih al-Mursala (Considerations of Public Interest)": "As for the schools of Malik and Ibn Hanbal, they both consider welfare as an independent principle in fiqh and state that the texts of the Lawgiver in their judgements only bring what is benefit, even if there is no text to define it, and if something is not known by text, its goal is known by the general texts of the Shari'a, like the words of the Prophet, 'No harm and no causing injury.'" Available at www.ourworld.compuserve.com/homepages/Abewley/usul10.html.

72. On husbands who have disappeared or are held in captivity in non-Muslim regions, see the French colonial codification of Maliki laws by Edouard Sautayra and Eugène Cherbonneau, *Du statut personnel et des successions* (Paris: Maisonneuve, 1873–74), 1: 22–23, 226; 2: 208.

73. Abdullahi Ahmed An-Naʻim, "The Right to Reparation for Human Rights Violations and Islamic Culture(s)," in *Seminar on the Right to Restitution, Compensation and Rehabilitation for Victims of Gross Violations of Human Rights and Fundamental Freedoms*, ed. Netherlands Institute of Human Rights (Amsterdam: SIM Special, 1992), 174–81.

74. Parallel to Islamic rules are the uses of *ḥadīth* in modern Moroccan law, which Rudiger Lohlker notes: "Due to the destruction of the older system of knowledge this new form of using hadith in legal literature means a reduction of the complex nature of Islamic law in former times to a library of texts to be used—consciously—to reconstruct an Islamic identity but no more needed for the juridical argumentation itself. Hadith has become a symbol, not part of a living religious practice. To avoid arguing in the vein of cultural pessimism we have to state that hadith has still a place in the lives of the Muslim people and in the field of law." See his "Hadith and Islamic Law," *Oriente moderno* 21, 1 (2002): 28.

75. The most quoted formulation is by a colonial official, Roger Gaudefroy-Demombynes, *L'oeuvre française en matière d'enseignement au Maroc* (Paris: P. Geuthner, 1928), 119: "It is necessary with all the means in our power to fight against the invasion of Arabic and even Islam in border regions that are bilingual. It is in the interest of the Protectorate and the populations that it is in charge of directing. It is French and not Arabic, not even Berber, that must replace Arabic as the common language and as the language of civilization. We must also at the same time maintain Berber institutions. It would be dangerous in fact to allow the formation of a compact bloc of Natives whose language and institutions are in common. We must utilize to our advantage the formula, followed previously by the Makhzen, 'divide and rule.' The presence of the Berber element is a useful counter-weight to the Arab element that we may use against the Makhzen."

76. On French discourse about the "good Berber" and the "bad Arab," see Patricia Lorcin, *Imperial Indignities: Stereotyping, Prejudice and Race in Colonial Algeria* (London: I.B. Tauris, 1995).

77. See Edmund Burke, III, "The Image of the Moroccan State in French Ethnological Literature: A New look at the Origin of Lyautey's Berber Policy," in *Arabs and Berbers*, ed. Ernest Gellner and Charles Micaud (London: Duckworth, 1973), 175–99.

78. For detailed examples of Berber trials by collective oath, see Ernest Gellner, *Saints of the Atlas* (Chicago: University of Chicago Press, 1969).

79. Alain Plantey, "La justice coutoumière marocaine," *Revue Juridique et Politique de l'Union Française* 6 (1952): 20–56, 189–211, and Dale F. Eickelmann, "Islam and the Impact of the French Colonial System in Morocco," *Humaniora Islamica* 2 (1974): 215–35.

80. Georges Surdon, "Droit musulman, droit coutumier berbère, legislations nord-africains," *Actes du sixième congrès de l'Institut des Hautes Études Marocaines*, 10–12 April 1928, lvii–lxiv.

81. See Jacques Berque, *Structures sociales du Haut Atlas* (Paris: Presses Universitaires de France, 1955) on "droit communal," 369–84. In the Berber-speaking Rif region, heavy fines known as *ḥaqq* (literally "truth, right") or *inṣāf* ("justice, equity") were the rule, as opposed to blood money compensation elsewhere, according to David Hart, "Murder in the Market: Penal Aspects of Berber Customary Law in the Precolonial Moroccan Rif," *Islamic Law and Society* 3 (1996): 343–71.

82. Martha Minow, *Between Vengeance and Forgiveness: Facing History After Genocide and Mass Violence* (Boston: Beacon, 1998), 116.

83. Malika Oufkir and Michèle Fitoussi, *Stolen Lives: Twenty Years in a Desert Jail* (New York: Hyperion, 1999), 281.

84. Malika Oufkir, the Geneviève McMillan-Reba Stewart lecture delivered at the Massachusetts Institute of Technology, 2 May 2002.

85. Norbert Frei, *Adenauer's Germany and the Nazi Past: The Politics of Amnesty and Integration* (New York: Columbia University Press, 2002), xi–xv.

86. Frei, 303–12.

87. Interview with Aziz El Ouadie, Casablanca, 4 August 1999.

88. Interview with Abdennaceur Bnouhachem, Rabat, 28 November 2003.

89. Interview with Hassan Elhasni Alaoui, Casablanca, 30 November 2003.

90. Mohamed Moustaid, "L'approche marocaine est la moins réfléchie," *Le Journal* (25–31 December 1999): 10.

Chapter 2. Disappearance

1. Al-Majlis al-Istishārī li-Ḥuqūq al-Insān (Advisory Committee on Human Rights), *Bayān* (Communiqué: On the Dossier of Some Prisoners and the So-Called Disappeared), 9 ms. pages, issued 15 October 1998.

2. Naima El Ouassouli is quoted in Fédération Internationale des Ligues des Droits de l'Homme (FIDH), "Les disparitions forcées au Maroc: Répondre aux exigencies de vérité et de justice," *Rapport* 298 (November 2000): 9. A formal reply to ACHR sent by Abdelkarim El Ouassouli demands his brother's address and declares: "Our brother remains disappeared and we consider the Moroccan authorities responsible. Moreover the appearance of his name on these lists constitutes an acknowledgment of this fact." Letter dated 12 November 1999, and posted by El Ouassouli on "Maghreb des droits de l'Homme" list, 18 April 2000.

3. Antonius C. G. M. Robben, "The Assault on Basic Trust: Disappearance, Protest, and Reburial in Argentina," in *Cultures Under Siege: Collective Violence and Trauma*, ed. Antonius C. G. M. Robben and Marcelo M. Súarez-Orozco (Cambridge: Cambridge University Press, 2000), 89.

4. Nigel S. Rodley, "The International Legal Consequences of Torture, Extralegal Execution, and Disappearance," in *New Directions in Human Rights*, ed. Ellen L. Lutz, Hurst Hannum and Kathryn L. Burke (Philadelphia: University of Pennsylvania Press, 1989), 187.

5. *Jacobellis v. Ohio*, 378 U.S. 476 (1964).

6. Declaration on the Protection of All Persons from Enforced Disappearances, General Assembly Resolution 47/133, UN GAOR, 47th Sess., Supp. No. 49, U.N.Doc. A/47/49 (1992). For a history of definitions and laws, see Reed Brody and Felipe González, "Nunca Más: An Analysis of International Instruments on 'Disappearance,'" *Human Rights Quarterly* 19 (1997): 365–405.

7. Declaration on the Protection of All Persons from Enforced Disappearance, United Nations General Assembly RES 47/133, adopted December 18, 1992; Parliamentary Assembly of the Council of Europe, Resolution 828/84; and OAS General Assembly Resolution 666 (XXIII-O/83).

8. Priscilla B. Hayner, *Unspeakable Truths: Facing the Challenge of Truth Commissions* (New York: Routledge, 2002), 177 and citing Argentina, Law No. 24,321, 11 May 1994.

9. See dahir no. 1-60-141 of 10 August 1960, in *Bulletin Officiel* no. 2495 of 19 August 1960. Mohamed Anik, "Décès judiciairement déclarés," *Al Bayane* (4 February 2000): 3. Anik notes that although judges and prosecutors could always set in motion an investigation into the circumstances of disappearances (article 2), these kind of judicial inquiries were initiated only in 2000 and in response to the creation of the Moroccan Indemnity Commission.

10. For an overview of the problems and case study, see Alison Brysk, "The Politics of Measurement: The Contested Count of the Disappeared in Argentina," *Human Rights Quarterly* 16 (1994): 676–92.

11. Annie Dillard, "The Wreck of Time: Taking Our Century's Measure," *Harper's* (January 1998): 54.

12. Sietske de Boer, *Jaren van lood: Een Marokkaanse familiekroniek (1913–1999)* (Amsterdam: Bulaaq, 2000), 8–9. The story of Houcine El Manouzi, in the context of the extraordinary El Manouzi family of resistance fighters, activists, and intellectuals, is narrated in direct speech. For a comprehensive file of testimonies and documents about Houcine El Manouzi, see the 126-page special issue of the journal *al-Suʾāl al-Milaff* issued October 2002 to mark the thirtieth anniversary of his disappearance. Approaches that link memorializing and writing Moroccan history are offered by Ahmed Herzenni, "Kitābat al-dhākirah min al-naḥīyah al-naẓarīyah (Writing memory from a theoretical viewpoint)," *al-Suʾāl al-Milaff* (October 2002): 152–53.

13. Interview with Sion Assidon, 11 September 1999. Reports about Assidon's prison escape, capture, and trial, including details of family members and friends kept in garde à vue, are in Comité de lutte contre la répression au Maroc, *Bulletin* 15 (September–October 1979): 7–9.

14. Interview with Ahmed Nadrani, Casablanca, 20 May 2000.

15. Interview with Ahmed Haou, Casablanca, 22 May 2000.

16. Interview with Amina Boukhalkhal, Casablanca, 16 November 1999.

17. There is a growing body of literature and case studies about torturers, for example, Martha K. Higgins, Mika Haritsos-Fatouros, and Philip G. Zimbardo, *Violence Workers: Police Torturers and Murderers Reconstruct Brazilian Atrocities* (Berkeley: University of California Press, 2002).

18. Ahmed Boukhari, *Le secret: Ben Barka et le Maroc: un ancien agent des services spéciaux parle* (Paris: Michel Lafon, 2002), 13–14.

19. *Le Monde*'s dossier on the Ben Barka case is available at www.lemonde.fr/res_rech_tld/1,681,00.html.

20. For an English summary, see Stephen Smith, Aboubakr Jamai, and Ali Amar, "Ben Barka 'died under torture,'" *Guardian Weekly* (12 July 2001): 27. On the life and death of General Mohamed Oufkir, see the biography by Stephen Smith, *Oufkir: Un destin marocain* (Paris: Calmann-Levy, 1999).

21. Ahmed Boukhari interview with Radio France Internationale's Isabelle Broz, 14 February 2000, available at www.radiofranceinternationale.fr.

22. Interview with Muhammad El Atlas, Casablanca, 24 October 1999 and Marrakesh, 7 November 1999.

23. Smith, *Oufkir*, 197: "De la campagne militaire des FAR, entre novembre 1958 et février 1959, aucun récit circonstancié n'est disponsible et même le bilan global de cette 'pacification' est impossible à établir: selon les auteurs, il varie entre deux et huit milles morts."

24. Juan Pando, *Historia secreta de Annual* (Madrid: Ediciones Temas de Hoy-Historia, 1999), cited in Ali Lamrabet, "Mohammed VI se penche sur la misère du Rif," *Le Journal* (23–29 October 1999): 5.

25. Maati Monjib, "L'Istiqlal, UNFP et le pouvoir au Maroc, 1955–65" (Ph.D. dissertaton, Université Paul Valéry Montpellier III, 1989), 130.

26. Jamal Berraoui, "Lettre ouverte à M. Jospin: dites-nous la vérité," *La Gazette de Maroc* 138 (3–9 November 1999): 11.

27. Khadija Rouissi, "Sans la vérité nous refusons toute indemnisation," *Le Journal* (24–30 July 1999): 7.

28. Boukhari, *Le secret*, 91.

29. Marguerite Feitlowitz, "The Scilingo Effect," in *A Lexicon of Terror: Argentina and the Legacies of Torture* (Oxford: Oxford University Press, 1998), 193–255.

30. Preparatory Committee, Working Paper for the Moroccan Forum for Truth and Equity, 5 ms. pages, issued for the conference October 1999. See also website of the Forum Marocain pour la Vérite et la Justice, where the French translation is "ceux qui ne sont plus disparus" (those no longer disappeared).

31. I first heard oral testimony about the Bnouhachem Group on 29 October 1999 at the headquarters of the Moroccan Association for Human Rights (AMDH) in Rabat on the occasion of commemorations for the "Day of the Disappeared." Oral testimony at that event was given by Abderrahmane Kounsi of the Bnouhachem Group, by Omar El Ouassouli, whose brother Abdelhak disappeared in 1984, and by Mohammed Raiss, imprisoned eighteen years in Tazmamart.

32. Mohammed Nadrani, *Kalaat-M'gouna: Disappeared Among the Roses* (London: Amnesty International UK Section: n.d.)

33. Elizabeth Hodgkin, "Introduction" to Mohamed Nadrani, *Kalaat-M'gouna: Disappeared Among the Roses*, 13. See also Nadrani's testimony published in France, where he received refugee status: Myriam Barbera, "L'un des 'disparus' des bagnes marocains témoigne: C'était l'enfer. J'ai pensé devenir fou," *L'Humanité* (14 January 1992): 18–19.

34. Hodgkin, 29.

35. Nadrani, *Kalaat-M'gouna*, 15; Abdellatif Laabi, *Sous le bâillon: Le poème* (Paris L'Harmattan: 1981), 23–25; reprinted in a collection of prison poetry, the poem "Tiens bon camarade" was originally composed in 1972. The poem is based on Laabi's experience of torture after he was arrested 27 January 1972, according to Abraham Serfaty, with whom he was arrested as coeditors of the journal, *Souffles*. See Abraham Serfaty and Christine Daure-Serfaty, *La mémoire de l'autre* (Paris: Stock, 1993), 101–3. My translation by permission of Abdellatif Laabi.

36. Hasan Najmy and Khalid al-Mouhtary, "Majmūʿat Bnūhāshim (Bnouhachem Group)" (part 2 of 4), *Ittiḥād Ishtirākī* (27 April 2000): 5.

37. "Le Groupe du 'complexe' se manifeste," *Al Bayane* (12 October 1999):

3, and "Communiqué du groupe du complexe à l'opinion publique nationale et internationale," *Le Journal* (16–22 October 1999): 8.

38. One group is 378 Sahrawis, who were disappeared in 1975 in the secret prisons of Kalaat M'Gouna and Agdz (where 57 died), and then reappeared in 1991. They formed a committee of survivors to dispute ACHR findings and addressed their situation in a letter to the 56th session of the United Nations Commission on Human Rights (letter posted on "Maghreb des droits de l'Homme" list, 4 April 2000).

39. Hasan Najmy and Khalid al-Mouhtary, "Majmūʿat Bnūhāshim" (part 2 of 4), *Ittiḥād Ishtirākī* (27 April 2000): 5.

40. Malika Oufkir and Michèle Fitoussi, *Stolen Lives: Twenty Years in a Desert Jail* (New York: Hyperion, 1999), 215.

41. Myriam Oufkir, "L'Opprimée," *Afrique Magazine* 184 (January 2001): 6. Translated and reproduced with author's permission.

42. Interview with Malika Oufkir, Live Chat, 20 June 2001, transcript available at http://oprah.com/com/chat/transcript/obc/chat_trans_moufkir_2.0010620.html. See also Catherine Perry, "L'innommable dans *La Prisonnière* de Malika Oufkir et Michèle Fitoussi," *La revue francaise* 10 (2000): 77–102.

43. See also by Malika Oufkir's mother, Fatéma Oufkir, *Les jardins du roi: Oufkir, Hassan II et nous* (Neuilly-sur-Seine: Lafon, 2000).

44. "After the Show With Malika Oufkir," http://oprah.com/obc/pastbooks/malika_oufkir/obc_20010620_aftertrans.html.

45. Hasan Najmy and Khalid al-Mouhtary, "Majmūʿat Bnūhāshim" (part 1 of 4), *Ittiḥād Ishtirākī* (24 April 2000): 5.

46. Interview with Abdelaziz Mouride, Casablanca, 23 June 2000. On cultures of fear sustained by silence, see Michael Taussig, "Culture of Terror—Space of Death: Roger Casement's Putumayo Report and the Explanation of Torture," *Comparative Studies in Society and History* 26 (1984): 467–97. On fear in Moroccan society, see Kevin Dwyer, *Arab Voices: The Human Rights Debate in the Middle East* (Berkeley: University of California Press, 1991), 137–39.

47. Abdellah Hammoudi, *Master and Disciple: The Cultural Foundations of Moroccan Authoritarianism* (Chicago: University of Chicago Press, 1997), xiv. See also his "The Reinvention of *Dar al-mulk*: The Moroccan Political System and Its Legitimation," in *In the Shadow of the Sultan: Culture, Power and Politics in Morocco*, ed. Rahma Bourqia and Susan Gilson Miller (Cambridge, Mass.: Harvard University Press, 1999), 129–75: "The intelligentsia is digested en masse by the apparatus of the state, is reclassified, becomes déclassé, or is physically eliminated" (161).

48. Jeffrey A. Sluka, "Introduction: State Terror and Anthropology," in *Death Squad: The Anthropology of State Terror*, ed. Jeffrey A. Sluka (Philadelphia: University of Pennsylvania Press, 2000), 22–23.

49. Letter originally published by the *Comité de lutte contre la répression au Maroc*. Text in Mohammed Raiss, *De Skhirat à Tazmamart: Retour du bout de l'enfer* (Casablanca: Afrique-Orient, 2002), 156.

50. Raiss, 146–47.

51. On the history and formation of the AMDH, see Marguerite Rollinde, *Le mouvement marocain des droits de l'Homme* (Paris: Karthala, 2002), 205–15.

52. Comité de lutte contre la répression au Maroc, "Les détenus militaires: Tazmamart le 5 aout 1980," *Bulletin* 42 (April 1982): 1–2. The author of the letter is identified in Gilles Perrault, *Notre ami le roi* (Paris: Gallimard, 1990), 268, and letters frame the chapter "Les morts vivants de Tazmamart," 267–78.

53. A report on Tazmamart based on interviews with three prisoners immediately after their 1991 release is in Johannes Wier Foundation, *Soins medicaux dans les prisons du Maroc: Témoignages sur la prison de Tazmamart. Rapport d'investigation d'une mission médicale novembre 1991* (Amersfoot, Netherlands: Johannes Wier, 1992). The report cites prisoners' understandable fear of being interviewed and calls Tazmamart Morocco's "national secret" (24). In 1993, a second mission was undertaken and a more comprehensive medical report was issued based on 21 prisoners interviewed. See Johannes Wier Foundation, *Tazmamart: Fort-militaire secret du Maroc, conséquences d'un internement de 18 années, mission médicale néerlandaise mai 1993* (Amersfoot, Netherlands: Johannes Wier, 1993).

54. See preface by Ignace Dalle in Ahmed Marzouki, *Tazmamart, cellule 10* (Casablanca: Tarik, 2000), 9–14.

55. Tahar Ben Jelloun, *This Blinding Absence of Light* (New York: Free Press, 2002), 23.

56. See the review of both books by Nicolas Beau, "Le cafard du bagnard," *Le canard enchaîné* (10 January 2001): 6.

57. Although Ben Jelloun does not identify the exception, Moroccans know that the parliamentarian is Mohamed Ben Said Ait Idder, who was a member of Liberation Army of the South during Morocco's struggle for independence from France.

58. Florence Aubenas and José Garcon, "Ben Jelloun s'enferre dans Tazmamart," *Libération* (15 January 2001), available at www.liberation.fr/archives.

59. Abdelhak Serhane, "La chienne de Tazmamart," in *Des nouvelles du Maroc* (Casablanca: Eddif, 1999), 62.

60. Christine Daure-Serfaty, *Tazmamart: Une prison de la mort au Maroc* (Paris: Stock, 1992), 104. Marzouki furnishes telling details about improvements to the prison regime, praising Touil's generosity in scrupulously sharing his food and medicines, and creating conduits for exchanges of letters. See Marzouki, 147.

61. Interview with Abdallah Aagaou, Casablanca, 22 February 2000. See also the report by psychiatrist Abdellah Ziou Ziou, "Psychothérapie de groupe pour les rascapés de Tazmamart et de Kalaat Mgouna," *Al Karama 4* (June 1999): 9–10.

62. Raiss, *De Skhirat à Tazmamart*, 288.

63. Driss Dahak, then president of ACHR, announced the release of 40 million dirhams provisional indemnification. See Brahim Moukhlis, "Droits de l'Homme: Le CCDH plus autonome," *Le Reporter* (20–26 April 2000): 7. The article is accompanied by a photograph of Mary Robinson and Mohamed Aoujar, minister of human rights, inaugurating the Centre de Documentation, d'Information et de Formation en Droits de l'Homme (CDIFDH, a library and documentation center on human rights in Rabat).

64. Association des familles des victimes des événements de Skhirat, *Le massacre de Skhirat 10 juillet 1971: "Crime contre l'humanité"* (Rabat: El Maarif al Jadida,

2002). Amale Samie, "Mohamed Ziane, avocat des victimes du putsch: 'L'état doit demander pardon,'" *Maroc Hebdo International* (18–24 January 2002): 1, 7.

65. Rabéa Bennouna, *Tazmamart Côté Femme: Témoignage* (Casablanca: al-Dār al-ʿĀlamīyah lil-Kitāb, 2003).

66. More is emerging on Tazmamart, for example the story of three North African brothers, French citizens who were disappeared there in 1981. See Midhat René Bourequat, *Mort vivant: Témoignage* (Paris: Pygmalion, 2000).

67. Marzouki, *Tazmamart, cellule 10*, 334.

68. Edward Alexander Westermarck, *Ritual and Belief in Morocco* (London: Macmillan, 1926), 1: 168–69, 199–206.

69. This was true for subsequent pilgrimages to secret detention centers such as the *caravanes* to Kalaat M'Gouna, 1–2 June 2002 and 11–12 October 2003. None could enter. Dale Eickelman notes that banning or restricting a particular ziyārah was a common tactic employed by the Moroccan sultan in pre-Protectorate Morocco, by French authorities under the colonial system, and by the postcolonial Moroccan government. See Dale F. Eickelman, *Moroccan Islam: Tradition and Society in a Pilgrimage Center* (Austin: University of Texas Press, 1976), 173.

70. The guard's statement was reported by Karim Boukhari, "Tazmamart? C'etait bien la peine," *Vie Économique* (6–12 October 2000). Interview with Fatna El Bouih, Cambridge, Massachusetts, 13 March 2001.

Chapter 3. Prison

Epigraphs: Mustapha Kamal, unpublished prison poem, 1981, English translation by Mustapha Kamal reprinted with author's permission. In prison, Kamal wrote poetry in Arabic, French, and Spanish. After his release, he wrote a few sonnets in English. Currently he writes poems in Arabic, English, and French. Dahbi Machrouhi, *Nabsh fī al-ḥā'iṭ* (Wall scratchings) (Rabat: Machrouhi, 1999), 9, translated with author's permission.

1. Published in Morocco as part of a path-breaking journal issue devoted to torture in Morocco. See "Non à la torture," *Al Karama* 4 (1999): 11.

2. Abdelaziz Mouride, *Fī aḥshā' balādī* (Paris: n.p., 1982), 61.

3. Sara Vidal, *Le jeu du pendu* (Paris: L'Harmattan, 1990), 121.

4. For sketches smuggled out of Kenitra and published in the newsletter of the French prisoner support group, see Comité de lutte contre la répression au Maroc, "Dans les prisons," *Bulletin* 26 (November 1982): 6–10.

5. Driss Bouissef Rekab, *À l'ombre de Lalla Chafia* (Paris: L'Harmattan, 1989), 188. Translated by author's permission.

6. Interview with Abdallah Zaazaa, Casablanca, 15 September 1999.

7. Abdellatif Derkaoui, *La parole confisquée* (Paris: L'Harmattan, 1982), 90.

8. Abdellatif Laabi, *Le chemin des ordalies* (Paris: Editions Denoel, 1982); *Rue de Retour*, translated by Jacqueline Kaye (London: Readers International, 1989), 50–51. English translation extracts published by permission of Readers International, Inc.

9. Hassan II, king of Morocco, "Discours prononcé à l'occasion de la fête de la jeunesse" (8 July 1994), in *Le Maroc et les droits de l'Homme,* ed. Driss Basri, Michel Rousset, and Georges Vedel (Paris: L'Harmattan, 1994), vii.

The image of a new page was repeated by the king in a speech to the ACHR on 19 July 1994: Hassan II, king of Morocco, "Allocution pronouncé lors de l'audience accordée aux membres du Conseil Consultatif des Droits de l'Homme": "Je crois en ce qui concerne aussi bien la justice que le barreau, çela [abrogation du Dahir de 1935] ouvrira une nouvelle page dans les rapports entre les juges, les avocats, et les procureurs" (*Le Maroc,* ix).

10. Abdellatif Mansour, "Vérité, indemnisation, et réconciliation," *Maroc Hebdo International* (3–9 December 1999): 6.

11. B. Elkhader, "Les disparus, à la recherche de la vérité," *Le Reporter* (2–8 December 1999): 7. See also Comité preparative, Document de travail, "Projet de plate-form constitutive du symposium marocain pour la vérité et l'équité, Complexe Maarif, Casablanca, 27–28 November 1999," translated from Arabic to French by Houria Slami; and Salah El Ouadie, "Risālah maftūḥah ilā jallād muʿtaqal Darb Mawlāy Sharīf" (Open letter to the torturer of prisoners in Derb Moulay Cherif) *al-Munaẓẓamah* (18–19 April 1999): 10. Selections translated from Arabic to French by François Trouin, "Lettre à mon tortionnaire," *Maroc Répression* (23 Mars 1999).

12. Salah El Ouadie, "Il faut écouter les victimes de la répression . . . ," *Le Reporter* (16–23 December 1999): 6.

13. El Ouadie.

14. Abdelkader El Aine, "On peut extorquer un aveu sous la torture, mais jamais un pardon," *Al Bayane* (29 December 1999): 7.

15. My translation of Salah El Ouadie, "The Bridegroom" (*al-ʿArīs*) first appeared as "Prison Literature and Human Rights," in *Everyday Life in the Muslim Middle East,* ed. Donna Lee Bowen and Evelyn Early (Bloomington: Indiana University Press, 2002), 360–65. I thank Ahmed Jebari, Latifa El-Morabitine, Ahmed Jebari, Ahmed Goughrabou, and Mustapha Kamal for their advice. Translated by permission of the author and reprinted by permission of the author and of Indiana University Press.

16. Abdelaziz Mouride, *On affame bien les rats!* (Casablanca: Tarik, 2000), 11–14.

17. Abdelkader Chaoui, *Kāna wa-akhawātuhā* (Casablanca: Dār al-Nashr al-Maghribīyah, 1986), 2nd. ed. (Rabat: al-Ghād, 2000). Selections translated and sketch reprinted by permission of Abdelkader Chaoui. A literal translation of Chaoui's book title is "Was and its sisters" or "The sisters of (the verb) *kāna.*" His title resonates with each student of literary Arabic as a basic rule of grammar that governs the past tense of a linked group of verbs: *aṣbaḥa* (to become), *baqiya* (to remain), *mā zāla* and *ẓalla* (to continue), and *laysa* (it is not). Insertion of the verb *kāna* (to be) shifts a sentence from the present to the past tense: the subject carries the vowel mark of the nominative case while the object is now in the accusative case. One characteristic of these verbs is to give the sense of past time continuing into the present, as in Bouissef Rekab, who chose to translate Chaoui's title from Arabic to French as *Le passé inachevé* (The incomplete past).

18. Interview with Abdelkader Chaoui, Rabat, 24 November 1999.

19. Chaoui's Arabic translation of Bouissef Rekab's book was finally published in 2002 in Morocco: Driss Bouissef Rekab, *Taḥta zilāl Lallā Shāfiyah* (Casablanca: Tarik, 2002).

20. Interview with Abdelkader Chaoui, Rabat, 21 February 2000.

21. Chaoui, *Kāna wa-akhawātuha*, 21–22.

22. Driss Bouissef Rekab, *Le passé inachevé*, unpublished manuscript. Bouissef Rekab completed his doctorate in Spanish literature while in Kenitra Central Prison: "L'univers carcéral dans l'Espagne franquiste; Romans et témoignages" (Doctorat 3 cycle, University of Toulouse II, 1986).

23. Maria Charaf, *Être, au feminine* (Casablanca: Éditions La Voie Democratique, 1997), 77.

24. Interview with Maria Charaf, Casablanca, 9 February 2000.

25. Charaf, *Être*, 73–74.

26. Ibid., 5.

27. Ibid., 78.

28. Oral testimony of Abdelhak Moussadak, "al-Yūsfī Qaddūr: huwa al-mas'ūl ʿan taʿdhīb ḥattā mawt al-shahīd Amīn Tahānī" (Youssfi Kaddour: he is responsible for torture until the martyr Amine Tahani died) in *Man qatala al-shahīdayni?* (Who killed the two martyrs?), unpaginated booklet printed to commemorate the anniversary of the deaths of Amine Tahani and Abdellatif Zeroual, November 1999.

29. Abdellatif Zeroual poetry fragment is in Chaoui, *Kāna wa-akhawātuhā*, 22. The complete poem is "Shahīd," *Aqlām* (May 1972): 133; a French translation is in *La parole confisquée* (Paris: L'Harmattan, 1982), 21.

30. Jaouad Mdidech, *La chambre noire ou Derb Moulay Cherif* (Casablanca: Éditions Eddif, 2000), 190–91. A first draft of Mdidech's manuscript was written in Kenitra Central Prison, according to fellow political prisoner Abdullah Zaazaa, who read the manuscript. Interview with Abdullah Zaazaa, Casablanca, 15 September 1999.

31. These verses were recited by Abdelkader Chaoui during a taped interview, Rabat, 23 November 1999. For an account of events leading to the creation of his poem and for the full text, see Chaoui, *Kāna wa-akhawātuhā*, 56–57. Translated by permission of the author.

32. Interview with Salah El Ouadie, Casablanca, 21 November 1999. El Ouadie, "Arīnī ʿuyūnak," *Jirāḥ al-ṣadr al-ʿālī* (Casablanca, n.p., 1985), 27–28. Translated by permission of the author.

33. Interview with Mostefa Temsamani, Tangier, 25 June 1997. According to Mustapha Kamal, interview, Chicago, 12 October 2003, he himself was present at the declamation of these poems in Derb Moulay Cherif along with Ahmed Habchi, Fouad Hilal, Noureddine Saoudi, Rahal Jbiha, Aissaoui, Mustapha Neflouss, Husni, and Kadi.

34. On the political life of Moroccan Jews, see Simon Levy, "Les juifs et la libération nationale au Maroc," in Simon Levy, *Essais d'histoire et de civilisation judéo-marocaines* (Rabat: Centre Tarik Ibn Zyad, 2001), 63–67, reprinted from *Perspectives Nouvelles* (1981): 87–90; "La communauté juive dans le contexte de l'histoire du Maroc du 17e siècle à nos jours," *Juifs du Maroc: Identité et dialogue* (Gre-

noble: La Pensée Sauvage, 1980), 105–52; and "Entre l'intégration et la diaspora (de l'indépendance à nos jours)," in *Les juifs du Maroc: Images et texts,* ed. André Goldenberg (Paris: Éditions du Scribe, 1992), 90–95.

35. Abraham Serfaty, "Face aux tortionnaires," *Les temps modernes* 477 (1986): 2–3.

36. Barbara Harlow, "Sappers in the Stacks: Colonial Archives, Land Mines, and Truth Commissions," in *Edward Said and the Work of the Critic: Speaking Truth to Power*, ed. Paul Bové (Durham, N.C.: Duke University Press, 2000), 165–86.

37. "Shumūʿ tabḥathu ʿan al-ḥaqīqah" (Candles Search for Truth), *Al-Aḥdath al-Maghribīyah* (6 March 2000):,1, 9.

38. Mohammed Mouaquit, *Liberté et liberté publiques* (Casablanca: Eddif, 1996), 149. The term "French Makhzen," according to Mouaquit, is owed to Jacques Berque, *Le Maghreb entre les deux guerres* (Paris: Seuil, 1962), 251.

39. Robert Bontine Cunninghame Graham, *Mogreb-El-Acksa: A Journey in Morocco* (Marlboro, Vt.: Marlboro Press, 1985), 33–35, originally published in 1898. I am grateful to David Crawford for this reference. See photograph in Said Mouline, *Repères de la mémoire: El Jadida* (Rabat: Royaume du Maroc, Ministère de l'Habitat, 1996), 6.

40. Cunninghame Graham, *Mogreb-El-Acksa*, 186–87. A 1900 photograph is said to show the archeological remains of an underground prison in Casablanca. See Jean-Louis Cohen and Dominique Eleb, *Casablanca: mythes et figures d'une aventure urbaine* (Paris: Hazan, 1998), 18.

41. *Morocco Prisons and Cruelties, 1893* (London: Howard Association, 1893), p. 3. As noted in a Howard Association pamphlet, McKenzie's observations were previously published in the Letters to the Editors section of *The Times* (10 January 10, 1893) thereby reaching a wide audience.

42. *Morocco Prisons and Cruelties*, 1.

43. Ibid., 4. Through their consular offices, the various colonial powers had instituted a "protégé system in which locals bought foreign citizenship to protect them from their own government." This has been well analyzed as a part of the successful destabilization of Morocco. See Mohammed Kenbib, *Les protégés* (Casablanca: Najah al-Jadidah, 1996).

44. Edward M. Peters, "Prison Before the Prison: The Ancient and Medieval Worlds," in *The Oxford History of the Prison: The Practice of Punishment in Western Society*, ed. Norval Morris and David J. Rothman (Oxford: Oxford University Press, 1998), 35–36.

45. On consequences of the state of emergency and the suspension of juridical order, supposedly temporary, see Giorgio Agamben, *Means Without End: Notes on Politics* (Minneapolis: University of Minnesota Press, 2000).

46. Daniel Rivet notes that, although Lyautey envisioned Morocco as a laboratory for France to improve and modernize French legal institutions, nonetheless, military officers were accorded immense powers not only as officers but also as judges and prosecuting attorneys based on the French colonial model in Indochina. See Daniel Rivet, *Lyautey et l'institution du Protectorat français au Maroc, 1912–1925*, (Paris: L'Harmattan, 1996), vol.1: 227–29.

47. Prison decrees are the dahir of 11 April 1915, in *Bulletin Officiel* no. 131 of

26 April 1915; the *arrêté viziriel* of 15 July 1927, in *Bulletin Officiel* no. 771 of 2 August 1927; and the dahir of 26 June 1930, in *Bulletin Officiel* no. 928 of 8 August 1930; finally revised forty-nine years later by dahir no. 1-99-200 of 25 August 1999, in *Bulletin Officiel* no. 4726 of 16 September 1999 promulgating Law no. 23-98 on the organization and functioning of the prison system.

48. Janet L. Abu-Lughod, *Rabat: Urban Apartheid in Morocco* (Princeton, N.J.: Princeton University Press, 1980).

49. Daniel Rivet, *Lyautey et l'institution du Protectorat français au Maroc, 1912–1925* (Paris: L'Harmattan, 1996), vol. 2: 156.

50. Abdellatif Laabi, *Le chemin des ordalies* (Paris: Éditions Denoel, 1982); *Rue de Retour*, English translation by Jacqueline Kaye (London: Readers International, 1989), 19.

51. Michel Foucault, *Discipline and Punish: The Birth of the Prison* (New York: Vintage, 1977), 200–209.

52. An architectural plan and analysis of La Petite Roquette can be found in Odile Foucaud, "Iconographie de l'architecture: La prison française du xixe siècle; Dernier avatar du couvent," *Gazette des Beaux-Arts* 125 (November 1994): 155–214.

53. Mohamed Raoudi, *Prisons du Maroc: Étude critique de la population pénale et du système pénitentiaire marocain (1975–1984,)* available at http://www.prison.eu.org/article.php3?id_article=2537.

54. Quoted in George W. Pierson, *Tocqueville in America* (New York: Doubleday Anchor, 1959), 60.

55. Gustave de Beaumont and Alexis de Tocqueville, *On the Penitentiary System in the United States and Its Application in France* (1833; New York: A.M. Kelley, 1970), 5.

56. Randall McGowen, "The Well-Ordered Prison: England, 1780–1865," in *The Oxford History of the Prison*, ed. Norval Morris and David J. Rothman (Oxford: Oxford University Press, 1998), 91.

57. Abraham Serfaty and Christine Daure-Serfaty, *La mémoire de l'autre* (Paris: Stock, 1993), 215–16. In Tunisia, political prisoner Chérif Ferjani describes blocks of individual cells reserved for homosexuals, dangerous and mentally unstable prisoners, death row inmates, and political prisoners. During hunger strikes, prominent among political prisoner demands was reassignment from isolated cells to group wards; see Chérif Ferjani, "Espace d'exclusion, espace de parole publique: Témoignage sur une expérience de détenus politiques dans la Tunisie des années soixante-six," in *Espaces publics, paroles publiques au Maghreb et au Machrek*, ed. Hannah Davis Taieb, Rabia Bekkar, and Jean-Claude David (Paris: L'Harmattan, 1997), 141–58.

58. Dahir of 29 June 1935, in *Bulletin Officiel* no. 1184 of 5 July 1935: "relatif à la répression des manifestations contraires à l'ordre et des atteintes au respect du à l'autorité," and only abrogated by dahir no. 1-94-288 of 25 July 1994. Dahir of 26 July 1939, in *Bulletin Officiel* no. 1399 of 18 August 1939.

59. Abdellatif Laabi, *Rue de Retour*, English translation by Jacqueline Kaye (London: Readers International, 1989), 19. English translation extracts published by permission of Readers International, Inc.

60. See Abdelfattah Fakihani, "Khawāṭir sarīʿah ḥawla istishhād Jbiha," *al-*

Badīl 2 (1982): 43, and French translation "Considérations rapides sur le martyre de Jbiha," in *La parole confisquée* (Paris: L'Harmattan, 1982), 99.

Chapter 4. The Casablanca Uprising of 1981 and Its Aftermath

Composed shortly after the 1981 Casablanca uprising by Hassan El Bou (political prisoner, 1976–89) during his stay at Ar-Razi psychiatric hospital, Salé, and published in "Lettre à son ami Lyazami," in *La parole confisquée* (Paris: L'Harmattan, 1982), 91–92, with a later version in Hassan El Bou, *Peindre la déchirure* (Rabat: Impérial, 1999), 7–8.

1. Jane Caplan, "'This or That Particular Person': Protocols of Identification in Nineteenth-Century Europe," in *Documenting Individual Identity: The Development of State Practices in the Modern World*, ed. Jane Caplan and John Torpey (Princeton, N.J.: Princeton University Press, 2001), 49–66.

2. The decree is in Robert Estoublon and Adolphe Lefébure, *Code de l'Algérie annoté: recueil chronologique des lois, ordonnances, décrets, arrêtés, circulaires, etc., formant la législation algérienne actuellement en vigueur, avec les travaux préparatoires et l'indication de la jurisprudence* (Algier: A. Jourdan, 1896), 500. Article 5 appears on 574.

3. Hassan Rachik, "Nom relatif et nom fixe," *Méditerranéans* 11 (1999–2000): 223–28.

4. Paul Decroux, "L'état civil et les Marocains," *Revue juridique et politique de l'union française* 6 (1952): 12.

5. William MacGuckin de Slane and Charles Gabeau, *Vocabulaire destiné a fixer la transcription en français des noms de personnes et de lieux usités chez les indigènes de l'Algérie* (Paris: Imprimerie Impériale, 1868).

6. On the chaos of identity brought about by burning the city records, see Alphonse Bertillon, *L'identité des récidivistes et la loi de relégation* (Paris: G. Masson, 1883), 5. On the family passbook, see "Historique du livret de famille," available at http://pays-aigre.chez.tiscali.fr/genea/textes/questions/lelivretdefamille.htm.

7. On the history and law of family names see Mohamed Chafi, "Le nom de famille au Maroc," *Revue juridique et politique* 1 (1989): 3–17, and *al-Ism al-ʿā'ilī bi-al-Maghrib* (Marrakesh: Dār Walīlī, 1999).

8. See the dahir of 14 February 1925, published in Pierre Vuillet, *Code Marocain du Travail* (Rabat: Publications Juridiques Marocaines, 1936), 22–24.

9. Decroux, "L'état civil et les Marocains," 1–18.

10. Sabine Filizzola, *L'organisation de l'état civil au Maroc* (Rabat: Librairie Générale de Droit et de Jurisprudence, 1958), 23.

11. Mounira Charrad, "State and Gender in the Maghrib," in *Women and Power in the Middle East*, ed. Suad Joseph and Susan Slyomovics, (Philadelphia: University of Pennsylvania Press, 2001), 64.

12. André Adam, *Casablanca* (Paris: CNRS, 1968), vol. 1: 85–95.

13. The most powerful description of the notion of "reciprocal exclusivity"

between native Arab and colonial European urban sectors is found in Frantz Fanon, *The Wretched of the Earth* (New York: Grove Press, 1963), 38–39.

14. See Jean-Louis Cohen and Monique Eleb, *Casablanca: Mythes and figures d'une aventure urbaine* (Paris: Hazan, 1998) and Gwendolyn Wright, *The Politics of Design in French Colonial Urbanism* (Chicago: University of Chicago Press, 1991), 85–160.

15. Janet L. Abu-Lughod, *Rabat: Urban Apartheid in Morocco* (Princeton, N.J.: Princeton University Press, 1980), 152–54.

16. English translation of Ecochard by Abu-Lughod, *Rabat*, 227. See also Michel Ecochard, *Casablanca: Le roman d'une ville* (Paris: Editions de Paris, 1955), 104–6.

17. Based on the evidence of his poems, Zrika was convicted of contempt for the king, morality, and religion (*outrage au roi, aux bonnes moeurs et à la religion*), with eight of his poems as evidence. See Comité de lutte contre la répression au Maroc, "Meknès," *Bulletin* 21 (April 1980): 5.

18. Abdallah Zrika, "A Letter in Ben Msik," in Liliane Dayot, *Morocco International Amnesia* (Paris: Méditerranée, 1999), 17.

19. Robert Montagne, *Naissance du prolétariat marocain, enquête collective exécutée de 1948 à 1950* (Paris, Peyronnet, 1952), 180.

20. Abdelkader Kaioua, *Casablanca: L'industrie et la ville* (Tours: URA 365 du CNRS URBAMA, Université François Rabelais, 1996), 1: 301 n. 87.

21. Mehdi Ben Barka, *Option révolutionnaire au Maroc* (Paris: Maspero, 1966), 35, 38.

22. Jean-François Clement, "Les révoltes urbaines," in *Le Maroc actuel*, ed. Jean-Claude Santucci (Paris: CNRS, 1992), 393–406, and Guy Delanoe, *Lyautey, Juin, Mohammed V, fin d'un protectorat* (Paris: L'Harmattan, 1988).

23. See Paul Buttin, *Le drame du Maroc* (Paris: Éditions du Cerf, 1955), 112–27.

24. Comité de lutte contre la répression au Maroc, "Bilan de la repression," *Bulletin* 37 (November 1981): 3–4.

25. Edward P. Thompson, "The Moral Economy of the English Crowd in the Eighteenth Century," *Past and Present* 50 (1971): 76–78.

26. The literature on riots in the Arab world emphasizing Moroccan riots as crucial political and social indicators are Edmund Burke, III, "Understanding Arab Protest Movements," *Arab Studies Quarterly* 8 (1987): 333–45; *Émeutes et mouvements sociaux au Maghreb*, ed. Didier Le Saout and Marguerite Rollinde (Paris: Karthala, 1999); and René Gallisot, "Les émeutes, phénomène cyclique au Maghreb: rupture ou reconduction du système politique," *Annuaire de l'Afrique du Nord* 28 (1989): 29–39. For a review of the literature on riots, see Abderrahmane Rachik, "Sciences sociales et violence collective urbaine au Maghreb," *Prologues* 16 (1999): 19–25.

27. Clement, "Les révoltes urbaines," 393–406.

28. Larbi Sadiki, "Popular Uprisings and Arab Democratization," *International Journal of Middle East Studies* 32 (2000): 71–95. Manuel Castells, *The City and the Grassroots: A Cross-Cultural Theory of Urban Social Movements* (London: Edward Arnold, 1983), charts similar demands centered on housing and schooling in a wide range of urban revolts historically and crossculturally.

29. Mostefa Bouaziz, "Mouvements sociaux et mouvement national au Maroc," in Le Saout and Rollinde, *Émeutes et mouvements sociaux*, 73.

30. Hasan Bazwi, *L'UMT, le rêve, et la réalité*, quoted by Jaafar Staoui in "Casablanca 1981, l'histoire d'une émeute sanglante," *Le Journal* (17–23 June 2000): 12.

31. Quoted by Zakya Daoud, "La situation explosive de Casablanca," *Lamalif* 127 (July–August 1981): 20–26, esp. n. 14.

32. Abderrahmane Rachik, *Ville et pouvoirs au Maroc* (Casablanca: Afrique Orient, 1995), 113–21 and "Casablanca ensanglantée," *Su'āl* 1 (1981): 83–90. The French newspaper *Le Monde* extensively chronicled events; see 21 June–31 July 1981.

33. "Ce n'est pas grave," were Hassan II's words reported by Roland Delcour, "Les émeutes de Casablanca," *Le Monde* (June 14 1981): 1, 4.

34. Aziz Khamliche, "Réactions: De la guerre des positions à la confrontation politicienne," *Le Journal* (17–23 June 2000): 13.

35. For a chronology of union activism, see Mohammed Benhlal, "Le syndicat comme enjeu politique au Maroc (1955–81)," *Annuaire de l'Afrique du Nord* 26 (1982), 217–58.

36. Interview with Mohamed Karam, Casablanca, 26 September 1999. On 26 March 1973, Karam was arrested and accused of participating in the 1973 uprisings against the monarchy. He spent three months in Derb Moulay Cherif, was tried in the military tribunal of 26 June–30 August, acquitted, kidnapped from Kenitra Central Prison (along with the other 80 people acquitted), and forcibly disappeared to Temara military camp for six months until 1 January 1974, retried in February 1974 on new charges of plotting against the royal heir, and released on provisional libery (*liberté provisoire*) on 10 May 1974. In interviews Karam does not speak of his torture; he is currently writing a book on Morocco's political trials.

37. Hervé Martin, "Le témoignage d'un manifestant," *Le Monde* (27 June 1981): 4.

38. Hassan II, king of Morocco, "Conference de presse du chef de l'État de juillet 1981," in *Discours et interview de S.M. Hassan II* (Rabat: Ministère de l'Information, de la Jeunesse et du Sport, 1981), 167.

39. On the origins of *récidivisme*, see Simon A. Cole, *Suspect Identities: A History of Fingerprinting and Criminal Identification* (Cambridge, Mass.: Harvard University Press, 2001), 15.

40. Laetitia Grotti, "Au dessus de toute soupçon," *Tel Quel* (Morocco) (17 February 2003) available at www.telquel-online.com/.

41. Jacques Vergès, *De la stratégie judiciaire* (Paris: Minuit, 1968), 19.

42. Vergès, 104–14.

43. Louis Anthes, "Publicly Deliberative Drama: The 1934 Mock Trial of Adolf Hitler for 'Crimes Against Civilization,'" *American Journal of Legal History* 42 (1998): 391–410.

44. Paul Schiff Berman, "The Globalization of Jurisdiction," *University of Pennsylvania Law Review* 151 (2002): 311–545, esp. 506–12.

45. Vergès, 183–99.

46. I taped and photographed the mock trial. Witness testimony quoted in the text is based on my English translation of Arabic audiotapes transcribed by Abdessamad Bouabid. The event was also videotaped by al-Muntadā.

47. Comité de lutte contre la répression au Maroc, "Retour du Maroc de J. P. Mignard," *Bulletin* 34 (July 1981): 6, 16.

48. The death of Cuquel, described as a Frenchman of Casablanca, was reported by Roland Delcour, "Les émeutes déclenchées à la suite de la grève ont fait une vingtaine des morts," *Le Monde* (23 June 1981): 29.

49. On the photographers' arrest, trial (as rioters), and imprisonment (7 and 5 years in Essaouira Prison), see Comité de lutte contre la répression au Maroc, "Procès," 36 *Bulletin* (October 1981): 8.

50. James Scott, *Seeing like a State: How Certain Schemes to Improve the Human Condition Have Failed* (New Haven, Conn.: Yale University Press, 1998), 65.

51. See Michael Herzfeld, *The Social Production of Indifference: Exploring the Symbolic Roots of Western Bureaucracy* (Chicago: University of Chicago Press, 1992), 143 passim.

52. Sandra S. Phillips, "Identifying the Criminal," in Sandra S. Phillips, Mark Haworth-Booth, and Carol Squiers, *Police Pictures: The Photograph as Evidence* (San Francisco: Chronicle Books, 1997), 20.

53. An *arrêté viziriel* was issued to establish anthropometry on 30 September 1913 and came into force when published in the *Bulletin Officiel*, no. 52, on 24 October 1913. The Service anthropométrique was transferred to the prison system in 1920 according to the *Bulletin Officiel*, no. 385 on 9 March 1920; for complete texts see Paul-Louis Rivière, *Traités, codes, lois et règlements du Maroc; (Dahirs, arrêtés viziriels et résidentiels, ordres, ordonnances, circulaires, instructions et avis)* (Paris: Sirey, 1923), 24–25.

54. Michel Foucault, *Discipline and Punish: The Birth of the Prison* (New York: Vintage, 1977), 195–228, and John Tagg, "A Means of Surveillance: the Photograph as Evidence in Law," in *The Burden of Representation: Essays on Photographies and Histories* (Minneapolis: University of Minnesota Press, 1988), 66–102.

55. See Alison Dundes Renteln, "The Rights of the Dead: Autopsies and Corpse Mismanagement in Multicultural Societies," *South Atlantic Quarterly* 100 (2001): 1005–27.

56. Comité de lutte contre la répression au Maroc, "Information," *Bulletin* 38 (December 1981): 2.

57. In an extraordinary conjuncture that brought together the mourning family member, the identity card, and the body in a mass grave in Iraq, see the photograph caption to Anne Barnard, "Rush for Remains Seen Jumbling Evidence," *Boston Globe* (5 May 2003): 1: "Nabiha Mohammad Abboud wailed after finding the identity card of her sister, Hayat, at a mass grave site in Hillah. The graves are believed to date to 1991."

58. See sentencing schema in pullout by Aḥmad Miftāḥ al-Baqālī, *Muʾassasat al-sujūn fī al-Maghrib* (Rabat: Maṭābiʿ Mithāq, 1979).

59. Susan Ossman, *Picturing Casablanca: Portraits of Power in a Modern City* (Berkeley: University of California Press, 1994), 136–141.

60. On witnessing in Islamic law, see Brinkley Messick, *The Calligraphic State: Textual Domination and History in a Muslim Society* (Berkeley: University of California Press, 1993), 161–63.

61. The many purposes of a mock trial are cogently presented in publications

emerging from a mock trial about gender in the Arab world, namely the Arab Court of Women staged in Beirut, 29–30 June 1995. See *Justice Through the Eyes of Women: Testimonies on Violence Against Women in the Arab World, Beirut, Lebanon, 28–30 June 1996*, Khadija Cherif et al., ed. (Tunis: El Taller, 1995).

62. Interview with Jamal Lakouis, Casablanca, 21 June 2000. The chapter subtitle, "Comment devenir un prisonnier politique malgré lui," was suggested by Lakouis. All subsequent quotes by Lakouis are from this interview conducted two days after the mock trial.

64. Interview with Mohamed Srifi, Tangier, 2 July 1997.

65. Comité de lutte contre la répression au Maroc, "Lettre des familles des prisonniers politiques du Maroc adressée au colloque sur la répression au Maroc du 5 décembre 1981," *Bulletin* 39 (January 1982): 8–9.

65. Abdellah Lehzam, *Le logement urbain au Maroc* (Rabat: Imprimerie Toumi, 1994), 138–40.

Chapter 5. Rānī nimḥik*: Women and Testimony*

1. Fatna El Bouih, *Ḥadīth al-ʿatamah* (Casablanca: Le Fennec, 2001), 21. My translation by permission of Fatna El Bouih.

2. See section on definitions of human rights abuses in Marguerite Feitlowitz, *A Lexicon of Terror: Argentina and the Legacies of Torture* (Oxford: Oxford University Press, 1998), 51–62.

3. El Bouih, *Ḥadīth*, 14–15.

4. Widad Bouab, "al-Sijn alladhī kāna malādhan baʿd ʿuzlati al-makhāfir" (The prison that was a refuge after the isolation of secret detention), in El Bouih, *Ḥadīth*, 115. Bouab's testimony, reprinted in El Bouih's book, was first published as a newspaper article in *Ittiḥād Ishtirākī* (5 November 1994): 5.

5. Aicha Alqoh, "Fatna El Bouih: Ma prison à moi," *Demain* 18 (7–21 July 2000): 48–49.

6. Latifa Jbabdi, "al-Makhfar wa-al-taʿdhīb wa-al-sijn wa-al-jallādūn: shahādat Latifa Jbabdi" (Secret detention, torture, prison and the executioners: Latifa Jbabdi's testimony), in El Bouih, *Ḥadīth*, 123. Jbabdi's testimony was first published as a newspaper article in *Ittiḥād Ishtirākī* (5 November 1994): 6.

7. El Bouih was raped by a prison guard, who threatened her with more savage treatment should she talk: "You are neither the first nor the last. Me, I will teach you liberation." See Comité de lutte contre la répression au Maroc, "Textes de prison: à propos d'un viol," *Bulletin* 21 (April 1980): 10–11.

8. El Bouih, *Ḥadīth*, 14.

9. El Bouih, *Ḥadīth*, 38, 44–45.

10. Interview with Fatna El Bouih, Casablanca, 3 October 1999. See also Fatna El Bouih, "Un sommeil court, peuplé de cauchemars," *Le Journal* (5–11 June 1999): 8.

11. Interview with Widad Bouab and Maria Ezzaouini, Marrakesh, 11 Decem-

ber 1999. See also Widad Bouab, "Fī Darb Mawlāy Sharīf" (In Derb Moulay Cherif), *al-Aḥdāth al-Maghribīyah* (27 August 2001): 4.

12. El Bouih interview.

13. El Bouih, Casablanca.

14. El Bouih, *Ḥadīth*, 26.

15. El Bouih interview.

16. El Bouih, *Ḥadīth*, 23.

17. El Bouih interview.

18. El Bouih interview.

19. El Bouih, *Ḥadīth*, 24–25.

20. Writing on the body by Moroccan women offers a radical contrast to Franz Kafka's *The Penal Colony*, in which a bureaucrat demonstrates a torture machine that writes on the body of the victim, using needles to inscribe the captive's body with minute letters that ultimately cause the prisoner to bleed to death. Franz Kafka, *The Penal Colony* (New York: Schocken, 1948).

21. El Bouih, "Un sommeil court," 8.

22. Interview with Fatna El Bouih, Casablanca, 3 February 2000.

23. El Bouih, *Ḥadīth*, 30–31.

24. Nezha Bernoussi, a teacher in Casablanca, was listed as disappeared on 4 November 1985, and Kabil two days after, according to the names published by Association de soutien aux comités de lutte contre la répression au Maroc, "Les arrestations d'Octobre 1985," *Maroc Répression* 75 (December 1985): 5–9. Eighty-five names were noted with ages and occupation; most detainees were young and educated. Saadia Kabil is the daughter of political activists: her father, Mohamed Kabil, was a member of the Black Crescent, an urban nationalist liberation group that took up arms against the French while her mother, Zohra, was responsible for arms caches. Interview with Saadia Kabil, Casablanca, 24 November 1999.

25. Interview with Saadia Kabil, Casablanca, 12 October 1999. Drawing and photograph reproduced by permission of Saadia Kabil.

26. Fatna El Bouih, "Témoignage, la commémoration de quarante jours de la mort de Ahmed Jaouhar," Complexe Culturel Hay Mohammedi, Casablanca, 29 January 2000. Translated from Arabic to French by Fatna El Bouih, oral communication: "Si la page est noir, il faudrait d'abord la saisir, la lire, et l'écrire. L'écriture est un moyen de délivrance. Beaucoup de femmes ont subit la torture, ont étaient des victimes d'une injustice et sombrent dans le silence et la méconnaissance. Beaucoup de jeune filles, beaucoup de femmes innocentes partout dans le Maroc figurent dans les listes des victimes mais n'osent pas parler, ni témoigner, ni écrire de ce qu'elles ont subit."

27. El Bouih, "Un sommeil court," 8. El Bouih is referring to Rabéa Ftouh, Fatima Okacha, Saida Menebhi, Khadija El Boukhari, Widad Bouab, Maria Ezzaouini, Fatna El Bouih, Nguia Boudaa, Hayat Zirari, Amina Mezdaoui, Nezha Bernoussi, Saadia Kabil, and Latifa Jbabdi. See also Marguerite Rollinde, "Les militant(e)s des droits de l'Homme et le discours sur les femmes au Maroc," in *Parcours d'intellectuels maghrébins*, ed. Aissa Kadri (Paris: Karthala, 1999), 309–20.

28. El Bouih, "Un sommeil court," 8: "Les femmes ont fait preuve de beaucoup de courage et de résistance face à la torture, aux multiples formes de torture.

Elles ont vécu des expériences exaltantes, très dures aussi, qu'elles ont su surmonter avec courage et dignité."

29. Doris Summer, "'Not Just a Personal Story': Women's *Testimonios* and the Plural Self," in *Life/Lines: Theorizing Women's Autobiography*, ed. Bella Brodski and Celeste Schenk (Ithaca, N.Y.: Cornell University Press, 1988), 110.

30. See two-page spread with El Bouih on women political prisoners, El Bouih, "Araʾū mā lā urīdu" (I saw what I don't want to see), *Ittiḥād Ishtirākī* (5 November 1994): 5–6.

31. Interview with Fatna El Bouih reprinted in Susan Slyomovics, "This Time I Choose When to Leave," *MERIP/Middle East Report* 218 (2001): 42–43.

32. El Bouih, "Témoignage."

33. Many prison testimonies by women activists in the Arab-Muslim world have been published. The Egyptian writers Latifa Zayyat, Zaynab al-Ghazali, Farida Naqqash, and Nawal El Saadawi are known in Morocco. In the monthly newspaper *Thamāniyah Mārs*, Latifa Jbabdi republished excerpts from the lives and works of Farida Naqqash (number 6, April 1984: 13); El Saadawi (number 14, January 1985: 16; number 15, February 1985: 16); as well as articles about Algerian, Moroccan, and Palestinian women fighters.

34. John Beverley, "The Margin at the Center: On *Testimonio* (Testimonial Narrative)," *Modern Fiction Studies* 35 (1989): 14.

35. Daniel Gimaret, "Shahāda," *Encyclopaedia of Islam*, new ed., (Leiden: E.J. Brill, 1997), 9: 201. Gimaret also notes that the term refers to the Islamic profession of faith when a believer professes: "There is no god but God, and Muḥammad is the Messenger of God."

36. See Brinkley Messick, "Evidence: From Memory to Archive," *Islamic Law and Society* 9 (2002): 231–70, and Lawrence Rosen, "Responsibility and Compensatory Justice in Arab Culture and Law," in *Semiotics, Self and Society*, ed. Benjamin Lee and Greg Urban (Berlin: Mouton, 1989), 101–20.

37. Mohammad Fadel, "Two Women, One Man: Knowledge, Power, and Gender in Medieval Sunni Thought," *International Journal of Middle East Studies* 29 (1997): 185–204.

38. Fatna El Bouih, "Pathways to Human Rights in Morocco," the Geneviève McMillan-Reba Stewart lecture delivered at the Massachusetts Institute of Technology, 13 March 2001.

39. "Autour d'un café avec Fatna El Bouih," *Femmes du Maroc* 69 (September 2001): 30. See Observatoire Marocain des Prisons, *Rapport annuel 2001/2002* (Mohammedia: El Mouttakki, 2002).

40. Fatema Mernissi, *Scheherazade Goes West: Different Cultures, Different Harems* (New York: Simon and Schuster, 2001), 55, and Melissa Matthes, "Shahrazad's Sisters: Storytelling and Politics in the Memoirs of Mernissi, El Saadawi and Ashrawi," *Alif: Journal of Comparative Poetics* 19 (1999): 68–96.

41. Abdellatif Laabi, *Le chemin des ordalies* (Paris: Denoel, 1982), 61. My translation differs from the published English translation in *Rue du Retour* (London: Readers International, 1989), 46.

42. Laabi, *Rue de Retour*, 121; for entire tale see Laabi, *Le chemin des ordalies*,

135–43. English translation extracts published by permission of Readers International Inc.

43. See the memoir of Saida Menebhi's last days by her sister, Khadija Menebhi, "Istihshād imraʾah" (A woman's martyrdom), *Nawāfid* 3 (1999): 121–27.

44. Saida Menebhi, *Poèmes, lettres, écrits de prison* (Paris: Comité de lutte contre la répression au Maroc, 1978), 81. The term "forward," in French, *en avant*, is a reference to Ilā al-Amām, the name of the Marxist organization to which Menebhi belonged.

45. Mohamed Belmejdoub, "Préface à l'édition de l'an 2000," in Saida Menebhi, *Poèmes, lettres, écrits de prison* (Rabat: Éditions Feed-Back, 2000), 10–11.

46. "Li-mādhā jarīdat Thamāniyah Mārs?" (Why the newspaper 8 March?) *Thamāniyah Mārs* 1 (April 1983): 1.

47. Interview with Fatna El Bouih, Casablanca, 3 October 1999. See also Latifa Akharbach and Narjis Rerhaye, "Latifa Jbabdi: L'étoffe d'une pasionaria," *Femmes en politique* (Casablanca: Le Fennec, 1992), 99–105.

48. Fatna El Bouih, *La tortionnaire en déroute* (Rabat: Synergie civique, 2001), 23.

49. Leila Abouzeid, *Year of the Elephant: A Moroccan Woman's Journey Toward Independence and Other Stories* (Austin: University of Texas Press, 1989), 9, 50. The novel was first published in 1983 in Arabic, *ʿĀm al-fīl.*

50. Abouzeid, *Year of the Elephant*, v.

51. Mohamed El Mansour, "Moroccan Historiography Since Independence," in *The Maghrib in Question: Essays in History & Historiography*, ed. Michel Le Gall and Kenneth J. Perkins (Austin: University of Texas Press, 1997), 102–20.

52. Mikhail M. Bakhtin, *The Dialogic Imagination* (Austin: University of Texas Press, 1981).

53. Scholarly writings in English on women in the Arab world and the project of oral history include Ellen L. Fleischmann, "Crossing the Boundaries of History: Exploring Oral History in Researching Palestinian Women in the Mandate Period," *Women's History Review* 5 (1996): 351–71; and the special issue of *Al-Jana* (2002), edited by Rosemary Sayigh, especially her article and bibliography, "The History of Palestinian Oral History: Individual Vitality and Institutional Paralysis," *Al-Jana* (2002): 2–4, 64–72. On Morocco, see Alison Baker, *Voices of Resistance: Oral Histories of Moroccan Women* (Albany: State University of New York Press, 1998) with accompanying film; and Liat Kozma, "Moroccan Women's Narratives of Liberation: A Passive Revolution?" *Journal of North African Studies* 8 (2003): 112–30.

54. Other writings by and about the mothers, sisters, and wives are Halima Zayn al-Abidin (former wife of a Marxist political prisoner), *Hājis al-ʿawdah* (The idea of return) (Rabat: n.p., 1999), and a novel by Khadija Marouazi set in the leftist milieu of the 1970s and 80s, *Sīrat al-ramād* (A life of ashes) (Casablanca: Afrique Orient, 2000). A group of political prisoners are in the process of authoring a collective work in Arabic and French to honor their families, entitled *Portraits de femmes: Mères, soeurs, épouses. . . .*

55. Andrea Malin, "Mothers Who Won't Disappear," *Human Rights Quarterly* 15 (1993): 187–213.

56. Interview with Layla Chaouni, Casablanca, 3 August 1999.

57. Interview with Khadija Rouissi, Casablanca, 6 April 2000. Moroccan shirts and kerchiefs are customized with the addition of names of secret detention sites visited by al-Muntadā. Algerian ones prefer *al-mafqūdūn* for "those disappeared" but both Algerian and Moroccan employ red, green, and black lettering.

58. Kamal Lahbib, "Mouvements sociaux et mouvements de droit," lecture delivered at the conference "État et formation nationale, University of Hassan II, Ain Chock, Casablanca, 1 September 1999. For the Algerian case, Paul Silverstein points to a postwar gendered discourse of martyrdom where women perform the role of mourning their fallen men. See his "Martyrs and Patriots: Ethnic, National and Transnational Dimensions of Kabyle Politics," *Journal of North African Studies* 8 (2003): 87–111, esp. n. 7.

59. Sophocles, *Antigone*, trans. Hugh Lloyd-Jones (Cambridge, Mass.: Harvard University Press, 1994), 2: 11. In the Arabic-speaking world, Antigone is best known through Berthold Brecht's play, translated into Arabic and a staple of Arab theater. Abdellatif Laabi notes that for the 1963 Moroccan university theater season in Rabat, a cycle of Brecht's plays were staged. See his *Rimbaud et Shéhérazade* (Paris: Différance, 2000), 7.

60. Judith Butler, *Antigone's Claim: Kinship Between Life and Death* (New York: Columbia University Press, 2000), 79–81.

61. Abraham Serfaty and Christine Daure-Serfaty, *La mémoire de l'autre* (Paris: Stock, 1993). See 161–62 for consequences to his family.

62. Evelyne Serfaty, "Témoignage d'Evelyne Serfaty," *Souffles* (Paris edition) 1 (1973); in Morocco reprinted over two decades later in "Tu parles ou on te tue" (special issue on torture) *Al Karama* 4 (June 1999): 15 and in *Shahādāt ʿan al-taʿdhīb fī al-Maghrib* (Casablanca: Publications of al-Muntadā al-Maghribī min Ajl al-Ḥaqīqah wa-al-Inṣāf, 2000), 1–6.

63. Abdellatif Laabi, *Histoire des sept crucifiés de l'espoir & Oraisons marquées au fer rouge* (Cesson-la-Forêt: La Table Rase, 1980), 37. My translation by permission of Abdellatif Laabi.

64. Interview with Abdelaziz Mouride, Casablanca, 23 June 2000.

65. Chaoui, *Kāna wa-akhawātuhā*, 16.

66. Chaoui, 17.

67. Interview with Zoubida Bouabid, Mohammedia, 29 May 2000. All subsequent quotes are from this interview. Present during the interview was her son, Abdessamad, who for the first time heard his mother's narratives of struggle on his behalf. I thank Abdessamad Bouabid, who transcribed the taped interview in the summer of 2003, a second hearing and close reading that he describes as moving and difficult.

68. The terms *al-munāḍilah* and *al-munāḍilāt* are the singular and plural feminine forms.

Chapter 6. Islamist Political Prisoners

1. See Vaclav Havel, "The Power of the Powerless," in *Open Letters: Selected Writings 1965–1990* (New York: Vintage, 1992), 181–82.

2. The Arabic term Islāmīyūn translates into English as "Islamic" or "Islamist." Employing the French *islamiste*, political prisoners pointed out to me the importance of attaching the term "Islamist" to "political prisoner." Islamism is interpreted as political activism, the possibilities of *ijtihād* (defined in this context as "renewal") that govern human reason and human error, whereas "Islamic" (French *islamique*) is concerned with religion, doctrine, culture, and history, in other words, they include an ideal.

3. Moti has always denied any connection to Benjelloun's murder, instead accusing the Moroccan government. See his interviews in François Burgat, *L'islamisme au Maghreb: La voix du Sud* (Paris: Karthala, 1988), 189–91.

4. Members of Faction al-Jihād are close and appreciative readers of the work of Moroccan scholar Muhammad Tozy, notably his book *Monarchie et islam politique au Maroc*, 2nd ed. (Paris: Presses de Sciences Politiques, 1999). Interviewed in Casablanca in 2000, they point to several errors in Tozy's information about their Faction al-Jihād, chronicled on 231–32. Their corrections to Tozy's text are (1) Naamani's group is called al-Moudjahidine (al-Mudjāhidīn), not al-Djihad (al-Jihād), and its newspaper is *al-Sarāyā*; (2) more controversially, they insist that al-Moudjahidine had nothing to do with bombs placed in Marrakesh's Hotel Atlas Asni in 1994 that killed several tourists but the incident is to be understood as an example of intergovernmental settling of accounts at the highest levels between Algeria and Morocco with the Islamists falsely accused; (3) *al-Moudjahid* is the newspaper of al-Shabībah al-Islāmīyah; and (4) The Group al-Jihād that appeared and disappeared mysteriously between 1984 and 1988 should never be confused, as Tozy does, with their own Faction al-Jihād.

5. After their arrest, a communiqué issued from prison and signed by twenty-nine shabibistes declared that they had no affiliation with any Islamist group whatsoever. See "Lā ʿalāqah lanā bi-munaẓẓamat al-Shabībah al-Islāmīyah" (We have no connection to the organization al-Shabībah al-Islāmīyah), *Anoual*, (22 August 1985): 6.

6. See Muhammad Darif, *al-Islāmīyūn al-Maghāribah: ḥiṣābat al-siyāsah fī al-ʿamal al-Islāmī, 1969–1999* (Casablanca: al-Majallah al-Maghribīyah, 1999); Henry Munson, Jr., "Morocco's Fundamentalists," *Government and Opposition* 26 (1991): 331–44; and Tozy, *Monarchie et islam politique au Maroc*. Naamani was reported in exile, although Islamist circles claim he was kidnapped by Moroccan secret services from Europe and brought to Morocco in 1994 and forcibly disappeared. Newspaper articles reported Naamani's arrest in Morocco in 2003. See "Arrestation de Abdelaziz Naamani: Il a preparé en 1975 l'assassinat de Omar Benjelloun," *Al Bayane* (13 June 2003), but Islamist circles maintained that Naamani had been kidnapped abroad by the Moroccan secret service as early as 1994, and was forcibly disappeared in Morocco. The newspaper article is interpreted as a government disinformation campaign to test public reactions in the post-16 May 2003 Casablanca bombings.

7. Taieb Chadi, "Entretien: Belkacem Hakimi, activiste islamiste détenu à Oukacha," *Maroc Hebdo International* 41 (24–30 March 2000): 18.

8. Taieb Chadi, "Entretien."

9. See Moroccan Penal Code, article 209, concerning *non-révelation* in cases

of state security. Offenses are punishable by two to five years prison and a fine ranging from 1,200 to 10,000 dirhams. Antiterrorist laws of 28 May 2003 passed by Parliament in the aftermath of the Casablanca bombings of 16 May 2003 increased prison terms.

10. Parenthetically, interviews were principally undertaken in the newly opened public spaces of meetings, reunions, commemorations, and at a Casablanca courthouse where the performance of human rights can now be enacted in Morocco. I met Abderrazak Trigui (Group 26) at the Casablanca headquarters of the Moroccan Association for Human Rights (AMDH) on 28 October 1999 during an "open house" campaign to register information about all victims of human rights abuses. Trigui introduced himself with the phrase: "They call me an Islamist political prisoner." Other occasions were on 29 October 1999, at the national "Day of the Disappeared" demonstration held in front of Parliament in Rabat, when I was introduced to many political prisoners; on 10 December 1999 during the anniversary of the Universal Declaration of Human Rights held at the house of the El Manouzi family on behalf of the Comité de coordination des familles des disparus et victimes de la disparition au Maroc. While seated next Abderrazzak Trigui, I was introduced to Ahmed Haou (Group 71). Interviews and further meetings were conducted thanks to introductions by Ahmed Haou during additional public performances, such as the sit-in on 4 March 2000 in front of Casablanca's major torture center Derb Moulay Cherif, and at several political prisoners' funerals and their subsequent fortieth day (al-ʿarbaʿīn) commemoration services. In addition, long hours were spent with the legal and human rights community of activists, especially with Abdessamad Bouabid and Hassan Elhasni Alaoui (Group 71), as observers to the May–June 2000 trial of three Islamists political prisoners still in prison and accused of attempted escape from Casablanca's Oukacha Prison.

11. Mohamed Hakiki, "Yawmīyāt sajīn (1)" (A prisoner's diary 1), *al-Jisr* 28 (July–August 1995): 12.

12. According to Fatima Mernissi, *Islam and Democracy* (New York: Addison-Wesley, 1992), 106: "*Taghiya* is a favorite word in the language of modern Islamic fundamentalists; it is the insult they throw most often at the heads of contemporary rulers."

13. I thank Ahmed Haou for a copy of his indemnity dossier filed with ACHR, dated 28 December 1999, 8 ms. pages.

14. Interview with Ahmed Haou, Rabat, 15 December 1999. See Haou's prison memoirs published while he was still incarcerated: "Nabsh fī dhākirat al-ẓill: 1-al-Qāʿ al-saḥīq" (Exploration of the memory of darkness: The bottomless pit), *al-Jisr* 17 (May 1994): 7; "2-al-Wilādah al-thāniyah" (Second birth), *al-Jisr* 18 (June 1994): 13; and "al-Muḥākamah" (The trial), *al-Jisr* 19 (July 1994): 13.

15. Hakiki, "Yawmīyāt sajīn (1)," 12.

16. Valerie J. Hoffman, "An Islamic Activist: Zaynab al-Ghazali," in *Women and the Family in the Middle East: New Voices of Change*, ed. Elizabeth Warnock Fernea (Austin: University of Texas Press, 1985), 233–54; Timothy Mitchell, "L'expérience de l'emprisonnement dans le discours islamiste," in *Intellectuels et militants de l'Islam contemporain*, ed. Gilles Kepel and Yann Richard (Paris: Seuil, 1990), 193–212; and Miriam Cooke, *Women Claim Islam* (New York: Routledge, 2001), 83–106.

17. Islamist political prisoners had read al-Ghazali's book, easily available in Morocco. Hassan Elhasni Alaoui recounts that as he waited for his torture sessions to begin while blindfolded and manacled in Derb Moulay Cherif, he saw the events described by al-Ghazali as if it were a film unfolding before him. Interview with Hassan Elhasni Alaoui, Casablanca, 30 November 2003. Works by Sayyid Qutb, Egyptian author and member of the Muslim Brotherhood, are widely read, notably his prison memoir *Maʿālim fī al-ṭarīq*, available in English under the title *Milestones* (Indianapolis: American Trust, 1990).

18. Hakiki, "Yawmīyāt sajīn (1)," 12.

19. For the events of 1983, see Jean-Claude Santucci, "Maroc," *Annuaire de l'Afrique du Nord* 25 (1984): 899–906.

20. See Haou, "al-Muḥākamah," 13.

21. I thank Khalid Bakhti for providing me with a photocopy of his four-page handwritten Amnesty International "Questionnaire au sujet des détenus," dated 7 June 1990. Only after 1990, observes Haou, did Amnesty International take up their cases, following long written exchanges with the Islamist prisoners, who had to persuade the outside world that they were indeed nonviolent prisoners of conscience. Unlike Moroccan Marxist political prisoners, there was no organized partisan Moroccan human rights movement for Islamists, who were uniformly tarred with the label of Khomeini–followers.

22. See entire issue of Comité de lutte contre la répression au Maroc, "Janvier 1984," *Bulletin* 59 (February 1984).

23. "Hassan II: discours à la nation," *Le Matin du Sahara* (22 January 1984): 1; David Seddon, "Winter of Discontent: Economic Crisis in Tunisia and Morocco," *MERIP/Middle East Reports* 14/8 (1984): 8 and "Riot and Rebellion in North Africa: Political Responses to Economic Crisis in Tunisia, Morocco, and Sudan," in *Power and Stability in the Middle East*, ed. Berch Berberoglu (London: Zed, 1989), 114–35; Jean-Claude Santucci, "Soulèvements urbains, procès en chaine et répression politique," *Annuaire de l'Afrique du Nord* 25 (1984): 899–919 and "Chronique marocaine," *Annuaire de l'Afrique du Nord* (1985): 650–52.

24. Interview with Abdessamad Bouabid, Casablanca, 22 May 2000. The works of James C. Scott offer analyses of groups resisting extreme physical coercion. See his *Weapons of the Weak: Everyday Forms of Peasant Resistance* (New Haven, Conn.: Yale University Press, 1986) and *Domination and the Arts of Resistance: Hidden Transcripts* (New Haven, Conn.: Yale University Press, 1990).

25. Interview with Ahmed Haou, Casablanca, 22 May 2000.

26. Ahmed Haou, Belkacem Hakimi, Abdellah Maazi, Abderrazak Rowane, Mohamed Nabah, Hamid Margiche, Abderrahim Maknassi, Abderrahim Chkir, Nourredine Bouabid, Said Kardadi, Abdelali Harit, Mustapha Marjaoui, Ahmed Chatah, Hassan Elhasni Alaoui, Mustapha Rtibi, Mustapha Ait Najim, Mustapha Rouani, Abdelghani Boutahar, Abdellah Belkrad, Redouane Zaidi, Mohamed Hansali, Mustapha Brakez, Mustapha Faouzi, Mustapha Raji, Abdallah Laamari, Mohammed Bahaj and Abderrahim Rifla completed legal studies.

27. Bouchaib Belamine and Abdelhafid Seriti, "Hiwār maʿa zawjat al-muʿtaqal al-Islāmī Ahmed Haou" (Interview with the wife of Islamist prisoner Ahmed

Haou), *al-Naba*ʾ 4 (January 1998): 7. Prison photographs reproduced by permission of Ahmed Haou.

28. Interview with Abderrahmane Naim, 31 May 2000, Tribunal Sidi Othmane-Ben M'sik, Casablanca, during the May–June trial. Naim is a founding member of Tamkine. I thank Abderrahmane Naim for a copy of his indemnity claim, which includes a comprehensive listing of each hunger strike by date, duration (from 24 hours to 67 days), category (limited or unlimited), and the reason for the hunger strike.

29. For a report on the joint Marxist-Islamist hunger strike of October 1985, see Hélène Jaffé, "Aux cotés des victimes de la répression," in *Droits de l'Homme et violences au Maghreb et en Europe* (Paris: Publication Hourriya/Liberté, 1997), 78–81.

30. Jamal Lakouis of the 1981 Casablanca Group describes the Islamists' removal from Kenitra Central Prison to Safi Prison: "They [Islamists] refused the decision to be transferred because they wanted to stay there [Kenitra]. At the same time the group of Islamist demanded their rights, for example to direct visits, radio, newspapers, concerning the situation of their lives. Then the decision of the administration came after their demands. At a certain moment during the night, around eight or nine in the evening, they came to get them by force. It was hard because they used tear gas and all. The guards came with clubs, they beat them, and they massacred them. We were shut in but we heard the screams, the voices, and the noises. In the morning we saw, there was blood on the ground, everywhere, and we knew they had been massacred. It wasn't that far away because their section was 100 meters away, cells here, ward there. We could hear everything and imagine what was happening. There was also the [Islamist] group of Omar Benjelloun who could see out of their cell grilles. They saw it like a film and the next morning they told us what had happened. There were guards who talked about it, because there are even guards who are against the regime. Understand? They were against what had happened there." Interview with Jamal Lakouis, Casablanca, 2 June 2000.

31. Belkacem Hakimi, prison diary dated Monday, 7 March/24 Ramadan 1994. Translated from Arabic to French by Belkacem Hakimi, reproduced by permission of author. See also Belkacem Hakimi, "Baynī wa-bayna al-mawt" (Between me and death), *al-Mishkāt* (November–December 1988): 108–9, and Hakimi, "Lettre à Aragon . . . d'un homme à mourir," *L'Infini* 23 (1997): 62.

32. Ahmed Haou correspondence with La Magdeleine High School, La Prairie, Québec, Amnesty International 1994 postcard campaign. Translated and reprinted by permission of Ahmed Haou.

33. See tenth-anniversary commemorative article by Ahmed Haou, "al-ʿĀlim al-mujāhid al-shahīd Muḥammad bin al-Ṭayyib al-Idrīsī," *al-Naba*ʾ 26 (January 2000): 4.

34. Abdessamad Bouabid, diary, Kenitra Central Prison, dated midnight 3 March 1993. Reproduced by permission of the author. Bouabid switched writing his diary from Arabic to French in prison to avoid the guards' intrusive reading.

35. Interview with Abdellatif Derkaoui, Casablanca, 25 January 2000.

36. See the prison memoirs of one signer of the 1986 pardon letter, Muḥammad al-Amīn Mishbāl, *Aḥlām al-ẓulmah* (Dreams of darkness) (Tetouan: al-Khalīj al-ʿArabī, 2003). Earlier in 1977, a group of Marxist political prisoners had sent a

pardon letter to the king that was never published. On pardon letters in France, see Natalie Zemon Davis, *Fiction in the Archives: Pardon Tales and Their Tellers in Sixteenth-Century France* (Stanford, Calif.: Stanford University Press, 1987). Zemon notes in her introduction that themes of "accepting responsibility and seeking rightful excuse" hold true for the twentieth century (viii).

37. As of the March 2000 trial, thirty-six Islamists claiming the status of political prisoner were serving sentences in Moroccan prisons, according to Lajnat al-Wafāʾ, founded on 5 March 2000 as an organization uniting former Islamist political prisoners. Prisoners belong to different organizations and were tried in a variety of political trials. See the Lajnat al-Wafāʾ communiqué, *Lāʾiḥat al-muʿtaqalīn al-siyāsīyīn al-Islāmīyīn* (List of Islamist political prisoners) (5 March 2000), published in *al-Ṣaḥīfah* (25–31 March 2000), 8. Additional political prisoners on their list are Aissa Saber condemned to twenty years; Abdelwahab Nabet, twenty-five years (Faction al-Mujāhidīn) condemned during the Marrakesh trials of 1985; Muhammad Boussouf, condemned to life imprisonment when he returned to Morocco after the general amnesty of 1994; twelve political prisoners from al-ʿAdl wa-al-Iḥsan (Oujda section), all condemned to twenty years in the trial of 10 January 1992, currently in Kenitra Central Prison; eight from 1994, eight from the 1996 Rabat military trial, including five Algerians considered members of the Front Islamique du Salut (FIS) condemned from six to twenty years for bringing arms to Morocco from Algeria.

38. Interview with Mostafa Lmouatissime, Casablanca, 30 November 2003.

39. Communiqué, al-Tajammu' min Ajl Karāmat al-Insān (Tamkine), *Balāgh min al-Jāmiʿah al-Huqūqīyah al-Waṭanīyah*) (12 May 2000). See also Qur'an Surah 28: 55 where the same word as a verb *numakkinu* (we establish) appears and is linked by Islamists to the story of Moses successfully opposing Pharaoh and "establishing a firm place for them in the land."

40. Ahmed Saad, Moustapha Oukil, and Belkacem Hakimi, Communiqué, "al-Muʿtaqalīn al-siyāsīyīn" (Political prisoners), Casablanca, 16 May 2000. See also Abderrafii Al Oumliki, "Le détenu victime d'un accident ne se souvient de rien devant le tribunal," *L'Opinion* (3 June 2000): 3.

41. See articles by Mohamed El Gahs, "Affront," *Libération* (15 May 2000): 1; Salah Sbyea, "Scandale à la prison: Outrage à la justice," *Libération* (16 May 2000): 1, 4; Said Mountasser, "Iʿtiqāl 3 ḥurrās wa-al-taḥqīq maʿa 4 ākharīn wa 4 sujanāʾ" *Ittiḥād Ishtirākī* (14 May 2000): 1 and "al-Ḥaqq wa-al istithnāʾ," *Ittiḥād Ishtirākī* (17 May 2000): 1. In contrast, the series of articles in *L'Opinion* by Abderrafii Al Oumliki were exemplary.

42. Susan E. Waltz, "Interpreting Reform in Morocco," in *In the Shadow of the Sultan: Culture, Power, and Politics in Morocco*, ed. Rahma Bourquia and Susan Gilson Miller (Cambridge, Mass.: Harvard University Press, 1999), 291.

43. Amnesty International, *Morocco: A Pattern of Political Imprisonment, Disappearances and Torture* (London: Amnesty International, 1991), 35, 90.

44. Although I am a mere dues-paying member of Amnesty International, as the only North American present during the trial, I was introduced by Islamist human rights activists to the presiding judges as an official observer from Amnesty International. Once, when I was late to a court session, an anonymous telephone

caller to my Casablanca home asked me to hurry to the tribunal because he claimed that it was as if America were present and watching in the courtroom.

45. Abderrafii Al Oumliki, "Procès des 'prisonniers libres' de Oukacha," *L'Opinion* (18 May 2000): 4.

46. Interviews with Mostefa al-Jid and Ahmed Haou, Tribunal of the First Instance, Casablanca, 5 June 2000.

47. Decades of mass political trials in postcolonial Morocco have lead to the common practice of eliminating original political affiliation and participation in a social movement. Political prisoners were renamed and designated according to first the number arrested, then the trial date. Moroccan political trials not only initiated the process to establish political prisoner status but also served to highlight and define publicly membership, for example, in already existing political parties, such as the UNFP and USFP trials; or affiliation with the sociopolitical movements such as the Marxists and socioreligious movements, such as the Islamists.

48. Interview with Ahmed Haou, Casablanca, 16 May 2000.

49. See my "Torture, Truth and Recovery in Morocco," in *Experiments with Truth: Transitional Justice and the Processes of Truth and Reconciliation, Documenta 11 Platform* 2, ed. Okwui Enwezor (Ostfildern-Ruit, Germany: Hatje Cantz, 2002), 213–30.

50. See "Création d'une Commission d'arbitrage indépendante," *Le Matin du Sahara et du Maghreb* (17 August, 1999): 1. The first hearings began 11 November 1999. See Abdelkader El Aine, "Les victimes peuvent savoir à quel saint se vouer," *Al Bayane* (30 September 1999): 2. Information and organization of the Indemnity Commission available at www.ccdh.org.ma.

51. Though members of the Group 71 were identified as Islamists belonging to al-Shabībah al-Islāmīyah (Islamic Youth), twenty-nine imprisoned political detainees, including Bakhti, claimed no affiliation with any Islamist group. See Slyomovics, "Torture, Truth and Recovery in Morocco," 213–30.

52. "La liste des détenus politiques," *Libération* (12 July 1984): 3. Khalid Bakhti, indemnity request, 6 ms. pages plus illustrations. Drawings by Khalid Bakhti are reprinted by permission of Khalid Bakhti. Bakhti's drawings were also included in the indemnity file submitted by Hassan Elhasni Alaoui, Group 71, 27 ms. pages.

53. See the list of forty methods of torture and their Arabic translations in Y. Nasser, "La sécurité comme stratégie de Domination," in *L'Integrité physique et mentale: Violences et torture dans le monde arabe*, ed. Haytham Manna (Paris: n.p., 1998), 133–49.

54. ACHR, Arbitration Decision number 3320, Indemnity File number 2551, Case of Ahmed Haou, 23 January 2003, 3 ms. pages. I thank Ahmed Haou for copies of his case and permission to translate and reprint selections.

55. Interview with Ahmed Haou, Temara, 29 November 2003.

56. Oral report by Abdelaziz Benzakour, Conference on Lajnah al-Inṣāf wa-al-Muṣālaḥah, Rabat, 1 December 2003.

57. Interview with Abdullah Laamari, Casablanca, 3 May 2000.

58. A similar intellectual trajectory has been followed by the Tunisian Islamists of the Mouvement de la Tendance Islamiste (MTI), which in 1981–82 began to

speak of human rights as part of its political platform. As documented by Mohamed Karem, three main elements contribute to a recognition of the diversity of opinion and liberty of expression among certain Tunisian Islamists: "The repression that fell on MTI activists, the support of the Tunisian League for Human Rights (LTDH) because they defended them and denounced this repression, and finally the internal debates within the movement on questions of referents, identity, strategy, and kinds of actions to adopt." See Mohamed Karem, "La notion des droits de Homme au Maghreb" (Ph.D. dissertation, Université d'Aix-Marseille, 1991), 231.

59. At the beginning of the trial of Belkacem Hakimi, Moustapha Oukil, and Ahmed Saad, both the Association Marocaine des Droits de l' Homme (AMDH) and an ad hoc committee of human rights activists drawn from the left was formed in support of the former two. Many human rights activists pointedly excluded Ahmed Saad, an Islamist political prisoner incarcerated since 1975 and implicated in the murder of the leftist militant Omar Benjelloun. While acknowledging that even the 1975 facts are open to question, and despite the obvious absurdity of the 2000 trial twenty-five years later that all three Islamists political prisoners were forced to undergo, "les blessures de la gauche" (the wounds of the left) were in evidence based on the 1975 murder. See communiqués in support of Hakimi and Oukil published in various newspapers, for example, *al-Nachra* (5–11 June 2000): 3. In contrast, communiqués and letters to the Moroccan ministers of justice and of human rights sent by la Comité de Parrainage des Prisonniers Politiques au Maroc (CPPPM) and by Tamkine were in support of all three.

60. John Rawls, *Political Liberalism* (New York: Columbia University Press, 1993), 133.

61. Many English translations of the Qur'an employ more commonly "children of adam."

62. Ahmed Haou's views are echoed in the programs of the Islamist association Harakah min Ajl al-Ummah, founded in 1998 and called "leftists Islamists." See Mohamed Chibani, "Mouvement pour la nation: Ce que pense la gauche islamique," *Le Quotidien* (17–23 September 1999): 4. Haou's position on *ijtihād* is controversial, even heretical according to many, and endorsed by a minority of Islamic scholars, notably Abdullahi Ahmed An-Na'im, *Toward an Islamic Reformation* (Syracuse, N.Y.: Syracuse University Press, 1990).

63. Moutapha Khalfi, "L'exception marocaine," *al-Tajdīd* (20 June 2003). The reporter is quoting from a television speech by Ahmed Toufik, historian, novelist, and minister of religious affairs.

64. "Chambre des conseillers: adoption du projet de loi antiterroriste," *Le Matin du Sahara et du Maghreb* (28 May 2003), available at www.lematin.ma/rech/rsarticle.asp?tb = article&id = 23018.

65. Lisa Hajjar, "From Nuremberg to Guantanamo: International Law and American Power Politics," *MERIP/Middle East Report* 229 (2003): 8–15.

66. "Outsourcing" torture to Morocco is reported by Eyal Press, "Tortured Logic: Thumbscrewing International Law," *Amnesty Now* 29, 2 (2003): 20–23, 25, 28.

67. For an exposé of the secret prison in Temara, see "Rapport de la FIDH sur la lutte anti-terroriste au Maroc," excerpted in *Telquel* 113 (9 February 2004), available at www.telquel-online.

Chapter 7. Ḥattā lā yatakarraru hādhā: *Never This Again*

1. On the ACHR reorganization, see dahir (decree) no. 1-9-12, in *Bulletin Officiel* on 10 April 2001, and avowedly based on the Paris Principles: National Institutions for the Promotion and Protection of Human Rights conceived by the United Nations on 20 December 1993 and available at www.unhchr.ch/html/menu6/2/fs19.htm. The Universal Declaration of Human Rights, adopted by the United Nations on 10 December 1948, is available at www.un.org/Overview/rights.html

2. See www.ArabicNews.com (17 December 2002).

3. See *Le Matin de Maghreb et du Sahara* (7 November 2003) at www.lematin.org.ma. The full text of the recommendation is available on the ACHR website at www.ccdh.org.ma.

4. ACHR members with experience on the previous Indemnity Commission are Abdelaziz Benzakour and Mohamed Mustapha Raissouni, both lawyers; six other ACHR members are Ahmed Chaouki Benyoub, a lawyer; Mbarek Bouderka; Mahjoub El Haiba and Mohamed Berdouzi, university professors; Latifa Jbabdi (Marxist political prisoner, 1977–80) and head of Union de l'action feminine (UAF); and Mustapha Iznasni.

5. See ACHR, "Tawṣiyah: Hay'at al-Inṣāf wa-al-Mụsalaḥah" (Recommendation: Equity and Reconciliation Commission), item 6, available at www.ccdh.org.ma.

6. Public rejections of the new commission have been published by human rights lawyer Abderrahim Berrada, "Droits de l'Homme: 'N'avez-vous pas honte?'" *Telquel* (31 October 2003), available at www.telquel-online.com.

7. Position papers by the three organizations based on the Rabat 9–11 November 2001 conference were compiled and issued in November 2003.

8. The most famous case concerns the journalist Ali Lmrabet, editor of the magazines *Demain* and *Doumane*, sentenced to three years in June 2003 for "insulting the king's person" and "undermining the monarchy." Lmrabet had reported that one of the king's palaces was to be sold to tourist developers.

9. Narjis Rerhaye, "Entretien avec Driss Benzekri," *Le Matin* (10 December 2003): 4–5.

10. Driss Benzekri, "The Status of International Law in the Moroccan Legal System: Domestic Applicability and Attitudes of National Courts" (LLM, University of Essex, 1997), 23. See Susan Slyomovics, "Morocco: Self-Definition as Self-Determination," paper presented at the Workshop on Negotiating Self-Determination, Tufts University, 5 April 2002.

11. The notion of "experiential truth" is owed to Mohandas Ghandi, *An Autobiography: The Story of My Experiments with Truth* (Boston: Beacon Press, 1993).

12. Michelle Parlevliet, "Considering Truth: Dealing with a Legacy of Gross Human Rights Violations," *Netherlands Quarterly of Human Rights* 16 (1998): 141–74.

13. Interview with Driss Benzekri, Rabat, 1 December 2003.

14. During an interview in Rabat when Benzekri was secretary-general of the OMDH, he referred to unpublished short stories from prison written in his native Tamazight, 17 June 1997.

15. Interview with Hassan Elbou and Père Jo Mula, Fez, 11 April 2000. Watercolor reproduced by author's permission.

16. Jonathan Power, *Amnesty International: The Human Rights Story* (New York: McGraw-Hill, 1981), 125. A shorter version of this text is part of Amnesty International's campaign "Against Oblivion," and their publicity cards entitled "The Partners of Conscience Lapel Pin."

17. Jonathan Power, *Like Water on Stone: The Story of Amnesty International* (Boston: Northeastern University Press, 2001), 122. The Amnesty International logo was designed by British artist Diana Redhouse.

18. Linda Rabben, *Fierce Legion of Friends: A History of Human Rights Campaigns and Campaigners* (Brentwood. Md.: Quixote Center, 2002), 190.

19. M. Dernouny and B. Zoulef, "Naissance d'un chant protestaire, le groupe marocain Nas al-Ghiwane," *Peuples méditérranéens* 12 (1980): 3–31; M. Jibril, "Nas al-Ghiwane-Jil Jilala: Les limites d'une expérience," *Lamalif* 18 (1976): 12–18.

20. The full text in transliterated Moroccan Arabic with German translation of Cherif Ben Ali Ould Irzin (Sharīf Ben ʿAli Wuld Irzīn), "Chemaa," is in Sibylle Vocke, *Die marokkanische Malḥūnpoesie* (Wiesbaden: Otto Harrassowitz, 1990), 165–77.

21. Abdellatif Laabi, *L'oeil et la nuit*, 2nd ed. (Rabat: SMER, 1982), 10, 91.

22. Laabi, *L'oeil et la nuit*, 91, 25.

23. Al-Muntadā, press release dated 3 June 2003.

24. Hassan El Bou's text in French translation appears in Sara Vidal, *Le jeu du pendu* (Paris: L'Harmattan, 1990), 146. El Bou's painting of Kenitra Central Prison accompanied by this poem also appears in cards sold by the Paris-based Association des Victimes de la Répression (AVRE) where El Bou received physical and psychological treatment after his release from prison.

Bibliography

Abed al-Jabri, Mohammed. *Positions: Témoignages et mises en lumière.* Tetouan: Centre de Recherche et de Coordination Scientifique, 2003.

Abouzeid, Leila. *Year of the Elephant: A Moroccan Woman's Journey Toward Independence, and Other Stories.* Austin: University of Texas Press, 1989.

Abu-Lughod, Janet L. *Rabat: Urban Apartheid in Morocco.* Princeton, N.J.: Princeton University Press, 1980.

Adam, André. *Casablanca.* 2 vols. Paris: CNRS, 1968.

Afid, M'barek Bensalem. "Shahādah." In al-Muntadā al-Maghrībī min Ajl al-Ḥaqīqah wa-al-Inṣāf, *Shahādāt ʿan al-taʿdhīb* (Testimonies about Torture). Casablanca: al-Muntadā, 2002, 11–13.

Afoulous, S. "Mais, qui a interdit Choukri?!" *L'Opinion* (19 November 1999): 6.

Agamben, Giorgio. *Means Without End: Notes on Politics.* Minneapolis: University of Minnesota Press, 2000.

Aḥmad ibn Yahyā al-Wansharīsī. *Le livre de la magistrature.* Rabat: Felix Moncho, 1937.

Akharbach, Latifa and Narjis Rerhaye. "Latifa Jbabdi: L'étoffe d'une pasionaria." *Femmes en politique.* Casablanca: Le Fennec, 1992, 99–105.

Al Oumliki, Abderrafii. "Le détenu victime d'un accident ne se souvient de rien devant le tribunal." *L'Opinion* (3 June 2000): 3.

———. "Procès des 'prisonniers libres' de Oukacha." *L'Opinion* (18 May 2000): 4.

Alqoh, Aicha. "Fatna El Bouih: Ma prison à moi." *Demain* 18 (7–21 July 2000): 48–49.

Amnesty International. *Morocco: A Pattern of Political Imprisonment, Disappearances and Torture.* London: Amnesty International, 1991.

———. *Report of an Amnesty International Mission to the Kingdom of Morocco, 10–13 February 1981.* London: Amnesty International Publications, c 1982.

Amzazi, Mohieddine. "National Monographs: Morocco." In *International Encyclopaedia of Laws, Criminal Law,* ed. Lieven Dupont and Cyrille Fijnault, vol. 3: 1–184. The Hague: Kluwer International, 1997.

An-Naʿim, Abdullahi Ahmed. "The Right to Reparation for Human Rights Violations and Islamic Culture(s)." In Netherlands Institute of Human Rights, *Seminar on the Right to Restitution, Compensation and Rehabilitation for Victims of Gross Violations of Human Rights and Fundamental Freedoms,* ed. Netherlands Institute of Human Rights. Amsterdam: SIM Special, 1992, 174–81.

———. *Toward an Islamic Reformation: Civil Liberties, Human Rights, and International Law.* Syracuse, N.Y.: Syracuse University Press, 1990.

Anik, Mohamed. "Décès judiciairement déclarés." *Al Bayane* (4 February 2000): 3.
Anthes, Louis. "Publicly Deliberative Drama: The 1934 Mock Trial of Adolf Hitler for 'Crimes Against Civilization.'" *American Journal of Legal History* 42 (1998): 391–410.
Arcel, Libby Tata, Mi Christiansen, and Eric Roque. "Reparation for Victims of Torture: Some Definitions and Questions." *Torture* 10 (2000): 89–91.
Archdiocese of São Paulo. *Torture in Brazil: A Shocking Report on the Pervasive Use of Torture by Brazilian Military Governments, 1964–1979.* Austin: University of Texas Press, 1985.
Association de soutien aux comités de lutte contre la répression au Maroc. "Les arrestations d'Octobre 1985." *Maroc Répression* 75 (December 1985): 5–9.
Association des familles des victims des évènements de Skhirat. *Le massacre de Skhirat 10 juillet 1971: "Crime contre l'humanité".* Rabat: El Maarif al Jadida, 2002.
Aubenas, Florence and José Garcon. "Ben Jelloun s'enferre dans Tazmamart." *Libération* (15 January 2001), available at www.liberation.fr/archives.
"Autour d'un café avec Fatna El Bouih." *Femmes du Maroc* 69 (September 2001): 30.
Baker, Alison. *Voices of Resistance: Oral Histories of Moroccan Women.* Albany: State University of New York Press, 1998.
Bakhtin, Mikhail M. *The Dialogic Imagination.* Austin: University of Texas Press, 1981.
al-Baqālī, Aḥmad Miftāḥ. *Muʾassasat al-sujūn fī al-Maghrib.* Rabat: Maṭābiʿ Mithāq, 1979.
Barbera, Myriam. "L'un des 'disparus' des bagnes marocains témoigne: C'était l'enfer. J'ai pensé devenir fou." *L'Humanité* (14 January 1992): 18–19.
Barnard, Anne. "Rush for Remains Seen Jumbling Evidence." *Boston Globe* (5 May 2003): 1.
Basri, Driss, Michel Rousset, and Georges Vedel, eds. *Le Maroc et les droits de l'Homme.* Paris: L'Harmattan, 1994.
Bassiouni, Cherif. "Final Report of the special Rapporteur, Professor M. Cherif Bassiouni submitted in accordance with Commission resolution 1999/33." U.N. Doc. E/CN.4/2000/62.
"Bavure judiciaire." *Le Journal* (6–13 January 2003).
Beau, Nicolas. "Le cafard du bagnard." *Le canard enchainé* (10 January 2001): 6.
Beaumont, Gustave de and Alexis de Tocqueville. *On the Penitentiary System in the United States and Its Application in France.* 1833. Reprint New York: A.M. Kelley, 1970.
Belamine, Bouchaib and Abdelhafid Seriti. "Hiwār maʿa zawjat al-muʿtaqal al-Islāmī Ahmed Haou" (Interview with the wife of Islamist prisoner Ahmed Haou). *al-Nabaʾ* 4 (January 1998): 7.
Belmejdoub, Mohamed. "Préface à l'édition de l'an 2000." In Saida Menebhi, *Poèmes, letters, écrits de prison.* Rabat: Éditions Feed-Back, 2000, 9–17.
Ben Barka, Mehdi. *Option révolutionnaire au Maroc.* Paris: Maspero, 1966.
Ben Jelloun, Tahar. *That Blinding Absence of Light.* New York: Free Press, 2002.
Benameur, Abderrahim. "Man huwa al-muʿtaqal al-siyāsī?" (What is a political detainee?). *Al-Taḍamūn* 3 (February 1983): 8–9.

———. "Quelques remarques sur la détention politique." *Attadamoun* 2 (February 1982): 3–4.

Benchemsi, Ahmed R. "Dessine-moi l'horreur." *Jeune Afrique/L'Intelligent* (23–29 May 2000): 34–37.

Benhlal, Mohammed. "Le syndicat comme enjeu politique au Maroc (1955–81)." *Annuaire de l'Afrique du Nord* 26 (1982): 217–58.

Bennouna, Rabéa. *Tazmamart Côté Femme: Témoignage.* Casablanca: al-Dār al-ʿĀlamīyah lil-Kitāb, 2003.

Benseghir, M. A. "La liberté individualle, les fonctionnaires publics et le droit penal." *Revue marocaine de droit et d'economie du développement* 29 (1993): 77–113.

Benzakour, Abdelaziz. "Intervention lors du seminaire de la Fédération Internationale des Droits de l'Homme." Casablanca 4–8 January 2001.

Benzekri, Driss. "Poésie berbère de résistance dans les années trentes." DEA, Université de Marseilles, Aix-en-Provence, 1987.

———. "The Status of International Law in the Moroccan Legal System: Domestic Applicability and the Attitudes of National Courts." LLM dissertation, University of Essex, 1997.

Berman, Paul Schiff. "The Globalization of Jurisdiction." *University of Pennsylvania Law Review* 151 (2002): 311–545.

Berque, Jacques. *Le Maghreb entre deux guerres.* Paris: Seuil, 1962.

Berrada, Abderrahim. "Droits de l'homme: 'N'avez-vous pas honte?'" *Tel Quel* (31 October 2003), available at www.telquel-online.com/.

Berraoui, Jamal. "Lettre ouverte à M. Jospin: Dites-nous la vérité." *La Gazette de Maroc* 138 (3–9 November 1999): 11.

Berrechid, Abdelkrim. *Ḥudūd al-kāʿin wa-al-mumkin fī al-masraḥ al-iḥtifālī* (Boundaries of being and possibility in festive theater). Casablanca: Dār al-Thaqāfah, 1985.

Berque, Jacques. *Structures sociales du Haut Atlas.* Paris: Presses Universitaires de France, 1955.

Bertillon, Alphonse. *L'identité des récidivistes et la loi de relégation.* Paris: G. Masson, 1883.

Beverley, John. "The Margin at the Center: On *Testimonio* (Testimonial Narrative)." *Modern Fiction Studies* 35 (1989): 11–28.

Blanc, François-Paul and Rabha Zeidguy. *Dahir formant code des obligations et contrats: Édition synoptique franco-arabe.* Casablanca: Sochepress, 1983.

———. *Les libértés publiques en droit marocain.* Casablanca: Sochepress, 1995.

Boer, Sietske de. *Jaren van lood: Een Marokkaanse familiekroniek* (1913–1999). Amsterdam: Bulaaq, 2000.

Bouab, Widad. "Fī Darb Mawlāy Sharīf" (In Derb Moulay Cherif). *al-Aḥdāth al-Maghribīyah* (27 August 2001): 4.

———. "al-Sijn alladhī kāna malādhan baʿd ʿuzlatī al-makhāfir" (The prison that was a refuge after the isolation of secret detention). *Ittiḥād Ishtirākī* (5 November 1994): 5.

Bouaziz, Mostefa. "Introduction à l'étude du mouvement marxiste-leniniste marocain (1985–1974)." DEU, Ecoles des Hautes Etudes en Science Sociale, Paris, 1981.

———. "Mouvements sociaux et mouvement national au Maroc." In *Émeutes et mouvements sociaux au Maghreb*, ed. Didier Le Saout and Marguerite Rollinde. Paris: Karthala, 1999, 67–78.

Bouisef Rekab, Driss. *À l'ombre de Lalla Chafia*. Paris: L'Harmattan, 1989.

———. *Taḥta zilāl Lallā Shāfiyah*. Casablanca: Tarik, 2002.

———. "L'univers carcéral dans l'Espagne franquiste; Romans et témoignages." Doctorat 3 cycle, Université de Toulouse II, 1986.

Boukhari, Ahmed. Interview by Isabelle Broz, Radio France Internationale, 14 February 2000. Available at www.radiofranceinternationale.fr.

———. *Le secret: Ben Barka et le Maroc: un ancien agent des services spéciaux parle*. Paris: Michel Lafon, 2002.

Bourequat, Midhat René. *Mort vivant: Témoignage*. Paris: Pygmalion, 2000.

Bradley, Craig M. "Overview." In *Criminal Procedure: A Worldwide Study*, ed. Craig M. Bradley. Durham, N.C.: Carolina Academic Press, 1999, xv–xxiv.

Brody, Reed and Felipe González. "Nunca Más: An Analysis of International Instruments on 'Disappearance.'" *Human Rights Quarterly* 19 (1997): 365–405.

Brooks, Roy L. *When Sorry Isn't Enough: The Controversy over Apologies and Reparations for Human Injustice*. New York: New York University Press, 1999.

Brysk, Alison. "The Politics of Measurement: The Contested Count of the Disappeared in Argentina." *Human Rights Quarterly* 16 (1994): 676–92.

Bulletins Officiels du Royaume du Maroc [electronic resource], Casablanca: Artémis Conseil, CD-ROM version of *Bulletin Officiel*, based on edition no. 10, covering 1912–2003.

Burgat, François, *L'islamisme au Maghreb: La voix du Sud*. Paris: Karthala, 1988.

Burke, Edmund, III. "The Image of the Moroccan State in French Ethnological Literature: A New look at the Origin of Lyautey's Berber Policy." In *Arabs and Berbers*, ed. Ernest Gellner and Charles Micaud. London: Duckworth, 1973, 175–99.

———. "Understanding Arab Protest Movements." *Arab Studies Quarterly* 8 (1987): 333–45.

Butler, Judith. *Antigone's Claim: Kinship Between Life and Death*. New York: Columbia University Press, 2000.

Buttin, Paul. *Le drame du Maroc*. Paris: Éditions du Cerf, 1955.

Caplan, Jane. "'This or That Particular Person': Protocols of Identification in Nineteenth-Century Europe." In *Documenting Individual Identity: The Development of State Practices in the Modern World*, ed. Jane Caplan and John Torpey. Princeton, N.J.: Princeton University Press, 2001, 49–66.

Castells, Manuel. *The City and the Grassroots: A Cross-Cultural Theory of Urban Social Movements*. London: Edward Arnold, 1983.

Chadi, Taieb. "Entretien: Belkacem Hakimi, activiste islamiste détenu à Oukacha." *Maroc Hebdo International* 41 (24–30 March 2000): 18.

Chafee, Zechariah. *Documents on Fundamental Human Rights*. Cambridge, Mass.: Harvard University Press, 1951.

———. "The Most Important Right in the Constitution." *Boston University Law Review* 32 (April 1952): 143–61.
Chafi, Mohamed. *al-Ism al-ʿāʾilī bi-al-Maghrib*. Marrakesh: Dār Walīlī, 1999.
———. "Le nom de famille au Maroc." *Revue juridique et politique* 1 (1989): 3–17.
"Chambre des conseillers: adoption du projet de loi antiterroriste." *Le Matin du Sahara et du Maghreb* (28 May 2003), available at www.lematin.ma/rech/rsarticle.asp?tb = article&id = 23018.
Chaoui, Abdelkader. *Kāna wa-akhawātuhā,* Casablanca: Dār al-Nashr al-Maghribīyah, 1986.
———. *al-Yasār fī al-Maghrib, 1970–1974* (The Left in Morocco). Rabat: Manshūrat ʿAli al-ʿAql, 1992.
Charaf, Maria. *Être, au feminine.* Casablanca: Éditions La Voie Démocratique, 1997.
Cherif, Khadija et al., eds. *Justice Through the Eyes of Women: Testimonies on Violence Against Women in the Arab World, Beirut, Lebanon, 28–30 June 1996.* Tunis: El Taller, 1995.
Charrad, Mounira. "State and Gender in the Maghrib." In *Women and Power in the Middle East,* ed. Suad Joseph and Susan Slyomovics. Philadelphia: University of Pennsylvania Press, 2001, 61–71.
Chibani, Mohamed. "Mouvement pour la nation: Ce que pense la gauche islamique." *Le Quotidien* (17–23 September 1999): 4.
Choukri, Mohamed. *For Bread Alone.* London: P. Owen, 1973.
———. *Le pain nu.* Paris: Maspero, 1980.
Clement, Jean-François. "Les révoltes urbaines." In *Le Maroc actuel,* ed. Jean-Claude Santucci. Paris: CNRS, 1992, 393–406.
Code de procédure pénale: mesures transitoires en matière de procédure pénale, extradition. Rabat: Publications de la Revue marocaine d'administration locale et de développement, 1997.
Cohen, Jean-Louis and Dominique Eleb. *Casablanca: Mythes et figures d'une aventure urbaine.* Paris: Hazan, 1998.
Cole, Simon A. *Suspect Identities: A History of Fingerprinting and Criminal Identification.* Cambridge, Mass.: Harvard University Press, 2001.
Comité de lutte contre la répression au Maroc. "Bande dessinée," *Bulletin* 31 (April 1981): 1.
———. "Bilan de la repression." *Bulletin* 37 (November 1981): 3–4.
———. "Dans les prisons." *Bulletin* 26 (November 1982): 6–10.
———. "Les détenus militaires: Tazmamart le 5 août 1980." *Bulletin* 42 (April 1982): 1–5.
———. "Information." *Bulletin* 38 (December 1981): 2.
———. "Janvier 1984." *Bulletin* 59 (February 1984).
———. "Lettre des familles des prisonniers politiques du Maroc adressée au colloque sur la répression au Maroc du 5 décembre 1981." *Bulletin* 39 (January 1982): 8–9.
———. *Le Maroc des procès.* Paris: Comité de lutte contre la répression, 1977.
———. "Meknès." *Bulletin* 21 (April 1980): 5.
———. "Procès," 36 *Bulletin* (October 1981): 8.
———. "Retour du Maroc de J. P. Mignard." *Bulletin* 34 (July 1981): 6, 16.

———. "Textes de prison: à propos d'un viol." *Bulletin* 21 (April 1980): 10–11.

"Communiqué du groupe du complexe à l'opinion publique nationale et internationale." *Le Journal* (16–22 October 1999): 8.

Cooke, Miriam. *Women Claim Islam: Creating Islamic Feminism Through Literature.* New York: Routledge, 2001.

"Création d'une Commission d'arbitrage indépendante." *Le Matin du Sahara et du Maghreb* (17 August 1999): 1.

Cunninghame Graham, Robert Bontine. *Mogreb-El-Acksa: A Journey in Morocco.* Marlboro, Vt.: Marlboro Press, 1985.

Daoud, Zakya. "La situation explosive de Casablanca." *Lamalif* 127 (July–August 1981): 20–26.

Darif, Muhammad. *al-Islamīyūn al-Maghāribah: ḥiṣābat al-siyāsah fī al-ʿamal al-Islāmī, 1969–1999.* Casablanca: al-Majallah al-Maghribīyah, 1999.

Daure-Serfaty, Christine. *Tazmamart: Une prison de la mort au Maroc.* Paris: Stock, 1992.

Davis, Natalie Zemon. *Fiction in the Archives: Pardon Tales and Their Tellers in Sixteenth-Century France.* Stanford, Calif.: Stanford University Press, 1987.

Decroux, Paul. "L'état civil et les Marocains." *Revue juridique et politique de l'union française* 6 (1952): 1–18.

Delanoe, Guy. *Lyautey, Juin, Mohammed V, fin d'un protectorat.* Paris: L'Harmattan, 1988.

Delcour, Roland. "Les émeutes de Casablanca." *Le Monde* (June 14 1981): 1, 4.

———. "Les émeutes déclenchées à la suite de la grève ont fait une vingtaine des morts," *Le Monde* (23 June 1981): 29.

Deprez, J. "Pérennité de l'islam dans l'ordre juridique au Maghreb." In *Islam et politique au Maghreb*, ed. Ernest Gellner and Jean-Claude Vatin. Paris: CNRS, 1981, 315–53.

Derkaoui, Abdellatif. In *La parole confisquée.* Paris: Harmattan, 1982, 84–90.

Dernouny, M. and B. Zoulef. "Naissance d'un chant protestaire, le groupe marocain Nas al-Ghiwane." *Peuples méditérannéens* 12 (1980): 3–31.

Dillard, Annie. "The Wreck of time: Taking Our Century's Measure." *Harper's* (January 1998): 51–56.

Dwyer, Kevin. *Arab Voices: The Human Rights Debate in the Middle East.* Berkeley: University of California Press, 1991.

Ecochard, Michel. *Casablanca: Le roman d'une ville.* Paris: Éditions de Paris, 1955.

Eickelmann, Dale F. "Islam and the Impact of the French Colonial System in Morocco." *Humaniora Islamica* 2 (1974): 215–35.

———. *Moroccan Islam: Tradition and Society in a Pilgrimage Center.* Austin: University of Texas Press, 1976.

El Aine, Abdelkader. "On peut extorquer un aveu sous la torture, mais jamais un pardon." *Al Bayane* (29 December 1999): 7.

———. "Les victimes peuvent savoir à quel saint se vouer." *Al Bayane* (30 September 1999): 2.

El Bou, Hassan. "Lettre à son ami Lyazami." In *La parole confisquée.* Paris: L'Harmattan, 1982, 91–92.

———. *Peindre la déchirure.* Rabat: Impérial, 1999.

El Bouih, Fatna. "Arā'u mā lā urīd" (I saw what I didn't want to see). *Ittiḥād Ishtirākī* (5 November 1994): 5–6.

———. *Ḥadīth al-ʿatamah*. Casablanca: Le Fennec, 2001.

———. "Pathways to Human Rights in Morocco." The Geneviève McMillan-Reba Stewart lecture delivered at the Massachusetts Institute of Technology, 13 March 2001.

———. "Témoignage, la commémoration de quarante jours de la mort de Ahmed Jaouhar," Complexe Culturel Hay Mohammedi, Casablanca, 29 January 2000.

———. *La tortionnaire en déroute*. Rabat: Synergie civique, 2001.

———. "Un sommeil court, peuplé de cauchemars." *Le Journal* (5–11 June 1999): 8.

El Gahs, Mohamed, "Affront." *Liberation* (15 May 2000): 1.

El Mansour, Mohamed. "Moroccan Historiography Since Independence." In *The Maghrib in Question: Essays in History & Historiography*, ed. Michel Le Gall and Kenneth J. Perkins. Austin: University of Texas Press, 1997, 102–20.

Elkhader, B. "Les disparus, à la recherche de la vérité." *Le Reporter* (2–8 December 1999): 7.

El Ouadie, Aziz. "Du jamais lu: La revue du détenu." *Libération* (25–26 May 1996): 3.

El Ouadie, Salah. "Risālah maftūḥah ilā jallād muʿtaqal Darb Mawlāy Sharīf" (Open letter to the torturer of prisoners in Derb Moulay Cherif). *al-Munaẓẓamah* (18–19 April 1999): 10.

———. "Il faut écouter les victimes de la répression . . ." *Le Reporter* (16–23 December 1999): 6.

——— *Jirāḥ al-ṣadr al-ʿālī*. Casablanca: n.p., 1985.

———. "Prison Literature and Human Rights." In *Everyday Life in the Muslim Middle East*, ed. Donna Lee Bowen and Evelyn Early. Bloomington: Indiana University Press, 2002, 360–65.

Essaid, Mohammed-Jalal. "Le conseil consultative des droits de l'Homme: Representations des courants politiques au sein du CCDH." In *Le Maroc et les droits de l'Homme*, ed. Driss Basri, Michel Rousset, and Georges Vedel. Paris: L'Harmattan, 1994, 409–48.

———. *La présomption d'innocence*. Rabat: Éditions La Porte, 1971.

Estoublon, Robert and Adolphe Lefébure. *Code de l'Algérie annoté: Recueil chronologique des lois, ordonnances, décrets, arrêtés, circulaires, etc., formant la législation algérienne actuellement en vigueur, avec les travaux préparatoires et l'indication de la jurisprudence*. Algiers: A. Jourdan, 1896.

Fadel, Mohammad. "Two Women, One Man: Knowledge, Power, and Gender in Medieval Sunni Thought." *International Journal of Middle East Studies* 29 (1997): 185–204.

Fakihani, Abdelfattah. "Khawātir sarīʿah ḥawla istishhād Jbiha." *al-Badīl* 2 (1982): 43.

———. "Considérations rapides sur le martyre de Jbiha." In *La parole confisquée*. Paris: L'Harmattan, 1982, 99.

Fanon, Frantz. *The Wretched of the Earth*. New York: Grove Press, 1963.

Fédération Internationale des Ligues des Droits de l'Homme (FIDH). "Les disparitions forcées au Maroc: Répondre aux exigencies de vérité et de justice." *Rapport* 298 (November 2000): 1–115.

Feitlowitz, Marguerite. *A Lexicon of Terror: Argentina and the Legacies of Torture.* Oxford: Oxford University Press, 1998.

Ferjani, Chérif. "Espace d'exclusion, espace de parole publique: Témoignage sur une expérience de détenus politiques dans la Tunisie des années soixante-six." In *Espaces publics, paroles publiques au Maghreb et au Machrek*, ed. Hannah Davis Taieb, Rabia Bekkar, and Jean-Claude David. Paris: L'Harmattan, 1997, 141–58.

Filizzola, Sabine. *L'organisation de l'état civil au Maroc.* Rabat: Librairie Générale de Droit et de Jurisprudence, 1958.

Fleischmann, Ellen L. "Crossing the Boundaries of History: Exploring Oral History in Researching Palestinian Women in the Mandate Period." *Women's History Review* 5 (1996): 351–71.

Foucaud, Odile. "Iconographie de l'architecture: La prison française du xixe siècle. Dernier avatar du couvent." *Gazette des Beaux-Arts* 125 (November 1994): 155–214.

Foucault, Michel. *Discipline and Punish: The Birth of the Prison.* New York: Vintage, 1977.

Forché, Carolyn. *Against Forgetting: Twentieth-Century Poetry of Witness.* New York: W.W. Norton, 1993.

Frei, Norbert. *Adenauer's Germany and the Nazi Past: The Politics of Amnesty and Integration.* New York: Columbia University Press, 2002.

"From the Editors." *MERIP/Middle East Report* 90 (September 1980): 2.

Gallisot, René. "Les émeutes, phénomène cyclique au Maghreb: rupture ou reconduction du système politique." *Annuaire de l'Afrique du Nord* 28 (1989): 29–39.

Gaudefroy-Demombynes, Roger. *L'oeuvre française en matière d'enseignement au Maroc.* Paris: P. Geuthner, 1928.

Geertz, Clifford. *Islam Observed: Religious Development in Morocco and Indonesia.* Chicago: University of Chicago Press, 1968.

Gellner, Ernest. *Saints of the Atlas.* Chicago: University of Chicago Press, 1969.

Ghailani, Mokhtar. "Morts suspectes." *Libération* (9 December 1999): 1, 6.

Ghandi, Mohandas K. *An Autobiography: The Story of My Experiments with Truth.* Boston: Beacon Press, 1993.

Gimaret, Daniel. "Shahāda." *Encyclopaedia of Islam*, new ed. Leiden: Brill: 1997, vol. 9: 201.

Ginsborg, Paul. *A History of Contemporary Italy: Society and Politics, 1943–1988.* New York: Penguin Books, 1990.

Glendon, Mary Ann. *A World Made New: Eleanor Roosevelt and the Universal Declaration of Human Rights.* New York: Random House, 2001.

Grotti, Laetitia. "Au dessus de toute soupçon." *Tel Quel* (Morocco) (17 February 2003), available at www.telquel-online.com.

"Le Groupe du 'complexe' se manifeste." *Al Bayane* (12 October 1999): 3.

Hajjar, Lisa. "From Nuremberg to Guantánamo: International Law and American Power Politics." *MERIP/Middle East Report* 229 (2003): 8–15.

Hakiki, Mohamed. "Yawmīyāt sajīn (1)" (A prisoner's diary 1). *al-Jisr* 28 (July–August 1995): 12.

Hakimi, Belkacem. "Baynī wa-bayna al-mawt" (Between me and death). *al-Mishkāt* (November–December 1988): 108–9.

———. "Lettre à Aragon . . . d'un homme à mourir." *L'Infini* 23 (1997): 62.

Hamdouchi, Miloud. *La régime juridique de l'enquête policière: Étude critique*. Casablanca: Éditions Maghrébines, 1999.

Hammoudi, Abdellah. *Master and Disciple: The Cultural Foundations of Moroccan Authoritarianism*. Chicago: University of Chicago, 1997.

———. "The Reinvention of *Dar al-mulk*: The Moroccan Political System and its Legitimation." In *In the Shadow of the Sultan: Culture, Power, and Politics in Morocco*, ed. Rahma Bourqia and Susan Gilson Miller. Cambridge, Mass.: Harvard University Press, 1999, 129–75.

Haou, Ahmed. "al-ʿĀlim al-mujāhid al-shahīd Muḥammad bin al-Ṭayyib al-Idrīsī." *Al-Nabaʾ* 26 (January 2000): 4.

———. "al-Muḥākamah" (The trial). *Al-Jisr* 19 (July 1994): 13

———. "Nabsh fī dhākirat al-ẓill: 1-al-Qāʿ al-saḥīq" (Exploration of the memory of darkness: The bottomless pit). *Al-Jisr* 17 (May 1994): 7.

———. "2-al-Wilādah al-thāniyah" (Second birth). *Al-Jisr* 18 (June 1994): 13.

Harkin, Tom. "A Pardon for Sion Assidon." *Congressional Record*—Extensions of Remarks (23 April 1980): E 2009.

Harlow, Barbara. *Barred: Women, Writing, and Detention*. Middletown, Conn.: Wesleyan University Press, 1992.

———. *Resistance Literature*. New York: Methuen, 1987.

———. "Sappers in the Stacks: Colonial Archives, Land Mines, and Truth Commissions." In *Edward Said and the Work of the Critic: Speaking Truth to Power*, ed. Paul Bové. Durham, N.C.: Duke University Press, 2000, 165–86.

Hart, David. "Murder in the Market: Penal Aspects of Berber Customary Law in the Precolonial Moroccan Rif." *Islamic Law and Society* 3 (1996): 343–71.

Hassan II, king of Morocco. "Conference de presse du chef de l'État de juillet 1981." In *Discours et interview de S. M. Hassan II*. Rabat: Ministère de l'Information, de la Jeunesse et du Sport, 1981.

Havel, Václav. "The Power of the Powerless." In *Open Letters: Selected Writings 1965–1990*. New York: Vintage, 1992, 127–214.

Hayner, Priscilla. "Fifteen Truth Commissions—1974–1994: A Comparative Study." *Human Rights Quarterly* 16 (1994): 597–655.

———. *Unspeakable Truths: Facing the Challenge of Truth Commissions*. New York: Routledge, 2002.

Herzenni, Ahmed. "Kitābat al-dhākirah min al-naḥiyah al-naẓarīyah (Writing memory from a theoretical viewpoint). *Al-Suʾāl al-Milaff* (October 2002): 152–53.

Herzfeld, Michael. *The Social Production of Indifference: Exploring the Symbolic Roots of Western Bureaucracy*. Chicago: University of Chicago Press, 1992.

Higgins, Martha K., Mika Haritsos-Fatouros, and Philip G. Zimbardo. *Violence Workers: Police Torturers and Murderers Reconstruct Brazilian Atrocities*. Berkeley: University of California Press, 2002.

Hoffman, Valerie J. "An Islamic Activist: Zaynab al-Ghazali." In *Women and the Family in the Middle East: New Voices of Change*, ed. Elizabeth Warnock Fernea. Austin: University of Texas Press, 1985, 233–54.

The Holy Quran: Text, Translation and Commentary. Translated by Abdullah Yusuf Ali. New York: Hafner, 1946.

Human Rights Watch. "The Pinochet Precedent: How Victims Can Pursue Human Rights Criminals Abroad." Available at www.hrw.org/campaigns/chile98/precedent.htm.

"Inter-American Court of Human Rights, San José, Judgment of 21 July 1989—*Velásquez Rodríguez Case*, Compensatory Damages." *Human Rights Law Journal* 11 (1990): 127–33.

Jaffé, Hélène. "Aux côtés des victimes de la répression." In *Droits de l'Homme et violences au Maghreb et en Europe*. Paris: Publication Hourriya/Liberté, 1997, 78–81.

Jamai, Aboubakr. "Brahim Hallaoui: 'Archane m'a torturé,'" *Le Journal* (20–26 November 1999): 11.

Jbabdi, Latifa. "al-Makhfar wa-al-taʿdhīb wa-al-sijn wa-al-jallādūna: shahādat Latifa Jbabdi" (Secret detention, torture, prison and the executioners: Latifa Jbabdi's testimony). *Ittiḥād Ishtirākī* (5 November 1994): 6.

Jibril, M. "Nas al-Ghiwane-Jil Jilala: Les limites d'une experience." *Lamalif* 18 (1976): 12–18.

Johannes Wier Foundation. *Soins medicaux dans les prisons du Maroc: témoignages sur la prison de Tazmamart. Rapport d'investigation d'une mission médicale novembre 1991.* Amersfoot, Netherlands: Johannes Wier, 1992.

———. *Tazmamart: fort-militaire secret du Maroc, conséquences d'un internement de 18 années, mission médicale néerlandaise mai 1993.* Amersfoot, Netherlands: Johannes Wier, 1993.

Joinet, Louis. "The Question of the Impunity of Perpetrators of Human Human Rights Violations." Principle 36, U.N. Doc. E/CN.4/SUB.2/1997/20.

Kadhim, Hussein. *The Poetics of Anti-Colonialism in the Arabic Qaṣīdah.* Leiden: Brill, 2004.

Kafka, Franz. *The Penal Colony.* New York: Schocken, 1948.

Kahera, Akel I. and Omar Benmira. "Damages in Islamic Law: Maghribi Muftis and the Built Environment." *Islamic Law and Society* 5 (1998): 131–64.

Kaioua, Abdelkader. *Casablanca: L'industrie et la ville.* 2 vols. Tours: URA 365 du CNRS URBAMA, Université François Rabelais, 1996.

Kapchan, Deborah A. "Performance." *Journal of American Folklore* 108 (1995): 479–508.

Karem, Mohamed. "La notion des droits de l'Homme au Maghreb." Ph.D. dissertation, Université d'Aix-Marseille, 1991.

Kenbib, Mohammed. *Les protégés.* Casablanca: Najah al-Jadidah, 1996.

Khamliche, Aziz. "Réactions: de la guerre des positions à la confrontation politicienne." *Le Journal* (17–23 June 2000): 13.

Kingdom of Morocco, Ministry of Communication website. "The Constitution adopted on September 13, 1996." Available at www.mincom.gov.ma/english/generalities/state_st/constitution.htm.

"Kin of Nazi Victims to Be Paid: France Announces Compensation Plan." *Boston Globe* (7 September 2003): A13.

Kozma, Liat. "Moroccan Women's Narratives of Liberation: A Passive Revolution?" *Journal of North African Studies* 8 (2003): 112–30.

"Lā 'alāqah lanā bi-munaẓẓamat al-Shabībah al-Islāmīyah" (We have no connection to the organization al-Shabībah al-Islāmīyah). *Anoual* (22 August 1985): 6.

Laabi, Abdellatif. *Le chemin des ordalies.* Paris: Éditions Denoel, 1982.

———. *Histoire des sept crucifiés de l'espoir & Oraisons marquées au fer rouge.* Cesson-la-Forêt: La Table Rase, 1980.

———. *L'oeil et la nuit.* 2nd ed. Rabat: SMER, 1982.

———. *La poésie palestinienne de combat.* Honfleur: Oswald, 1970.

———. *Rimbaud et Shéhérazade.* Paris: Différance, 2000.

———. *Rue de Retour.* Translated by Jacqueline Kaye. London: Reader's International, 1989.

———. *Sous le bâillon: Le poème.* Paris L'Harmattan: 1981.

Lahbib, Kamal. "Mouvements sociaux et mouvements de droit." Lecture delivered at the conference, "État et formation nationale," University of Hassan II, Ain Chock, Casablanca, 1 September 1999.

Lamrabet, Ali. "Mohammed VI se penche sur la misère du Rif." *Le Journal* (23–29 October 1999): 5.

Landman, Todd. "Comparative Politics and Human Rights." *Human Rights Working Papers* 10 (2000): 1–40.

Le Saout, Didier and Marguerite Rollinde. *Émeutes et mouvements sociaux au Maghreb.* Paris: Karthala, 1999.

Lehzam, Abdellah. *Le logement urbain au Maroc.* Rabat: Imprimerie Toumi, 1994.

Levy, Simon. "La communauté juive dans le contexte de l'histoire du Maroc du 17e siècle à nos jours." In *Juifs du Maroc: Identité et dialogue.* Grenoble: La Pensée Sauvage, 1980, 105–52.

———. "Entre l'intégration et la diaspora (de l'indépendance à nos jours)." In *Les Juifs du Maroc: Images et texts*, ed. André Goldenberg. Paris: Éditions du Scribe, 1992, 90–95.

———. "Les juifs et la libération nationale au Maroc." In *Essais d'histoire et de civilisation judéo-marocaines.* Rabat: Centre Tarik Ibn Zyad, 2001, 63–67.

"Li-mādhā jarīdat Thamāniyah Mārs?" (Why the newspaper 8 March?) *Thamāniyah Mārs* 1 (April 1983): 1.

"La liste des détenus politiques." *Libération* (12 July 1984): 3.

Lohlker, Rudiger. "Hadith and Islamic Law." *Oriente moderno* 21, 1 (2002): 19–29.

Lorcin, Patricia. *Imperial Indignities: Stereotyping, Prejudice and Race in Colonial Algeria.* London: I.B. Tauris, 1995.

MacGuckin de Slane, William and Charles Gabeau. *Vocabulaire destiné a fixer la transcription en français des noms de personnes et de lieux usités chez les indigènes de l'Algérie.* Paris: Imprimerie Impériale, 1868.

Machrouhi, Dahbi. *Nabsh fī al-ḥā'iṭ* (Wall scratchings). Rabat: Machrouhi, 1999.

al-Majlis al-Istishārī li-Ḥuqūq al-Insān (Advisory Committee on Human Rights). *Bayān* (Communiqué), article 12, 3.

———. *Bayān* (Communiqué: On the Dossier of Some Prisoners and the So-Called Disappeared). 15 October 1998.

———. "Tawṣiyah: Hayʾat al-Inṣāf wa-al-Muṣalaḥah" (Recommendation: Equity and Reconciliation Commission), item 6, available at www.ccdh.org.ma.

Mālik bin Anas. *Al-Muwatta of Imam Malik ibn Anas: The First Formulation of Islamic Law*. London: Kegan Paul, 1981.

Malin, Andrea. "Mothers Who Won't Disappear." *Human Rights Quarterly* 15 (1993): 187–213.

Mansour, Abdellatif. "Vérité, indemnisation, et reconciliation." *Maroc Hebdo International* (3–9 December 1999): 6.

Marouazi, Khadija. *Sīrat al-ramād* (A life of ashes). Casablanca: Afrique Orient, 2000.

"Maroc: Une plainte devait être déposé." *Le Monde* (17 November 1999): 5.

Martin, Hervé. "Le témoignage d'un manifestant." *Le Monde* (27 June 1981): 4.

Marzouki, Ahmed. *Tazmamart, cellule 10*. Casablanca: Tarik, 2000.

Matthes, Melissa. "Shahrazad's Sisters: Storytelling and Politics in the Memoirs of Mernissi, El Saadawi and Ashrawi." *Alif: Journal of Comparative Poetics* 19 (1999): 68–96.

McGowen, Randall. "The Well-Ordered Prison: England, 1780–1865." In *The Oxford History of the Prison*, ed. Norval Morris and David J. Rothman. Oxford: Oxford University Press, 1998, 71–99.

Mdidech, Jaouad. *La chambre noire ou Derb Moulay Cherif*. Casablanca: Editions Eddif, 2000.

Menebhi, Khadija. "Istihshād imraʾah" (A woman's martyrdom). *Nawāfiḍ* 3 (1999): 121–27

Menebhi, Saida. *Poèmes, lettres, écrits de prison*. Paris: Comité de lutte contre la répression au Maroc, 1978.

Mernissi, Fatema. *Islam and Democracy*. New York: Addison-Wesley, 1992.

———. *Scheherazade Goes West: Different Cultures, Different Harems*. New York: Simon and Schuster, 2001.

Messick, Brinkley. *The Calligraphic State: Textual Domination and History in a Muslim Society*. Berkeley: University of California Press, 1993.

———. "Evidence: From Memory to Archive." *Islamic Law and Society* 9 (2002): 231–70.

Minow, Martha. *Between Vengeance and Forgiveness: Facing History After Genocide and Mass Violence*. Boston: Beacon Press, 1998.

Mishbāl, Muḥammad al-Amīn. *Aḥlām al-ẓulmah* (Dreams of darkness). Tetouan: al-Khalīj al-ʿArabī, 2003.

Mitchell, Timothy. "L'expérience de l'emprisonnement dans le discours islamiste." In *Intellectuels et militants de l'Islam contemporain*, ed. Gilles Kepel and Yann Richard. Paris: Seuil, 1990, 193–212.

Monjib, Maati. "L'Istiqlal, UNFP et le pouvoir au Maroc, 1955–65." Ph.D. dissertation, Université Paul Valéry Montpellier III, 1989.

Montagne, Robert. *Naissance du prolétariat marocain, enquête collective exécutée de 1948 à 1950*. Paris: Peyronnet, 1952.

"Morocco." *Critique* (May 1985): 67–69.

Morocco Prisons and Cruelties, 1893. London: Howard Association, 1893.
Mouaquit, Mohammed. *Liberté et liberté publiques*. Casablanca: Eddif, 1996.
Moukhlis, Brahim. "Droits de l'Homme: Le CCDH plus autonome." *Le Reporter* (20–26 April 2000): 7.
Mouline, Said. *Repères de la mémoire: El Jadida*. Rabat: Royaume du Maroc, Ministère de l'Habitat, 1996.
Mountasser, Said. "al-Ḥaqq wa-al istithnāʾ." *Ittiḥād Ishtirākī* (17 May 2000): 1.
———. "Iʿtiqāl 3 ḥurrās wa al-tahqīq maʿa 4 ākharīn wa-4 sujanāʾ." *Ittiḥād Ishtirākī* (14 May 2000): 1.
Mouride, Abdelaziz [pseud. Rahhal]. *Fī ʿaḥshāʾ baladī* (In the bowels of my country). Paris: n.p., 1982.
———. *On affame bien les rats!* Casablanca: Tarik, 2000.
Moustaid, Mohamed. "L'approche marocaine est la moins réfléchie." *Le Journal* (25–31 December 1999): 10.
Muhammad VI, king of Morocco. "Premier Discours du Trône." *Le Matin du Sahara et du Maghreb* (1 August 1999): 1.
Munson, Henry, Jr. "Morocco's Fundamentalists." *Government and Opposition* 26 (1991): 331–44.
Naciri, Khaled. "Le droit constitutionnel marocain ou la maturation progressive d'un système évolutif." In *Les constitutions des pays arabes, colloque de Beyrout*. Brussels: Bruylant, 1999, 109–26.
Nadrani, Mohammed. *Kalaat-M'gouna: Disappeared Among the Roses*. London: Amnesty International UK Section, n.d.
Najmy, Hasan and Khalid al-Mouhtary. "Majmūʿat Bnūhāshim" (part 1 of 4). *Ittiḥād Ishtirākī* (24 April 2000): 5.
———. "Majmūʿat Bnūhāshim" (Bnouhachem Group, part 2 of 4). *Ittiḥād Ishtirākī* (27 April 2000): 5.
Nasser, Y. "La sécurité comme stratégie de domination." In *L'Integrité physique et mentale: Violences et torture dans le monde arabe*, ed. Haytham Manna. Paris: n.p., 1998, 133–49.
al-Nawāwī, Muḥyī al-Dīn. *An-Nawawi's Forty Hadith: An Anthology of the Sayings of the Prophet Muhammad*. Translated by Ezzedin Ibrahim and Denys Johnson-Davies. Beirut: Holy Koran Publishing House, 1982.
"Non à la torture." *Al Karama* 4 (1999): 11.
Nouaydi, Abdelaziz. "Elite and Transition to Democracy in Morocco: The Example of the Advisory Council of Human Rights." Paper presented at the Middle East Studies Association annual meeting, Washington, D.C., 16–19 November 2000.
———. "The Right to a Fair Trial in the Moroccan Criminal Procedure." In *The Right to a Fair Trial*, ed. David Weissbrod and Rudiger. Wolfrum. Berlin: Springer, 1998, 165–218.
Nunca más: Report of the Argentine National Commission on the Disappeared. New York: Farrar, Straus, and Giroux, 1986.
Observatoire Marocain des Prisons. *Rapport annuel 2001/2002*. Mohammedia: El Mouttakki, 2002.

Ossman, Susan. *Picturing Casablanca: Portraits of Power in a Modern City*. Berkeley: University of California Press, 1994.

Oufkir, Fatéma. *Les jardins du roi: Oufkir, Hassan II et nous*. Neuilly-sur-Seine: Lafon, 2000.

Oufkir, Malika and Michèle Fitoussi. After the Show With Malika Oufkir. Available at http://oprah.com/obc/pastbooks/malika_oufkir/obc_20010620_aftertrans.html.

———. Live Chat, 20 June 2001. Transcript available at http://oprah.com/com/chat/transcript/obc/chat_trans_moufkir_20010620.html.

———. *Stolen Lives: Twenty Years in a Desert Jail*. New York: Hyperion, 1999.

Oufkir, Myriam. "L'opprimée." *Afrique Magazine* 184 (January 2001): 6.

Parlevliet, Michelle. "Considering Truth: Dealing with a Legacy of Gross Human Rights Violations." *Netherlands Quarterly of Human Rights* 16 (1998): 141–74.

Perrault, Gilles. *Notre ami le roi*. Paris: Gallimard, 1990.

Perry, Catherine. "L'innommable dans *La Prisonnière* de Malika Oufkir et Michèle Fitoussi." *La revue française* 10 (2000): 77–102.

Peters, Edward M. "Prison Before the Prison: The Ancient and Medieval Worlds." In *The Oxford History of the Prison: The Practice of Punishment in Western Society*, ed. Norval Morris and David J. Rothman. Oxford: Oxford University Press, 1998, 3–43.

Phillips, Sandra S. "Identifying the Criminal." In Sandra S. Phillips, Mark Haworth-Booth, and Carol Squiers, *Police Pictures: The Photograph as Evidence*. San Francisco: Chronicle Books, 1997, 11–31.

Pierson, George W. *Tocqueville in America*. New York: Doubleday Anchor, 1959.

Plantey, Alain. "La justice coutumière marocaine." *Revue juridique et politique de l'union française* 6 (1952): 20–56; 189–211.

Power, Jonathan. *Amnesty International: The Human Rights Story*. New York: McGraw-Hill, 1981.

———. *Like Water on Stone: The Story of Amnesty International*. Boston: Northeastern University Press, 2001.

Press, Eyal. "Tortured Logic: Thumbscrewing International Law." *Amnesty Now* 29, 2 (2003): 20–23, 25, 28.

Prieur, Cécile. "La réforme de la garde à vue soulève l'opposition des policiers." *Le Monde* (1 March 2000): 12.

Qutb, Sayyid. *Milestones*. Indianapolis: American Trust, 1990.

Rabben, Linda. *Fierce Legion of Friends: A History of Human Rights Campaigns and Campaigners*. Brentwood. Md.: Quixote Center, 2002.

Rachik, Abderrahmane. "Casablanca ensanglantée." *Su'āl* 1 (1981): 83–90.

———. "Sciences sociales et violence collective urbaine au Maghreb." *Prologues* 16 (1999): 19–25.

———. *Ville et pouvoirs au Maroc*. Casablanca: Afrique-Orient, 1995.

Rachik, Hassan. "Nom rélatif et nom fixe." *Méditerranéans* 11 (1999–2000): 223–28.

———. *Symbole et nation*. Casablanca: Le Fennec, 2003.

Raiss, Mohammed. *De Skhirat à Tazmamart: Retour du bout de l'enfer*. Casablanca: Afrique-Orient, 2002.

Raoudi, Mohamed. *Prisons du Maroc: Étude critique de la population pénale et du système pénitentiaire marocain (1975–1984).* Available at http://www.prison.eu.org/article.php3?id_article=2537.

"Rapport de la FIDH sur la lutte anti-terroriste au Maroc." *Tel Quel* 113 (9 February 2004). Available at www.telquel-online.

Rawle, William. *A View of the Constitution of the United States.* Philadelphia: P.H. Nicklin, 1829.

Rawls, John. *Political Liberalism.* New York: Columbia University Press, 1993.

Renteln, Alison Dundes. "The Rights of the Dead: Autopsies and Corpse Mismanagement in Multicultural Societies." *South Atlantic Quarterly* 100, 4 (2001): 1005–27.

Rerhaye, Narjis. "Entretien avec Driss Benzekri." *Le Matin du Sahara et du Maghreb* (10 December 2003): 4–5.

Rivet, Daniel. *Lyautey et l'institution du Protectorat français au Maroc, 1912–1925.* 3 vols. Paris: L'Harmattan, 1996.

Rivière, Paul-Louis. *Traités, codes, lois et règlements du Maroc: (Dahirs, arrêtés viziriels et résidentiels, ordres, ordonnances, circulaires, instructions et avis).* Paris: Sirey, 1923.

Robben, Antonius C. G. M. "The Assault on Basic Trust: Disappearance, Protest, and Reburial in Argentina." In *Cultures Under Siege: Collective Violence and Trauma*, ed. Antonius C. G. M. Robben and Marcelo M. Suárez-Orozco. Cambridge: Cambridge University Press, 2000, 70–101.

Rodley, Nigel S. "The International Legal Consequences of Torture, Extra-Legal Execution, and Disappearance." In *New Directions in Human Rights*, ed. Ellen L. Lutz, Hurst Hannum, and Kathryn L. Burke. Philadelphia: University of Pennsylvania Press, 1989, 167–94.

Rollinde, Marguerite. "Les militant(e)s des droits de l'Homme et le discours sur les femmes au Maroc." In *Parcours d'intellectuels maghrébins*, ed. Aissa Kadri. Paris: Karthala, 1999, 309–20.

———. *Le mouvement marocain des droits de l'Homme: Entre consensus national et engagement citoyen.* Paris: Karthala: 2002.

Rosen, Lawrence. "Responsibility and Compensatory Justice in Arab Culture and Law." In *Semiotics, Self and Society*, ed. Benjamin Lee and Greg Urban. Berlin: Mouton, 1989, 101–20.

Rouissi, Khadija. "Sans la vérité nous refusons toute indemnisation." *Le Journal* (24–30 July 1999): 7.

Sadiki, Larbi. "Popular Uprisings and Arab Democratization." *International Journal of Middle East Studies* 32 (2000): 71–95.

Ṣamad, Wāḍiḥ. *al-Sujūn wa-atharuhā fī al-adab al-ʿArabīyah* (Prison and its influence on Arabic literature). Beirut: al-Muʾassasah al-jamīʿīyah lil-Dirāsāt wa-al-Nashr wa-al-Tawzīʿ, 1995.

Samie, Amale. "Mohamed Ziane, avocat des victims du putsch: 'L'état doit demander pardon.'" *Maroc Hebdo International* (18–24 January 2002): 1, 7.

Santucci, Jean-Claude, "Chronique marocaine." *Annuaire de l'Afrique du Nord* (1985): 650–52.

———. "Maroc." *Annuaire de l'Afrique du Nord* 25 (1984): 899–906.

———. "Soulèvements urbains, procès en chaine et répression politique." *Annuaire de l'Afrique du Nord* 25 (1984): 899–919.
Sautayra, Edouard and Eugène Cherbonneau. *Du statut personnel et des successions.* 2 vols. Paris: Maisonneuve, 1873–74.
Sayigh, Rosemary. "The History of Palestinian Oral History: Individual Vitality and Institutional Paralysis." *Al-Jana* (2002): 2–4, 64–72.
Sbyea, Salah. "Scandale à la prison: Outrage à la justice." *Libération* (16 May 2000): 1, 4.
Scarry, Elaine. *The Body in Pain: The Making and Unmaking of the World.* New York: Oxford University Press, 1985.
Scott, James C. *Domination and the Arts of Resistance: Hidden Transcripts.* New Haven, Conn.: Yale University Press, 1990.
———. *Seeing like a State: How Certain Schemes to Improve the Human Condition Have Failed.* New Haven, Conn.: Yale University Press, 1998.
———. *Weapons of the Weak: Everyday Forms of Peasant Resistance.* New Haven, Conn.: Yale University Press, 1986.
Seddon, David. "Riot and Rebellion in North Africa: Political Responses to Economic Crisis in Tunisia, Morocco, and Sudan." In *Power and Stability in the Middle East*, ed. Berch Berberoglu. London: Zed, 1989, 114–35.
———. "Winter of Discontent: Economic Crisis in Tunisia and Morocco," *MERIP/Middle East Report* 14 (1984): 7–16.
"Le sens de la reclusion." *Libération* (25–26 May 1996): 3.
Serfaty, Abraham. "Face aux tortionnaires." *Les temps modernes* 477 (1986): 1–27.
Serfaty, Abraham and Christine Daure-Serfaty. *La mémoire de l'autre.* Paris: Stock, 1993.
Serhane, Abdelhak. "La chienne de Tazmamart." In *Des nouvelles du Maroc.* Casablanca: Eddif, 1999, 47–63.
al-Shābbi, Abū al-Qāsim. *Works.* 6 vols. Tunis: Dār al-Maghrib al-ʿArabī, 1994.
"Shumuʿ tabḥathu ʿan al-haqīqah" (Candles search for truth). *Al-Aḥdath al-Maghribīyah* (6 March 2000): 1, 9.
Silverstein, Paul. "Martyrs and Patriots: Ethnic, National and Transnational Dimensions of Kabyle Politics." *Journal of North African Studies* 8 (2003): 87–111.
Slyomovics, Susan. "Malika Oufkir, Stolen Lives: Twenty Years in a Desert Prison." *Boston Review of Books* (December 2001–January 2002): 53–56.
———. "Morocco: Self-Definition as Self-Determination." Paper presented at the Workshop on Negotiating Self-Determination, Tufts University, 5 April 2002.
———. *The Object of Memory: Arab and Jew Narrate the Palestinian Village.* Philadelphia: University of Pennsylvania Press, 1998.
———. "This Time I Choose When to Leave: An Interview with Fatna Elbouih," *MERIP/Middle East Report* 218 (2001): 42–43.
———. " 'To Put One's Fingers in the Bleeding Wound': Palestinian Theatre Under Israeli Censorship." *Drama Review* (1991): 18–38.
———. "Torture, Truth and Recovery in Morocco." In *Experiments with Truth: Transitional Justice and the Processes of Truth and Reconciliation, Documenta 11 Platform 2*, ed. Okwui Enwezor. Ostfildern-Ruit, Germany: Hatje Cantz, 2002, 213–30.

———. "A Truth Commission for Morocco." *MERIP/Middle East Report* 218 (2001): 18–21.

Sluka, Jeffrey A. "Introduction: State Terror and Anthropology." In *Death Squad: The Anthropology of State Terror*, ed. Jeffrey A. Sluka. Philadelphia: University of Pennsylvania Press, 2000, 1–45.

Smith, Stephan. *Oufkir: Un destin marocain*. Paris: Calmann-Levy, 1999.

Smith, Stephan, Aboubakr Jamai, and Ali Amar. "Ben Barka 'died under torture.'" *Guardian Weekly* (12 July 2001): 27.

Sophocles. *Antigone*. Translated by Hugh Lloyd-Jones. Cambridge, Mass.: Harvard University Press, 1994.

Staoui, Jaafar. "Casablanca 1981, l'histoire d'une émeute sanglante." *Le Journal* (17–23 June 2000): 12.

Summer, Doris. "'Not Just a Personal Story': Women's *Testimonios* and the Plural Self." In *Life/Lines: Theorizing Women's Autobiography*, ed. Bella Brodski and Celeste Schenk. Ithaca, N.Y.: Cornell University Press, 1988, 107–30.

Surdon, Georges. "Droit musulman, droit coutumier berbère, legislations nord-africains." In *Actes du sixième congrès de l'Institut des Hautes Études Marocaines*, 10–12 April 1928, lvii–lxiv.

Tagg, John. "A Means of Surveillance: The Photograph as Evidence in Law." In *The Burden of Representation: Essays on Photographies and Histories*. Minneapolis: University of Minnesota Press, 1988, 66–102.

Taussig, Michael. "Culture of Terror—Space of Death: Roger Casement's Putumayo Report and the Explanation of Torture." *Comparative Studies in Society and History* 26 (1984): 467–97.

Thompson, Edward P. "The Moral Economy of the English Crowd in the Eighteenth Century." *Past and Present* 50 (1971): 76–136.

Torpey, John. "'Making Whole What Has Been Smashed': Reflections on Reparations." *Journal of Modern History* 73 (2001): 333–58.

Tozy, Muhammad. *Monarchie et islam politique au Maroc*. 2e ed. Paris: Presses de Sciences Politiques, 1999.

U.S. State Department. *Morocco Report on Human Rights Practices for 1996*. Bureau of Democracy, Human Rights, and Labor, January 30, 1997.

Van Boven, Theo. "Draft Basic Principles and Guidelines on the Right to Reparation for Victims of Gross Violations of Human Rights and Humanitarian Law." U.N. Doc. E/CN.4/1997/64.

———. "The Right to Restitution, Compensation and Rehabilitation for Victims of Gross Violations of Human Rights and Fundamental Freedoms." U.N. Doc. E/CN.4/SUB.2/1993/8

Vergès, Jacques. *De la stratégie judiciaire*. Paris: Minuit, 1968.

Vidal, Sara. *Le jeu du pendu*. Paris: L'Harmattan, 1990.

Vocke, Sibylle. *Die marokkanische Malḥūnpoesie*. Wiesbaden: Otto Harrassowitz, 1990.

Vuillet, Pierre. *Code marocain du travail*. Rabat: Publications Juridiques Marocaines, 1936.

Waltz, Susan E. *Human Rights and Reform: Changing the Face of North African Politics*. Berkeley: University of California Press, 1995.

———. "Interpreting Reform in Morocco." In *In the Shadow of the Sultan: Culture, Power and Politics in Morocco*, ed. Rahma Bourquia and Susan Gilson Miller. Cambridge, Mass.: Harvard University Press, 1999, 282–305.

Westermarck, Edward Alexander. *Ritual and Belief in Morocco*. 2 vols. London: Macmillan, 1926.

Wright, Gwendolyn. *The Politics of Design in French Colonial Urbanism*. Chicago: University of Chicago Press, 1991.

Zeroual, Abdellatif. "Le martyre." In *La parole confisquée*. Paris: L'Harmattan, 1982, 21.

Ziou Ziou, Abdellah. "Psychothérapie de groupe pour les rascapés de Tazmamart et de Kalaat Mgouna." *Al Karama 4* (June 1999): 9–10.

Zrika, Abdallah. "A Letter in Ben Msik." In *Morocco International Amnesia*, ed. Liliane Dayot. Paris: Méditerranée, 1999, 13–24.

Zweig, Ronald W. *German Reparations and the Jewish World: A History of the Claims Conference*. London: Frank Cass, 2001.

Index

Acknowledgments

Research in Morocco (summers of 1996 and 1997, and 1999–2000) was funded by grants from the American Institute of Maghribi Studies (AIMS) and in 1999–2000 by a Fulbright Senior Scholar Award. The Richard B. Salomon Faculty Research Award from Brown University funded extended residence in France and Morocco in 1997. At the Massachusetts Institute of Technology, I thank Philip Khoury and the Dean's Office of the School of Humanities, Arts, and Social Sciences for funding my leaves, additional research trips to Morocco in 2003, and a book subvention from the Dean's Fund for Faculty Development. I am very grateful to my colleagues in MIT's programs in Anthropology, Women's Studies, and Foreign Languages and Literature for providing me with a stimulating scholarly environment of lectures and meetings, especially to Margaret Burnham, Odile Cazenave, Isabelle de Courtivron, Heghnar Watenpaugh, James Howe, Jean Jackson, Nasser Rabbat, Marjorie Resnick, and Susan Silbey.

During the academic year 2002–2003, support for writing came from the National Endowment for the Humanities grant and the Rita Hauser Fellowship from the Radcliffe Institute for Advanced Studies. Residency at the Radcliffe Institute introduced me to a vibrant academic community and I thank Jean Comaroff, John Comaroff, Caridad Svich and Richard Wolf for their critical insights and company. A fall 2003 semester MIT Dean's leave enabled me to complete the book.

Two intellectual communities have sustained me most over the years: AIMS and *MERIP/Middle East Report.* My thanks to colleagues from the American Institute of Maghribi Studies, notably Donna Lee Bowen, Miriam Cooke, Susan Gilson Miller, Richard Serrano, and Mark Tessler, to *MERIP* editor Chris Tensing, and editorial committee members Joel Beinin, Sheila Carapico, Lisa Hajjar, Joe Stork, and Ted Swedenburg.

For their unfailing support, advice and friendship during our stays in Morocco, I am profoundly grateful to Daoud Casewit, Executive Secretary of the Moroccan-American Commission for Educational and Cultural Exchange (Fulbright), to Saadia Maski, Program Assistant, and the entire Fulbright staff in Rabat, as well as to Nabil Khoury, United States consul in Casablanca. Hassan Rachik, Professor of Anthropology at Hassan II University, Ain Chok in Casablanca, warmly hosted me at his university and his home. Hamadi Safi and Abderrahmane Rachik of the King Abdul Aziz Al-Saoud Foundation and Library in Casablanca ably assisted me with my research. Many friends and colleagues in Morocco advised, discussed, and aided my research and welcomed me into their homes. I benefited from the critical insights, extensive discussions, and hospitality of Fatna El Bouih and Youssef Madad in Casablanca, the Haou family in Rabat, the Bouabid family in Mohammedia, and in Tangier, Mohammed Srifi and Rabia Ftouh, Mostefa Temsamani and family. I thank Driss Benzekri, Ahmed Herzenni, Fatema Mernissi, Hamadi Safi and Fatima Oukacha, Abdelhak Moussadak and family, Mostafa Miftah and family, Salah El Ouadie and Meriem Maroufi, Asthma El Ouadie, Assia El Ouadie, Aziz El Ouadie and Khadija Boutni, Abdelaziz Mouride and family, Khadija Rouissi and Hassan Hilal, Maria Charaf and family, Abdelkader Chaoui, Abdellatif Derkaoui, Abraham Serfaty and Christine Daure-Serfaty, Bensalem Himmich, Abdelfattah Kilito, Mohamed Saib, Simon Levy, Abdennaceur Bnouhachem and family, Belkacem Hakimi and family, Hassan Elhasni Alaoui and family, Khalid Bakhti and family, Jenine Abboushi, Jamal Lakouis, Driss Oumhand, Abderrahim Afarki, Abdellah Lehzam, Bouazza Bagui, Abdelbaki Youssefi, Amina Boukhalkhal, Abdelaziz Nouaydi, Guy Martinet, Widad Bouab, Maria Ezzaouini, Ahmed Habchi, Kenneth Brown, Susan Ossman, Omar Jbiha, Mohamed Karam and family, Saadia Kabil, Jaouad Mdidech and family, Khadija Seddouk, Hassan Elbou, Père Jo Mula, Abdelilah Zaazaa, Dahbi Machroukhi, Mostafa Bouaziz, Abdelali El Yazami, Mohamed Tozy, Hassan Semlali, Bachir Znagui, Okwui Enwezor, and Ute Meta Bauer. I extend my special thanks to Sion Assidon, who inspired and aided my research.

For additional close readings and comments on the manuscript at various stages, I thank Roger Abrahams, Jon Anderson, Jamaa Baida, Jacqueline Bhabha, Joan Biella, Abdessamad Bouabid, Fran Buntman, Zeynep Celik, Joshua Cohen, David Crawford, Jane Dunphy, Dale Eickelman, Fatna El Bouih, Mia Fuller, Eric Goldstein, Abdellah Hammoudi, Ahmed Haou, Mustapha Kamal, Ian Lague, Abderrahman Lakhsassi, Abdulhay Moudden, Hassan Rachik, Hamadi Safi, Helen Schmierer, Susan Silbey, Sarah Wright, and Richard A. Wilson.

Anda Bordean and Iliana Montauk, students from the Radcliffe Institute's Research Partnership Program, transcribed French-language interview tapes, and Abdessamad Bouabid transcribed Arabic-language audiotapes. Isabelle de Courtivron, Abdessamad Bouabid, Ahmed Jebari, Mustapha Kamal, and Hamadi Safi expertly reviewed my translations from Arabic or French. Kristina M. Holton, funded by MIT's Anthropology Program, helped produce the index. Peter Agree, editor at the University of Pennsylvania Press, and his able staff guided this volume to publication.

Portions of this text have been presented at several conferences: the Fulbright Commission conference in Rabat, March 2000; Homage to Clifford Geertz conference in Sefrou, Morocco, 3–6 May 2000; Documenta 11 in New Delhi, India, 7–14 May 2001; 2001 and 2002 Middle East Studies Association annual meetings; Radcliffe Institute for Advanced Study, 12 February 2003; and the Centre for Cross-Cultural Understanding, Rabat, on 28 November 2003, as well as presentations at Rice University, University of Florida in Gainesville, and the Mershon Center at Ohio State University. I thank the organizers, respondents, and participants for their comments.

Permission to use or translate specific passages, clandestine prison photographs, and artwork is included in notes and captions. Unless otherwise noted, translations and photographs are mine.

I dedicate this book with love and gratitude to my family, Nadjib and Sandy Berber, who were always with me in Morocco.